THE

WESTERN GATE

CITY & COUNTRY

READERS SERIES

Edited by John Farrar and Roger W. Straus, Jr.

ALREADY PUBLISHED

Robert N. Linscott • *Boston Reader*

Etolia S. Basso • *New Orleans Reader*

Henry Beston • *Maine Reader*

IN PREPARATION

Richard Rovere • *New York Reader*

T. D. Clark • *Blue Grass Reader*

Harlan Hatcher • *Buckeye Reader*

NEW YORK • 1952

The
WESTERN GATE

A SAN FRANCISCO READER

Edited by Joseph Henry Jackson

———

"Thou drawest all things, small or great,

To thee, beside the Western Gate"

— Bret Harte
San Francisco from the Sea

FARRAR, STRAUS AND YOUNG

FOR CHARLOTTE

Also by JOSEPH HENRY JACKSON

TINTYPES IN GOLD

THE CHRISTMAS FLOWER

ANYBODY'S GOLD

CONTINENT'S END

PREFACE

Frank norris once said—and dozens of wirters have repeated it at one time or another—that San Francisco, like New York and New Orleans, was a "story city." Since any story, if it is good enough in itself, may be set anywhere (within limits), what Norris meant by his statement was simply that San Francisco, New York, and New Orleans seemed to him romantic.

Purely subjective as his observation was, others have felt the same about San Francisco and said so according to their lights and in their various ways. It was the egregious Willie Britt, brother of the prizefighter Jimmy Britt and his manager, and later a man-about-town and wit, who is credited with the remark, "I'd rather be a busted lamp-post on Battery Street, San Francisco, than the Waldorf-Astoria!" And Rudyard Kipling, young and eager to put San Francisco in its place (he didn't like the city's newspapers, its politics, its drinking-customs, or its citizens' habit of high-flown oratory), was unable to resist at least a left-handed compliment, writing, "San Francisco is a mad city, inhabited by perfectly insane people whose women are of a remarkable beauty."

It is plain enough that San Francisco does have something special about it, a quality which is clearly difficult to put into words, since so many have attempted it and have come up with such widely different answers. Perhaps this volume, representing the viewpoints of many kinds and conditions of people, will help to pin down that quality. Here are admirals, historians, trained newspapermen, novelists and military men, priests, philosophers and poets, each with his bit to add, his view of what he saw in San Francisco and what he thought of it. Here is the Visiting Englishman, without whose slightly acid contribution to correct the over-sweetness of the worshiping versifier this collection might lack balance; here is the objective reporter, setting down the facts; here are the humorists, sometimes playful and some-

times savage, telling the world what they feel about the city. Omitted
as going altogether too far are the outright fearful poetasters whose
rhymes, in the manner of the Sweet Singer of Michigan, have all too
often managed to get into print. It was one such, happily never committed to type (I saw the manuscript, however), who, moved to
uncontrolled rhapsody by the beauties of San Francisco's harbor,
included in his apostrophe the couplet—

> "That Bay where magic islands float,
> Angel, Alcatraz—and Goat!"

But the reader will discover these things for himself in the pages
to follow, and he may make up his mind, if he can, about the true
inner nature of a city so young yet so old, so rowdy and so vigorous,
on occasion so virtuous and sometimes so blandly wicked, so stimu-
lating always, yet so conservative often, and so oddly sure of itself
that Bret Harte could call it, in exasperation, "indifferent of Fate."
San Francisco is all these things and more. That, in a continent just
now realizing that a new world-orientation is taking place, San Francisco, as Harte saw almost a century ago is also its country's "Western
Gate," is perhaps a further reason why it is worth while to try to
understand the city. Whatever the pressures and however powerful
the pull of the past, America is irresistibly changing its focus, swinging
toward the Pacific. And at the gateway to the Pacific—not to be too
solemnly prophetic about it—San Francisco sits on its hills at the
continent's end and considers the future. Even if Harte had not
thought of it first, it is quite likely that *Western Gate* would have
suggested itself as the title of this volume.

As with all collections of this kind, the editor must acknowledge
help from dozens if not hundreds of people who have interested themselves in the project. It is impossible to name all of them; many,
indeed, made good suggestions of which I could not take advantage
simply because there has to be a limit somewhere to the sheer physical
size of any book. I should like particularly, however, to acknowledge
the help of Miss Caroline Wenzel of the California State Library at
Sacramento; Dr. George P. Hammond, Director of the Bancroft
Library at the University of California in Berkeley, his assistant,
Eleanor Bancroft and others of the staff, notably Frank Brezee; Mrs.
Edna Rogers Parratt, Secretary of the California Historical Society;

Miss Dolores Caddell of the Reference Room of the San Francisco Public Library; Edmund D. Coblentz, Publisher of the San Francisco Call-Bulletin, who was one of the handful of newspapermen who got out the combined Call-Chronicle-Examiner announcing the disaster on the day after the earthquake of 1906, and whose knowledge of San Francisco's past is encyclopedic; Richard O'Connor, Historian of the Bohemian Club, who found for me an elusive poem of George Sterling's that I wanted to use in this book; Robert O'Brien, whose books and newspaper columns have reminded today's San Franciscans of their history, particularly in its odd and too frequently half-forgotten aspects; Oscar Lewis, who knows the feel of old San Francisco as well as the facts; Julia Cooley Altrocchi, author of *The Spectacular San Franciscans,* and many other books, whose helpful suggestions led me to make some useful discoveries of material I might otherwise have missed; Edwin Grabhorn, fine printer, whose rescuing of so many early-day San Francisco classics in his own limited editions aided me in short-cutting; Jane Grabhorn, in whose beauiful Colt Press books I found such tidbits as the Trollope, De Quincey, and Kipling selections included here; and finally, Marjorie Brown, Librarian of the San Francisco Chronicle, and her staff, whose friendly and long-continued assistance in digging up old files and verifying references made this task far easier than it might have been.

JOSEPH HENRY JACKSON

Berkeley, California
March, 1952

The editor and publisher wish to acknowledge the following publishers or holders of copyright material for permission to reprint selections:

Mary Elizabeth Buckley for "San Francisco Harbor" by Nancy Buckley.

The estate of Gelett Burgess for the "Ballad of the Hyde Street Grip" by Mr. Burgess.

Stanton A. Coblentz for "From the Golden Gate Bridge" by Mr. Coblentz.

Mary Carolyn Davies for "San Francisco" by Miss Davies.

Lawrence W. Harris (and "The Family") for "The Damndest Finest Ruins" by Mr. Harris.

Houghton Mifflin Company for "San Francisco by the Sea" and "What the Engines Said" by Bert Harte.

Wallace Irwin for "At the Stevenson Fountain," "San Francisco" and "Telygraft Hill" by Mr. Irwin.

Juanita J. Miller for "San Francisco Bay" by Joaquin Miller.

J. J. Newbegin and the estate of Thomas C. Russell for *The Indolent San Franciscans, Russia Looks at Nueva California, San Francisco is the Point* and *Voyage Down the Bay.*

Nestor H. Palladius and the heirs of Asbury Harpending for *The Great Diamond Hoax* by Asbury Harpending.

Frederick Hanley Seares for "San Francisco Bay" by Clarence Urmy.

Avis P. Spring for "City by the Sea" and "The Cool, Grey City of Love" by George Sterling.

Sunset Magazine for "San Francisco" by S. J. Alexander, "San Francisco" by Philip Anspacher and "Barriers Burned" by Charles K. Field.

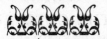

CONTENTS

Preface, BY JOSEPH HENRY JACKSON

I BEFORE THE GOLD

II THE GOLD RUSH

III THE CITY GROWS UP

IV CITY OF OUR TIMES

I

BEFORE THE GOLD

INTRODUCTION

A NYONE who examines the beginnings of San Francisco must get two important points straight in his mind. Both are confusing, and both involve the kind of fact that slips away from the reader even as he thinks he has a sure grip on its tail.

The first is that San Francisco Bay was named before it was found.

The second is that after the true bay was discovered and the name was at last firmly tacked to that body of water, it was nearly three-quarters of a century before the settlement on its shore was called San Francisco.

One other set of facts may be useful here. As American cities go, San Francisco is young. When the little group of 450 settlers—including men, women and children, Indians, Negroes and Sandwich Islanders—decided that the name Yerba Buena would not do, and that "San Francisco" had better be the official name, such cities as Boston, Philadelphia, New York and New Orleans were already looking back on several generations of respectable tradition. Even Chicago had been platted and incorporated for a decade and a half. Yet the name of San Francisco Bay was on a map a dozen years before the Jamestown colony was founded, and a full twenty-five years before the Plymouth landing.

There is a good reason why these historical odds and ends are difficult to keep placed. For generations, American history was lopsidedly taught. Few young Americans were told that by the time of the Jamestown experiment the Spaniards were old hands in the Western Hemisphere. Still fewer realized that the *conquistadores* and their descendants ranged much farther north than Mexico, or that one such leader had penetrated the very center of what is now the United States long before a handful of wandering Englishmen courageously decided to begin a new life on the none-too-hospitable Atlantic coast of North America. And very few indeed, even if they knew vaguely of such explorations, had any idea that four hundred years ago master mariners were nosing up and down what is now the American Pacific Coast in search of a rumored bay that was said to be the most magnificent harbor in the world, nor that after it was discovered several other European countries beside Spain cast covetous eyes on that harbor and the land to which it gave access.

The selections in Part I of this volume will at least highlight this aspect of our history and so provide for the mirroring of a great city some of the early background—the quicksilver coating, so to put it, on the other side of the glass.

The story properly begins with the Portuguese, Juan Rodríguez Cabrillo, sent out by Mexico's viceroy to see what he could find, including the mythical Straits of Anian.

California had already acquired its name, though nobody was quite sure where it might be. An early sixteenth-century novel had described it as lying "on the right hand of the Indies" and very close to the Terrestrial Paradise, stating further that it was inhabited by Amazons, that griffins roamed the land, and that it was notable for gold and precious stones. It was said to be an island, moreover, and one or two of Cortes' men had made casts toward the north, hoping to find gold if not Amazon queens. But it was Cabrillo, in 1542, who made the discovery of what is now California, lying sheltered from a three-day September storm behind Point Loma in a bay he named San Miguel, now the harbor of San Diego. What further might have happened if Cabrillo had not broken an arm is a matter for speculation. In spite of this accident, however, Cabrillo sailed stubbornly northward, finding another bay—which may have been the one in which Drake later anchored or may have been the Bay of Monterey—and then being forced south again by storms, finally dying of his injury in January, 1543. His second in command, one Ferrelo, carried on, getting occasional glimpses of the coast near San Francisco Bay but missing the entrance, and perhaps reaching a point near what is now the Oregon line. But storms forced him back too, and that was that.

Sir Francis Drake came next, nearly four decades later. In the *Golden Hind* he spent a month on the northern California coast, repairing and provisioning his vessel and taking possession of what he called New Albion. Perhaps because of fog, he missed the narrow gate to San Francisco Bay; his landing—maybe in the little bay that now bears his name, maybe not—resulted in his setting up a wooden post and a "plate of brasse" on the shores of the "convenient and fit harborough" which, wherever it may have been, was not the present Bay of San Francisco. Some historians, in view of the two-hundred-odd voyages that had already been made by the Spanish galleons to the Philippines, feel that Drake's voyage has been over emphasized, and perhaps it has. At any rate, Drake landed somewhere and gave today's Californian a link, however tenuous, with old England.

It was at about this time that another Mexican viceroy decided that the Manila galleons needed a port of call somewhere up the Pacific coast and sent Sebastián Rodríguez Cermeño to find one.

Cermeño sailed from Manila in the summer of 1595 and found the California coast easily enough. He found a bay, too. And it is with Cermeño that the familiar confusion begins. The bay he found was the one called today Drake's Bay—the pleasant *ensenada* where Drake may or may not have careened his *Golden Hind*. But Cermeño named it. He called it the Bay of San Francisco. Then, like others before him, and after, he had storm trouble. His *San Agustin* was driven ashore in that harbor and totally wrecked, adventurous salvagers have tried sporadically to find her remains ever since, but shifting shorelines have probably covered her deep. Cermeño and his men fitted out the ship's launch and headed intrepidly down the Pacific. And once more today's San Francisco Bay escaped discovery; though their launch sailed inside the Farallon Islands, straight across the space of sea outside today's Golden Gate, they saw nothing of an entrance. But a bay was named. And later the name was to draw further exploration in search of that harbor named San Francisco, even though it was not the right one.

The fourth near-discovery by sea came only a year later. This time the adventurer was Sebastián Vizcaino. He was a sailor to be sure. But he was also a businessman. His expedition was a business enterprise. It was known there were pearls to be had, and rumors of gold and silver died hard. A contract was drawn up. Vizcaino was to deliver to the king of Spain one-fifth of any pearls, gold or silver he found. Just so there might be a more practical basis for the agreement, it specified one other thing as well; the king would get one-tenth of any salt fish Vizcaino put down.

Vizcaino did well as an exploror. He followed the coast, gave today's names to San Diego, Santa Barbara, Point Concepcion and Monterey, traded with Indians. But he was looking for his pearls and gold, and he was also instructed to find a good port for the galleons. Monterey's harbor was all very well, but he hoped to find a better. His search took him north to Cermeño's Bay of San Francisco (he intended to see if he could find the wreck of the *San Agustin* but didn't get around to it), and probably up as far as what is is now Cape Mendocino. But once more storms came up, and fog. His men were sick and weak. Vizcaino too had an accident; in a particularly violent blow he fell against some boxes and broke several ribs. It was too much. He headed south again, and one more adventurer-by-sea had failed to find today's San Francisco Bay. That distinction was reserved for an adventurer-by-land, and a century and a half would elapse before the discovery was made.

It is not to the point here to elaborate on the factors that led Spain to lose interest in the Pacific shores of the continent north of the peninsula of Baja California. The point is that the day of the *conquistador*-leader passed, and the attention of Spain was focused upon working out her destiny on the Mexican land frontier. Throughout the seventeenth and early eighteenth centuries, that frontier was pushed slowly northward until it stretched like a bent bow up into what is now the United States—a dangerous frontier where sword and cross went hand in hand, the missionary fathers working patiently to convert the heathen, and the soldiers fighting, somewhat less patiently but quite as persistently, to protect the fathers and consolidate Spanish gains. No one else seemed to pay much attention, and New Spain, that vaguely defined region of the New World, went about its business for a hundred and fifty years. Then, in the 1760s, Spain shivered and woke up.

For one thing, the Russians were threatening; in their search for furs they were reaching down along the far northern Pacific coast. The British, too, were evincing an interest in the Pacific generally, and so were the Dutch. If New Spain was to be secure, something had better be done about Alta California—the California of today.

The story of the various expeditions is also another matter, related to California as a whole rather than to San Francisco. But the Franciscan missionaries and the soldiers moved steadily northward. And in 1769, a group exploring by land, priests and soldiers together, made the great discovery. Part of the purpose, on the orders of Viceroy Galvez, was to establish a mission in honor of St. Francis at the "Bay of San Francisco." (Remember that this was what is now called Drake's Bay.) But the little expedition, following Vizcaino's notes on the geographical features of the coast, somehow missed Monterey Bay and wandered north of it. The leader of the group, Gaspar de Portolá, might well have turned back when he realized he had come too far. Instead, he thought he might be close to the "Bay of San Francisco," and he had his orders to establish that mission if he could. He sent his sergeant out to scout the way to Point Reyes, which would identify the Bay for which he was looking. Meantime a small group went up into the hills to see what game they might shoot for the hungry party. It was those hunters who topped a crest and found themselves looking down on an inland body of water so incredibly great that a priest with the expedition, Father Crespi, wrote in his diary, "It is a harbor such that not only the navy of our most Catholic Majesty but those of all Europe could take shelter in it."

They hastened back to camp with the news. Shortly afterward Sergeant Ortega came in with confirmation from another direction. He and his men could not get to Point Reyes; an arm of the sea—today's Golden Gate—prevented them. The weary men sent other scouts along the shores of the new bay, hoping to find a way around. But they gave it up as a bad job and turned south again. On their way they identified Monterey Bay at last and then went on back to San Diego. They made it, but only by killing one of their beasts for food each night. It is of record that they reached Father Serra's San Diego camp "smelling frightfully of mules." But San Francisco Bay had been discovered, complete with the estuary that gave entry from the Pacific.

Setting up the California mission chain was slow work. It was another seven years before the Franciscan fathers came to establish their mission of St. Francis of Assisi by the pond called Laguna de Nuestra Señora de los Dolores. With them traveled the colonists and soldiers whose business was set up the military post, or *Presidio,* that

would guard the settlement and the entrance to the bay. Father
Francisco Palóu, faithfully keeping a journal of all the proceedings,
tells the story in the first prose selection in this volume, in which
the reader will note that although the primary purpose was to get the
Presidio under way, Palóu saw to it that before anything else was done
a brush shelter to serve as a chapel was built on the edge of the little
lagoon. There, on June 29, 1776, five days before the Thirteen
Colonies on the edge of the Atlantic adopted their Declaration of
Independence, the priest celebrated the first mass in what was to be
San Francisco. In this sense, though the party proceeded immediately
to the bay shore and set about constructing the Presidio, the city's
Mission Dolores, chronologically sixth among the great Junipero
Serra's California missions and nineteenth in geographical order from
south to north, had its real beginning.

Both mission and Presidio had their minor troubles with Indians,
with food, with the weather. But both prospered in the next thirty
years which were the great days of the entire mission establishment.
Then, in the spring of 1806, an ambitious young Russian arrived.

His name was Nicolai Petrovich Rezanov. He had bought his ship
Juno in Sitka from the "Bostonians" (they were Rhode Islanders),
and set out to see what the chances were for expanding Russian
trade. He had intended to explore the mouth of the Columbia, but
bad weather kept him off and half his crew was down with scurvy.
A providential north wind made it easier to run southward than to
wait, and so it was that on April 8 the first Russian set foot on the
soil of Nueva California. Rezanov's account, it seemed to me, was
worth excerpting at some length, first because of its unconscious reflection of arrogance (both personal and national), and second because
the reader will find in it a somewhat different interpretation of the
"romance" between Rezanov and the Spanish Comandante's daughter,
Concepcion Argüello, from that which has become one of California's
favorite love stories. Writing frankly, in his own report, Rezanov
makes it sadly clear that his romantic ardor stemmed largely from his
knowledge than an alliance with the Argüello family would help him
pursue his ambition to establish trade relations between Russia and
the new Spanish province.

With Rezanov on his ship was a German, Doctor Georg H. von
Langsdorff, traveling as the Russian emissary's personal physician.

Langsdorff, like others of his time, had a passion for diary-keeping, and in 1814 he published a narrative of his travels. I have selected for this volume his account of a trip by small boat down San Francisco Bay to the missions of San José and Santa Clara, made while his commander was firmly explaining to Don José Argüello and Don José Arrillaga, the governor of Nueva California, exactly what concessions he felt Russia should be given. Langsdorff, in his careful German way, was a shrewd observer, and his notes furnish a good, quickly sketched picture of the bay's lower reaches, the two missions, and the Indians in and around them.

Ten years later another Russian, Otto von Kotzebue, visited San Francisco in his ship *Rurick*. Like Rezanov, Kotzebue was domineering; as Rezanov had, he arrogantly sent orders for the Spanish governor to come up from Monterey to see him. But the young man had a sharp eye for what he saw and a sense of what was worth setting down. His account of a bull-and-bear fight, for example, is one of the earliest to describe that brutal sport, and he was at some pains to note the exceptional horsemanship of the Spaniards, which he graciously admitted was quite as skillful as that of the Russian Cossacks. Indirectly, by the way, Kotzebue was responsible for the difficult botanical name of the California poppy—Eschscholtzia. On the *Rurick* with him were a young French artist-botanizer who had Germanized his name to Adelbert von Chamisso, and the ship's doctor, Johann Friedrich Eschscholtz. It was Chamisso who named the poppy he found, and who chose to christen it in honor of his doctor friend.

The British had been in and out of San Francisco long before this. Vancouver, indeed, had visited the great port almost three decades earlier in the course of demonstrating that there was no Northwest passage south of the Arctic Circle. But explorers were still trying to find some shorter route, and in 1825 Parry and Franklin were again in the Arctic. It was decided in London that someone had better sail up to meet these expeditions and the ship *Blossom* was sent, under command of Captain Frederick William Beechey. In November, 1826, Beechey visited the Bay of San Francisco, asked and got permission to make a survey, drew a map, exchanged visits, and sailed away after some seven weeks during which he had improved the opportunity to examine most of the bay region. He had seen a good deal, though a scheduled bear-and-bull fight had not taken place after all (Beechey described the event anyhow), and he and his men had come to the conclusion that the sleepy little settlement was both "tedious and insipid." But because he was a conscientious officer, and perhaps because it had been hinted to him that detailed reports might be useful to the Admiralty, he wrote in colorful detail about the mission life and its economic foundation, the Indian neophyte and convert. Though the local government was now, and for more than three years had been, Mexican rather than Spanish, Captain Beechey has little to say about the change, other than to note that the Presidio fort was in poor repair and that the soldiers' pay was badly in arrears. As for secularization of the missions, this had lagged behind actual proclamations, and Beechey observed only that the padres were accustomed to pay a certain amount of tax and let it go at that. The process of disintegration had begun, however, and later visitors were to see its consequences.

Of these, the first really articulate one was Richard Henry Dana, sailing before the mast in 1834-36, a young Bostonian in search of health. Dana spent the Christmas of 1835 in the port of San Francisco, punctiliously recorded the trading enterprise of the first Englishman, William A. Richardson, (who had put up a board shanty and was doing business with Indians, soldiers, and such vessels as made their way into the bay), and set down his conviction that "If California ever becomes a prosperous country, this bay will be the center of its prosperity". Enough Americans said the same thing later, but Dana was one of the earliest. Twenty-four years afterward, Dana was to return and register his astonishment at the extent to which his modest prediction had been fulfilled; his report of San Francisco as he saw it in 1859 appears in Part II of this volume.

Already some Americans were beginning to come into California, by sea and by land. Some were sailors who simply jumped ship, hid until their captains sailed without them, and gradually learned the ways of this new country that had attracted them so irresistibly. Some filtered over the mountains, found the gentle climate to their liking and stayed. Some of both married into California families and became a part of California's ranch life; some settled near the missions and pueblos and merged with the Mexican and "Californio" population.

In the settlement of Yerba Buena on San Francisco Bay this was beginning to be noticed, at any rate enough so that in 1839 an English-man, Alexander Forbes, in the first book written in English on California, had some advice to give his countrymen. Much of his *History of Upper and Lower California* does not concern San Fran-cisco, but in it he has some remarks that suggest remarkable foresight. Briefing the political situation in California vis-a-vis Mexico, he pro-ceeds to a concrete proposal. Mexico is in debt to England in the sum of some fifty million pounds. What better way to settle this than by persuading Mexico to cede California? Forbes makes the proposal, openly, even blunty, and implements it with specific suggestions on methods of colonization, to begin in San Francisco and around the bay. Selections from his book appear in this Part I, and today's reader cannot help wondering what would have come of it if Forbes' fellow-Englishmen had taken his advice.

Yet another Englishman, Sir George Simpson, Governor-in-Chief of the Hudson's Bay Company's territories in North America, visited San Francisco shortly after this time and had his say about what he saw.

Sir George—a Scot by birth, actually—was able, upright, and a fearfully energetic man. It was his energy that brought him up in the world, and it was that same energy that led him to view the San Franciscans he met in the winter of 1841-42 with a thoroughly jaundiced eye. "The most indolent variety of an indolent species," he called them, with a fine and sweeping contempt for anyone who did not possess his own passion for getting things done. In the two weeks Sir George spent in port he wasted little time, visiting the Vallejo family up beyond the head of the bay at Sonoma, seeing the mission and the forts, asking questions wherever he went, shaking up his company's agents (he caught one of them in "a capital mis-take" and recorded the details), and departing with a brisk salute to Captain Wilson of the British bark *Index* just thirteen days after his arrival. The selection from his "Narrative" is included here both for the information Sir George so carefully gathered and precisely set down, and for its amusing reflection of a solid British businessman's irritation at what obviously seemed to him a horrifyingly slipshod way of living.

In this Part I, there remains only a single further selection requir-

ing comment. During 1846 the firm of Wiley & Putnan in New York
brought out a book, *Life in California,* which was important for many
reasons, including its first-hand, exact account of California ways in
the years before the American conquest. Its author, Alfred Robinson,
a Boston boy who had come to California in 1829 when he was
twenty-three years old, had spent his adult life in the state as a
comerciante, and was connected by marriage with two of the region's
oldest families, the de la Guerras and the Carrillos. His part in the
state's growth and development, both before and after the period of
the gold rush, was a significant one, and his book shows his powers
of observation and his methodical, well-organized habit of mind. But
the brief excerpt herein reprinted was chosen because, more than
anyone before him, Don Alfredo Robinson saw that the Americans
must and would soon take over California, and understood that the
little settlement of Yerba Buena, so soon to be renamed San Francisco,
was the vital point in such an annexation. "Here is your point," he
says, and hammers it home. "Annex! Settle!" and finally "It must
come to pass! The march of emigration is to the West. Naught will
arrest its advance but the mighty ocean!"

How rapidly his prediction was fulfilled the suceeding sections of
this book will show. Only a little more than two years after his book
appeared, the gold rush was on and half the world dropped what it
was doing and headed for a city practically nobody had heard of.
What happened to that city then is the basis for Part II of this volume.

SAN FRANCISCO BAY

by

JOAQUIN MILLER

Such room of sea! Such room of sky!
Such room to draw a soul-full breath!
Such room to live! Such room to die!
Such room to roam in after death!
White room, with sapphire room set round,
And still beyond His room profound;
    Such room-bound boundlessness o'erhead
    As never has been writ or said
Or seen, save by the favored few,
Where kings of thought play chess with stars
Across their board of blue.

FOUNDING THE PRESIDIO

by

FRAY FRANCISCO PALOU, O. F. M.

ON THE 17th day of June, 1776, about two in the afternoon, the company of soldiers and families from Sonora set out from Monterey. It was composed of its commander, Lieutenant Don José Joaquín Moraga, a sergeant, two corporals, and ten soldiers, all with their wives and families except the commander, who had left his in Sonora. In addition there were seven families of settlers, rationed and provisioned by the king; other persons attached to the soldiers and their families; five servant boys, muleteers and vaqueros, who conducted about two hundred of the king's cattle and some belonging to individuals, and the mule train which carried the provisions and utensils necessary for the road.

All of the foregoing belonged to the new presidio. And for whatever concerned the first mission that was to be founded, we two ministers, Father Fray Pedro Benito Cambón and I, went with two servants who conducted the loads, and three unmarried Indian neophytes, two of them from Old California and the other from the mission of Carmelo, who drove the cattle for the mission, numbering eighty-six head, which were incorporated with those for the presidio.

The officers of the vessels, with their pilots and chaplains, wished to accompany the expedition, and they all did so for about half a league. From this point the captain of the *Príncipe* and all the pilots turned back; but Don Fernando Quiros continued for the first day's

---

From *Historical Memoirs of New California,* edited and copyright 1926 by Herbert Eugene Bolton. By permission of the University of California Press.

march with the two father chaplains as far as the Monterey River, where the expedition halted and camped. On the following day, after having watched all the people cross the river and seen the line formed on that broad plain by all those people, the pack trains, cattle, and the horse herd, they returned to Monterey after taking farewell in the hope that we would soon meet in the port of Our Father San Francisco.

The expedition continued by the same road which was traveled in the exploration of that harbor in the year 1774. But the day's marches were shorter, in order not to fatigue the little children and the women, especially those who were pregnant, and for this reason it was even necessary to make several stops. On the whole way there was not a single mishap, thanks to God. We were well received by all the heathen whom we met on the road, who were surprised to see so many people of both sexes and all ages, for up to that time they had not seen more than some few soldiers on the occasions when they went to make explorations. And they were astonished at the cattle, which they had never seen before.

On the 27th day of June the expedition arrived in the neighborhood of the harbor, and the commander ordered the camp halted on the bank of a lagoon called by Señor Anza "Nuestra Señora de los Dolores", which is in sight of the bay of Los Llorones and the beach of the bay or arm of the sea which runs to the southeast, with the intention of waiting here for the bark in order to select the spot for the founding of the fort and presidio, and in the meantime to explore the land. On the following day he ordered a shelter of branches built to serve as a chapel in which to celebrate the holy sacrifice of the Mass. In it the first Masss was said on the 29th, the feast of the great, holy apostles, San Pedro and San Pablo, and we continued to celebrate in it every day until the camp was moved to the site which it occupies near the landing place, when the ground and the convenience of water permitted it.

As soon as the expedition halted, the heathen of the neighboring villages came to the camp, attracted by the novelty of seeing such neighbors in their country. They came to visit us frequently, bringing their rude gifts of mussels and wild seeds, which were always reciprocated with beads and some of our food, to which they soon took a liking, except the milk, which they did not wish to taste.

These natives are well formed, many of them being bearded, bald, and rather ugly, for they have a habit of pulling out the hair of their eyebrows by the roots, which makes them ugly. They are poor, and have no houses except little fences made of branches to shelter them somewhat from the heavy winds which prevail and are extremely annoying. The men go totally naked, though here and there one covers his shoulders with a sort of a little cape of beaver skins and pelican feathers. The women cover themselves only with plaited tules, for very few skins of animals are seen among them.

For an entire month the expedition remained in that camp, which was composed of field tents, waiting for the *San Carlos*. Meanwhile soldiers, citizens, and servants employed themselves in cutting logs in order to have this much done when the vessel should arrive. The lieutenant busied himself in exploring the land in the vicinity, where he found some springs of water, lagoons, pastures, and good sites for all kinds of stock. Near the white cliff he found two springs of water sufficient for the use of the presidio, and not far from them he found a good plain which is in sight of the harbor and entrance, and also of its interior. As soon as he saw the spot the lieutenant decided that it was suitable for the presidio; but he delayed moving the people there, as he was waiting day by day for the packet.

Seeing that it did not appear for a whole month, and as they wrote from Monterey, by the pack train which went to bring provisions, that it had sailed long ago, the lieutenant decided to move to that spot so that the soldiers might begin to build their huts for shelter, since it was nearer at hand for making a beginning of the houses. This he did on the 26th of July, setting to work immediately to construct some tule huts. The first was the one that was to serve as chapel, and in it I said Mass on the 28th of the same month.

Nothwithstanding that the order of the commander, which was sent from San Diego to the lieutenant, was to found the presidio only, yet, seeing that he had plenty of men, among soldiers and settlers; that the site of the first mission was so near the presidio; and that as far as he had observed the heathen in the vicinity there was no reason at that time to fear them, as they had shown signs of friendship, the lieutenant decided that we two missionaries should remain, with a guard of six soldiers, all the cattle, and the other things belonging to the mission, so that hand might be put to cutting timbers for a dwelling; and he charged the soldiers and one settler to do the same, so as to have a place to live in with their families.

It has already been said that when the expedition left Monterey the packet *San Carlos* remained at anchor loaded in that port, while its commander delayed sailing until the return of the messenger whom he had despatched to San Diego. As soon as the courier arrived the San Carlos sailed from that port bound for San Francisco, but immediately after leaving Monterey it began to experience contrary winds, so strong that it was driven down to the parallel of San Diego, but very far from the coast. From that point it went on gradually ascending and gaining altitude until it reached forty-two degrees, at which latitude it approached the shore and then descended as far as Point Reyes. There it put in between that point and the northern *farallones,* dropping anchor on the north coast in the Gulf of the Farallones on the night of the 17th of August. On the following day it successfully entered the harbor, and about two o'clock in the afternoon it anchored not very far from the spot where the soldiers were lodged, but not in sight of them, as the view was cut off by the point of the hill on whose skirts the camp was placed; but it was in sight of the white cliff and the entrance to the harbor.

As soon as the bark was made fast, the commander, pilots, and Father Nocedal went ashore. When they saw the site of the camp they were all of the opinion that it was a very suitable place for the fort and presidio, and they thought the same of the site of the Laguna de los Dolores for the mission. In view of the opinion of the captain of the bark and the pilots, work was begun on the building of the houses and the presidio. A square measuring ninety-two *varas* each way was marked out for it, with divisions for church, royal offices, warehouses, guardhouse, and houses for soldiers settlers, a map of the plan being formed and drawn by the first pilot.

And so that the work might be done as speedily as possible, the commander designated a squad of sailors and the two carpenters to join the servants of the royal presidio in making a good warehouse in which to keep the provisions, a house for the commanding officer of the presidio, and a chapel for celebrating the holy sacrifice of the Mass, while the soldiers were making their own houses for their families.

The work on the presidio being now under way, Captain Don

Fernando Quiros came to the site of the mission, accompanied by the chaplain, a pilot, the surgeon, and six sailors, to aid in building a church or chapel in which to celebrate Mass and a room to live in. With this assistance the buildings were begun, and everything progressed so well that by the middle of September the soldiers had their houses already made of logs, all with flat roofs; the lieutenant had his government house; and a warehouse was finished of the same material, large enough to store all the provisions brought by the bark.

It was then decided that the formal act of possession should take place, the day appointed for it being that on which our Mother Church celebrates the impression of the stigmata of Our Seraphic Father San Francisco, that is, the 17th of September, a most appropriate day, since he is the patron of the harbor, the new presidio, and the mission. And for taking formal possession of the mission the 4th of October was designated, which is the day dedicated to Our Seraphic Father San Francisco. The commander of the packet, his two pilots, and the greater part of the crew were present at the ceremony of taking formal possession, only those who were absolutely necessary remaining on board; and with the people from the presidio, troops as well as citizens, they made up a goodly number of Spaniards. There were also present four friar priests, all of our College, that is, the two missionary ministers of this mission, the chaplain of the bark, and Father Fray Tomás de la Peña, who had come from Monterey to examine the site for the second mission, of which he had been named minister.

A solemn Mass was sung by the ministers, and when it was concluded the gentlemen performed the ceremony of taking formal possession. This finished, all entered the chapel and sang the *Te Deum Laudamus,* accompanied by peals of bells and repeated salvos of cannon, muskets, and guns, the bark responding with its swivel-guns, whose roar and the sound of the bells doubtless terrified the heathen, for they did not allow themselves to be seen for many days. The ceremony concluded, the commander of the presidio invited to it all the people, conducting himself with all the splendor that the place permitted, and supplying with his true kindness what would have been missed in other parts, for which all the people were grateful, expressing their gratitude in the joy and happiness which all felt on that day.

RUSSIA LOOKS AT
NUEVA CALIFORNIA

by

NIKOLAI PETROVICH REZANOV

EMBRACING at once the opportunity offered by a favoring wind and tide to enter the port of San Francisco the following morning (April 8, 1806), and the suspicious nature of the Spanish government being known to me, I thought it best to go straight through the gate and by the fort.

As we neared the fort a great commotion was observed among the soldiers, and when abreast of it one of them asked, through a speaking trumpet, "What ship is that?" "Russian," we replied. They shouted to us several times to anchor, but we merely replied, "Si, Señor!" and simulated an active effort to comply with their demand, but in the meantime we had passed the fort and were running up the *puerto*. At a cannon-shot's distance we complied.

Some twenty horsemen, among whom were the commandante and one *misionero,* soon after this demanded the surrender of the ship, but we were not alarmed as their calvary was within reach of our grape-shot. I dispatched Lt. Davidov to inform them that I was the Russian officer of whose coming I hoped they had been notified; that I should have proceeded to Monterey had not my ship been damaged by storms, which compelled me to seek shelter in the first port; that I should leave as soon as the repairs were made.

The answer back was that orders had been received from the Spanish sovereign to render us all necessary assistance, and that the *comandante* invited me to dine with him at the Presidio. I thereupon went ashore and was met by Don Luis Argüello, a son of the *coman-*

dante, temporarily in command in the absence of his father.

Don Luis informed me with marked courtesy and tact that he must send a courier to the *gobernador* at Monterey, the capital, to advise him of my arrival. By this same courier I also sent a letter in which I thanked the *gobernador* for his gracious manifestations of hospitality, and informed him that as soon as the vessel was repaired I should leave for Monterey. His reply was framed in the most courteous terms. He would not permit me to go to so much trouble; he would undertake the journey himself the following day, and he stated that he had sent orders that I should be assisted in everything.

Thereupon I recognized the suspicious nature of the Spanish government, which at every point prevents foreign visitors from gaining a knowledge of the interior of their country, and from observing the weakness of their military defenses.

In the meantime, the excellent climate of Nueva California, the abundance of breadstuffs there, the comparison of the resources of the country with our destitution, were hourly subjects of conversation among the members of our crew. On the third day after we arrived, three Bostonians and a Prussian, who, after we had purchased the *Juno,* entered the company's service as sailors, expressed to me their desire to stay. I told them I would consult the *comandante,* but he, when conferred with, refused to consent, whereupon I ordered their removal to a barren island, where they were held until the day of our departure.

In the meantime we placed pickets on shore and established rounds, and a mounted patrol was given us by the Spaniards, but in spite of every precaution, two of our most esteemed men, Mikhailo Kalianin and Peter Polkanov, seized the opportunity to escape when at the creek washing their clothes, vanishing without a trace. Subsequently I obtained the word of honor of the Spanish authorities that the deserters, if found, would be deported to Russia by way of Vera Cruz; but I ask your excellency that they be punished by being returned to America forever. Without severe punishment as an example, it will be hard to control the others.

While awaiting the arrival of the *gobernador* we made visits daily to the residence of the hospitable Argüellos, and soon became on intimate terms with them. Loveliest of the lovely sisters of Don Luis, the *comandante temporal,* the Doña Concepción is the universally recognized beauty of Nueva California, and your excellency will concur with me when I say that our past sufferings were thus delightfully requited, for our time was passed very joyously. (Pardon me, gracious sir, that in such a serious report I mingle something of the romantic—but I must be very sincere.)

In ten days Don José Joaquín Arrillaga, *gobernador* of Nueva California arrived. He was saluted from the fort with nine guns, and another battery behind our ship, which was not visible because of a point of land, opened fire with the same number.

No matter how weak the Spaniards are, since the visit of Vancouver in 1792 they have increased their artillery. We later secretly inspected the second battery above mentioned, and found five brass guns of twelve pounds' caliber. They say they have seven guns at the fort, but whether more or less is unknown to me as I was never there, and I did not allow others to go, in order to disarm suspicion.

It was nearly noon when two *misioneros* came to the ship to advise me that Don José Argüello, the *comandante* of the Presidio de San Francisco, who had arrived with the *gobernador,* invited me to dinner. With thanks for the compliment, I answered them that the proprieties demanded that I should go to him and thank him for the daily favors that had been accorded to me by his family, but that since at present the *gobernador,* with whom I was in official communication, was at his house, I begged him to pardon me for my delay in the discharge of my duties to him. One of the *misioneros* said to me, "You have not understood me correctly. The *gobernador* also sends you an invitation." In order that I should not prejudice our business interests, I decided to go.

When entering the Presidio, the officers met us at the gate, and the pickets saluted. The *gobernador* in full uniform came to meet us in the patio. After paying my compliments and thanking Comandante Argüello for the kind and gracious hospitality of his family, I candidly informed them that it was in their names I had been invited by the *misioneros,* and though I was not aware of the status of the holy padres, and had not given the matter my serious consideration, yet I had made all conventionalities subordinate to my desire to secure the benefits that had attracted me to Nueva California.

The *gobernador* spoke French quite well. He was confused when I had spoken and apologized for the precipitancy of the *misioneros.*

"It is true," he said, "that I meant to have the honor of inviting you, but I could not venture to do so without first notifying you of my arrival, and although everything in California is subject to my commands, yet my right foot" (on which he could hardly step) "refuses obedience, and in this state of affairs, the *misioneros,* knowing your kindliness, undertook the duty."

"That being the case," I said, "I am under more obligations to the *misioneros,* since they hastened our meeting."

The unreserved manner of the *gobernador,* the mutual exchange of compliments at the table, and my intimacy with the Argüello family, combined, very soon created in us a sincere mutual regard.

On my requesting a business interview, the *gobernador* complied, and made an appointment for the following day, but, upon my persuasion, he met me the same evening.

When I had disclosed myself personally to him, I proceeded to tell him that my presence in Nueva California had for its primary object the welfare of the American posssessions of both Russia and Spain, and, entering at once into the matter, I impressed upon his mind the wants of Nueva California, as well as those of the Russsian colonies, which could be supplied by mutual commercial intercourse; that only in that way could lasting bonds of comity be established between the courts of both countries; that the American colonies of both would flourish, and that our coasts would form a tie between us, which would always be equally protected by both powers, and that nobody would dare to settle in the unoccupied territory between us.

I further explained to him that the possessions of his Catholic majesty in the New World were of such vast extent that it was impossible to protect them, and that, on account of their weak means of defense, they would sooner or later fall a victim to the rapacity and aggressiveness of others, and that perhaps the war in Europe was now saving them. As to the suspicions long entertained by the court of Spain that the Russians wanted to colonize in Spanish territories, I could assure him that even if California were gratuitously given to us, it would, on account of the expense of keeping it, never bring us such advantages as we could expect would accrue from mutual commercial intercourse.

"Dismiss from your mind this erroneous idea," I told him. "In their furs alone, the possessions of our monarch in the north have an inexhaustible source of wealth. The growing demand for these furs, as an article of use as well as of luxury, among the northern peoples enhances their value every year, and forbids all thoughts of quitting a country that enriches us, and of such vastnesss that for ages to come its supplies cannot be exhausted. Therefore the situation of Russia, as well as its interests, must convince you that the southern parts of America are not necessary to us. Even were it otherwise, you must acknowledge that so strong a power would not need to disguise its intentions, and you could never prevent it from carrying them out. I frankly tell you we need breadstuffs. These we can procure at Canton, but Nueva California being nearer to us, and having a surplus that it cannot sell, I came here to negotiate with you with a view to purchase, as the supreme authority in Nueva California. Assuredly we can agree upon the preliminary conditions, and send them to our respective courts for examination and approval. That is the true motive of my voyage, and I respectively ask you to decide speedily in the matter, so that I shall not lose valuable time."

I perceived that the *gobernador* listened to me with much pleasure, and he said, "We have already learned of the confidence reposed in you by your emperor, and the full powers conferred upon you with regard to America, and are acquainted with your instructions in regard to commercial affairs. Therefore I am exceedingly pleased to know you personally; but my position is altogether different from yours, and for many reasons I cannot give you an answer decisively and at once. In the mean time permit me to ask you if it is long since you have had letters from Europe."

"Ten months," I answered him. Though it was a fabrication, yet, fortunately, since my arrival, with the aid of the *misioneros* I had happily succeeded in perfecting my knowledge of late political news.

"Do you know," he asked, "that you are at war with Prussia?"

"Perhaps," I replied, "on account of the purchase of Pomerania."

"But the latest news that I have received from Europe—five and a half months old—shows that Russia's relations with France are not amicable, nor are they amicable with other powers allied to the latter."

"That may also be so," said I; "but the threats of European cabinets must not always be taken at their face value. You will acknowledge that you and I are at present in such an out-of-the-way corner of the world that we may hear of a war when peace has perhaps already been declared."

"True," said he; "but you take this too calmly."

"Men like us," said I, "who are inured to all kinds of dangers, must not take much notice of rumors."

I reverted to the previous subject, and he asked me to give him until the next day to consider, and at the same time told me very politely that, though there were no doubts as to my character, formality demanded that I should send him the documents conferring upon me plenipotentiary powers, so that he could properly make his report to the viceroy.

"With pleasure," I said; "and then we shall talk seriously together to-morrow morning."

Thanks to my close intimacy with the house of Argüello, I was told, the next day, word for word, all that had been said there after I left. My frank declaration had met the assent of the *gobernador*. He acknowledged the merits of my conclusions as to the wants of Nueva California, and consulted with the *misioneros,* who were all on my side. He divulged to them the unfriendly attitude shown by our European cabinets, and admitted that he wished nothing better than to get rid speedily, in some way, of such visitors as we, on whose account he might compromise himself in the eyes of their suspicious government, whether we were received kindly or unkindly. However, they had spent the evening in committing my arguments to paper.

I met the *gobernador* according to appointment, and was courteously received. I addressed him at once on my subject, and handed him the registers of various powers, which I possessed in duplicate, saying that the Spanish register had been given over by me to the ships returning to Russia, as I did not at that time expect to visit Nueva California. He made merely a copy of the register of the French court and a copy of my credentials from the Russian American Company, and returned everything.

"Your talk last night interested me greatly," said he. "I acknowledge that I wish you success with all my heart, but I cannot conceal the fact that I hourly expect a report of a total breach of concord between our governments. I do not know how to meet and consider your project, and I must tell you frankly that it would be very agreeable to me if you would hasten your departure in a friendly manner before the arrival of the courier expected by me."

"I am astonished at your haste," said I. "You have received instructions as to how I should be received, but even if you should receive other instructions, it seems to me that, coming here as I did, with the most friendly intentions, the law of nations would allow you the means of parting with me in a like friendly way. Only appoint a time within which I must leave."

"Oh, of that you can be assured."

"Then let us put aside," said I, "this disagreeable concept while as yet there is nothing to prevent us from occupying ourselves with what concerns the interests of both powers."

"You wish to purchase at this *puerto* a cargo of breadstuffs. But tell me why you want such a large quantity, since you do not need so much to provision your ship for your return voyage."

"I will at once explain to you my reasons. First, my ship is in need of repairs, and hence the ballast must be discharged, and it is desirable that, in place thereof, breadstuffs shall be loaded. Second, I want to purchase the breadstuffs in order to learn, upon their distribution in the possessions of Russia in America and in Kamchatka, if the purchase price would be suitable, and to determine the needs of each place, and in the general plan the total quantity required, as we now know in detail what Nueva California can supply, and the amount. At the same time you yourself admit that a cargo of five thousand *pouds* (= 200 tons) is no great object in trade."

"I acknowledge that," he said; "but I hear that you have brought goods."

"None at all," I replied. "The ship's commissary has a small quantity, which I permitted him to take on board, and I do not deny that this was done for the purpose of barter, if you will permit this."

"All I can do for you," said the *gobernador,* "is to allow you to pay for the breadstuffs in piastres, but with regard to trade in general, you will pardon me if I tell you that I cannot consent to that, on account of strict orders from the government. With regard to the purchase of breadstuffs, the granting to you of permission to do so is very difficult. I must ask you to state your requirements in writing, without mentioning other matters, and I also respectfully ask you to state briefly the particulars of your travels from Saint Petersburg."

"I am very sorry," said I, "that you cannot grant my last request. The goods, the inhabitants tell me, are very much needed by them, and it is my wish that my commissary can sell them, as in that case we should gain more room in the ship for breadstuffs. But it makes no difference to me whether I pay the purchase price of the grain to the *misioneros* or to my commissary. I am only sorry that on my first visit the wants of the population cannot be satisfied, it being so easy for you to consent thereto, and thus give general satisfaction. The *misioneros* will supply the grain, the piastres will be paid to them by me, a receipt being taken therefor, which you will send to the viceroy. As to how the holy padres use the money, that is a matter that does not, it appears to me, concern either of us."

"No, no," said he; "that is equivalent to trading. After living sixty years without reproach, I cannot take that upon my conscience."

"But," said I, "it is not love of gain, but merely a desire to benefit your countrymen, that would urge you to infringe slightly on the regulations. Here you are in a better position to see the needs of the country than the people in Madrid, and really I see no crime in it, especially," said I, with a smile, "when the holy padres will bend the knee in prayers for you."

"Oh, I see very clearly that the holy padres have already bent the knee for you," smilingly remarked the *gobernador;* "but, jokes apart," he continued, "you cannot imagine how strictly the regulations prohibiting all trading are enforced here. I will give you an instance. Some five years ago a Boston vessel wintered here. Running in debt to us, and having no ready cash, I accepted in payment some goods we needed. But first I had reported to the viceroy, who replied that for that time the transaction would be permitted, but that in future such trading would not be, as it would give foreign vessels a pretext for visits to our ports."

"To convince you," said I, "that I am desireless of being the cause of any trouble to you, I will not pursue this discussion further, but will merely ask you to give me ground to hope that I shall get the necessary quantity of grain."

"You shall have it," said he.

"And in order to lose no time, I will order that the ship be disarmed."

"With God's help," answered the *gobernador.*

Thereupon, in his presence, I sent orders to that effect to the ship. Congratulating myself on having made a beginning, I left to time the carrying out of my experiment in trading, certain of its successful termination.

On the following day I presented the *gobernador* with the written statement requested by him, but some five days passed without a single grain being delivered. Meanwhile rumors of the war between Russia and France had day by day grown so that they were taken to be true, and a frigate, on a cruise from San Blas, was expected. I also heard that a part of the Monterey garrison had been transferred to the Misión Santa Clara de Asís, a day's march from this *puerto*. The inclination of our men to prove treasonable and to leave us, and the actual desertion of two men at that time, rendered our position still more critical. But the respect always manifested by the Spaniards showed no signs of diminishing. I had a dragoon at all times as a guard of honor; the Spanish pickets always saluted; the *gobernador* met and took leave of me graciously every day and the general courtesy everywhere manifested disarmed me of all suspicion.

From day to day, though in a way imperceptible to the *gobernador,* the graciousness of the house of Argüello towards me inspired in him a feeling of increasing confidence in me, and he apologized for not yet having visited me on my ship.

"Let us," said I, "set aside all useless formality of etiquette. I know the ways of your government, and I am sure that if you had followed the impulses of your heart you would have visited me long ago, but, anyway, I am with you every day."

"We have become accustomed to your presence," said the *gobernador,* "and I assure you that the good family of my friend Argüello appreciates the pleasure of seeing you in their house just as highly as they are grateful to you for the manifestation of your benevolence."

Here I must lay open to your excellency some purely personal affairs. Seeing that our situation was not getting better, expecting every day that some serious unpleasantness would arise, and having but little confidence in my own men, I decided that I should assume a serious bearing where I had before been but formally polite and gracious.

Associating daily with and paying my addresses to the beautiful Spanish señorita, I could not fail to perceive her active, venturesome disposition and character, her unlimited and overweening desire for rank and honors, which, with her age of fifteen years, made her, alone among her family, dissatisfied with the land of her birth. She always referred to it jokingly; thus, as "a beautiful country, a warm climate, an abundance of grain and cattle,—and nothing else."

I described Russia to her as a colder country, but still abounding in everything, and she was willing to live there, and at length I imperceptibly created in her an impatient desire to hear something more explicit from me, and when I proffered my hand she accepted.

My proposal was a shock to her parents, whose religious upbringing was fanatical. The difference in religion, besides the prospective separation from their daughter, was, in contemplation, a dreadful blow to them.

They sought the counsel of the *misioneros,* who did not know what to do. The parents forced their daughter to church and had her confessed. They urged her to refuse me, but her brave front finally quieted them all. The holy padres decided to leave the final decision to the throne of Rome.

Not being able to bring about the marriage, I had a written conditional agreement made, and forced a betrothal. Consent was given on condition that the agreement be kept secret pending the decision of the pope. Thereafter my deportment in the house of Comandante Argüello was that of a near relative, and I managed this *puerto* of his Catholic majesty as my interests called for. The *gobernador* was now very much perplexed, and perceived that he had made a mistake when he assured me of the high esteem with which I was regarded by the family of the *comandante,* as he now found himself to be in fact my guest.

A rare friendship, of thirty years' standing, existed between the *gobernador* and the *comandante.* The latter was consulted in everything. Every official document received by Gobernador Arrillaga passed through the hands of Comandante Argüello, and consequently through mine. The *gobernador* was soon won over, and he placed a like confidence in me, and at length they did not keep the slightest secret from me.

I conversed better in Spanish every hour, and was in Comandante Argüello's house from morning till evening, and when his subordinate officers saw that I had almost become Hispaniolized, each vied with the other to be the first to apprise me of any new occurence, so that now information of the possible arrival of any courier was not dreaded.

Meanwhile I wondered why the *misioneros* did not deliver the grain, and so I managed to have the *gobernador* perceive my dissatisfaction. He told me frankly that the holy padres expected a courier, and that they thought that thereupon they could obtain the ship's cargo for nothing; hence the delay. I told him just as frankly that he personally was the cause of the delay. "Do you not still keep the Monterey garrison at Misión Santa Clara?" I assured him that as soon as he should order the garrison to return to Monterey, all rumors would at once cease.

The *gobernador* was surprised to learn that even his secret orders were known to me, and, turning it off as a joke, sent orders at once for the troops to return, while the *misiones* were again advised that those of them that desired to supply grain should deliver it, as otherwise he would be obliged to take different measures.

At the same time he ordered, upon request, a detail of *inválidos* from the pueblo, where, with the assistance of Concepción's brother, the grain was ready for the first shipment. As soon as the first shipment was on the way, the *misiones* began to send in such quantities that I was driven to request them to stop hauling, as, on account of the ballast, the ordnance, and the cargo of goods, the ship could not take on more than four thousand five hundred *pouds* (*poud*=40 pounds). With the grain I received four hundred and seventy *pouds* of tallow and butter, and one hundred *pouds* of salt and other things.

Our account was computed in piastres, but the prices, as fixed in California by the government, were known to me, and on that basis my purchase was made without any mistake. I shall speak of the prices in the proper place, but I was very anxious to make an experiment in trading, and I urged the *gobernador* in every way to this end, promising him the good-will of my emperor.

The venerable don hesitated a long time in this connection, and on one day went so far as to ask me to tell him candidly how he could comply with my wish and at the same time be free from suspicion.

"Very easily," said I. "Let the *misioneros* and the other inhabitants present a petition to you, of which you will advise me; then send some of your officers to examine the quality of the goods and ascertain the prices. The latter I shall make as favorable as possible, in the interests of the inhabitants, if you will give orders that the original Mexican invoices for such goods shall be shown me. Thereupon I will transfer the piastres to my commissary, from whom you will receive the goods and apportion them as required by the people."

This plan was carried out to the letter. The goods were inspected and accepted, and the transfer was made. My name did not appear in the transaction, except where I signed the general invoice of goods purchased, certifying that such goods belonged to the commissary, Panaev, and that, for the purpose of supplying the wants of the inhabitants of Nueva California and to favor the Spanish government, I had permitted such sale, and had deposited in the office of the *puerto* a declaration to that effect.

This, gracious sire, is our first experiment in trade in Nueva California, which, at a low estimate, may amount to a million rubles yearly. In the future the needs of our American possessions will be supplied; Kamchatka and Okhotsk, with grain and other provisions; the Yakuts will not be obliged to carry grain long distances; the government expenses for army and navy supplies will be diminished; the price of bread in Irkutsk will be much lower when a considerable portion of grain, formerly shipped to the distant provinces, can be kept at home for local consumption; the custom-houses will bring new revenue to the crown; the industries of interior Russia will receive a new impulse when the number of factories will have to be increased on account of the California trade alone, and in the mean time ways will be found for trade with India by way of Siberia; and your excellency may believe that with a good and well-considered beginnings all this will be brought about in a short time.

I have already, in my last reports to the general administration, written sufficiently concerning the means of expanding the trade here to dimensions worthy of a great empire. I shall only briefly refer to them here, and declare my sincere belief that it is too soon for us, or, rather, unprofitable, to send ships back to Russia by way of Canton. Above all other matters, I considered the strengthening of New Archangel, the sending of ships from there to Canton, and then back to Siberia and America, as thus they could make quicker, safer, and more profitable voyages.

No ships with goods should be sent here (New Archangel) from Saint Petersburg, unless they are to remain here. Then both America and its fleet will be strengthened. Siberia will be awakened by this trade, and when it is impossible for Russia to dispose of all its goods, time will show us the proper moment to attempt world trade; otherwise I must acknowledge it would be only factitious glitter and little profit.

If you can obtain permission to trade with Nueva California, the company could, from the profits accruing, erect granaries, and, after encouraging the savages in the proposed southern colonies, it would not be long before their increased population would make it necessary to use our own system of agriculture and cattle-raising, and with our trade with Canton fully organized, we could settle Chinese laborers there.

Your excellency perhaps may laugh at my far-reaching plans, but I am certain that they will prove exceedingly profitable ventures, and if we had men and means, even without any great sacrifice on the part of the treasury, all this country could be made a corporeal part of the Russian empire; and when you consider the conditions and investigate their interrelations, you will concur in my opinion that our trade would make notable and even gigantic strides. All great plans appear visionary on paper, but, viewed and considered comprehensively, their execution compels admiration. Not through petty enterprise, but by great undertakings, have mighty commercial bodies achieved rank and power.

If the Russian government had thought earlier of this part of the world, and estimated adequately its potentialities, and if it had pursued continuously the far-reaching plans of Peter the Great, who, with insignificant resources, dispatched the expedition commanded by Bering, it is safe to say that Nueva California would never have been Spanish territory, the Spaniards having only turned their attention to it since 1760, and it was only by the zeal and energy of the Franciscan *misioneros* that this incomparable territory was permanently incorporated into their kingdom. Even now there still is left an unoccupied intervening territory fully as rich, and if we allow it to slip through our fingers, what will succeeding generations say? I, at least, shall not be arraigned before them in judgment.

Should fate decree the completion of my romance,—not begun in hot passion, which is not becoming at my age, but arising under the pressure of conditions,—remoteness, duties, responsibilities,—perhaps also under the influence of remnants of feelings that in the past were a source of happiness in my life,—then, and in such case, I shall be in a position to serve my country once again, as by a personal examination of the harbor of Vera Cruz, Mexico, and by a trip through the interior parts of America. This could not be accomplished by, nor would permission be granted to, any one else, the suspicious Spanish temperament forbidding such investigations. I should also be able to inform you fully, gracious sire, as to their trade, their surplus, and their needs. Upon becoming acquainted with the viceroy of Nueva España, I could be of benefit to my countrymen in making an attempt to secure an entrance for Russian vessels to the eastern ports, as I hope that during the reign of such a gracious emperor the Russians will inaugurate trade from Saint Petersburg in natural and industrial products. At the same time I can investigate the prospects of trading with the United States, upon visiting that country, and seek to establish business connections with our company.

Here, gracious sire, you will see that I sacrifice myself for the good of others, and only hope that my strength shall equal my intentions.

[1806]

VOYAGE DOWN THE BAY

by

G. H. von LANGSDORFF

MISIONES de San Francisco de Asís, Santa Clara de Asís, San José, the three most northerly of the Franciscan *misiones* of Nueva California, lie near the southeast part of the Puerto de San Francisco; and although water-communication from one to the other would be of the utmost benefit, it seems almost incredible that in not one of them, no, not even in the Presidio or Puerto de San Francisco, is there a vessel or boat of any kind.

Perhaps the *misioneros* are afraid that if they had boats the escape of the Indians, who never wholly lose their love of freedom, or attachment to their original habits, might be facilitated, and therefore consider it better to confine their communication with one another to the means afforded by land,—to the horse.

The Spaniard, as well as his nursling the Indian, is but seldom forced to trust himself to the waves, and this may be the reason that communication by water here is hardly yet in its infancy. When such an occasion does arise, they make a kind of boat of straw, reeds, and rushes, bound so compactly that it is water-tight, and in this they manage to go very well from one shore to the other. It is called by the Spaniards "balsa." The oar used is a long, narrow pole, somewhat wider at the ends, with which they row, sometimes on one side and sometimes on the other.

This total lack of vessels, which are, so to speak, keys to all their southern and eastern possessions, is a strong proof of the recklessness of the Spanish government. It is because of this lack that they had to wait so long on shore on the day of our arrival, and were thus precluded from all communication with us until we sent out our ship's boat.

As *Misión* San José lies on the opposite or southeastern shore of the *puerto,* at a distance of sixteen leagues, communication by water would prove of infinite benefit to the *misioneros.* Notwithstanding that this convenience is so easily within their reach, they have no other means of intercourse than that by land. Thus they are obliged to go round the bay, at least three times the distance.

The difficulty of conveyance by land, the small number of *neófitos* at the *Misión* San José, and the breaking out, this year, of an infectious disease—the measles—hitherto unknown in California, which had spread from Antigua California to the northern settlements, and had for some weeks attacked great numbers of the Indians in the contiguous *misiones,* caused much delay in the delivery of the supplies agreed upon. Count Rezanov therefore applied to *Gobernador* Arrillaga for permission to send our ship's boats to *Misión* San José, so that the delivery of the supplies might be expedited. The advantage accruing, in saving the labor of men and horses, was so obvious that the *gobernador* readily consented.

According, on the 12th of April, several boats were held in readiness, and a courier was sent by land to the *Misión* San José to inform them of our coming, and with an order from the *gobernador* to make a signal-fire at the landing-place on the 14th to indicate its locale. Without such a fire, we were assured by the *gobernador* and the *comandante,* it would not be posssible to find it. Lieutenant Davidow commanded on this occasion, and permitted me to accompany him.

At about noon on the 14th we left the ship and availed ourselves of the flood-tide to run into the large arm of the *puerto* stretching to the southeast. When we reached the point of land lying northeast of the Presidio we saw thereon the battery of five cannon that protected the south-southeastern and southwestern division of the *puerto.* The shore on our left, or eastern shore, presents a low, extensive plain stretching several miles inland, and is bounded by a chain of hills of moderate height, intersected by deep valleys, covered only in some places with timber. The western shore is bounded by hills partly bare and partly covered with brush. This shore has many points of land and small bays, and near one of the latter lies *Misión* San Francisco de Asís. As far as this place the water is deep enough for large vessels, but a little farther on it is much shallower, not having a depth of five feet. This was shown by a great change in the color of the water. We now proceeded for several nautical miles, sounding all the way quite frequently, and saw high land on the southern horizon, which appeared to rise like an island in the midst of the water, and soon after this we saw pretty clearly, to the southeast, upon a rising eminence, the *Misión* San José. At the same time we saw smoke toward the south, upon what we had supposed to be an island. As this smoke was so far to the south, we were of the opinion that it could not be the signal intended for us, regarding it as a chance-fire, and kept on the lookout for ours on the nearer eastern shore.

Only at sunset did we find out our mistake, and discover that what we had supposed to be an island was connected by a narrow neck of land to a plain lying farther east. But, having had a fresh southwest wind, we were now so near the eastern shore that it was impossible, either by rowing or with a sail, to reach the signal-fire. When night came on, it was so dark that we were forced to anchor in a shallow place, in three feet of water. We were now separated from and entirely out of sight of the other boats.

On the morning of the 15th we endeavored in vain to reach the high point of land, and as the wind still blew strong from the southwest, nothing now remained but to return to the ship. The longboat having battled all day both winds and waves, we considered ourselves fortunate on the 16th to reach the harbor of (the Presidio de) San Francisco. The third boat, having lost its mast, had taken refuge in a small bay. The same squally weather, with rain, continued until the 19th, when it cleared, and the wind changed to the north and northwest.

My desire to visit *Misión* San José was not abated in consequence of this unsuccessful attempt, and I requested and obtained the *gobernador's* consent to make another attempt. On the 20th, therefore, with a sailor and a huntsman, I set out in a three-seated bidarka that I had brought from Sitka. We left San Francisco early in the morning, and about noon reached the plain lying in front of the *Misión*. We then sought for the principal channel, which is supposed to be in the vicinity of several hills, and these are indeed the principal guides in finding it. They stretch from the northwest to the southeast, and are surrounded by a muddy shallow extending a con-

siderable distance along the shore, to avoid which one must steer
to the west until the southern hills, which on our first attempt on
the 14th we had mistaken for an island, lie to the east. The channel
that must then be taken winds among the heights, and the lowest
two of these left to the north, and the others, which are much higher,
to the south. This channel runs at first in a northwesterly direction,
and then, after many windings, southeasterly into the interior. At
flood-tide the depth of water is from six to nine feet, but even at
ebb-tide it is navigable by small boats. At low water it is almost impossible to land, on account of the muddy shore, and at high water
the landing is not unattended with difficulty. The many little channels
intersecting this flat land make it an absolute labyrinth, and as we
were not acquainted with the terrain, we were mistaken at many
times, and had to turn back, often missing the main by turning into
a side channel.

Wearied at length by continually going astray, I ascended a hill
near by, where I could get a better view of the terrain, and saw a
landing-place from which we could proceed overland to the *Misión,*
which lay three and a half leagues east-north-east. The country now
to be traveled over rises gradually over the low-lying plain, and is
bounded by a chain of moderately high hills, which stretch from the
north-northwest to the south-southeast. Numerous herds of horses and
cattle were running wild here, without any attention being paid to
them. The bulls even render the country unsafe for foot-passengers.
We also saw many foxes, and a large wolf that ran away frightened.
The foxes seemed to live on the most peaceful terms with the young
calves, and followed the cows like the calves.

Shortly before sunset we arrived at the *Misión,* very much fatigued.
It was now under the charge of two *misioneros,* Padre Luis (Gily
Taboada) and Padre Pedro De la Cueva. The latter only was at the
Misión. He received us with open arms, and sent at once horses to
the shore to fetch our baggage and the sailor. We had left the sailor
to take care of the bidarka, and he was now relieved by some Indians.
Fray Luis was now at San Francisco on a short visit. On the morning
of the 21st all the Indian *neófitos* were assembled to receive from Fray
Pedro their allotted work for the day. He had promised, when I saw
him at San Francisco, to entertain me with an Indian dance at his
Misión, and he therefore now announced to them that they should

have a holiday, and that they might dress themselves in their best and prepare for the dance. He distributed, for this purpose, a number of ornaments among the best dancers, who immediately withdrew with them to make the necessary preparations.

In the mean time Fray Pedro showed me about the buildings and grounds belonging to his *Misión*. They are of considerable extent, although it is only eight years since work was begun on them. Grain in the storehouses, as to quantity, greatly exceeded my expectations, there being over two thousand fanegas of wheat, and a proportionate quantity of maize, barely, pease, beans, etc. The kitchen-garden is exceptionally well laid out, and kept in very good order. The soil is everywhere productive, and the fruit-trees, although still small, are doing very well. A rivulet runs through the garden, with sufficient water to irrigate. Some vineyards have been planted within the past few years, with vines now yielding exceedingly well. The wine is sweet, and resembles Malaga.

The site of the establishment is exceedingly well chosen, and the common opinion is that the *Misión* will in a few years be one of the richest and best in Nueva California. The one and only disadvantage is an entire lack of forests of tall timber. The native Indians have, now and then, thoughtlessly, simply to make a bonfire, set fire to the forests, and burned down large tracts, leaving few trees standing; hence timber for building purposes must be brought from a distance of several miles. But, in comparison with other *misiones,* this disadvantage is compensated by the presence, in the neighborhood, of chalk-hills and an excellent clay, whereby brick-kilns may be erected and the main structures built of brick.

The interior arrangement and organization of this *Misión* is entirely the same as that of *Misión* San Francisco. The habitations of the Indians—*las rancherías*—are not yet finished, so that the *neófitos* live for the most part in families, in straw huts of a conical form.

Fray Pedro, who showed me about everywhere, invited me, when we had seen all that was worth seeing, to go and see the Indians getting ready for the dance. We went to a rivulet, by the side of which the dancers were gathered, very busy in smearing their bodies over with charcoal, red clay, and chalk. While one Indian was ornamenting his own breast, abdomen, and thighs, another was painting his back with various regular figures. Some were covering their nude bodies all over

with down, which gave them rather the appearance of monkeys than
of human beings. Their heads, ears, and necks were set off with a
great variety of ornaments, but except a covering tied around the
waist, their entire bodies were nude. The women were at the same
time, in their huts, performing the offices of the toilet, and were all,
consistently with the customs of decorum, dressed. Their faces and
necks, only, were painted, and they were adorned with a profusion of
shells, feathers, corals, etc.

The Indians assembled in the courtyard toward noon. They are
very different from the Indians of *Misión* San Francisco, as to size,
appearance, and build. The men were well built, and almost all are
above middling stature. Very few indeed are what may be called
undersized. Their complexions are dark, but not negro-like, and if
their physiognomy cannot absolutely be called pleasing, there is nothing
about it that would provoke aversion. I thought that they strongly
resembled the northern tribes. They have very coarse black hair, and
some are possessed of extraordinary strength. In general, the women
seem proportionately taller than the men, and many are over five feet
high.

If there were not any, either among the men or women, that I
could call handsome, I did not note in one the dull, heavy, and
repugnant look of the *neófitos* of San Francisco. The Indians of this
Misión are indeed generally considered the handsomest in Nueva
California, and hence the Spanish soldiers, in the absence of Spanish
women, often marry the Indian women of this *Misión*.

The dancers were divided into two companies. Each distinguished
itself by specific ornaments and a special kind of song. One of these
companies was composed of Indians inhabiting the coast, and the other
of Indians belonging to inland tribes. The coast Indians were not so
well made, nor so strong, nor so good-looking, as those of the interior.
These neighboring tribes formerly lived at great mutual enmity.
Although they are now united here by the bond of religion, yet the
old hostility is so rooted in them that it is still apparent. As an instance of this, the *misioneros* cannot induce them to inter-marry.
They will unite themselves with only those of their own tribe, and it
is an exception that they mingle or associate with members of any
tribe other than their own.

In their dances the Indians remain almost always in the same place, endeavoring, partly with their bows and arrows, partly with the feathers they hold in their hands and wear on their heads, and also by measured springs, by different movements of their bodies, and by facial contortions, to imitate scenes of battle or of domestic life. Their music consists of singing, and clapping with a stick at one end. The women have their own particular song, and their own particular manner of dancing. They hop about near the men, but never in time with them. Their principal action or practice is in pressing the abdomen with the thumb and forefinger, first to one side and then to the other, in regular measure. As soon as the men begin to dance, the women also begin, and cease the moment the men cease.

At about two o'clock we sat down to a very fine dinner, and afterwards went again to see the Indians, who were still engaged in dancing, and were now about to enact a mock battle. A large straw figure represented the enemy, and a number of men, armed with bows and arrows, sprang and danced about with fierce gesticulations and contortions to defy their adversary, who, had he been able, would have done likewise. One of the Indians finally gave a signal, and at the same moment the straw figure was pierced with many arrows, whereupon it was presented in triumph to the man who personated the chief.

Upon this occasion I perceived that most of the Indians were skillful marksmen. Yet it appeared to me that if the enemy was courageous, and would attend more to the use of his weapons and less to gesticulations, he could hardly fail to win. These people were never in the habit of eating the enemy killed in battle, the greatest endeavor of each party being to steal the young girls and the wives of the enemy.

Another party of Indians danced before a large fire, from which each one, apparently for his own gratification, took, now and then, a glowing ember as large as a walnut, and without further ceremony put it into his mouth and swallowed it. It was not deception. I watched them very closely, and saw it done repeatedly, although it is utterly beyond my comprehension how it could be done without the mouth being burned.

I was also entertained with a representation of a hunting party. The Indians fasten the horns of a deer on their heads, and throw a portion of the skin over their shoulders. Thus disguised, they lurk in the high grass, where the stags and the roes come to feed, imitating their actions so well that, though naturally shy and timid, they are duped, and allow the Indians, with their bows and arrows, to come within a few feet of them. Several are often killed without the others having any idea of their peril.

Directly east, about seven leagues from *Misión* San José, there is an arm of a great river that first winds toward the north, and then, making a turn to the west, empties itself at last into the Bay of San Francisco at its northeastern part. In the region of this river there are numerous Indian villages, but the natives do not yet consort with the Spaniards or the baptized Indians. When *Misión* San José was first founded they became troublesome from time to time. Only a year and half before I was there they had murdered five soldiers and dangerously wounded one of the padres and another soldier. Upon this a strong military expedition was sent out against them, and a great slaughter of the Indians was the result, whereupon they were compelled to conclude a peace. There has been no trouble with them since. The Spaniards and the Indian *neófitos* occasionally go among these Indians, remaining with them for perhaps a fortnight or longer, with the intention of gaining *neófitos*, if possible. Some of them make visits to the *Misión,* at which times they always return home enriched with presents of various kinds.

Three leagues from the *Misión* San José, to the southwest, lies the Pueblo de San José de Guadalupe. The word "pueblo" is used here to indicate a sort of village composed of *inválidos,* who are released from military service. They cultivate the soil and raise cattle, and live in the midst of plenty. There are several pueblos such as this, in different parts of Nueva and Antigua California, and here there is a yearly increase in population. Gobernador Arrillaga assured me that in twenty years the population of the Pueblo de San José de Guadalupe had increased from one hundred to seven hundred. It is peculiar that, conversely, and nothwithstanding their good treatment, there is a continuous diminution in the number of the *Misión* Indian *neófitos.*

On the 23d I took leave of Fray Pedro, to whom I owe my public acknowledgments for his kindly reception and hospitality. He had horses saddled for us, and we went, accompanied by a soldier, in search of our bidarka, which we found at the very spot where we had left it. Some wild bulls followed us on our way, and caused us much uneasiness. A number of foxes, on the contrary, ran off terrified.

We rowed in shallow water, through the channel that winds among the hills, down to the bay. The muddy banks that stretched on either side were overspread with sandpipers, snipes, wild ducks, and sea-mews; but we did not attempt to shoot any of them, as it would have been impossible to get them out of the deep mire. We saw also a great number of sea-otters, one of which we shot, but as it took refuge in one of the smaller channels, we had not the disposition to lose time in its pursuit.

Scarcely had we reached the open waters of the bay than a strong north wind arose. It was now an impossibility to proceed. Wet through and through by the dashing waves, held back by the rush of the current, and suffering from hunger and thirst, we were forced at sunset to relinquish all hope of going forward, and resign ourselves to the probability of passing the night in the open, in a low boggy place near the landing. Not having anticipated such a condition, we had brought with us provisions for only one day, and now nothing was left but a little bread and cheese, and an insignificant quantity of brandy. We laid ourselves down to rest with empty stomachs, not being able even to quench our thirst, since we were surrounded by the saline tidewater. We endeavored to shelter ourselves somewhat from the force of the strong winds by means of our wet sailcloth, and in this situation, and stiff with cold, waited for daybreak.

By the morning our clothes, which had been wet through by the storm yesterday, were tolerably dry, and at ten o'clock were were ready to leave. But we found that on account of the tide being still at low ebb there was still a larger extent of muddy shore than it was possible to cross. Nor would it admit of our re-embarking until about noon. Scarcely, then, had we seated ourselves in the boat than the same north and northwest wind returned, and left not a probability of our being able, even on that day, to reach the (Presidio harbor of) San Francisco. We consequently decided to row to the opposite shore, which looked to be much higher and well wooded, and reached that side at about three o'clock in the afternoon. But here we found a low boggy plain, overgrown merely by a saltwort (Salsola), and, like the plain on the eastern shore, intersected by many little channels, so that there was no possibility of our reaching the woods on foot.

However, we followed, in our bidarka, the widest channel, and, row-ing amidst the many windings for about three quarters of an hour, were lucky enough to find a place to land, and from which there was reason to hope that we might soon reach the wood, where we hoped to find fresh water. Armed with guns and pistols, and taking with us our last morsel of bread and cheese and an empty bottle, we went on our way. Infinitely annoyed, we traveled about in search of some brook or spring where we might quench our thirst. We reached the wood before nightfall, after walking more than a German mile, but nowhere found a drop of water. We at length saw a numerous herd of bulls and cows, feeding wild among luxuriant wild grass in a meadow. Keeping these off with our guns and pistols, we searched in a thorough manner for water, but all in vain,—again not a drop could we find. Exhausted by fatigue and suffering from hunger and thirst, in listless despair we laid ourselves down, when suddenly we heard, at some distance, the croak of a frog. Never did the tuneful notes of the nightingale sound to our ears half so delightful. We started up, and, following the call and seeming invitation of this creature, soon found ourselves, in the darkness of the night, by the side of a little stream of excellent water. As for two days we had been upon a short allowance of food, and with nothing to quench our thirst, we drank the water with such avidity that in two hours we consumed fourteen bottlefuls. It should be stated that we were a party of only three.

The night was cool and damp. So we made a fire to warm ourselves, and rested till midnight, when, the moon being very bright, we decided to return to our bidarka. On the way we encountered several bears and wild bulls, which we kept off with our guns, and at about three o'clock in the morning we reached our bidarka. It was then perfectly calm. In a very fine morning we set out upon our return to (the harbor of the Presidio de) San Francisco. The channel that we followed to reach the bay was full of sea-otters and sea-dogs. Many were lying on the muddy shores, and many swimming, their heads just above the water. The trials of the past few days were so fresh in our memories, and the craving of our stomachs for nourishment so insistent, that we renounced all the joys and advantages that might accrue from a chase of these animals. Despite this, three sea-otters, that lay sleeping almost beside our bidarka, presented a temptation that could not be resisted. These we did kill and carry off with us.

Towards noon we were pretty near the *Misión* San Francisco, but a northwest wind, that arose at the moment, again retarded us so much that we did not reach the ship until about three, exhausted by hunger, thirst, and fatigue.

To my inexpressible regret, a number of objects of natural history, collected by me on my journey, chiefly plants and birds, had become a prey to the stormy waters, and I brought nothing back with me but the three sea-otters.

SAN FRANCISCO

FROM THE SEA

by

BRET HARTE

Serene, indifferent of Fate,
Thou sittest at the Western Gate;
Upon thy heights so lately won
Still slant the banners of the sun;
Thou seest the white seas strike their tents,
O Warder of two Continents!
And scornful of the peace that flies
Thy angry winds and sullen skies,
Thou drawest all things, small or great,
To thee, beside the Western Gate.

O, lion's whelp, that hidest fast
In jungle growth of spire and mast,
I know thy cunning and thy greed,
Thy hard high lust and wilful deed,
And all thy glory loves to tell
Of specious gifts material.
Drop down, O fleecy Fog, and hide
Her skeptic sneer, and all her pride!
Wrap her, O Fog, in gown and hood
Of her Franciscan Brotherhood.
Hide me her faults, her sin and blame,
With thy grey mantle cloak her shame!
So shall she, cowléd, sit and pray
Till morning bears her sins away.
Then rise, O fleecy Fog, and raise

The glory of her coming days;
Be as the cloud that flecks the seas
Above her smoky argosies.
When forms familiar shall give place
To stranger speech and newer face;
When all her throes and anxious fears
Lie hushed in the repose of years;
When Art shall raise and Culture lift
The sensual joys and meaner thrift,
And all fulfilled the vision, we
Who watch and wait shall never see—
Who, in the morning of her race,
Toiled fair or meanly in our place—
But, yielding to the common lot,
Lie unrecorded and forgot.

ST. FRANCIS' BAY

by

OTTO von KOTZEBUE

ON THE 1st of October, at midnight, we descried by moonlight the Cape de los Reyes, and at four o'clock P.M. we dropped anchor in the port of St. Francisco, opposite the government house.

Our *Rurick* seemed to throw the place in no small alarm, for, on approaching the fort of St. Toaquin, situated on a neck of land formed of high rocks, on the southern entrance, we saw several soldiers on horse and foot, and in the fort itself they were loading the cannon. The entrance to the harbour is so narrow, that ships are compelled to sail within musket-shot from the fort. On approaching it, we were asked, through the speaking-trumpet, to what nation we belonged, our flag being unknown to them. Having answered that we were Russians and friends, I saluted them with five guns, and was answered by the same number. More than an hour elapsed after we had cast anchor, without any one approaching us, the whole of the military train having left the fort, and ranged themselves opposite our anchorage. At last it occurred to me that Vancouver had not found any boats here; I therefore sent my lieutenant with Mr. Chamisso on shore, to announce our arrival to the commandant, Don Louis d'Argüello, lieutenant of the cavalry, who received them in a friendly manner, promising to provide our ship daily with fresh provisions. A basket of fruit, which he sent me, I found a great treat, not having tasted any so long. He also immediately dispatched a courier to Monterez, to inform the governor of California of our arrival.

The 3d of October: This morning we were visited by the artillery officer of the fort, as a messenger from the commandant, accompanied

From *Voyage of Discovery in The South Sea*, London, 1821.

by a clergyman of the mission. They both offered us every possible assistance; the former in the name of the commandant, and the latter in the name of the mission. At noon they sent us a fat ox, two sheep, cabbage, pumpkins, and a great quantity of fruit; of the latter I made my men eat as much as they could daily, to counteract any tendency to the scurvy that might have been produced in their system. I found the *praesidio* as Vancouver described it; the garrison consists of one company of calvary, of which the commandant is the chief, and who has only one officer of the artillery under his command.

On the 4th we went ashore, in order to ride with the commandant to the mission-house, whither we had been invited to the feast of St. Francisco. We were accompanied by ten horsemen, all fine dexterous men, who use their carbines and lances with the skill of our Cossacks. They owe their skill to the constant practice in which they are kept, for the military in California only serve to protect the mission against the attacks of the savages, and assist the clergy in enlisting Christians among these people, and to keep the converted in the new faith. We arrived in about an hour, although above half our road lay among sand and hills, which were scantily covered with a few shrubs; in the neighbourhood of the mission we came to a delightful country, and recognized the rich vegetation of California. After having rode through a street inhabited by Indians, (for thus the natives are denominated by the Spaniards,) we stopped at a large building, near the church, inhabited by the missionaries; and here we were met by five priests, three of whom belong to this mission, and two others came from St. Clara, in honour of the solemnity; they led us into a large room, plainly furnished, where we were received very respectfully. On the clock striking ten we entered the church, built of stone, and neatly ornamented, where we already found some hundreds of half-naked Indians upon their knees, who, although they neither understand Spanish nor Latin, are not allowed to miss one mass after their conversion. As the missionaries, on their side, do not endeavour to learn the language of the natives, I cannot conceive in what manner they have been taught the Christian religion; and the confusion in the heads and hearts of these poor people, who only know how to mimic some external ceremonies, must indeed be very great. The rage of converting savage nations is now spreading over the whole of the South-Sea, and produces great mischief, since the missionaries never think to humanize them before they make them Christians, and thus that which was to have been productive of happiness and peace, becomes the ground of bloody warfare: for instance, on the Friendly Islands, where the Christians and heathens constantly strive to exterminate each other.

It struck me that, during the whole ceremony, the unbaptized were not allowed to rise from their knees; for this exertion, however, they were indemnified by the church-music, which seemed to give them much pleasure, and which undoubtedly was the only part of the ceremony in which they felt interested. The choir consisted of a violoncello, a violin, and two flutes; which instruments were played by little half-naked Indians, who gave us many false notes.

From the church we went to dinner, where we found no lack of provisions and wine, the latter of which the missionaries make themselves. After dinner we were shown the dwelling-places of the Indians, consisting of long, low, clay-built houses, forming several streets. The filthy state of these barracks was beyond conception, which is probably the cause of the great mortality among the inhabitants, since, of the 1000 Indians that are in Fort Francisco, 300 die annually. The Indian girls, of whom there are 400 in the mission, live, separate from the men, likewise in similar barracks; both parties are obliged to work hard. The men cultivate the ground; the produce of which is received by the missionaries, who keep it in granaries, from which the Indians receive just enough to subsist on. The soldiers of the settlement are likewise kept from it, but they must pay for the flour with ready cash. The women constantly spin wool and weave a coarse stuff, which is party used for their ordinary dress, and some is sent to Mexico, where it is exchanged for other necessary articles. This being a holiday, the Indians were not at work; and instead of which they were playing at various games, one of which required particular skill: two of them sit opposite each other on the ground, each of them holding in his hand a bundle of sticks; and, while they, at the same time, throw them up in the air with great dexterity, they guess whether the number is even or odd; near each player a person is sitting, who scores the gain and loss. As they are always playing for something, and having nothing besides their clothes, which they are not permitted to stake, they work with great labour small white shells, which are used by them instead of money.

The coast of California is so rich in various tribes, that there are often more than ten tribes together, each of which has its peculiar language. On leaving the mission, we were surprised by two groups of Indians, who also consisted of several nations. They came in battle-array, quite naked, and painted with various colours; the heads of most them were adorned with feathers and other finery, some had covered their long wild hair with down, and painted their faces in a frightful manner. There was nothing remarkable in the warlike dance, but I regretted I could not understand the words of their song. The physiognomy of these Indians is ugly, stupid, and savage; besides they are well-made, rather tall, and of a dark brown colour; the women are very small and ugly: they have much of the negro in their faces, except that a negro-head, in comparison with theirs, may be called beautiful; what particularly distinguishes them from the negro, is their long straight hair, of the darkest black.

The missionaries assured us that their stupidity made it a very diffi-cult task to instruct them; but I rather think that the gentlemen do not trouble themselves much about it; they all told us that the Indians came far from the interior, submitting to them of their own accord (which we also doubted): the religious instruction, they said, was then immediately begun, and, according to their capacities, they were sooner or later baptized. California costs the Spanish government a great sum, without any other advantage than the annual conversion of some hundreds of Indians, but who soon die in their new faith, as they cannot easily accustom themselves to a new mode of life. Twice a year they are permitted to go home, which short time is for them the happiest; and I have sometimes seen them going, in large numbers, shouting on the road. The sick, who cannot undertake the journey, at least accompany their fortunate countrymen to the shore, where they embark, and remain sitting for days together, casting their sorrow-ful eyes on the distant hills that surround their habitations; they often stop for several days in this spot, without taking any food, so much are these new Christians attracted by their lost homes. Every time some of those which are on furlough take flight, and probably they would flee away altogether, were it not for fear of the soldiers, who take them, and bring them back like criminals to the mission: but this fear is so great that seven or eight dragoons are enough to keep in check hundreds of Indians.

Two considerable rivers fall in the Bay of St. Francisco, of which that in the north is the largest, and is called by the Spaniards Rio-grande. This river, the missionaries say, is the finest in the world, and is navigable by the largest vessels; at the same time its banks are fruitful, the climate is mild, and the population numerous. The missionaries frequently make excursions upon it, in large well-armed boats, in order to get recruits for their faith, in which, however, they seldom succeed, the inhabitants being brave and well-armed.

We had just come back to the *Rurick,* when a messenger from the governor of Old California, Don Paolo Vicente de Sola arrived from Monterey, bringing me a polite letter from the governor, in which, among the rest, he promised to come himself to St. Francisco, as soon as his business would allow. At the same time I obtained permission to send a messenger to Mr. Kuskoff, for some articles I wanted, and which he could immediately supply me, being in trade with American ships. Mr. Kuskoff, an agent of the Russo-American Company, has settled, by order of Mr. Baranof, who is at the head of all these possessions in America, at Bodega, in order to supply the possessions of the colony with provisions from that place. Bodega is half a day's voyage from St. Francisco, and is called by the Spaniards Port Bodega. The harbour is only fit for small vessels. Kuskoff's larger possessions are a little north of Port Bodega.

The 5th.—The *Rurick* required several repairs, which I left to the care of my lieutenant, while I occupied myself with the instruments, which I took on shore under a tent. Our naturalists and draughtsmen were very busy; and, after the days quickly passed in various occupations, we met in the evening to enjoy together the beauty of the climate, in which the officers of the settlement joined us. The military seem to be dissatisfied both with the government and the mission, having received nothing for these seven years, and being almost entirely without clothing; at the same time, the inhabitants are entirely deprived of European goods, since no trading vessel is allowed to enter any port of California; and it is truly lamentable to see this beautiful country thus neglected.

On the 16th, the governor arrived in the fort.

On the 17th, a large baydare from Mr. Kuskoff arrived, loaded with all necessary articles. At noon the governor dined with us in our

tent on shore. We found him a very amiable gentleman, and afterwards spent many pleasant days in his company.

On the 18th, I sent word to Mr. Kuskoff, that the governor wished
to see him here respecting his establishment at Bodega. The governor
told me there were several Russian prisoners in California; they were
part of the crew of a vessel belonging to the Company, which had
been carrying on trade upon this coast, contrary to the Spanish laws,
and had been seized by the soldiers, while they were on shore, without suspecting any danger, and were thrown into prison. By the express command of the Viceroy of Mexico, the governor was inter-
dicted from surrendering them to Mr. Kuskoff, but he had no objection
to give them up to me, if I would carry them away; but my ship being
too small, I could only take three of them, and I selected those who
had been some time in the service of the Company. Besides these,
I took on-board Mr. Elliot, with the intention of leaving him, at
his own request, on the Sandwich Islands. *John Elliot de Castro,* a
Portuguese by birth, came to Sitka on-board an American vessel, in
which he had been engaged by Mr. Baranof, to accompany the ship
destined for the coast of California, as supercargo, and had been taken
with the rest.

On the 23d, the governor amused us with some interesting sport
between a bull and a bear; the latter are so frequent in this country,
that on going only a mile from the houses into the woods, we could
meet with them in great numbers. The species differs from ours by
a pointed head, and of an ash-grey colour; they are also more active
and daring. Nevertheless, the dragoons here are so dexterous and
courageous that they are sent out into the wood for a bear, as we
should order a cook to fetch in a goose. They go on horseback, with
nothing but a rope with a running-knot in their hands, which is sufficient to overpower a bear. As soon as the enraged animal is about
to rush on one of them, another throws the knot, which is fixed to
the saddle by a strong curve, round one of his fore-paws, and, gallop-
ing off, throws him down; immediately the other throws a knot around
his hind-leg, and thus the third is able to tie his fore-legs together,
after which they carry him home without danger. In this manner,
the dragoons had brought one to-day, while others had gone in the
same way to fetch a bull. The cattle being, upon the whole, abandoned
to themselves, have become savage, and are likewise caught with

knots by a few horsemen, when they are wanted to be killed. The battle between these two animals was very remarkable; and, although the bull several times tossed his furious opponent, he was overpowered at last.

On the 29th, the governor returned to Monterey. One of the Russians, whom I had taken here on board, being out a-hunting, was so injured by the explosion of the powder-horn, that he died in consequence of it.

On the 1st of November, the *Rurick* being in excellent trim, well furnished with provisions, and my men in perfect health, we heaved anchor, and at ten o'clock A.M. were out of the bay. At a distance of two miles in sea, we heard the piercing howlings of the sea-lions that lay upon the stones on shore.

A LUXURIANT COUNTRY

by

CAPTAIN FREDERICK WILLIAM BEECHEY

Harbor and Presidio

WHEN the day broke, we found ouselves about four miles from the land. It was a beautiful morning, with just sufficient freshness in the air to exhilarate without chilling. The tops of the mountains, the only part of the land visible, formed two ranges, between which our port was situated, though its entrance, as well as the valleys and the low lands, were still covered with the morning mist condensed around the bases of the mountains. We bore up for the opening between the ranges, anxious for the rising sun to withdraw the veil that we might obtain a view of the harbour, and form our judgment of the country in which we were about to pass the next few weeks. As we advanced, the beams of the rising sun gradually descended the hills, until the mist, dispelled from the land, rolled on before the refreshing sea wind, discovering cape after cape, and exhibiting a luxuriant country apparently abounding in wood and rivers. At length two low promontories, the southern one distinguished by a fort and a Mexican flag, marked the narrow entrance of the port.

We spread our sails with all the anxiety of persons who had long been secluded from civilized society, and deprived of wholesome aliment; but after the first effort of the breeze, it died away and left us becalmed in a heavy N. W. swell.

Off the harbour of San Francisco there is a bar which extends from the northern shore, gradually deepening its water until it approaches

From *Narrative of a Voyage to the Pacific*, the Colt Press, San Francisco, 1941.

the peninsula on the opposite side, where nine fathoms may be carried over it. Of this bar, however, we were ignorant, and naturally steered directly for the harbour, in doing which the depth of water gradually diminished to five fathoms. This would have been of no consequence, had it not been for a swell which rolled so heavily over the bank that it continually broke; and though our depth of water was never less than 4½ fathoms, the ship on two or three occasions disturbed the sand with her keel. The tide was unfortunately against us, and the swell propelled the ship just sufficiently fast for her to steer without gaining any ground, so that we remained in this situation several hours.

At length a breeze sprung up, and we entered the port, and dropped our anchor in the spot where Vancouver had moored his ship thirty-three years before. As we passed the entrance, a heavy sea rolling violently upon a reef of rocks on our left bespoke the danger of approaching that side too close in light or baffling winds; while some scattered rocks with deep water round them skirting the shore on our right, marked that side also as dangerous; so that the entrance may be justly considered difficult. Beyond these rocks, however, near the fort, there is a bay in which, if necessary, ships may drop their anchor.

The fort, which we passed upon our right, mounts nine guns, and is built upon a promontory on the south side of the entrance, apparently so near to the precipice, that one side will, before long, be precipitated over it by the gradual breaking away of the rock. Its situation, nevertheless, is good, as regards the defence of the entrance; but it is commanded by a rising ground behind it. As we passed, a soldier protruded a speaking-trumpet through one of the embrasures, and hailed us with a stentorian voice, but we could not distinguish what was said. This custom of hailing vessels has arisen from there being no boat belonging to the garrison, and the inconvenience felt by the governor, in having to wait for a report of arrivals, until the masters of the vessels could send their boats on shore.

The port of San Francisco does not show itself to advantage until after the fort is passed, when it breaks upon the view, and forcibly impresses the spectator with the magnificence of the harbour. He then beholds a broad sheet of water, sufficiently extensive to contain all the British navy, with convenient coves, anchorage in every part, and, around, a country diversified with hill & dale, partly wooded and partly disposed in pasture lands of the richest kind, abounding in herds of cattle. In short, the only subjects wanting to complete the interest of the scene are some useful establishments and comfortable residences on the grassy borders of the harbour, the absence of which creates an involuntary regret that so fine a country, abounding in all that is essential to man, should be allowed to remain in such a state of neglect. So poorly did the place appear to be peopled that a sickly column of smoke rising from within some dilapidated walls, misnamed the presidio or "protection," was the only indication we had of the country being inhabited.

The harbour stretches to the S. E. to the distance of thirty miles, and affords a water communication between the missions of San José, Santa Clara, and the presidio, which is built upon a peninsula about five miles in width. On the north the harbour is contracted to a strait, which communicates with a basin ten miles wide, with a channel across it sufficiently deep for frigates, though they cannot come near the land on account of the mud. A creek on the N. W. side of this basin leads up to the new mission of San Francisco Solano; and a strait to the eastward, named Estrecho de Karquines, communicates with another basin into which three rivers discharge themselves, and bring down so large a body of water than the estrecho is from ten to eleven fathoms deep. These rivers are named Jesús María, El Sacramento, and San Joachin: the first, I was informed, takes a northerly direction, passes at the back of Bodega, and extends beyond Cape Mendocino. El Sacramento trends to the N. E., and is said to have its rise in the rocky mountains near the source of the Columbia. The other, San Joachin, stretches to the southward, through the country of the Bolbones, and is divided from the S. E. arm of the harbour by a range of mountains.

As we opened out the several islands and stopping places in the harbour, we noticed seven American whalers at anchor at Sausalito, not one of which showed their colours; we passed them and anchored off a small bay named Yerba Buena, from the luxuriance of its vegetation, about a league distant from both the presidio and the mission of San Francisco. I immediately went on shore to pay my respects to Don Ignacio Martinez, a lieutenant in the Mexican army, acting governor in the absence of Don Luis, and to the priest, whose name was Tomaso, both of whom gave me a very hospitable and friendly reception, and offered their services in any way they might be required.

We were happy to find the country around our anchorage abounding in game of all kinds, so plentiful, indeed, as soon to lessen the desire of pursuit; still there were many inducements to both the officers and seamen to land and enjoy themselves; and as it was for the benefit of the service that they should recruit their health and strength as soon as possible, every facility was afforded them. Horses were fortunately very cheap, from nine shillings to seven pounds apiece, so that riding became a favourite amusement; and the Spaniards finding they could make a good market by letting out their stud, appeared with them every Sunday opposite the ship, ready saddled for the occasion, as this was a day on which I allowed every man to go out of the ship. Some of the officers purchased horses and tethered them near the place, but the Spaniards finding this to interfere with their market, contrived to let them loose on the Saturday night, in order that the officers might be compelled to hire others on the following day. The only difficulty to the enjoyment of this amusement was the scarcity of saddles & bridles, some of which cost ten times as much as a decent horse. The ingenuity of the seamen generally obviated these difficulties, while some borrowed or hired saddles of the natives; for my own part, I purchased a decent looking horse for about thirty-five shillings sterling, and on my departure presented it to a Spaniard, who had lent me the necessary accoutrements for it during my stay, which answered the purpose of both parties, as he was pleased with his present, and I had my ride for about a shilling a day: a useful hint to persons who may be similarly circumstanced.

Martinez was always glad to see the officers at the presidio, and made them welcome to what he had. Indeed, nothing seemed to give him greater pleasure than our partaking of his family dinner; the greater part of which was dressed by his wife and daughters, who prided themselves on their proficiency in the art of cooking. It was not, however, entirely for the satisfaction of presenting us with a well-prepared repast that they were induced to indulge in this humble occupation: poor Martinez, besides his legitimate offspring, had eighteen others to provide for out of his salary, which was then eleven years in arrears. He had a sorry prospect before him, as, a short time previous to our visit, the government, by way of paying up these arrears, sent a brig with a cargo of paper cigars to be issued to the troops in lieu of dollars; but, as Martinez justly observed, cigars would not satisfy the families of the soldiers, and the compromise was refused. The cargo was, however, landed at Monterey & placed under the charge of the governor, where all other tobacco is contraband; and as the Spaniards are fond of smoking, it stands a fair chance, in the course of time, of answering the intention of the government, particularly as the troops apply for these oftener than they otherwise would, under the impression of clearing off a score of wages that will never be settled in any other manner. Fortunately for Martinez and other veterans in this country, both vegetable and animal food are uncommonly cheap, and there are no fashions to create any expense of dress.

The governor's abode was in a corner of the presidio, and formed one end of a row, of which the other was occupied by a chapel; the opposite side was broken down, and little better than a heap of rubbish and bones, on which jackals, dogs, and vultures were constantly preying; the other two sides of the quadrangle contained storehouses, artificer's shops, and the gaol, all built in the humblest style with badly burnt bricks, and roofed with tiles. The chapel & the governor's house were distinguished by being whitewashed.

Whether viewed at a distance or near, the establishment impresses a spectator with any other sentiment than that of its being a place of authority; and but for a tottering flag-staff, upon which was occasionally displayed the tri-coloured flag of Mexico, three rusty field pieces, and a half accoutred sentinel parading the gateway in charge of a few poor wretches heavily shackled, a visitor would be ignorant of the importance of the place. The neglect of the government to its establishments could not be more thoroughly evinced than in the dilapidated condition of the building in question; and such was the dissatisfaction of the people that there was no inclination to improve their situation, or even to remedy many of the evils which they appeared to us to have the power to remove.

The Mission System

The missions have hitherto been of the highest importance to California, and the government cannot be too careful to promote their welfare, as the prosperity of the country in a great measure is dependent upon them, and must continue to be so until settlers from the mother country can be induced to resort thither. As they are of such consequence, I shall enter somewhat minutely into a description of them. In Uppper California there are twenty-one of these establishments, nine of which are attached to the presidios of Monterey and San Francisco, and contain about 7000 converts.

Each mission has fifteen square miles of ground allotted to it. The buildings are variously laid out, and adapted in size to the number of Indians which they contain; some are inclosed by a high wall, as at San Carlos, while other consist merely of a few rows of huts, built with sunburnt mud-bricks; many are whitewashed and tiled, and have a neat and comfortable appearance. It is not, however, every hut that has a white face to exhibit, as that in a great measure depends upon the industry and good conduct of the family who possess it, who are in such a case supplied with lime for the purpose. It is only the married persons and officers of the establishment who are allowed these huts, the bachelors and spinsters having large places of their own, where they are separately incarcerated every night.

To each mission is attached a well-built church, better decorated in the interior than the external appearance of some would lead a stranger to suppose: they are well supplied with costly dresses for processions and feast days, to strike with admiration the senses of the gazing Indians, and on the whole are very respectable establishments. In some of these are a few tolerable pictures, among many bad ones; and those who have been able to obtain them are always provided with representations of hell and paradise: the former exhibiting in the most disgusting manner all the torments the imagination can fancy, for the purpose of striking terror into the simple Indians, who look upon the performance with fear and trembling. Such representations may perhaps be useful in exhibiting to the dull senses of the Indians what could not be conveyed in any other way, and so far they are desirable in the mission; but to an European the one is disgusting, and the other ludicrous. Each establishment is under the management of two priests if possible, who in Upper California belong to the mendicant order of San Francisco. They have under them a major domo, and several subordinate officers, generally Spaniards, whose principal business is to overlook the labour of the Indians.

The object of the missions is to convert as many of the wild Indians as possible, and to train them up within the walls of the establishment in the exercise of a good life, and of some trade, so that they may in time be able to provide for themselves and become useful members of civilised society. As to the various methods employed for the purpose of bringing proselytes to the mission, there are several reports, of which some were not very creditable to the institution: nevertheless, on the whole I am of opinion that the priests are innocent, from a conviction that they are ignorant of the means employed by those who are under them. Whatever may be the system, and whether the Indians be really dragged from their homes and families by armed parties, as some assert, or not, and forced to exchange their life of freedom and wandering for one of confinement and restraint in the missions, the change according to our ideas of happiness would seem advantageous to them, as they lead a far better life in the missions than in their forests, where they are in a state of nudity, and are frequently obliged to depend solely upon wild acorns for their subsistence.

Immediately the Indians are brought to the mission they are placed under the tuition of some of the most enlightened of their countrymen, who teach them to repeat in Spanish the Lord's Prayer and certain passages in the Romish litany; and also, to cross themselves properly on entering the church. In a few days a willing Indian becomes a proficient in these mysteries, and suffers himself to be baptized, and duly initiated into the church. If, however, as it not unfrequently happens, any of the captured Indians show a repugnance to conversion, it is the practice to imprison them for a few days, and then to allow them to breathe a little fresh air in a walk round the mission, to observe the happy mode of life of their converted countrymen; after which they are again shut up, and thus continue to be incarcerated until they declare their readiness to renounce the religion of their forefathers.

I do not suppose that this apparently unjustifiable conduct would be pursued for any length of time; and I had never an opportunity of ascertaining the fact, as the Indians are so averse to confinement that they very soon become impressed with the manifestly superior and more comfortable mode of life of those who are at liberty, and in a very few days declare their readiness to have the new religion explained to them. A person acquainted with the language of the parties, of which there are sometimes several dialects in the same mission, is then selected to train them, and having duly prepared them takes them to the padre to be baptized and to receive the sacrament. Having become Christians they are put to trades, or if they have good voices they are taught music, and form part of the choir of the church. Thus there are in almost every mission weavers, tanners, shoemakers, bricklayers, carpenters, blacksmiths, and other artificers. Others again are taught husbandry, to rear cattle and horses; and some to cook for the mission: while the females card, clean, and spin wool, weave, and sew; and those who are married attend to their domestic concerns.

In requital of these benefits, the services of the Indian, for life, belong to the mission, and if any neophyte should repent of his apostasy from the religion of his ancestors and desert, an armed force is sent in pursuit of him, and drags him back to punishment apportioned to the degree of aggravation attached to his crime. It does not often happen that a voluntary convert succeeds in his attempt to escape, as the wild Indians have a great contempt and dislike for those who have entered the missions, and they will frequently not only refuse to readmit them to their tribe, but will sometimes even discover their retreat to their pursuers. This animosity between the wild and converted Indians is of great importance to the missions, as it checks desertion, and is at the same time a powerful defence against the wild tribes, who consider their territory invaded, and have other just causes of complaint. The Indians, besides, from political motives, are, I fear, frequently encouraged in a contemptuous feeling towards their unconverted countrymen by hearing them constantly held up to them in the degrading light of *bestias!* and in hearing the Spaniards distinguished by the appellation of *gente de razón*.

The produce of the land and of the labour of the Indians is appropriated to the support of the mission, and the overplus to amass a fund which is entirely at the disposal of the padres. In some of the establishments this must be very large, although the padres will not admit it, and always plead poverty. The government has lately demanded a part of this profit, but the priests who, it is said, think the Indians are more entitled to it than the government, make small donations to them, and thus evade the tax by taking care there shall be no overplus. These donations in some of the missions are greater than in others, according as one establishment is more prosperous than another; and on this also, in a great measure, depends the comforts of the dwellings, & the neatness, the cleanliness, and the clothing of the people. In some of the missions much misery prevails, while in others there is a degree of cheerfulness and cleanliness which shows that many of the Indians require only care and proper management to make them as happy as their dull senses will admit of under a life of constraint.

The two missions of San Francisco and San José are examples of the contrast alluded to. The former in 1817 contained a thousand converts, who were housed in small huts around the mission; but at present only two hundred and sixty remain—some have been sent, it is true, to the new mission of San Francisco Solano, but sickness & death have dealt with an unsparing hand among the others. The huts of the absentees, at the time of our visit, had all fallen to decay, and presented heaps of filth and rubbish; while the remaining inmates of the mission were in as miserable a condition as it was possible to conceive, and were entirely regardless of their own comfort. Their hovels afforded scarcely any protection against the weather, and were black with smoke: some of the Indians were sleeping on the greasy floor; others were grinding baked acorns to make into cakes, which constitute a large portion of their food. So little attention indeed had been paid even to health that in one hut there was a quarter of beef suspended opposite a window in a very offensive and unwholesome state, but its owners were too indolent to throw it out. San José, on the other hand, was all neatness, cleanliness, and comfort; the Indians were amusing themselves between the hours of labour at their games; and the children, uniformly dressed in white bodices and scarlet petticoats, were playing at bat and ball. Part of this difference may arise from the habits of the people, who are of different tribes. Langsdorff observes that the Indians of the mission of San José are the handsomest tribe in California, and in every way a finer race of men; and terms the neophytes of San Francisco pigmies compared with them. I cannot say that this remark occured to me, and I think it probable that he may have been deceived by the apparently miserable condition of the people of San Francisco.

The children & adults of both sexes, in all the missions, are carefully locked up every night in separate apartments, and the keys are delivered into the possession of the padre; and as, in the daytime, their occupations lead to distinct places, unless they form a matrimonial alliance, they enjoy very little of each other's society. It, however, sometimes happened that they endeavour to evade the vigilance of their keepers, and are locked up with the opposite sex; but severe corporeal punishment, inflicted in the same manner as is practised in our schools with a whip of a rod, is sure to ensue if they are discovered. Though there may be occasional acts of tyranny, yet the general character of the padres is kind and benevolent, and in some of the missions the converts are so much attached to them that I have heard them declare they would go with them, if they were obliged to quit the country. It is greatly to be regretted that with the influence these men have over their pupils, and with the regard those pupils seem to have for their masters, that the priests do not interest themselves a little more in the education of their converts, the first step to which would be in making themselves acquainted with the Indian language. Many of the Indians surpass their pastors in this respect and can speak the Spanish language, while scarcely one of the padres can make themselves understood by the Indians. They have besides, in general, a lamentable contempt for the intellect of these simple people, and think them incapable of improvement beyond a certain point. Nothwithstanding this, the Indians are, in general, well clothed and fed; they have houses of their own, and if they are not comfortable, it is, in a great measure, their own fault; their meals are given to them three times a day, and consist of thick gruel made of wheat, Indian corn, and sometimes acorns, to which at noon is generally added meat. Clothing of a better kind than that worn by the Indians is given to the officers of the missions, both as a reward for their services, and to create an emulation in others.

If it should happen that there is a scarcity of provisions, either through failure in the crop, or damage of that which is in store, as they have always two or three years in reserve, the Indians are sent off to the woods to provide for themselves, where, accustomed to hunt and fish, and game being very abundant, they find enough to subsist upon, and return to the mission, when they are required to reap the next year's harvest.

Having served ten years in the mission, an Indian may claim his liberty, provided any respectable settler will become surety for his future good conduct. A piece of ground is then allotted for his support, but he is never wholly free from the establishment, as part of his earnings must still be given to them. We heard of very few to whom this reward for servitude and good conduct had been granted; and it is not improbable that the padres are averse to it, as it deprives them of their best scholars. When these establishments were first founded, the Indians flocked to them in great numbers for the clothing with which the neophytes were supplied; but after they became acquainted with the nature of the institution, and felt themselves under restraint, many absconded. Even now, notwithstanding the difficulty of escaping, desertions are of frequent occurrence, owing probably, in some cases, to the fear of punishment—in others to the deserters having been originally inveigled into the mission by the converted Indians or neophytes, as they are called by way of distinction to Los Gentiles, or the wild Indians—in other cases again to the fickleness of their own disposition.

Some of the converted Indians are occasionally stationed in places which are resorted to by the wild tribes for the purpose of offering them flattering accounts of the advantages of the mission, and of persuading them to abandon their barbarous life; while others obtain leave to go into the territory of the Gentiles to visit their friends, and are expected to bring back converts with them when they return. At a particular period of the year, also, when the Indians can be spared from the agricultural concerns of the establishment, many of them are permitted to take the launch of the mission, and make excursions to the Indian territory. All are anxious to go on such occasions, some to visit their friends, some to procure the manufactures of their barbarous countrymen, which, by the by, are often better than their own; and some with the secret determination never to return. On these occasions the padres desire them to induce as many of their unconverted brethren as possible to accompany them back to the mission, of course, implying that this is to be done only by persuasion; but the boat being furnished with a cannon and musketry, and in every respect equipped for war, it too often happens that the neophytes, and the *gente de razón,* who superintend the direction of the boat, avail themselves of their superiority, with the desire of ingratiating themselves with their masters, and of receiving a reward. There are, besides, repeated acts of aggression which it is necessary to punish, all of which furnish proselytes. Women and children are generally the first objects of capture, as their husbands and parents sometimes voluntarily follow them into captivity. These misunderstandings & captivities keep up a perpetual enmity amongst the tribes, whose thirst for revenge is almost insatiable.

We had an opportunity of witnessing the tragical issue of one of those holyday excursions of the neophytes of the mission of San José. The launch was armed as usual, and placed under the superintendence of an *alcalde* of the mission, who, it appears from one statement (for there were several), converted the party of pleasure either into one of attack for the purpose of procuring proselytes, or of revenge upon a particular tribe for some aggression in which they were concerned. They proceeded up Río San Joachin until they came to the territory of a particular tribe named Cosemenes, when they disembarked with the gun, and encamped for the night near the village of *Los Gentiles,* intending to make an attack upon them the next morning; but before they were prepared, the Gentiles, who had been apprised of their inattention, and had collected a large body of friends, became the assailants, and pressed so hard upon the party that, nothwithstanding they dealt death in every direction with their cannon and musketry, and were inspired with confidence by the contempt in which they held the valour and tactics of their unconverted countrymen, they were overpowered by numbers, and obliged to seek their safety in flight, and to leave the gun in the woods. Some regained the launch and were saved, and others found their way over land to the mission; but thirty-four of the party never returned to tell their tale.

A Bull and Bear Fight

While we remained in San Francisco refitting the ship, the boats were constantly employed sounding and surveying the harbour, in which duty we received every assistance from Martinez, the governor, who allowed us to enter the forts, and to take what angles and measurements we pleased, requiring only in return for this indulgence a copy of the plan when finished for his own government: his proposal seemed so fair that I immediately acceded to it, and on my return to the place the following year, fully complied with his request. It is impossible to pass unnoticed the difference between this liberal conduct of Martinez and that of the former Spanish authorities, who watched all Vancouver's actions with the greatest suspicion, and whose jealously had been the subject of animadversion of almost every voyager who has touched at this port.

On the 12th of December a salute was fired from the battery; high mass was said in all the missions, and a grand entertainment, to which all the officers were invited, was given at the presidio, in honour of Santa Señora Guadaloupe. There was also to have been a fight between a bear and a bull, but for some reason not known to us—probably the trouble it required to bring the animal so far, as the bears do not come within many miles of the presidio—it did not take place; and we were all greatly disappointed, as we had offered to reward the soldiers for their trouble, and had heard so much of these exhibitions from everybody, that our curiosity had been highly excited. This is a favourite amusement with the Californians, but it is of rare occurrence, as there is much trouble in getting a bear alive to the scene of combat, and there is also some risk and expense attending it. We were informed that when a fight is determined upon, three or four horsemen are despatched with lassos to the woods where the bears resort, and that when they come to an advantageous spot they kill a horse or a bullock as a bait, and hide themselves in the wood. Sometimes they have to wait a whole day or more before any of these animals appear, but when they come to partake of the food, the men seize a favourable opportunity, and rush upon them at different points with their lassos, and entangle one of them until he is thrown upon the ground, when they manage to suspend him between the horsemen, while a third person dismounts and ties his feet together; he is then extended upon a hide and dragged home; during which time it is necessary, they say, to keep him constantly wet to allay his thirst and rage, which amounts almost to madness—and woe to him who should be near if he were to break away from his fastenings. The entangling of the animal in the first instance appears to be by no means devoid of risk, as in case of the failure of a lasso it is only by speed that a rider can save himself and his horse. The bear being caught, two or three men are despatched for a wild bull, which they lasso in an equally dexterous manner, catching him either by the horns or by whichsoever legs they please, in order to trip him up and retain him between them.

It is necessary to begin the fight as soon as the animals are brought in, as the bear cannot be tempted to eat, and is continually exhausting himself in struggling for his liberty. The two animals are then tied together by a long rope, and the battle begins, sometimes to the disadvantage of the bear, who is half dead with exhaustion, but in the end almost always proves fatal to the bull. It is remarkable that all the bears endeavour to seize the bull by the tongue, for which purpose they spring upon his head or neck and first grapple with his nose, until the pain compels the bull to roar, when his adversary instantly seizes his tongue, pierces it with his sharp talons, and is sure of victory. These battles were the everlasting topic of conversation with the Californians, who indeed have very little else to talk about, and they all agreed as to the manner of the fatal termination of the spectacle.

By Christmas day we had all remained sufficiently long in the harbour to contemplate our departure without regret: the eye had become familiar to the picturesque scenery of the bay, the pleasure of the chase had lost its fascination, and the roads to the mission and presidio were grown tedious and insipid. There was no society to enliven the hours, no incidents to vary one day from the other, and to use the expression of Doña Gonzales, California appeared to be as much out of the world as Kamschatka.

On the 26th, being ready for sea, I was obliged to relinquish the survey of this magnificent port, which possesses almost all the requisites for a great naval establishment, and is so advantageously situated with regard to North America and China, and the Pacific in general, that it will, no doubt, at some future time, be of great importance. We completed the examination of those parts of the harbour which were likely to be frequented by vessels for some years to come, in which it is proper to mention, in order to give as much publicity to the circumstance as possible, that we discovered a rock between Alcatraz & Yerba Buena Islands, dangerous to both shipping and boats, in consequence of its rising from about seven fathoms so near to the surface, as to occasion strong overfalls with the tides. A shoal was also found to the eastward of the landing-place off the presidio, which ought to be avoided by boats sailing along shore. In my nautical remarks I purpose giving directions for avoiding both these dangers, which are the only hidden ones in that part of the harbour which is at present frequented.

On the 28th, we took leave of our hospitable and affable friends, Martinez and Padre Tomaso, full of gratitude for their kindness and attention to our wants; weighed anchor, and bade adieu to the Port of San Francisco, in which we had all received material benefit from the salubrity of its climate, the refreshing product of its soil, and the healthy exercise we had enjoyed there. In the ship's company in particular there was the most apparent amendment; some of them, from being so emaciated on their arrival that the surgeon could scarcely recognize them, were now restored to their former healthy appearance, and we had the satisfaction of sailing without a single case of sickness on board.

SAN FRANCISCO

by

S. J. ALEXANDER

And She said, "I am She who was set at the marches of sea and land,
With the crowns of the world on my brow, and girt with the sword
of command.
And the many come to my gateways, they enter, abide and pass
Like shadows on wind-driven water, or seeds from wind-shaken
grass . . . .
Ye are lords in your far-lying lands, and great in your lordships,
yet still
Ye are tools of the Gods in my hands to hew to the lines of my will.
From nethermost deeps I have called; ye have followed the path
of the sun:
Ye are four where your rule is supreme, but to serve and obey me
but one . . . .
And as sister to brothers, I charge ye depart from me now to your
lands,
That ye dazzle the eyes of the Gods with the gifts of your brotherly
hands.
That the sails like a white crested torrent stream out on the limitless
blue,
With the gifts that shall top and exceed and better the best that I
knew."

[1835]

THE CITY
FROM BEFORE THE MAST

by

RICHARD HENRY DANA

After a passage of twenty days, we arrived at the mouth of the Bay of San Francisco.

Our place of destination had been Monterey, but as we were to the northward of .it when the wind hauled ahead, we made a fair wind for San Francisco. About thirty miles from the mouth of the bay, and on the southeast side, is a high point, upon which the Presidio is built. Behind this point is the little harbor, or bight, called Yerba Buena in which trading-vessels anchor, and, near it, the Mission of Dolores. There was no other habitation on this side of the Bay, except a shanty of rough boards put up by a man named Richardson, who was doing a little trading between the vessels and the Indians.* Here, at anchor, and the only vessel, was a brig under Russian colors, from Sitka, in Russian America, which had come down to winter and to take in a supply of tallow and grain, great quantities of which latter article are raised in the Missions at the head of the bay. The second day after our arrival we went on board the brig, it being Sunday, as a matter of curiosity; and there was enough there to gratify it. Though no larger than the *Pilgrim,* she had five or six officers, and a crew of between twenty and thirty; and such a stupid and greasy-looking set, I never saw before. Although it was quite comfortable weather

---

From *Two Years Before the Mast,* Harper & Brothers, New York, 1840.

* The next year Richardson built a one-story adobe house on the same spot, which was long afterwards known as the oldest house in the great city of San Francisco.

and we had nothing on but straw hats, shirts, and duck trousers, and were barefooted, they had, every man of them, double-soled boots, coming up to the knees, and well greased; thick woollen trousers, frocks, waistcoats, pea-jackets, woollen caps, and everything in true Nova Zembla rig; and in the warmest days they made no change. The clothing of one of these men would weigh nearly as much as that of half our crew. They had brutish faces, looked like the antipodes of sailors, and apparently dealt in nothing but grease. They lived upon grease; eat it, drank it, slept in the midst of it, and their clothes were covered with it. To a Russian, grease is the greatest luxury. They looked with greedy eyes upon the tallow-bags as they were taken into the vessel, and, no doubt, would have eaten one up whole, had not the officer kept watch over it. The grease appeared to fill their pores, and to come out in their hair and on their faces. It seems as if it were this saturation which makes them stand cold and rain so well. If they were to go into a warm climate, they would melt and die of the scurvy.

The vessel was no better than the crew. Everything was in the oldest and most inconvenient fashion possible: running trusses and lifts on the yards, and large hawser cables, coiled all over the decks, and served and parcelled in all directions. The topmasts, top-gallant-masts, and studding-sail booms were nearly black for want of scraping, and the decks would have turned the stomach of a man-of-war's-man. The galley was down in the forecastle; and there the crew lived, in the midst of the steam and grease of the cooking, in a place as hot as an oven, and apparently never cleaned out. Five minutes in the forecastle was enough for us, and we were glad to get into the open air. We made some trade with them, buying Indian curiosities, of which they had a great number; such as bead-work, feathers of birds, fur moccasins, &c. I purchased a large robe, made of the skins of some animal, dried and sewed nicely together, and covered all over on the outside with thick downy feathers, taken from the breasts of various birds, and arranged with their different colors so as to make a brilliant show.

A few days after our arrival the rainy season set in, and for three weeks it rained almost every hour, without cessation. This was bad for our trade, for the collecting of hides is managed differently in this port from what it is in any other on the coast. The Mission of Dolores, near the anchorage, has no trade at all; but those of San José, Santa Clara, and others situated on the large creeks or rivers, which run into the bay, and distant between fifteen and forty miles from the anchorage, do a greater business in hides than any in California. Large boats, or launches, manned by Indians, and capable of carrying from five to six hundred hides apiece, are attached to the Missions, and sent down to the vessels with hides, to bring away goods in return. Some of the crews of the vessels are obliged to go and come in the boats, to look out for the hides and goods. These are favorite expeditions with the sailors in fine weather; but now, to be gone three or four days, in open boats, in constant rain, without any shelter, and with cold food, was hard service. Two of our men went up to Santa Clara in one of these boats, and were gone three days, during all which time they had a constant rain, and did not sleep a wink, but passed three long nights walking fore and aft the boat, in the open air. When they got on board they were completely exhausted, and took a watch below of twelve hours. All the hides, too, that came down in the boats were soaked with water, and unfit to put below, so that we were obliged to trice them up to dry, in the intervals of sunshine or wind, upon all parts of the vessel. We got up tricing-lines from the jib-boom-end to each arm of the fore yard, and thence to the main and cross-jack yard-arms. Between the tops, too, and the mast-heads, from the fore to the main swifters, and thence to the mizzen rigging, and in all directions athwartships, tricing-lines were run, and strung with hides. The head stays and guys, and the spritsail yard were lined, and, having still more, we got out the swinging-booms, and strung them and the forward and after guys with hides. The rail, fore and aft, the windlass, capstan, the sides of the ship, and every vacant place on deck, were covered with wet hides, on the least sign of an interval for drying. Our ship was nothing but mass of hides, from the cat-hairpins to the water's edge, and from the jib-boom-end to the taffrail.

One cold, rainy evening, about eight o'clock, I received orders to get ready to start for San José at four the next morning, in one of these Indian boats, with four days' provisions. I got my oil-cloth clothes, southwester, and thick boots ready, and turned into my hammock early, determined to get some sleep in advance, as the boat was to be alongside before daybreak. I slept on till all hands were called in the morning; for, fortunately for me, the Indians, intentionally, or from mistaking their orders, had gone off alone in the night, and were far out of sight. Thus I escaped three or four days of very uncomfortable service.

Four of our men, a few days afterwards, went up in one of the quarter-boats to Santa Clara, to carry the agent, and remained out all night in a drenching rain, in the small boat, in which there was not room for them to turn round; the agent having gone up to the Mission and left the men to their fate, making no provision for their accomodation, and not even sending them anything to eat. After this they had to pull thirty miles, and when they got on board were so stiff that they could not come up the gangway ladder. This filled up the measure of the agent's unpopularity, and never after this could he get anything done for him by the crew; and many a delay and vexation, and many a good ducking in the surf, did he get to pay up old scores, or "square the yards with the bloody quill-driver."

Having collected nearly all the hides that were to be procured, we began our preparations for taking in a supply of wood and water, for both of which San Francisco is the best place on the coast. A small island, about two leagues from the anchorage, called by us "Wood Island," and by the Mexicans "Isla de los Angeles," was covered with trees to the water's edge; and to this two of our crew, who were Kennebec men, and could handle an axe like a plaything, were sent every morning to cut wood, with two boys to pile it up for them. In about a week they had cut enough to last us a year, and the third mate, with myself and three others, were sent over in a large, schooner-rigged, open launch, which we had hired of the Mission, to take in the wood, and bring it to the ship. We left the ship about noon, but owing to a strong head wind, and a tide which here runs four or five knots, did not get into the harbor, formed by two points of the island, where the boats lie, until sundown. No sooner had we come-to, than a strong southeaster, which had been threatening us all day, set in, with heavy rain and a chilly air. We were in rather a bad situation: an open boat, a heavy rain, and a long night; for in winter, in this latitude, it was dark nearly fifteen hours. Taking a small skiff which we had brought with us, we went ashore but discovered no shelter, for everything was open to the rain; and, collecting a little wood, which we found by lifting up the leaves and brush, and a few mussels, we put aboard again, and made the best preparations in our power for passing the night. We unbent the mainsail, and formed an awning with it over the after part of the boat, made a bed of wet logs of wood, and, with our jackets on, lay down, about six o'clock, to sleep. Finding the rain running down upon us, and our jackets getting wet through, and the rough, knotty logs rather indifferent couches, we turned out; and, taking an iron pan which we brought with us, we wiped it out dry, put some stones around it, cut the wet bark from some sticks, and, striking a light, made a small fire in the pan. Keeping some sticks near to dry, and covering the whole over with a roof of boards, we kept up a small fire, by which we cooked our mussels, and ate them, rather for an occupation than from hunger. Still it was not ten o'clock, and the night was long before us, when one of the party produced an old pack of Spanish cards from his monkey-jacket pocket, which we hailed as a great windfall; and, keeping a dim, flickering light by our fagots, we played game after game, till one or two o'clock, when, becoming really tired, we went to our logs again, one sitting up at a time, in turn, to keep watch over the fire.

Toward morning the rain ceased, and the air became sensibly colder, so that we found sleep impossible, and sat up, watching for daybreak. No sooner was it light than we went ashore, and began our preparations for loading our vessel. We were not mistaken in the coldness of of the weather, for a white frost was on the ground, and—a thing we had never seen before in California—one or two little puddles of fresh water were skimmed over with a thin coat of ice. In this state of the weather, and before sunrise, in the gray of the morning, we had to wade off, nearly up to our hips in water, to load the skiff with the wood by armfuls. The third mate remained on board the launch, two more men stayed in the skiff to load and manage it, and all the water-work, as usual, fell upon the two youngest of us; and there we were with frost on the ground, wading forward and back, from the beach to the boat, with armfuls of wood, barefooted, and our trousers rolled up. When the skiff went off with her load, we could only keep our feet from freezing by racing up and down the beach on the hard sand, as fast as we could go. We were all day at this work, and toward sundown, having loaded the vessel as deep as she would bear, we hove up our anchor and made sail, beating out of the bay. No sooner had we got into the large bay than we found a strong tide setting us out to seaward, a thick fog which prevented our seeing the ship, and a breeze too light to set us against the tide, for we were as deep as a sand-barge. By the utmost exertions, we saved ourselves from being carried out to sea, and were glad to reach the leewardmost point of the island, where we came-to, and prepared to pass another night more uncomfortable than the first, for we were loaded up to the gunwale, and had only a choice among logs and sticks for a resting-place. The next morning we made sail at slack water, with a fair wind, and got on board by eleven o'clock, when all hands were turned-to to unload and stow away the wood, which took till night.

Having now taken in all our wood, the next morning a water-party was ordered off with all the casks. From this we escaped, having had a pretty good siege with the wooding. The water-party were gone three days, during which time they narrowly escaped being carried out to sea, and passed one day on an island, where one of them shot a deer, great numbers of which overrun the islands and hills of San Francisco Bay.

While not off on these wood and water parties, or up the rivers to the Missions, we had easy times on board the ship. We were moored, stem and stern, within a cable's length of the shore, safe from south-easters, and with little boating to do; and, as it rained nearly all the time, awnings were put over the hatchways, and all hands sent down between decks, where we were at work, day after day, picking oakum, until we got enough to calk the ship all over, and to last the whole voyage. Then we made a whole suit of gaskets for the voyage home, a pair of wheel-ropes from strips of green hide, great quantities of spun-yarn, and everything else that could be made between decks. It being now mid-winter and in high latitude, the nights were very long, so that we were not turned-to until seven in the morning, and were obliged to knock off at five in the evening, when we got supper; which gave us nearly three hours before eight bells, at which time the watch was set.

As we had now been about a year on the coast, it was time to think of the voyage home; and, knowing that the last two or three months of our stay would be very busy ones, and that we should never have so good an opportunity to work for ourselves as the present, we all employed our evenings in making clothes for the passage home, and more especially for Cape Horn. As soon as supper was over and the kids cleared away, and each man had taken his smoke, we seated ourselves on our chests round the lamp, which swung from a beam, and went to work each in his own way, some making hats, others trousers, others jackets, &c., &c., and no one was idle. The boys who could not sew well enough to make their own clothes laid up grass into sinnet for the men, who sewed for them in return. Several of us clubbed together and bought a large piece of twilled cotton, which we made into trousers and jackets, and, giving them several coats of linseed oil, laid them by for Cape Horn. I also sewed and covered a tarpaulin hat, thick and strong enough to sit upon, and made myself a complete suit of flannel underclothing for bad weather. Those who had no southwester caps made them; and several of the crew got up for themselves tarpaulin jackets and trousers, lined on the inside with flannel. Industry was the order of the day, and every one did something for himself; for we knew that as the season advanced, and we went further south, we should have no evenings to work in.

Friday, December 25th. This day was Christmas; and, as it rained all day long, and there was no hides to take in, and nothing especial to do, the captain gave us a holiday (the first we had had, except Sundays, since leaving Boston), and plum-duff for dinner. The Russian brig, following the Old Style, had celebrated their Christmas eleven days before, when they had a grand blowout, and (as our men said), drank, in the forecastle, a barrel of gin, ate up a bag of tallow, and made a soup of the skin.

Sunday, December 27th. We had now finished all our business at this port, and, it being Sunday, we unmoored ship and got under way, firing a salute to the Russian brig, and another to the presidio, which were both answered. The *comandante* of the presidio, Don Guadalupe Vallejo, a young man, and the most popular, among the Americans and English, of any man in California, was on board when we got under way. He spoke English very well, and was suspected of being favorably inclined to foreigners.

We sailed down this magnificent bay with a light wind, the tide, which was running out, carrying us at the rate of four or five knots. It was a fine day; the first of entire sunshine we had had for more than a month. We passed directly under the high cliff on which the presidio is built, and stood into the middle of the bay, from whence we could see small bays making up into the interior, large and beautifully wooded islands, and the mouths of several small rivers. If California ever becomes a prosperous country, this bay will be the centre of its prosperity. The abundance of wood and water; the extreme fertility of its shores; the excellence of its climate, which is as near to being perfect as any in the world; and its facilities for navigation, affording the best anchoring-grounds in the whole western coast of America,—all fit it for a place of great importance.

The tide leaving us, we came to anchor near the mouth of the bay, under a high and beautifully sloping hill, upon which herds of hundreds and hundreds of red deer, and the stag, with his high branching antlers, were bounding about, looking at us for a moment, and then starting off, affrighted at the noises which we made for the purpose of seeing the variety of their beautiful attitudes and motions.

At midnight, the tide having turned, we hove up our anchor and stood out of the bay, with a fine starry heaven above us.

AN ENGLISHMAN'S PROPOSAL

by

ALEXANDER FORBES, ESQ.

IN THE YEAR 1836, the inhabitants of Monterey and the vicinity rose, and, declaring themselves independent, attacked the garrison and forced the commandant and troops to capitulate. At a public meeting of the inhabitants called subsequently, on the 7th November, at Monterey, the following Resolutions were passed as the basis of a provisional government:—

1st.—Upper California is declared to be independent of Mexico during the non-re-establishment of the Federal system which was adopted in the year 1824.

2nd.—The said California shall be erected into a free and governing state, establishing a Congress which shall dictate all the particular laws of the country and elect the other supreme powers necessary, declaring the actual "Most Excellent Deputation" constituent.

3rd.—The Religion shall be the Roman Catholic Apostolic; without admitting the exercise of any other; but the government will not molest any persons for their particular religious opinions.

4th.—A Constitution shall regulate all the branches of the Administration "provisionally," in conformity, as much as possible, with the expressed declaration.

5th.—Until what is contained in the foregoing articles be put in execution, Senor Don Mariano Guadalupe Vallejo shall be called on to act as Commandant General.

6th.—The President of the "Most Excellent Deputation" shall pass the necessary communications to the municipalities of the territory.

They followed up these proceedings by expelling the whole officials

---

From the original edition, London, 1839.

of the Mexican government, and all the troops from the country, and transporting them to the Mexican territory.

On receiving notice of this revolution, the Mexican government immediately had recourse to their usual mode of warfare, fulminating furious proclamations and addresses to the citizens, appealing to their patriotism, and ordering to be prepared, without delay, a formidable expedition to proceed against such audacious and unnatural sons of the Republic, whom it was incumbent on them to put down and chastise as their treason deserved. The first patriotic ebullition however soon subsided; no expedition was prepared, California was soon forgotten, and it has remained for nearly two years to do as it pleases, to have a government of its own manufacture, or to live without a government at all. Being thus left to the freedom of their own will, the Californians, true to the spirit which has animated all the Spanish American colonies since their emancipation, immediately began to divide themselves into parties; and although there are only about five thousand Spanish creoles in the whole country, they had their party of the north, which declared for an entire independence on Mexico, and the party of the south, which adhered to Mexico on certain conditions. The want of frequent communication with Mexico renders it quite uncertain what may at present (June, 1838) be the state of the country; but it is, at least, evident now, if there was any doubt formerly, that it is at this moment in a state which cannot prevent its being taken possession of by any foreign force which may present itself. The British government seem lately to have had some suspicion that California would be encroached upon, if not taken entire possession of, by the Russians who are settled so close upon its northern frontier; but by the latest accounts no encroachment has been made, nor has any augmentation been made either in the number of people in the colony, or in the fortifications.

The danger does not lie there. There is another restless and enterprising neighbour from whom they will most probably soon have to defend themselves, or rather to submit to: for although the frontiers of North America are much more distant than the Russians, yet to such men as the Back-settlers, distance is of little moment, and they are already well acquainted with the route. The northern American tide of population must roll on southward, and overwhelm not only California, but other more important states. This latter event, however, is in the womb of time: but the invasion of California by American settlers is daily talked of; and if Santa Anna had prevailed against Texas, a portion of the inhabitants of that country, sufficient to overrun California, would now have been its masters.

There have been some thoughts of proposing to the Mexican government that it should endeavour to cancel the English debt—which now exceeds fifty millions of dollars—by a transfer of California to the creditors. This would be a wise measure on the part of Mexico, if the government could be brought to lay aside the vanity of retaining large possessions. The cession of such a disjointed part of the republic as California would be an advantage. In no case can it ever be profitable to the Mexican republic, nor can it possibly remain united to it for any length of time, if it should even be induced to rejoin this state, from which at present it is to all intents and purposes separated. Therefore, by giving up this territory for the debt, Mexico would get rid of this last for nothing. But would the English creditors accept of it? I think they might, and I think they ought. They have lately displayed an inclination to treat and to receive lands as a part of the debt where no land exists belonging to Mexico. In the settlement made with Lizardi and Co. as agents for the Mexican government in London, lands are stipulated to be delivered at a certain price per acre, in Texas in which Mexico does not possess an acre, in the state of New Mexico which is many hundred leagues inland, in Sonora, and God knows where. To the good fortune however of the English creditors this contract has been disapproved of by the Mexican government, and it is hoped that some more rational scheme will be hit upon to give the creditors some sort of tangible security for at least a part of what they have been so scandalously fleeced out of. If California was ceded for the English debt, the creditors might be formed into a company, with the difference that they should have a sort of sovereignty over the territory, somewhat in the manner of the East India company. This in my opinion would certainly bring a revenue in time which might be equal to the interest of the debt, and under good management and with an English population, would most certainly realize all that has been predicted of this fine country.

Should such be the case, I know of no place, as I have already stated, better calculated for receiving and cherishing the superfluous population of Great Britain. Hitherto nothing could have been less encouraging to the settlement of strangers than the proceedings of the successive governments of republican Mexico. For although the different parties who have ruled the country have, in many public acts, held forth their great desire to encourage emigration to all parts of the country, all their laws, devised with this object, have been dictated too much in the old Spanish spirit to be really practically useful. By the multiplication of regulations and restrictions they contrived to envelope their meaning and provisions in such uncertainty that they could scarcely be understood, while most of them embraced some antiquated prohibitive principle which rendered the whole nugatory. In all of the acts relating to emigration, for instance, there have been such absurd clauses as that the emigrant must profess the Catholic religion, that he shall have a certain capital, a trade or profession, that he shall appear before the authority, shall have a regular passport, &c.

As yet few strangers have established themselves in Upper California. Such as have done so, have proceeded thither, as it were casually, in vessels trading to the coast, and are, consequently, chiefly seafaring men; but several mechanics and others have also established themselves, and all have been received with the utmost kindness by the natives, and the greater part of them have intermarried with them. The native inhabitants are indeed remarkable for their peaceable inoffensive character; and on their part no opposition is to be apprehended. It might be presumed that the chief opposition to the admission of strangers was to be expected from the missionaries: it would be supposed that from their education, and from the fear of losing the influence they possess, none could view the entrance of strangers with so much jealousy as they; but it is a curious fact, that from the first establishment of these missions to the present day, as well in the time of the Spanish government as under the republican system, the reception of strangers has always been much more cordial by the missionaries than by the government officers! The different navigators who have touched on the coast of California since its first settlement, have unanimously borne testimony to this fact; and since the country has been opened to strangers indiscriminately, the hospitality and kindness of the missionaries have been the praise of every one who has been there. Foreign mechanics have been employed at almost all the missions, and the most cordial reception experienced by all of them. As, however, the greatest part of the lands to the southward of Monterey, and along the coast, are in the hands of the Missions, it is not to be expected that they could view with satisfaction any large number of emigrants landing in their territories, and which might require the cession of land, or interfere to disturb their peculiar system.

But, indeed, whenever circumstances permit foreign emigrants to establish themselves in Upper California, they ought to settle to the northward and eastward of the bay of San Francisco, and on the lands around that bay, and on the banks of the river Sacramento, and other streams which fall into it. These are the best lands, and in the best climate for settlers from the north of Europe. They are peculiarly favourable for the raising of wheat and other grain, and for the rearing of cattle. The immense tracts of fertile land not incumbered by forests, the facility of water intercourse by the country being intersected by the creeks on the Bay of San Francisco, and the various branches of the rivers which fall into it, render this situation highly advantageous; and its northerly situation, and the general distribution of the rains throughout the year, make it fitter for agricultural pursuits than the more southerly districts. It has also the advantage of being but little inhabited, and is unconnected with the possessions of the missionaries.

It ought also to be a fundamental principle in any plan of emigration to this country, that a sufficient number should go together, in order that they might form at first a society by themselves. Their lands should be selected as distinct from those of the missions and the present free towns as possible, so that no dispute as to territory or on any other account could ensue: for this reason, the lands on the bay of San Francisco, as before recommended, are the most proper. In the course of time the emigrants and the native settlers would become acquainted and approximate; their union would be the consequence, and this would tend to promote their mutual happiness and prosperity.

THE INDOLENT
SAN FRANCISCANS

by

SIR GEORGE SIMPSON

THE sheet of water, as already described, forms only a part of the inland sea of San Francisco. Whalers' Harbor (Sausalito Harbor), at its own northern extremity, communicates, by a strait (San Pablo Strait) of about two miles in width, with the Bay of San Pedro (San Pablo Bay), a circular basin of ten miles in diameter, and again, this extensive pool, at its northeastern end, leads, by means of a second strait (Carquinez Strait), into Freshwater Bay (Suisún) Bay, of nearly the same form and magnitude, which is full of islands, and forms the receptacle of the Sacramento and the San Joaquín. Large vessels, it is said, may penetrate into Freshwater (Suisún) Bay, and as the San Joaquín and the Sacramento, which drain vast tracts of country respectively to the southeast and to the northeast, are navigable for inland craft, the whole harbor, besides its matchless qualities as a port of refuge on this surf-beaten coast, is the outlet of a vast breadth of fair and fertile land.

In the face of all these advantages and temptations, the good folk of San Francisco, priests as well as laymen, and laymen as well as priests, have been contented to borrow, for their aquatic excursions, the native balsa, a kind of raft or basket, which, when wanted, can be constructed in a few minutes with the bulrushes that spring so luxuriantly on the margins of the lakes and rivers. In this miserable makeshift they contrive to cross the inland waters, and perhaps, in very choice weather, to venture a little way out to sea, there being, I believe, no other floating thing besides, neither boat nor canoe, neither barge nor scow, in any part of the harbor, or, in fact, in any part of Upper California, from San Diego on the south to San Francisco on the north. In consequence of this state of things, the people of the bay have been so far from availing themselves of their internal channels of communication, that their numerous expeditions into the interior have all been conducted by land, seldom leading, of course, to any result commensurate with the delay and expense.

But, inconvenient as the entire want of small craft must be to the dwellers on such an inlet as has been described, there are circumstances which do, to a certain extent, account for the protracted endurance of the evil. Horses are almost as plentiful as bulrushes; time is a perfect glut with a community of loungers; and, under the plea of having no means of catching fish, the faithful enjoy, by a standing dispensation, the comfortable privilege of fasting, at meager times, on their hecatombs of beef.

The world at large has hitherto made nearly as little use of the peculiar facilities of San Francisco as the Californians themselves. Though at one time many whaling-ships, as the name of Whalers' Harbor would imply, frequented the port, yet, through the operation of various causes, they have all gradually betaken themselves to the Sandwich Islands. In point of natural capabilities for such a purpose, the Sandwich Islands are, on the whole, inferior to San Francisco. If they excel it in position, as lying more directly in the track between the summer-fishing of the north and the winter-fishing of the south, and also as being more easy of access and departure by reason of the steadiness of the trade-winds, they are, in turn, surpassed in all the elements for the refreshing and refitting of vessels by a place where beef may be had for little or nothing, where hemp grows spontaneously, where the pine offers an inexhaustible supply of resin, and where suitable timber for ship-building invites the ax within an easy distance.

But though nature may have done more for San Francisco than for the Sandwich Islands, yet man has certainly done less to promote her liberal intentions. The Sandwich Islands afford to the refitting whaler an ample supply of competent labor, both native and foreign, at reasonable wages, while San Francisco, turning the very bounty of Providence into a curse, corrupts a naturally indolent population by the superabundance of cattle and horses, by the readiness, in short, with which idleness can find both subsistence and recreation. Moreover,

even on the score of fiscal regulations, the savage community has as
decidedly the advantage of the civilized as in point of industrious
habits. In the Sandwich Islands the whaler can enter at once into the
port which is best adapted for his purposes, while in San Francisco
he is by law forbidden to remain more than forty-eight hours, unless
he has previously presented himself at Monterey and paid duty on
the whole of his cargo. What wonder, then, is it that with such a
government and such a people Whalers' Harbor is merely an empty
name?

The trade of the bay, and in fact of the whole province, is entirely
in the hands of foreigners, who are almost exclusively of the English
race. Of that race, however, the Americans are considerably more
numerous than the British, the former naturally flocking in greater
force to neutral ground, such as this country and the Sandwich Islands,
while the latter find a variety of advantageous outlets in their own
national colonies. At present the foreigners are to the Californians
in number as one to ten, being about six hundred out of about seven
thousand, while, by their monopoly of trade and their command of
resources, to say nothing of their superior energy and intelligence,
they already possess vastly more than their numerical proportion of
political influence, and their position in this respect excites the less
jealousy, inasmuch as most of them have been induced, either by a
desire of shaking off legal incapacities or by less interested motives,
to profess the Catholic religion, and to marry into provincial families.

The Californians of San Francisco number between two thousand
and two thousand five hundred, about seven hundred belonging to
the village of pueblo of San José de Guadalupe and the remainder
occupying about thirty farms of various sizes, generally subdivided
among the families of the respective holders.

On the score of industry, these good folks, as also their brethren
of the other ports, are perhaps the least promising colonists of a new
country in the world, being in this respect decidedly inferior to what
the savages themselves had become under the training of the priests,
so that the spoliation of the missions, excepting that it has opened
the province to general enterprise, has directly tended to nip civilization in the bud.

In the missions there were large flocks of sheep, but now there are
scarcely any left, the Hudson's Bay Company, last spring, having

experienced great difficulty in collecting about four thousand for its northern settlements.

In the missions the wool used to be manufactured into coarse cloth, and it is, in fact, because the Californians are too lazy to weave or spin—too lazy, I suspect, even to clip and wash the raw material— that the sheep have been literally destroyed to make more room for the horned cattle.

In the missions soap and leather used to be made, but in such vulgar processes the Californians advance no further than nature herself has advanced before them, excepting to put each animal's tallow in one place and its hide in another.

In the missions the dairy formed a principal object of attention, but now neither butter nor cheese, nor any other preparation of milk whatever, is to be found in the province.

In the missions there were annually produced about eighty thousand bushels of wheat and maize, the former, and perhaps part of the latter also, being converted into flour; but the present possessors of the soil do so little in the way of tilling the ground, that, when lying at Monterey, we sold to the government some barrels of flour at the famine rate of twenty-eight dollars, or nearly six pounds sterling, a sack,—a price which could not be considered as merely local, for the stuff was intended to victual the same schooner which, on our first arrival, we had seen at anchor in Whalers' Harbor.

In the missions beef was occasionally cured for exportation; but so miserably is the case now reversed, that, though meat enough to supply the fleets of England is annually either consumed by fire or left to the carrion-birds, yet the authorities purchased from us, along with the flour just mentioned, some salted salmon as indispensable sea-stores for the one paltry vessel which constituted the entire line of battle of the Californian navy.

In the missions a great deal of wine was grown, good enough to be sent for sale to Mexico; but, with the exception of what we got at the *Misión* Santa Bárbara, the native wine that we tasted was such trash as nothing but politeness could have induced us to swallow.

Various circumstances have conspired to render these dons so very peculiarly indolent. Independently of innate differences of national tastes, the objects of colonization exert an influence over the character of the colonists. Thus the energy of our republican brethren, and the prosperity of the contiguous dependencies of the empire, are to be traced, in a great degree, to the original and permanent necessity of relying on the steady and laborious use of the ax and the plow; and thus also the rival colonists of New France—a name which comprehended the valleys of the Saint Lawrence and the Mississippi—dwindled and pined on much of the same ground, partly because the golden dreams of the fur trade carried them away from stationary pursuits to overrun half the breadth of the continent, and partly because the gigantic ambition of their government regarded them rather as soldiers than as settlers, rather as the instruments of political aggrandizement than as the germ of a kindred people. In like manner, Spanish America, with its sierras of silver, became the asylum and paradise of idlers, holding out to every adventurer, when leaving the shores of the old country, the prospect of earning his bread without the sweat of his brow.

But the population of California in particular has been drawn from the most indolent variety of an indolent species, being composed of superannuated troopers and retired office-holders and their descendants. In connection with the establishment of the missions, at least of those of the upper province, there had been projected three villages or pueblos as places of refuge for such of the old soldiers as might obtain leave to settle in the country; but as the priests were by no means friendly to the rise of a separate interest, they did all in their power to prevent the requisite licenses from being granted by the crown, so as to send to the villages as few denizens as possible, and to send them only when they were past labor, as well in ability as in inclination. These villages were occasionally strengthened by congenial reinforcements of runaway sailors, and, in order to avoid such sinks of profligacy and riot, the better sort of functionaries, both civil and military, gradually established themselves elsewhere, but more particularly at Santa Bárbara, while both classes were frequently coming into collision with the fathers, whose vexatious spirit of exclusiveness, even after the emancipation of the veterans, often prompted them nominally to preoccupy lands which they did not require.

Such settlers of either class were not likely to toil for much more than what the cheap bounty of nature afforded them,—horses to ride and beef to eat, with hides and tallow to exchange for such other supplies as they wanted. In a word, they displayed more than the pro-

verbial indolence of a pastoral people, for they did not even devote
their idle hours to the tending of their herds. As one might have expected, the children improved on the example of the parents through
the influence of a systematic education,—an education which gave
them the lasso as a toy in infancy and the horse as a companion in
boyhood, which, in short, trained them from the cradle to be mounted
bullock-hunters, and nothing else, and if anything could aggravate
their laziness, it was the circumstance that many of them dropped, as
it were, into ready-made competency by sharing in the lands and
cattle of the plundered missions.

SAN FRANCISCO
IS THE POINT

by

ALFRED ROBINSON

THE writer, in his preceding chapters, has given a correct and impartial account of the peculiar character of California and its inhabitants.

A portion of the country, however, most interesting in its natural features, has been, perhaps, but too little dwelt upon. It is that embracing the extensive Bay of San Francisco, into which flow the waters from the Sacramento, San Joaquín, Jesús María, and other lesser streams. The surrounding country, diversified by hills and plains, is very beautiful; the soil is rich and heavily timbered; and the high mountains which rise around are thickly adorned with cedar-trees. There are extensive prairies also, and large tracts of excellent tillage-ground on the banks of the rivers. It is the grand region for colonization, and if peopled by our industrious backwoodsmen, who are gradually emigrating from the Western States, it must hold, in a very few years, a conspicuous station among the nations of the earth. Its locations are well adapted to purposes of agriculture, and such is its mildness of climate that all tropical fruits might be raised there, if cultivated. The large rivers are navigable for steamboats for more than one hundred miles, and are well stocked with salmon and other fish. The cold, blustering winds and disagreeable temperature of the climate alluded to by other writers are solely confined to the lands adjacent to the sea-coast, for, a very few leagues beyond the limits of Yerba Buena, we find a totally different atmosphere.

As the traveler proceeds south from San Francisco, he passes through a similar description of country till beyond Monterey, when the plains become more contracted and less fertile, till he is forced at last upon a hard sandy beach. Riding through little openings among the hills, he enters again upon wider strips of land as the mountains retreat from the sea. In this way he may continue towards San Diego day after day, the face of the country varying until it becomes barren and cheerless.

There is a vast extent of land, however, beyond the mountains which is but imperfectly known to the Californians. This has been repeatedly visited by foreigners, who have said much in its favor. It it unoccupied, and is the only part of California, with the exception of land north and east of San Francisco, that is attainable for the purpose of colonization. All that portion that is within twenty or thirty miles of the sea-coast is at present either occupied by cattle-farms or by the much-restricted possessions of the Missions.

Now that Upper California remains in its unsettled state, it opens a field for immigration, and the unfriendly feelings of its inhabitants towards Mexico will undoubtedly lead them to favor other nations. *San Francisco, then, is the point,* as also the lands around the bay, the banks of the Sacramento and Jesús María. These are the best lands, and are well calculated for the raising of wheat and other grains, and for the rearing of cattle. These immense tracts of land, and the facility of water-intercourse between them and the bay by rivers and creeks, render their situation highly important.

The liberality of the Californians since their first opposition to Mexico has induced many foreigners to settle in the country, and several hundreds of Americans may be already found located at different points. Their industrious habits have procured for them many very promising settlements, where the lands under judicious management, produce abundance, and contribute greatly to the beauty of the surrounding country.

Agriculture, as may be supposed, has not much improved since its first introduction by the Spanish friars, for the same modes of cultivation are still adhered to which they introduced at the commencement of their labors in California.

The grains principally cultivated are, wheat, barley, maize, and several kinds of beans, or frijoles as they are called by the natives. Oats are not raised for any purpose whatever, but they grow spontaneously on the prairies and upon the hills, where they are left to dry and rot with the yearly pasturage. The sowing of grain commences in November, when the rains set in, and the harvest is in the months of July and August. Owing to inattention, perhaps, in procuring good seed, their wheat is not so fine as it might be, for in no part of the world can be found a soil and climate better adapted to its production.

Most kinds of vegetables are raised in gardens, and there is hardly a house in the country that has not its small patch of ground devoted to that purpose.

Both flax and hemp have been raised in California, and also cotton, to considerable advantage. The vine is thrifty, and is cultivated everywhere, from which is made very excellent wine and brandy.

Notwithstanding the immense number of domestic animals in the country, it is rather surprising that the Californians give so little attention to the dairy. Butter and cheese are extremely scarce, and but seldom used, and I have known instances in which the proprietor of three or four thousand cows has been obliged to send all over the village where he resided to obtain milk for his family. From this circumstance it may be supposed that they are totally ignorant of its value. Not so; for, since the introduction of foreign settlers, they have been well instructed in the art of making both butter and cheese, and it is only from sheer indolence that these articles are not more plentiful.

In the intercourse between California and the Sandwich Islands, which has considerably increased in latter years, large quantities of wheat, beans, flour, cheese, and soap have been annually exported from the former, the proceeds of which have usually returned in a variety of goods from the English and American markets.

The trade with California is, however, confined principally to American ships direct from the United States, for they have but two or three small vessels of their own, and not more than twenty or thirty on the whole extent of the Mexican coast.

Gold and silver mines have been found in Upper California, from which considerable quantities of ore were obtained. Skillful miners are only required to make them profitable. It is said coal has recently been discovered, which, if true, will greatly facilitate the introduction of steam-navigation in the Pacific, and be the means of making California one of the most important commercial positions on the west coast of America, particularly if a communication should ever be opened by means of a canal across the Isthmus of Panamá. That such an event may happen is not improbable. The day is not far distant, perhaps, when it will be realized, and one may visit this fertile and interesting country and return to the United States in one half of the time now required for the long and tedious outward navigation.

The resources of California, its magnificent harbors, climate, and abundance of naval stores, would make it the rendezvous for all the steamers engaged in the trade between Europe and the East Indies, as well as those from the United States, and the facilities for emigration would be such that soon the whole western coast of North America would be settled by emigrants, both from this country and Europe.

During the anarchy which existed in past years throughout this fertile country, there were many of the native Californians who would have been thankful for the protection of either England or America, and indeed a great many desired it, in preference to the detested administration of Mexico. Perhaps there are many who still feel as they did then, and in this age of "annexation" why not extend the "area of freedom" by the annexation of California? Why not plant the banner of liberty there, in the fortress at the entrance of the noble, the spacious Bay of San Francisco? It requires not the far-reaching eye of the statesman nor the wisdom of a contemplative mind to know what would be the result. Soon its immense sheet of water would become enlivened with thousands of vessels, and steamboats would ply between the towns which, as a matter of course, would spring up on its shores, while on other locations along the banks of the rivers would be seen manufactories and sawmills. The whole country would be changed, and instead of one being deemed wealthy by possessing such extensive tracts as are now held by the farming class, he would be rich with one quarter part. Everything would improve, population would increase, consumption would be greater, and industry would follow.

All this may come to pass, and indeed it must come to pass, for the march of emigration is to the West, and naught will arrest its advance but the mighty ocean.

NAMING THE GOLDEN GATE

by

JOHN CHARLES FRÉMONT

THE Bay of San Francisco has been celebrated, from the time of its first discovery, as one of the finest in the world, and is justly entitled to that character even under the seaman's view of a mere harbour. But when all the accessory advantages which belong to it—fertile and picturesque dependent country; mildness and salubrity of climate; connection with the great interior valley of the Sacramento and San Joaquin; its vast resources for ship-timber, grain and cattle—when these advantages are taken into the account, with its geographical position on the line of communication with Asia, it rises into an importance far above that of a mere harbour, and deserves a particular notice in any account of maritime California. Its latitudinal position is that of Lisbon; its climate is that of southern Italy; settlements upon it for more than half a century attest its healthiness; bold shores and mountains give it grandeur; the extent and fertility of its dependent country give it great resources for agriculture, commerce, and population.

The Bay of San Franicsco is separated from the sea by low mountain ranges. Looking from the peaks of the Sierra Nevada, the coast mountains present an apparently continuous line, with only a single gap, resembling a mountain pass. This is the entrance to the great bay, and is the only water communication from the coast to the interior country. Approaching from the sea, the coast presents a bold outline. On the south, the bordering mountains come down in a narrow ridge of broken hills, terminating in a precipitous point, against which the sea breaks heavily. On the northern side, the mountain

From *Geographical Memoir Upon Upper California,* 1849.

presents a bold promontory, rising in a few miles to a height of two or three thousand feet. Between these points is the strait—about one mile broad in the narrowest part, and five miles long from the sea to the bay. Passing through this gate,* the bay opens to the right and left, extending in each direction about thirty-five miles, having a total length of more than seventy, and a coast of about two hundred and seventy-five miles. It is divided, by straits and projecting points, into three separate bays, of which the northern two are called San Pablo and Suisún bays. Within, the view presented is of a mountainous country, the bay resembling an interior lake of deep water, lying between parallel ranges of mountains. Islands, which have the bold character of the shores—some mere masses of rock, and others grass-covered, rising to the height of three and eight hundred feet—break its surface, and add to its picturesque appearance. Directly fronting the entrance, mountains a few miles from the shore rise about 2000 feet above the water, crowned by a forest of the lofty cypress, which is visible from the sea, and makes a conspicuous landmark for vessels entering the bay. Behind, the rugged peak of Mount Diavolo, nearly 4000 feet high, overlooks the surrounding country of the bay and San Joaquín. The immediate shore of the bay derives, from its proximate and opposite relation to the sea, the name of *contra costa*, (counter-coast, or opposite coast.) It presents a varied character of rugged and broken hills, rolling and undulating land, and rich alluvial shores backed by fertile and wooded ranges, suitable for towns, villages, and farms, with which it is beginning to be dotted.

A low alluvial bottom land, several miles in breadth, with occasional open woods of oak, borders the foot of the mountains around the southern arm of the bay, terminating on a breadth of twenty miles in the fertile valley of St. Joseph, a narrow plain of rich soil, lying between ranges from two to three thousand feet high. The valley is openly wooded with groves of oak, free from underbrush, and, after the spring rains, covered with grass. Taken in connection with the

---

* Called *Chrysopylae* (golden gate) on the map, on the same principle that the harbour of *Byzantium* (Constantinople afterwards) was called *Chrysoceras* (golden horn.) The form of the harbour, and its advantages for commerce, (and that before it became an entrepot of eastern commerce,) suggested the name to the Greek founders of Byzantium. The form of the entrance into the Bay of San Francisco, and its advantages for commerce, (Asiatic inclusive,) suggest the name which is given to this entrance.

valley of San Juan, with which it forms a continuous plain, it is fifty-five miles long and one to twenty broad, opening into smaller valleys among the hills. At the head of the bay it is twenty miles broad, and about the same at the southern end, where the soil is beautifully fertile, covered in summer with four or five varieties of wild clover several feet high. In many places it is overgrown with wild mustard, growing ten or twelve feet high, in almost impenetrable fields, through which roads are made like lanes. On both sides the mountains are fertile, wooded, or covered with grasses and scattered trees. On the west it is protected from the chilling influence of the northwest winds by the *cuesta de los gatos*, (wild-cat ridge,) which separates it from the coast. This is a grassy and timbered mountain, watered with small streams, and wooded on both sides with many varieties of trees and shrubbery, the heavier forests of pine and cypress occupying the western slope. Timber and shingles are now obtained from this mountain; and one of the recently discovered quick-silver mines is on the eastern side of the mountain, near the Pueblo of San José. This range terminates on the south in the *Año Nuevo* point of Monterey Bay, and on the north declines into a ridge of broken hills about five miles wide, between the bay and the sea, and having the town of San Francisco on the bay shore, near its northern extremity.

Sheltered from the cold winds and fogs of the sea, and having a soil of remarkable fertility, the valley of St. Joseph (San José) is capable of producing in great perfection many fruits and grains which do not thrive on the coast in its immediate vicinity. Without taking into consideration the extraordinary yields which have sometimes occurred, the fair average product of wheat is estimated at fifty fold, or fifty for one sown. The mission establishments of Santa Clara and San José, in the north end of the valley, were formerly, in the prosperous days of the missions, distinguished for the superiority of their wheat crops.

The slope of alluvial land continues entirely around the eastern shore of the bay, intersected by small streams, and offering some points which good landing and deep water, with advantageous positions between the sea and interior country, indicate for future settlement.

Such is the bay, and the proximate country and shores of the Bay of San Francisco. It is not a mere indentation of the coast, but a little sea to itself, connected with the ocean by a defensible gate, opening out between seventy and eighty miles to the right and left, upon a breadth of ten to fifteen, deep enough for the largest ships, with bold shores suitable for towns and settlements, and fertile adjacent country for cultivation. The head of the bay is about forty miles from the sea, and there commences its connection with the noble valleys of the San Joaquín and Sacramento.

SAN FRANCISCO BAY

by

CLARENCE URMY

This is the Golden Gate; the rock-bound way
   Viscaino and Cabrillo failed to find,
   The port Sir Francis on the "Golden Hind"
Sailed past to anchor in a rough, bleak bay;
And we are Argonauts (or so we say),
   Shore-driven by fair Fortune's favoring wind,
   We enter, lo, a splendid harbor lined
With ships that flags of all the world display!

In amber air a hill-set city gleams,
   And fields of poppies wondrous to behold;
Afar through vine-clad vales come singing streams
   And river-tales of mountains filled with gold—
A land, a sea, a sky a-thrill with dreams
   That only Time and poets shall unfold.

THE *BROOKLYN*,
AND THE CITY'S FIRST
NEWSPAPER

by

E. C. KEMBLE

THE ship Brooklyn, of Mormon fame, landed her colony of 238 men, women and children on the beach of Yerba Buena during the first days of August, 1846.

When the tide served, the ship's launch and small boat set them ashore bag and baggage, on a strip of good, firm land between Clay and Washington streets, thirty yards from the line of the stores on the west side of Montgomery street, and about six feet below its hard earth level; at low tide the boats touched at the foot of the rocky bluff known later as Clark's Point.

At this rocky point, where this writer first went ashore in Yerba Buena, the principal store was Dickson & Hay's "Beehive." That name was added later and painted in large capitals across the front of their new store, one of the first notable building improvements in the Spring of the year following. Dickson & Hay were Englishmen, and their stock of miscellaneous goods selected for the native trade (not native trash, O satirical setters-up of these unfortunate pages, as your types made me say a week or two ago!) made up the fourth of the group of mercantile houses which gave Yerba Buena its commercial dignity in 1846. Besides this store, there were two or three sailor drinking houses on the point; and this was all.

From *Yerba Buena: 1846,* Johnck & Seeger, San Francisco, 1935.

I look through my "loophole" on the busy scene of the Brooklyn landing. The beach is strewn with goods and implements, such as never before were landed on this wild coast. There were Yankee plows of which I will venture to say not a dozen had ever before been introducd into California; for at the time of which I write even the enterprising Sutter stirred the soil of your own Sacramento—neighbor UNION—with the Mexican forked stick, though I believe he had also American plows in use. And to-day I read in the UNION's report of the annual address before the California State Fair, "In twenty-five years, we have passed from the cast-iron plow to the steel-gang, from the sickle to the header, and from the flail to the steam-power and horse-forks." After all, the metamorphosis wrought by your types when they changed the points of the compass in San Francisco is scarcely more incredible than the changes which these types of industry reveal, and there were harrows landed from the Brooklyn over which even many "foreigners" in Yerba Buena scratched their wise polls in puzzled meditation on their uses; for the youthful California of that period of Agriculture had never been combed by the harrow. Scythes, grain-cradlers, hoes and rakes, and all that in those days made up the complete outfit to the husbandman, with various mechanic implements and dairy utensils, cover the landing, and are being dragged on Yankee wheels by hand-power up the long hill at Washington street. In an enclosed space in the rear of the houses, near the junction of this street with Montgomery, the Mormon colony first pitched its tents; a few families are lodged in the few vacant houses about town. Headquarters are established at the adobe building on Dupont street between Clay and Washington, where were stored the company's goods and implements. And now the camp-fires are lighted and the new life in this strange land begins.

Around one of those evening camp-fires near the roadside (Washington street), a group of the new-comers are gathered, discussing with long faces the events of the day, and the prospects which have opened before them, some of which, to judge from certain sinister remarks, are as unexpected as they are unwelcome. The destination of this colony had been the Bay of San Francisco, and the muskets which had been put in their hands before starting it was understood were to be used to achieve their independence and win a heritage on the shores of the Pacific for the saints at Nauvoo.

Today these dreams of sovereignty and empire had been put to flight and they found themselves once more under the United States flag. This was bitterness number one. In their visions of the new land to which they were going, they had beheld a paradise in which all the ripe harvests of all their old homes were but as the bloom of the rich fruitage that awaited them. They had landed on bleak, treeless and apparently verdureless shores, and instead of the soft airs of the Italian clime which Fremont and Hastings and other writers had described, a cold wind swept around them and a gray fog distilled dampness and shrouded the strange landscape in gloom. And this was bitterness number two. "They call this place *Yerba Buno*," said one of the group, and it is a curious fact that until that day not a dozen of the Brooklyn colony had ever heard the name Yerba Buena before. "They say it means good herbs; but if anything good will grow on this soil, I'm mightily mistaken." And so thought all the company. "Here is some of the stuff the town takes its name from," said another speaker, producing a bunch of the little vine then so plentiful on the hills around the bay. "The people here make tea of it." And so indeed they did, nor were the Mormons of the Brooklyn long in following their example. In the Fall and Winter that followed their arrival, it became their chief beverage, not from choice, but because the Chinese product was both scarce and costly in the Yerba Buena market. "And here is the sort of grub we're coming to," added a third party present. "It's called jerky," and we were accordingly introduced to the staple of our future meat supplies—the dried beef of the country.

The Brooklyn colony set about their labor of preparing new homes with heavy hearts. A few abandoned the field in the outset and returned to the East in the first ship that sailed out of the harbor. Others separated from the company of the faithful and set up for themselves. The first school opened in Monterey, then the capital of the country, was established by a seceder from the Brooklyn colony. Two or three unprotected females opened pie shops in Yerba Buena. But the main body of Mormons formed themselves into a Farming, Trading and Manufacturing Company, elected a board of officers, and inaugurated their existence as a corporate body by taking a contract to supply a certain number of saw-logs from the redwoods near Bodega for Captain Smith's mills at that point. The Brooklyn had been chartered to load at Bodega, and a few weeks after their landing in California a select party of woodchoppers from the Brooklyn company found themselves again on board the old ship on their way up the coast. About the same time the new organization bought a ship's longboat, and sent her sloop-rigged up the San Joaquín, with a party on board to make the first venture in farming, and formed the first settlement in the San Joaquín valley. And now comes in the story of the mill on Clay street, from which was sent forth the first issue of the press in the embryo mistress of the Pacific. I doubt if ever a babe born in a mill was more royally couched. The first impress of the types was laid upon satin. It was the programme of a reception given to Commodore Stockton by the citizens of Yerba Buena, on the occasion of his arrival from the lower coast. The babe was born about the first of October, 1846.

The old mill was about the largest frame structure in town. It stood, as I have before described, on Clay street, north side, midway between Kearny and Montgomery streets. On the ground floor there had been set up—how many years before I know not—a single run of stones worked by mule power *arrastre*-wise. The second floor, or loft, was reached by a crazy stair-case on the outside. The Mormons hired the building soon after their arrival, and set one of their number to work with a mule, grinding wheat for the company. Let me pause for a moment to masticate the tough wheatcake of my recollection. Flour, even of the lowest unbolted grade, it never for a moment aspired to be called. It had a conscience as well as a hide, and just dropped from the mill a dirty mess of partially cracked wheat of a very inferior and damaged quality. That was our bread—our very ill bread—of those times that tired men's teeth. It was a fitting accompaniment to the herb tea and the wormy jerked beef—our unchangeable diet. Let us go on.

Up those outside stairs with incredible difficulty and no small danger of being buried beneath their wreck, with the frame of a No. 4 Washington press across our stomachs, my fellow printer and I lifted and pushed and dragged that Star printing machine. The name of the intended paper had been cut in wood six months before in the city of New York; yea, some of the type (a column Brandreth pill advertisement) had been set. We had half a dozen pairs of cases of old Long Primer and Brevier type, and two or three small fonts of job type. These, with the press, were set up in the loft of the mill, and the first printing office on the Bay of San Francisco was ready for business.

THE CITY IS CHRISTENED

An Ordinance.

"WHEREAS, the local name of Yerba Buena, as applied to the settlement or town of San Francisco, is unknown beyond the district; and has been applied from the local name of the cove, on which the town is built: *Therefore,* to prevent confusion and mistakes in public documents, and that the town may have the advantage of the name given on the public map;

"IT IS HEREBY ORDAINED, that the name of SAN FRANCISCO shall hereafter be used in all official communications and public documents, or records appertaining to the town.

"WASH'N A. BARTLETT,
"Chief Magistrate.

"Published by order,
"J. G. T. DUNLEAVY, *Municipal Clerk.*"
San Francisco, California
January 30, 1847.

SOME LAWS
OF THE TOWN COUNCIL
OF
SAN FRANCISCO

To Prevent Desertion of Seamen

BE IT ORDAINED by the Town Council of the Town of San Francisco, that if any person within the limits of this Town, shall entice or advise any Sailor or other person employed on board of any vessel within this harbor or bay, to leave the vessel on which he or they may be employed, upon conviction thereof, he shall be fined not exceeding five hundred dollars, nor less than twenty, and be imprisoned not exceeding three months.

Be it further Ordained, that if any person or persons shall feed, harbor or employ, any runaway Sailor within the limits of this town without permission from the Alcalde, such person or persons shall be fined on conviction thereof, not exceeding five hundred dollars, nor less than twenty, and be imprisoned not exceeding three months.

Be it further Ordained, that if any Sailor or other person employed on board of any vessel now in this bay, or which may hereafter come into it, run away and be caught within the town, such Sailor or other person shall, on conviction of having run away, be ordered to hard labor on the public works not exceeding six months.

Be it further Ordained, that this Ordinance take effect from and after the sixteenth day of September, A. D. 1847.

Police Regulations

Be it Ordained by the Town Council of the Town of San Francisco, that each and every member of the Council shall be a conservator of the peace within the limits of the town, and shall issue any process necessary to preserve the peace and morals of the place, upon application, or when they may deem it proper so to do, and all such process shall be made returnable to the Alcalde, and shall be charged and regarded by the Alcalde as if it had been issued by himself.

Be it further Ordained, that the members of the Council shall receive no compensation for the performance of the above duty.

Bt it Ordained by the Town Council of the Town of San Francisco, that if any person shall enter the house occupied by another, and assault the occupant or any other person within said house, such person so assaulting shall be fined, on proof thereof before the Alcade, not less than five nor more than fifty dollars; and on failure to pay the same, shall be put upon the public works until the same is paid.

Be it further Ordained, that any person who shall assault or strike another in any other house than the one occupied by him, or in any other place, such person so assaulting or striking shall be fined not less than five nor more than fifty dollars; and on failure to pay, shall be put on the public works until the same is paid.

Be it further Ordained, that the informer shall have one half the fine imposed by this ordinance.

Be it Ordained by the Council of the Town of San Franicsco that any person firing a gun or pistol within one mile of Portsmouth Square, shall be fined upon conviction thereof, not less than three nor more than five dollars.

Be it further Ordained, that any person killing or maiming the carrion fowls or birds within the limits of this town, shall be fined one dollar for each offence, upon conviction thereof.

Be it Ordained by the Council of the Town of San Francisco that from and after the 12th day of November, 1847, all property holders desiring to dig wells upon their premises, or who may now have them dug, shall, under a penalty of fifty dollars fine, carefully close and fence, or box them up.

Licenses

Be it Ordained by the Town Council of the Town of San Francisco, that any person or persons wishing to sell any merchandise or property at auction, shall first procure a license from the constituted authorities before selling, as hereby described.

Be it Ordained, that the Alcalde of this town shall, on application of any person or persons in writing, grant licenses to sell goods, wares and merchandise, real estate and every other description of property, for not less than one year; and for each of such licenses granted, the person or persons shall pay the sum of twenty five dollars in advance.

Be it further Ordained, that any person or persons acting in the capacity of an Auctioneer without first obtaining licenses, shall be fined not exceeding one hundred nor less than twenty five dollars, on conviction thereof, with cost of suit.

Be it further Ordained, that the Alcalde shall receive for his fees one dollar for every such license so granted. The above to take effect from and after the passage hereof, this 11th day of October, A. D. 1847.

Be it Ordained by the Town Council of the Town of San Francisco, that from and after the passage hereof, no person or persons shall sell or dispose of spirituous liquors in large or small quantities within the jurisdiction of this town, unless they have a license from the constituted authority.

Be it Ordained, that the Alcalde of this town, on the application of any person in writing, shall grant licenses to sell spirituous liquors for a term not exceeding one year, nor less than six months; and for every license so granted, the person or persons obtaining, shall pay the sum of fifty dollars every six months, in advance.

Be it Ordained, that no license shall be granted unless the petitioner shall procure and enter into competent bonds of two hundred and fifty dollars, to keep an orderly house.

Be it Ordained, that for the grant of any and every license as aforesaid, the Alcalde's fees shall be one dollar, and for the execution of the bonds one dollar.

Concerning Constables

Be it Ordained by the Town Council of the Town of San Francisco, that there shall be elected two Constables who shall constitute the chief police of the town.

Be it further Ordained, that the Constables shall perform all duties required of other ministerial officers within the town; shall faithfully execute all process directed to them in accordance with law, and make due return thereof; shall strictly enforce and obey every law, ordinance and resolution, passed by the Council.

Be it further Ordained, that the Constables shall receive for the service of any writ or other process, one dollar, to be paid out of the fines imposed upon cases; one dollar for the service of any writ or other process to be paid by the defeated party, also ten cents per mile for every mile which they may travel to serve any writ or other process beyond the limits of the town.

An Ordinance to amend an Ordinance concerning Constables.

Be it Ordained by the Town Council of San Francisco, that hereafter there shall be but one Constable for the Town, who shall receive, in addition to all the fees and perquisites of his office allowed by law, the sum of fifty dollars per month, and shall continue in office during good behaviour.

Be it further Ordained, that the Constable shall devote his entire time to his official duties, and is hereby empowered to arrest any one guilty of any crime, misdemeanor, or other improper conduct, and take him or them before the Alcalde for trial.

Be it further Ordained, that the Constable shall have power to call upon any citizen or citizens to assist him in the performance of his duties, and that any person refusing to assist as aforesaid, shall be fined not less than five nor more than fifty dollars.

THE FIRST OFFICIAL YEAR

F ROM the columns of the early papers we extract much curious information regarding the number and elements of the population of San Francisco in the latter part of June, 1847. The following table shows the total number of inhabitants, the sex and age of the whites, and the sex of the Indians, Sandwich Islanders, and negroes; excluding the officers and soldiers of the detachment of New York volunteers stationed there at the time:—

Whites	Males	Females	Total
Under 5 years of age	28	23	51
Over 5 and under 10 years	18	14	32
” 10 ” 15 ”	10	14	24
” 15 ” 20 ”	11	11	22
” 20 ” 25 ”	29	15	44
” 25 ” 30 ”	54	19	73
” 30 ” 40 ”	61	19	80
” 40 ” 50 ”	20	10	30
” 50 ” 60 ”	12	3	15
” 60 ” 70 ”	2	—	2
” 70 ” 80 ”	2	—	2
Total whites	247	128	375
Indians (of different ages)	26	8	34
Sandwich Islanders (of different ages)	39	1	40
Negroes (of different ages)	9	1	10
Total	321	138	459

From this table it will be seen that upwards of four-fifths of the whole population were under forty years of age; while more than one-half were between twenty and forty—the prime of life. Under

From *The Annals of San Francisco* by Soule, Gihon & Nisbet, D. Appleton, New York, 1855.

twenty, the sexes were nearly equal in number; but above that age, the vast majority were males. These circumstances must be borne in mind when the reader considers the restless enterprise, energy and capability exhibited by the comparatively small population of the town. We have already alluded to the mixture of foreigners who settled in San Francisco. We now give the birth-places of the above white population:—

Born in the United States, 228; in California, 38; other Mexican departments, 2; Canada, 5; Chile, 2; England, 22; France, 3; Germany, 27; Ireland, 14, Scotland, 14, Switzerland, 6; at sea, 4; Denmark, Malta, New Holland, New Zealand, Peru, Poland, Russia, Sandwich Islands, Sweden and West Indies, *one* each.

As of the number stated to have been born in California, eight were children of immigrant parents, it will be seen that the total population of Spanish or Mexican descent was only thirty-two. Three-fifths of the total inhabitants were of direct American origin; and perhaps one-fifth more was composed of people who had previously settled or lived in the United States. The Americans, however, as may be supposed, were from every State in the Union, and were often as different from each other in personal characteristics, as if they had been so many foreigners of separate countries.

The number who could not read and write was two hundred and seventy-three; those who could read, but not write, were thirteen; while those who could neither read nor write, were eighty-nine.

From these statements it appears that the number who could neither read nor write bore a near relation to the number of inhabitants under ten years of age. At that period, it may be mentioned, there was only one school in the place, and no proper facilities were as yet given for bestowing a suitable education upon the young.

The occupations or professions of the white males were as follows:—

1 minister; 3 doctors; 3 lawyers; 2 surveyors; 1 school-teacher; 11 agriculturists; 7 bakers; 6 blacksmiths; 1 brewer; 6 brick-makers; 7 butchers; 2 cabinet makers; 26 carpenters; 1 cigar-maker; 13 clerks; 3 coopers; 1 gardener; 5 grocers; 2 gunsmiths; 3 hotel-keepers; 20 laborers; 4 masons; 11 merchants; 1 miner; 1 morocco-case maker; 6 inland navigators; 1 ocean navigator; 1 painter; 6 printers; 1 saddler; 4 shoemakers; 1 silversmith; 4 tailors; 2 tanners; 1 watchmaker; 1 weaver.

The places in which the inhabitants conducted their business, were as follows., viz.:—shops, 1 apothecary, 2 blacksmith, 3 butcher, 1 cabinet maker, 2 carpenter, 1 cigar-maker, 2 cooper, 1 gun-smith, 1 shoemaker, 2 tailor, and 1 watchmaker; 8 stores; 7 groceries; 2 hotels; 1 wind-mill; 1 horse-mill; 2 printing-offiices and 3 bakeries.

The Indians, Sandwich Islanders, and negroes, who formed nearly one-fifth of the population, were mostly employed as servants and porters. Many of the Sandwich Islanders were engaged in navigating the bay, and were very expert boatmen.

II

THE GOLD RUSH

INTRODUCTION

THERE had been talk of gold in California long before the region was explored, or even properly identified.

As the reader will recall, Montalvo's romantic fifteenth-century novel, *The Exploits of Esplandián,* in which the name "California" was invented, spoke of the mythical island as being inhabited by a race of Amazons whose weapons were all of gold. The author was quite explicit about it: "The island everywhere abounded with gold and precious stones," he said, and added, "upon it no other metal was found."

This was fiction, to be sure, and recognized as such. But somehow the idea of gold in California never quite died. Sir Francis Drake knew nothing of the old Spanish novel. But after he had careened his ship and repaired her, at the same time taking possession of the country as New Albion, he sailed back to England and solemnly reported that gold was to be found in quantity in this marvelous land. Less was said about gold by the Spanish explorers, but they were after all members of a race whose far-flung enterprises had been undertaken for gold, and the precious metal could never have been far from their minds.

The Franciscan fathers, pushing farther northward, knew that there was some gold; that much is of record. Every now and then, as the missions grew and became prosperous, an Indian neophyte would come to one of the priests and show him a quill or perhaps an acorn-cup full of gold dust. When such things happened, the fathers took special pains to discourage the Indians. They had a difficult task managing the great mission properties as it was; there were all too few good Indians to pick the grapes, herd the cattle, render the tallow, and harvest the grain. No mission priest wanted to see a convert turn goldhunter. So nothing was said. Anyhow, the economy of California was of its own special kind, and when a Mexican settler down in the southern part of the state did make a discovery that amounted to something, pulling up a clump of wild onion and finding yellow par-

ticles clinging to the roots, the excitement was minor. Some few stam-
peded to San Feliciano Canyon in 1841, but they came back again
without having made their fortunes and that was that. The *Californio*
of the time had no particular inclination to grow rich; to accumulate
money for money's sake was alien to his nature. So the true "first"
gold mine was all but forgotten.

By the time of the big discovery, however, California was American, or near enough. As things fell out, the Treaty of Guadalupe
Hidalgo, which officially ended the war with Mexico and made California American, was signed on February 2, 1848. Just ten days earlier,
in a little foothill valley about a hundred and fifty miles from San
Francisco, James Wilson Marshall, carpenter for Captain John A.
Sutter, had picked up in his millrace the flakes that were to touch off
the greatest gold rush ever. By one of the oddest ironies of history the
Spaniards had missed their chance and the Americans cashed in.

The news took a long while to filter down to San Francisco—partly,
at least, because Sutter realized what it meant. His vast New Helvetia
grant, he saw, would be overrun; his properties would be ruined; his
whole life would be turned upside down. (All these things happened.)
And so he tried his best to keep the discovery quiet while he made
attempts to get title to the land where gold had been found.

He did not succeed, chiefly because California's military governor
was cautious about his legal right to confirm title to any property
until the treaty had been signed and new machinery was set up to do
such jobs correctly. For a time Sutter tried signing joint papers with
chiefs of the Indian tribes that lived in Coloma where he had set up
his sawmill, but such agreements were worth little. And eventually he
learned that a gold discovery does not remain secret. Some of his men
bragged. The Mormon, Sam Brannan, who was keeping store up the
Sacramento River near Sutter's Fort, heard about it, and quietly went
off into the hills to see what he could find. He found all he needed.
By the middle of May, 1848, he had his evidence—a quinine bottle
filled with dust. His store, on the road to the gold fields, was well
stocked, and he was ready to start business coming his way. He took
Sutter's little launch down the river to San Francisco. There he went
about the streets waving his dust-filled bottle and crying "Gold! Gold
from the American River!" That was enough. San Franciscans dropped
everything and headed for the mountains. The *Californian* suspended

publication; its publisher noted sadly that his advertisers had "closed
their doors and places of business and left town to look for gold,"—
and he himself left for Coloma the next day. And the rest of California, as quickly as the news got around, did the same thing. By the
first of June there were two thousand amateur gold-miners digging
and washing for thirty miles around Sutter's mill. As for Sutter, he
was forgotten. His lands were pre-empted; miners squatted as they
pleased; his crops were ruined; he had no workers left to run his vast
ranches. After a while he gave it up and retired to one of his smaller
properties. It was the end for him. His California had changed overnight.

Meantime, for a few months the rush was an all-California affair.
Communication was slow, and through the summer and autumn of
1848 the Californians had things pretty much to themselves.

This did not last much longer. The evidence of gold was sent east,
as was proper; an official messenger took $3,000 worth in a tea-caddy
to President Polk. In December the director of the mint in Philadelphia made his report on a larger "deposit of gold received from California." It had been brought from San Francisco over the Isthmus
route by one David Carter, and it totaled some 1,800 Troy ounces,
valued at $36,000. This and Polk's message to Congress in December
set off the real rush. The forty-niners were on their way before 1848
was over.

One of the natural results was a rash of "Guides to the Gold Fields,"
some worth the price asked, many utterly valueless. Most useful were
those which did not pretend to educate the miner in how to dig for
gold but simply advised him how to proceed to California. One might
go by sea, around Cape Horn; one might set out, prepared for Indians,
on the fatiguing Overland Route. Or one might sail to Chagres, cross
the Isthmus to the city of Panama, and take ship again northward to
San Francisco.

"Gregory's Guide for California Travellers" was one whose author
contented himself with describing this route and giving common sense
advice on what the gold-seeker should do if he planned to go via the
Isthmus. As the reader will see, even Gregory was not immune to the
infection of optimism. The journey, he writes, from New York to San
Francisco by way of the Isthmus, ought not to take more than five

or six weeks at the most. In the selection which comes immediately after Gregory's counsel, the reader will learn that the truth was far different. Hiram D. Pierce, whose admirably detailed and colorful journal is excerpted here, sailed from the Pacific side, embarking at Panama, on May 9, 1849, and it was August 1 when the ship dropped anchor in San Francisco Bay—just twice as many weeks as Gregory's outside estimate, not including the time spent coming down from New York to Chagres and the days it took the company to get through the mosquito-infested Isthmus jungles.

The Pierce journal is perhaps the best I have ever seen covering the weary voyage northward from Panama to San Franicsco. Its author, a city alderman in Troy, New York (Russell Sage served on the board at the same time), was an elder of the Second Presbyterian Church of Troy and a solid citizen. A wagonmaker and blacksmith, he had a good business and the California fever might not have had any effect upon him but for the fact that his health had been poor and his doctor talked about a sea voyage. He was almost forty years old; he had a wife and seven children. But what with the doctor's advice and the talk of gold—well, he decided to see what California might offer. His journal covers the whole story of his great adventure (from which, like many another, he returned as poor as when he went). For this volume I have chosen only the entries covering the twelve-weeks' voyage from Panama to San Franicsco. The reader will find Hiram Pierece a man with a sharp eye, upright and sensible, no great shakes on orthography but possessed of a fine sense of drama and enough humor to enable him to weather a rough experience for a man his age then. His record of the trip is reproduced here exactly as he wrote it.

News of California gold did not stop at America's Atlantic Coast Within a year or two the entire world knew about the discovery and a good part of the world was on the way to San Francisco, natura gateway to the mines.

In England, Thomas De Quincey made up his mind that the whole business was nine-tenths a Yankee hoax, and said so in a magazine called *Hogg's Weekly Instructor*. His remarks concerning the method by which the Yankee sharpers were spreading and supporting the hoax are reprinted here as "The Gold 'Swindle' " and his ingenious, satirica explanation of the operations of the top-ranking liar, stationed in San

Francisco, and his subordinates in perpetuating this "poetic hoax," is amusing reading, especially since there is at least a nubbin of truth in it all, though De Quincey himself was guilty of exaggeration when he wrote that the man who went to the California goldfields stood to get "nothing except perhaps a *soupcon* of catarrh."

De Quincey was only one of many who found difficulty in believing the tall tales that came back from San Francisco. There was one way to get the truth; this was to send a reliable man after it. Any newspaper might have had the idea, but it was Horace Greeley of the *Tribune* who sent his already famous correspondent, Bayard Taylor, then just twenty-four years old, to San Francisco to get the story. Taylor's correspondence describing the fantastic gold-rush city and the mines was one of the sensations of 1849 in New York, and was published in book form as *El Dorado, Or Adventures in the Path of Empire* the next year. The excerpt here was chosen for its double view of San Francisco—the city as Taylor saw it on his arrival, and again some months later when he returned from his tour of the mining regions and could scarcely believe the changes that had taken place in that short time. As a good reporter should, Taylor noted all he saw— carefully jotting down details of the incredible prices paid for everything, recording the menus at the best hotels, describing the dazzling gambling places, the colorful street crowds and such matters. His well-written, accurate report is still the best picture of San Francisco in 1849 the reader can find anywhere, and a "must" for inclusion in this volume.

As every reporter of the day took pains to note, San Franicsco in the first decade of the gold rush was one of the most mixed cities on earth, a polygot community in which the languages of all nations were heard. It was a diary-writing age, too, and it is not surprising that journals kept in the San Francisco of gold-rush days have turned up in almost every country of the world. One such came to light a few years ago in a Paris bookshop, and an American novelist, Clarkson Crane, translated and published that section of it in which a young Frenchman, Albert Benard de Russailh, recorded the life of the fifties in San Francisco as he saw it on his way to the mines. A sensible man, experienced in city life in his own Paris, he held no great opinion of one particular class of San Franciscans—the *nymphes du pave*—and expressed himself frankly. His comment on this side of San Francisco

life is so specific that it earns a place in this volume as "The Women
of the Town: 1851." De Russailh died of cholera only a little more
than a year after his arrival, but his reflection of San Francisco as
Mr. Crane has translated it in the scarce little book, *Last Adventure,*
has a flavor not quite like any other writing about the city in those
times.

During the fifties, of course, San Francisco's waterfront was the
busiest place in town. The bay was a forest of masts; ships moved in
and out constantly. And so fast did the city grow that frequently a
cargo never got as far as the establishment of the merchant who had
ordered it; buyers thronged the wharves and bid for items as they
were brought ashore. Of the landing places, the busiest was the city's
"Long Wharf," and a sharp, brief vignette of that blend of mart and
slum is reprinted here from Alonzo Delano's "Pen-Knife Sketches."
Delano, one of California's favorite humorists for half a lifetime, wrote
under the pseudonym of "Old Block," and from 1849, when he arrived
from Illinois to seek his fortune, until he died in 1878 in the mining
town of Grass Valley, he made his gentle combination of humor and
sound reportage famous through the newspapers and magazines of his
adopted state. The sketch here used appeared first in the Sacramento
Union and later in his "Pen-Knife" volume, published in that city
and reprinted in a small fine-press edition in San Francisco in 1934.

Perhaps the most famous episodes of the fifties in San Francisco
were the two Committees of Vigilance and the summary disposal they
made of the criminals who had begun to consider that they had the
city government in their pockets.

For the story of the Committee of 'Fifty-one, I have chosen the
account of California-born Harvard philosopher Josiah Royce, taking
it from his volume "California" in the American Commonwealth Series
published in the 1880s. Royce's volume is not primarily a history; it
was written as a study in the American character, and for this reason
he approaches the First Vigilance Committee as a social manifestation, an aspect of the period that produced it, and relates its work to
the picture of social change in the new California. For the sake of
contrast, I have chosen the account given in his "Memoirs" by that
tart military man and sometime banker, General William Tecumseh
Sherman, of the Second Vigilance Committee (the one of 1856), as
he saw it in operation in San Francisco. His view is a special one,

moreover, since he represented the Law-and-Order Party which—but for a wisely broken promise on the part of the officer in charge of the Benicia Arsenal—might well have come to bloody warfare with the Vigilantes. Unlike the philosophical Royce, General Sherman saw the vigilante principle simply as a wanton breach of the law, and he says so, though he admits that it was a necessity under the circumstances. Both Royce and Sherman, however, draw the same conclusion: The vigilante principle is a dangerous one, and must not be invoked until and unless all else fails.

San Francisco was a sufficiently naughty city in the fifties, yet it was oddly strait-laced too. The stage, aside from honky-tonks and the like, was in the hand of good people, for the most part hard-working actors and actresses who went all out to give the city the best theater they knew. When Lola Montez arrived, therefore, the reputation that had preceded her was what tickled the fancy of San Franciscans. She had been the mistress of a Bavarian King; she had told the press of the world she was Spanish, but that taradiddle was catching up with her; she had married and had been unmarried, and remarried. From her appearances in Paris and New York word had come to the Pacific Coast that she had no great talent as either actress or dancer, and San Franciscans generally knew that too. But perversely they were interested. Lola, shaking oversized whalebone-and-rubber insects from her dress in her notorious Spider Dance, might be worth watching for the sake of these acrobatics, or she might not. But as the Mid-Victorian Bad Girl she was a curiosity. Her sojourn in the city, brief as it was, turned out to be a seven-days' wonder, and when she took herself off in a fit of pique to live in a Sierra foothill mining town, San Francisco was still interested in her. Oscar Lewis, in the selection I have taken from his *Lola Montez in California,* does beautifully with the unsual personality of the exotic lady, and also with the prim, Nice-Nelly attitude of a town in which mere naughtiness should have been no great attraction.

As California grew by leaps and bounds, (the state was admitted to the Union very early in its career—in 1850), and as differences sharpened everywhere between the northern and southern states on the question of slavery and other issues, politics in San Francisco became a violent, rough-and-tumble business. The Republican party was

growing rapidly, but the state was still controlled by a half-split Democratic organization; the Lecomptonite wing, led, among others, by
California's Supreme Court Chief Justice, David S. Terry, and the
anti-Lecomptonite wing headed by David C. Broderick, self-made
man, U. S. Senator and friend of Stephen A. Douglas. It was inevitable that the two men should clash; as it happened, their clash was
sufficiently sharp so that it led to California's most famous duel. I
have here selected an account of that affair from an old history of
dueling, *The Field of Honor,* written by Ben C. Truman, California
newspaperman and a witness of the Terry-Broderick affair of which
he writes at first hand. Since Truman wrote his book, students have
corrected some of his statements, and anyone interested in the schol-
arly ins and outs of the matter should consult Carroll D. Hall's *Terry-
Broderick Duel,* published by The Colt Press of San Francisco in 1939.
Truman's account, however, is simply and dramatically written, and
for the purposes of this book more useful than any, in spite of minor
errors.

All in all, the California gold rush was so stupendous an affair that
only a stupendously energetic man could have captured the whole
story between covers. Such a man was Hubert Howe Bancroft. Originally a bookseller in the San Francisco of the rush, Bancroft quickly
made himself a historian, then a publisher. In the eighties his "History
Factory" was a streamlined wonder, a busy building in which scores
of workers transcribed the documents Bancroft had gathered, reworked
the personal-narrative accounts that their employer had sent them
throughout the state to get from the pioneers before these men vanished and took their precious eyewitness knowledge with them, and
organized the vast amount of material into a comprehensive history
of California running to a dozen volumes out of the thirty-odd which
constitute his historical "Works." One of these volumes, *California
Inter Pocula,* which is to say "California in Her Cups," contains a
survey of San Francisco during its gold-drunk decade, and it is a part
of that survey that I have chosen to reprint in this book as a sum-
ming up of the period in which San Francisco mushroomed from a
sleepy village into a vigorous, even roaring, boom town known everywhere as one of the world's great cities. For color, anecdote, detail
and general coverage, it is the most thorough picture of the fifties in
San Francisco ever painted, and because of this it has been source

material for hundreds who have written about the period and the place in the years since its publication sixty-odd years ago. Here, summed up and vividly drawn, is San Francisco in the first flush of its youth, and the reader will understand the city's beginnings better with Bancroft's help than he could in any other way.

Richard Henry Dana, whose view of San Francisco Bay in 1835 appears in Part I of this volume, provides the ideal conclusion for our composite picture of the gold rush years. Long after his *Two Years Before the Mast* had made him famous and his successul efforts to ameliorate the hard lot of American merchant seamen had brought him favorable attention in other quarters, Dana came back to visit the scene of his youthful adventure. He wrote the story of what he saw, and it was incorporated into later editions of his book as "Twenty-Four Years After." That essay, describing the San Francisco of 1859, logically closes Part II of this volume. It is by all odds the sharpest single summary of what ten years of gold-in-the-hills growth had brought about in the city that was the port of entry for, the supply center and financial heart of, the gold-mining regions of California.

Finally the reader will observe, scattered through Part II, various comments on San Francisco, none too good-natured, written by one Hinton Rowan Helper. These appeared, together with much more of the same vinegary sort, in a book called *The Land of Gold,* published in 1855 by a Carolinian who was to acquire an even wider reputation as a minority of one opposed to popular views when he scolded the South for its reliance upon the institution of Negro slavery in his sensational volume, *The Impending Crisis.* Helper came to California, saw San Francisco and the mines, and went away again in a passion of dislike and dissent. Some of his acid comments are scattered through this section simply as a kind of corrective, so the reader may discover for himself that not every articulate visitor to the Gold Rush City felt bound to praise what he saw there.

ONCE BY THE PACIFIC

by

ROBERT FROST

The shattered water made a misty din.
Great waves looked over others coming in,
   And thought of doing something to the shore
   That water never did to land before.
The clouds were low and hairy in the skies
Like locks blown forward in the gleam of eyes.
   You could not tell, and yet it looked as if
   The sand was lucky in being backed by cliff,
The cliff in being backed by continent.
It looked as if a night of dark intent
   Was coming, and not only a night, an age.
   Someone had better be prepared for rage.
There would be more than ocean water broken
Before God's last "Put out the light" was spoken.

From *West-Running Book* by Robert Frost. Copyright 1928 by Henry Holt and Company, Inc.

GOLD REACHES THE EAST

Mint U.S., Philadelphia, Dec. 11

SIR—On the 8th inst. we received, as I have already had the honour to inform you, the first deposit of gold from California. It was deposited by Mr. David Carter, who brought it from San Francisco, by the Isthmus route. It weighed 1804.59 ounces Troy; of which 1423.80 was from the lower surface mines, and 380.79 from those at Feather River. On the 9th inst., another deposit was sent, by the Secretary of War, which weighed 228 ounces.

The gold was of two sorts in external character, though apparently not different as to quality. The first, from the "dry diggings," was in grains, which averaged from one to two pennyweights; the other variety, from the swamps or margins of the streams, being in small flat spangles, of which, on an average, it would take six or seven to weigh one grain. Of these, by far the larger part of the deposits was composed.

The gold was melted in six parcels, and the loss by melting, due to the earthy and oxidable matter which disappears in this operation, averaged about 2½ per cent of the original weight. The loss thus reported is moderate, and shows that the gold had been carefully washed.

Assays of the melted gold were made with great care, and the results showed a variation in fineness from 892 to 897 thousandths, the average of the whole being 894. This is slightly below the standard fineness, which is 900.

The average value per ounce of the bullion, before melting, is $18.5-1/3; that of the same in bars, after melting, is $18.50.

The whole value of the gold in two deposits was $36,492, besides a few ounces reserved in the native state for the Secretary of War, at his request.

Very respectfully, your faithful servant,

R. M. Patterson, *Director*.

Hon. Robert J. Walker,
    Secretary of the Treasury.

[1849]

UP FROM PANAMA

by

HIRAM D. PIERCE

W ENSDAY, MAY 9th, 1849: Went on the Ship, & at 5 P M.
Waid Anchor, fair wind & Tide. We steered South S. W. The *Sophia*
made sail at the same time.

Thursday, 10th. A fair wind all night & by 12 today we had made
160 miles. In the afternoon a calm. I was Sea Sick. Our fare was
wretched, & I cast up all that I had eaten. The Ship was wretched
dirty & we were crowded in a sad plight. I confess that I wished myself in Troy.

Friday, 11th. I felt some better. eat for breakfast a small piece of
Sea bread & 1 cup of coffey. Continued sick through the day. Have
not yet kept anything on my stomach that I have taken on the Ship.
At noon it rained hard. So that those who went on deck for dinner
got drenched unless protected by oil cloth.

Saturday, 12. (3d D.O.) I felt some better in the morning. Cast
up some bile & felt better through the day. It was quite calm. Not
making over 2 or 3 knots. A meeting was held & means taken to
better the condition of the passengers. The passengers were divided
into 3 messes called 1st, 2d & 3d mess, to take their turns in beeing
served. At evening a shower & good breeze for an hour or two & then
lulled all knight.

Tuesday, 15th. (6th D.O.) Winds still fresh on our starboard beam.
Not verry well. The long voyage before us makes my Spirits sink.
Since starting on Pacific I can begin to realise that I have fairly
started for Cal. But while on the Isthmus I felt that I could go back

---

From *A '49'er Speaks,* published from the diary in 1930 by Sarah Wiswall
Meyer.

& had I received word from home that called for it I should have done so. O the loneliness. Saw a large School of Sperm Whale. Some rain & a fresh breeze on our Starboard beam.

Wensday, 15th. (7th D.O.) Some rain. Saw land on the Starboard about 3 deg. North the Equator. Last night the Sea presented a beautiful Sparkling appearance. The Sparks appearing many feet under water as well as at the Surface. They freequently have the appearance of large kernels of powder burned & sometimes remain for some seconds.

Thursday, 16th. (8th D.O.) Rained last night. Still beating to the South. Wind W.S.W. This morning a sail in sight far a way the first we had seen. Our fare for breckfast Coffey & hard bread & molases. For Dinner Pork Corned beef, & beans or rice some times. Supper Bread and Sugar. Butter is served but the sight is sufficient without the smell. Meals taken in hand, standing when we can & when we cannot we go down.

Sunday 20th. (11th D.O.) Wind fresh. Troy & its privileges. I strive to keep my mind from it. Comstock & 3 others have fitted up our Whale boat & covered it with Canvass & sleep in it along side. Comstock rose in the morning came from under the canvass & with a graceful bow said, Good morning Pacific. What agitates thy Bousom this morning. I have not seen the sun rise or set clear since I have ben on the Pacific. It has rained I think every night since we started. Day after day I look out on the blue expance of waters. Occasionally we see some of the Monsters of the deep. Our mode of liveing is truly brutish. Our Company is now divided into 2 messes, Starboard & Larboard. One mess first one day & the other the next. We form ourselves in two lines when we can, on that small part of the deck that is left clear. And a man passes through with the Coffey. Another with the Sugar. Another with a basket of bread. Another with a pan of Boiled meat. Another with a bottle of vinegar & molases, & then the grabbing commences. we ketch a piece of meat in the fingers & crowd like a lot of Swine. The ship perhaps so careened that you will need to hold on or stagger & pitch like a Drunken man. Many behave so swineish that I perfer to stay away unless driven to it by hunger. Often we get a lurch & go Scating across deck on back or belley, Coffey Sugar & Bread scattered in wild profusion.

Monday, 21st. (12th D.O.) Wind fresh West by S. Running down the coast. Saw some Turtle 5 or feet across. Engaged during the day in tacking & beating trying to get round a point of land that makes out some 20 or 30 miles. At evening the Sea was verry rugged.

Saturday, 2d. (24th D. O.) Fine morning. We are running along with a gentle breeze. I feel quite well. I think my Stomach has gained strength verry much. All on board quite well. In the evening there was quite a spree on deck. The assistant Dr of the Ship got beastly drunk, & got down betwene decks, & the passengers there were determined to rout him from there. So they got a rope round him & with great hevving hoisted him on deck, & took him to his hammoc & lashed him in. His hammoc was slung verry high & in the night he got out & was found suspended by his feet. The same worthy took a dose of medecine to a patient & haveing a bone in his hand knawing, he took the medicine & gave the bone to the patient.

Sunday, 3d. (25th D. O.) Stiff breeze S. W. Running in the same Driection. Religious Service was held at ½ past ten.

Monday, 4th. (26th D. O.) Breeze same. A flurry occured betwene the old Spanish Steward & a passenger in which the former was knocked down. A Booby was caught & the ships name, number of passengers, destinations &c fastend to its neck & it was let go. I was not verry well. Lat. 4 deg. 5 min. Long. 90 deg. 30 min. W.

Friday, 8th. (30th D. O.) Stiff breeze all night same direction. Making a good run some 7 or 8 nots. No appetite—boiled meat & wormey bread goes hard. Lat. 3—13 L. 96—64.

Saturday, 9th. (31st D. O.) Wind strong. Making about 8½ knott. The sea sparkled last evening beautifully. Lat 3. 45 Long 99. 41.

Sunday, 10th. (32d D. O.) Wind Strong Same direction Lulled in the afternoon. A Sermon was preached in the afternoon from the Subject of Naman the Assyrian. Discussion on Scripture were frequent. Any One not acquained with the habits of Southerners would be astonished at their profanity, even of their Doctors Judges and Lawers. It is mingled with all their conversation. Lt. 4 deg. 5 min. Long. 102 deg. 12½ min.

Monday, 11th. (33d D. O.) Wind verry Strong through the night. The Sea the roughest we had seen. Ship pitched badly. Tacking, our course. Breckfast would remind one of a stall of Swine. Sliping & Jostling about Spilling Coffey on each other. Sometimes going across the deck before they could bring up, some on the belley & Some otherwise. It seems as if all restraint is taken off and the Supreme Selfishness of the human heart showes its darkest colors. It is a good oppertunity to read carractor. The Sea rolled heavy all day. Lat. 3. 57. . Long 104. 18.

Thursday, 14th. (36th D.O.) The night was squalley, & in the forenoon. In the afternoon a calm & squall when the sails were handled nimbly. Two Porpoises & a Cowfish were caught & taken on board. they were harpooned. the cowfish would weigh about 500 lb. I think the porpois has the nicest shaped head & jaws & finest set of teeth that I ever saw. The head is shaped like the Pikes only it comes narrower forward, & is armed with 80 beautiful round teeth & shut so close as to nearly form a water joint. Roasted a little on the coals & it tasted well, but at home it would have ben rather dark. Lat. 8 deg. 21 min. Long. 110 deg. 21 min.

Friday, 15th. (37 D.O.) It was Squalley & some gusts of wind. There was quite an excitement about dinner. Capt. Butler, a passenger, made a cowfish chowder, putting in pork & crust. About two Barrels were made. As it was a fresh dish each one watched the pots with eagle eye untill about 2 P. M. when it was brought forth, their stomachs refusing to be comforted or fed on expectation any longer. Capt. B. meantime had crowded the fires out of pure compassion & nearly smoked his eyes out, & there beeing such a mass in the kettle, it was badly burned. Each in the exercise of his selfishness, loaded his plate, when on taisting, spitting & spewing & dumping of plates overboard commenced, & for a time it was a wrothy sene. Capt. B. shrunk from view, & was no whither. He never got over that chowder during the voyage.

Saturday, 16th. (38th D.O.) Freequent squalls occured attended with heavy rain. It kept the sea verry rough & kept the sailors stirring. Squalls would sometimes turn the ship on hur beam ends. The night was uncomfortable in the extreme, the rain drove the passengers betwene decks, & the air became fowl in the extreme. We are now passing through the variables.

Sunday, 17th. (39th D.O.) Freequent squalls, allmost impossible to get about decks. I felt verry unwell, but after snuffing the seabreeze I felt much better. I thought of Troy &c. About 11 a squall struck us with great violance.

Thursday, 21st. (43d D.O.) I feel poorly mornings with loss of appetite. Some murmuring. Lat. 13 55 Long. 116. 14. At night the wind increased. All Sail was taken in except a double reefed topsail & spencer, the latter a strong small sail to the mainmast. At 12 it blew a perfect gale & in the morning the sene was truly awful.

Friday, 22d. (44th D.O.) The gale seemd to increase & at 7 the gibboom & foretegaliant were carried away. the gibboom which usually rides some 20 or 30 feet high plunged into a swell & broke them away. It was a thing that the officers never saw before. The foretegaliant with the yard attached, & sail furled with all the rigging hung dangling. There was a rope strung along deck for the sailors & the few that were compelled to go on deck to pass by, as but few had the courage to go on deck, as a man could not keep his feet. The wind was sufficient to sweep most anything off not made fast, & as she rolled & pitched hur decks would be as steep as the roof of a house. Hur rail & bullworks would go under. I got out & looked around & the sene was such as no picture or Language can begin to describe. To see the fury of the Ocean, hissing & boiling & heaveing like a boiling Cauldren, the roar of its waters & of the tempest & the storm, the roar of the wind through the rigging & pitching of the ship combined to make a Sene truly appauling. The Spray was such that we could see but a short distance. The swells seemed thrown up in heaps, the wind having veard round to all points of the compass. The Ship lay for 30 hours at the mercy of the waves, only they kept hur laid to, broad side to the wind, otherwise hur decks would have ben swept. But as a Swell approached lifting hur whole length at a time she rode them like a duck. At 2 P.M. the Hatches were fastend down, & I tell you there were many thoughts on home & far away. The expectation of seeing Home at this time was small. Had the Ship foundred, probably not a Soul would have lived to tell the tale, as a boat could not have lived a moment. One boat was Stove hanging high above water at the stern, & a man could not have staid on any other object. The night was the most tedious that I had experienced. My bedfellow, Comstock was unwell & I gave him the berth untill after midnight & I hung on to the side of the berth to keep from beeing thrown across the deck as it was impossible to stand sit or lay without bracing or holding with a firm grasp. It was said by the Captain who had followed the sea 24 years that he had never seen but one Storm so severe & that of but few hours duration. And it was generally said that a vessel never lived through a harder one to tell the story. Eating was given up. All sat or lay in mute astonishment, & some at least who at other times could curse their Maker were willing afterwards to thank Him, & say nothing but the tender Mercies of Allmighty God had spared them, & to confess that they Praid, but they soon forgat their vows. For my part in the fore part of the storm I felt to look up to my Heavenly Father & commit to Him my Family & my Soul & bid adieu to the Senes of Earth, but when I saw the ability of the Ship to ride it I thought we should be Saved. Lat. 16, 30. Long. 116.

Saturday, 23d. (45th D.O.) The hatches were removed & the wind had verry much subcided & we began to make sail, though the Sea was verry rough & continued so for 2 days. Lat. 16. 25. Long. 116. 28.

Wensday, 27th. (49th D.O.) Morning cool looked like a storm. Running E.N.E. then tacked & ran W.S.W. In the evening I gave my Berth to Mr. Bristol who was sick & took his place in the Boat & in spite of all the covering I could master I Suffered much with the cold, & took cold.

Saturday, 30th. (52d D.O.) Thermometer 70 in the daytime, we beeing directly under the Sun. I find great difficulty in keeping warm nights. Wind N. & we are sailing close on the wind, making W. ½ N.W. Running within 6 points of the wind. We have about 12 days of water & are 1000 Miles from San Francisco, & with the present wind it is judged it will take 15 days at least to reach there. Home!! Lat. 21. 8. Long. 126. 21.

Sunday, July 1st. (53 D.O.) Great coat & flannel & mitens quite necessary Service at ½ past 10.

Monday, 2d. (54th D.O.) Wind light N.E. My bowels are very much out of order in consequence of Cold I had taken. I we reelected a commityman.

Tuesday, 3d. (55th D.O.) Cool. Running N.W. by N. I am quite unwell. My cold seems to have seteld in my whole Systom. Today a dozen or more were engaged in making & frying donuts. At 5 I went to bed & suffered severly all night with pain in my head & bowels. I was cold all night.

Wensday, 4th. (56th D.O.) Independence. I reckon I thought of Home. The morning verry cool & unpleasant, & I was quite sick. I ate no supper or breckfast. At 10 the Passengers asembled & comenced the Celebration of the day. Prair was offered by Mr. Fairchild & a

National Song was sung. After which the decleration was read by Judge Buoy, followed by a Most Eloquent Oration from Mr. Parbert of Geneva, Ny. It was recieved with enthuseasm followed by another Song & closed by the Benediction. After which Rice Donuts Honey & Panama Molases were served out, & we all enjoyed the day as well as we could under the circumstances. No liquor or gunpowder were used during the day!

Thursday, 5th. (57th D.O.) This day was a tedious day for me. I have Severe Cholic pain & a Diarea discharging a blooddy Slime & a Severe headache with other Symptoms of Foul Stomach. Occasioned I think by having eaten two freely of raw pork & a want of exercise, but more particularly by taking cold in the night which seteld on my Bowels. I suffer severely with the cold wearing flanel & a great coat. Lat. 26. 30. Long. 132 35.

Friday, 6th. (58th D.O.) This day was Still more tedious to me. I kept my berth all day & time hung heavy. I have commenced taking some pill that Dr. N. gave me, composed of Opeum Camphor & Calomel.

Saturday, 7th. (59th D.O.) My bowels are getting some better. I have ate nothing for 4 days. No appetite. Still cold. During the past few days Mr. Bristol has been failing very much.

Sunday, 8th. (60th D.O.) At 10 Service was held, after which we were put on allowance of one quart of water per day, or 1 pint of water & 1 pint of coffey.

Monday, 9th. (61st D.O.) Wind still N.E. We running 2 points N of E variation 1 point, leaving 1 makes our course E. I am much better. Mr. Bristol had a tedious night of it, but today is more comfortable.

Tuesday, 10th. (62d D.O.) A cold unpleasant day & rough Sea.

Wensday, 11th. (63d. D.O.) The night was verry boistrous, nearly all Sail was furled. Morning cold & unpleasant. There is some talk about going to the Sandwich Islands, as it seems impossible to get to San Francisco.

Sunday, 15th. (67th D.O.) Service was held at the usual hour. A Sail in Sight. Mr. Bristol is verry feeble. Our course is rather more favourable. The butt opened to us again this afternoon & another pint delt to each man, which seemed to spread joy through all our ranks as if we had found treasures.

Monday, 16th. (68th D.O.) This Morning at 6 Mr. Bristol Expired after a few weeks of most intense Suffering, brought on I think by scalding his fingers at the galley & taking cold in his hand. And not withstanding it is the blasting of all his worldly hopes & prospects, yet in view of his sufferings it seemed a sweet relief. His request was that his body might be sent home, & we commenced to make preparations accordingly. We asertained that spirits could be obtained at about $2. per gallon. We got a cask of the Captain. It would take about 40 gallons. A meeting of the passengers was called & it appointed a committy composed of the Phisicians on board, to concider & report the best mode of preservation. They reported it could best be done in spirits & then it was decided by the Surgon of the Ship & other Phisicians that his heart & vitals must be taken out, otherwise it would burst the cask. To this his friends objected & majority of our company voted against opening him, & that rather than have him cut to pieces we would bury him in the deep. So a commity was appointed to make the nessesary preperations, & at 6 P. M., he was brought to the waist of the Ship sewed up in canvass with his face exposed while the English Service was gone through in a Solom manner, after which all was sewed up & he was commited to the deep. The Ship passed on & in one moment he was hid from mortal eyes untill the morning of the Resurection. The Sene was a Solom one & many eyes were sufused with tears. Thus perished one of our most active & usefull members before we had reached the field of opperation It took place in Lat. 33. 33. Long. 130. 28.

Tuesday, 17th. (69th D.O.) Rather more mild & pleasant, wind strong N.E. I feel much better today. Lat. 33 deg. 51 min. Long. 127 deg. 18 min.

Wensday, 8th. (70th D.O.) The day was clowdy & cold. No observation. Running N.N.E. at an average of 4 knot. I done up some washing.

Thursday, 19th. (71st D.O.) Another batch of donuts was made. It is interesting to see the galley rangers. Some dozen or 20 are constantly buisy roasting bread or baking pancakes, & frying fritters & roasting pork. The day was cool. It averaged 63 degrees.

Sunday, 22d. (74th D.O.) Land was seen last evening. Wind strong all knight. This morning verry cool. Thermometor 55 degrees. At ¼ before 10 the coast of California was in Sight before us. We stood on our course running sharp on the wind untill within 2 miles & then tacked & ran 2 hours & tacked again & ran into the coast having made but 5 miles, & at 4 tacked & ran 9 hours, & then tacked in untill 12 having made 13 miles. Tacked West again the wind blowing quite a gale the whole time. Lat. 37 deg. 9 min.

Monday, 23d. (75th D.O.) Cold & cloudy. We found that we had made land in the gulf of Monteray. At 12 came near land 43 miles South of San Francisco by observation. Then tacked W.S.W. 10 hours, then tacked N.E. & stood on the course.

Tuesday, 24th. (76th D.O.) Still cold, during yesterday & last night it blew allmost a gale. At 12 came in sight of land again running nearly parallell with the Coast. Breakers were seen along the coast at the distance of 10 miles. At Sundown in 10 miles of the coast off & on during the night. The hills at a distance look red like burnt clay. At 3 A. M. I heard as I supposed sticks or kelp scrape the sides of bottom of the Ship & feeling a little uneasy got up & went on deck. The mate was throwing the lead. It had Shoaled to 7 fathom. The sails were immediately clued up & all hands called. The Captain came on deck in his shirt flaps & ordered the Anchor dropped in 6½ fathom. During the afternoon we saw a Whale close along Side. One throwed thimself out of the water finely. His flukes presented a formidable appearance.

Wensday, 25th. (77th D.O.) Laying at anchor Somewhere in the neighbourhood of the entrance to San Francisco but none can tell where, as the whether is thick & foggy. We knew we were near Shore but could see but a few rods. There was a current running some 4 or 5 knot. The Captain thought our situation unsafe as it blew fresh & at 6 got up the Anchor & stood out & ran up the coast. At 10 saw a sail, boarded it & learned that we had lain anchored at the entrance. We were now some 12 miles above. Bout ship & the wind lulled & at sundown came to anchor 4 miles abrest the entrance.

Thursday, 26th. (78th D.O.) Morning thick & foggy. Not able to see a mile. At ½ past 12 raised Anchor & got underway for the harbour. Wind & tide in favour. The Senery was most wild & desolate. Large naked rocks some of them covered with guana projecting out & towering up, the entrance beeing about one mile wide & tide running through 6 miles. A great abundance of fowls coverd the water. At 2 P. M. dropped anchor 3 miles from the landing, the wind blowing a gale. The bay stretches in one direction 60 miles & the other 10, & in clear weather we can easily see across it. It is interspersed with islands. At 4 miles from town we passed Guana Island,* perhaps of 2 acres. It towers up some 50 feet & looks like a great Snow bank beeing perfectly white with guana. There is said to be 175 Sail in the Harbour. All is life & bustle

---

* Now called Alcatraz Island.

Friday, 27th. Went ashore & found such a wild state of things as allmost to intoxicate a person without giveing 50 cts a glass. Money seemed of no account. Houses that would not cost over $100 in Troy rents for $300 per month. Others of the commonest class & cheapest construction rent for $800. per month. One house that might be rented in Troy for $200. rents as I am informed for $180,000.* Lumber is worth $450. per M. Brick $100 per M. Wages from $12 to $16 per day, & yet provisions & clothing in particular is comparatively cheap. Yet some articles is high enough to make up. Flour 6 to $12 per bbl. Choice Cheese 6/ per lb. Salaratus $12. per lb. Eggs $12. per dozen. I paid $1.50 for breckfast. Reports from the mines are verry encourageing. Men are coming in, some of them loaded with the dust. In the forenoon there is a thick cold fog, & about noon the Seabreeze begins to blow a gale untill in the evening. San Francisco is a miserable dusty dirty town of some 5000, out of every kindred tongue & people under Heaven.

---

* This evidently means per year.

Saturday, 28th. Morning bright & clear. The anchor was raised to run in nearer shore. I feel quite well. Rose & took notes, went ashore at 9, looked around, bought a chest of Tea at 40 cts, one cheese of 43 lb. at 55 cts, bread 25 cts per loaf, mince pies 4/. Returned to the Ship after a hard struggle. Wood is from 40 to $60. per cord.

Sunday, 29th. Staid a board & wrote home. A pleasant day but windy & cold. 2 Ships Came in, one that Started the midle of January.

Monday, 30th. Still at anchor. Today wrote three letters. One to my Wife, one to Mr. Boutwell & one to J. H. Austin. Mr. Bills came a board & took dinner with us today, & spent the afternoon.

August 1st. This morning we are verry buisy in packing up & getting readdy for a start up the rivers.

AFTER THIS, SEA

by

JOSEPHINE MILES

This is as far as the land goes, after this it is sea.
This is where my father stopped, being no sailor,
Being no Beowulf, not orient spice hungry
Here he let horizons come quietly to rest.
      What he fled is past and over,
      Raftered roof and quilted cover,
      The known street and the known face,
      The stale place.
This is as far as the land goes, here we are at length
Facing back on the known street and face, all flight
Spent before our time in building the new towns,
Letting these last horizons come quietly to rest.
      We have a special pressing need
      We of the outer border breed
      To climb these hills we cannot flee
      To swim in this sea.
This is as far as the land goes, here the coast ranges
Hard and brown stand down to hold the ocean,
Here the winds are named for saints and blow on leaves
Small, young, yellow, few, but bound to be ancestral.
      Nowhere are so still as here
      Four horizons, or so clear.
      Whatever we make here, whatever find,
      We cannot leave behind.

From *Lines at Intersection* by Josephine Miles. Copyright 1939 by the Macmillan Company and used with their permission.

A REPORTER'S STORY

by

BAYARD TAYLOR

Fifty-One Days from New York

AT LAST the voyage is drawing to a close. Fifty-one days have elapsed since leaving New York, in which time we have, in a manner, coasted both sides of the North-American Continent, from the parallel of 40° N. to its termination, within a few degrees of the Equator, over seas once ploughed by the keels of Columbus and Balboa, of Grijalva and Sebastian Viscaino. All is excitement on board; the Captain has just taken his noon observation. We are running along the shore, within six or eight miles' distance; the hills are bare and sandy, but loom up finely through the deep blue haze. A brig bound to San Francisco, but fallen off to the leeward of the harbor, is making a new tack on our left, to come up again. The coast trends somewhat more to the westward, and a notch or gap is at last visible in its lofty outline.

An hour later: We are in front of the entrance to San Francisco Bay. The mountains on the northern side are 3,000 feet in height, and come boldly down to the sea. As the view opens through the splendid strait, three or four miles in width, the island rock of Alcatraz appears, gleaming white in the distance. An inward-bound ship follows close on our wake, urged on by wind and tide. There is a small fort perched among the trees on our right, where the strait is narrowest, and a glance at the formation of the hills shows that this pass might

---

From *El Dorado, Or Adventures in the Path of Empire* by Bayard Taylor. G. P. Putnam, New York, 1850.

be made impregnable as Gibraltar. The town is still concealed behind the promontory around which the Bay turns to the southward, but between Alcatraz and the island of Yerba Buena, now coming into sight, I can see vessels at anchor. High through the vapor in front, and thirty miles distant, rises the peak of Monte Diablo, which overlooks everything between the Sierra Nevada and the Ocean. On our left opens the bight of Sausalito, where the U.S. propeller *Massachusetts* and several other vessels are at anchor.

At last we are through the Golden Gate—fit name for such a magnificent portal to the commerce of the Pacific! Yerba Buena Island is in front; southward and westward opens the renowned harbor, crowded with the shipping of the world, mast behind mast and vessel behind vessel, the flags of all nations fluttering in the breeze! Around the curving shore of the Bay and upon the sides of three hills which rise steeply from the water, the middle one receding so as to form a bold amphitheatre, the town is planted and seems scarcely yet to have taken root, for tents, canvas, plank, mud and adobe houses are mingled together without the least apparent attempt at order and durability. But I am not yet on shore. The gun of the *Panama* has just announced our arrival to the people on land. We glide on with the tide, past the U. S. ship *Ohio* and opposite the main landing, outside of the forest of masts. A dozen boats are creeping out to us over the water; the signal is given—the anchor drops—our voyage is over.

The *Ohio's* boat put us ashore at the northern point of the anchorage, at the foot of a steep bank, from which a high pier had been built into the bay. A large vessel lay at the end, discharging her cargo. We scrambled up through piles of luggage, and among the crowd collected to witness our arrival, picked out two Mexicans to carry our trunks to a hotel. The barren side of the hill before us was covered with tents and canvas houses, and nearly in front a large two-story building displayed the sign: "Fremont Family Hotel."

As yet, we were only in the suburbs of the town. Crossing the shoulder of the hill, the view extended around the curve of the bay, and hundreds of tents and houses appeared, scattered all over the heights, and along the shore for more than a mile. A furious wind was blowing down through a gap in the hills, filling the streets with clouds of dust. On every side stood buildings of all kinds, begun or

half-finished, and the greater part of them mere canvas sheds, open
in front, and covered with all kinds of signs, in all languages. Great
quantities of goods were piled up in the open air, for want of a place
to store them. The streets were full of people, hurrying to and fro,
and of as diverse and bizarre a character as the houses: Yankees of
every possible variety, native Californians in *sarapes* and sombreros,
Chileans, Sonorians, Kanakas from Hawaii, Chinese with long tails,
Malays armed with their everlasting creeses and others in whose
embrowned and bearded visages it was impossible to recognize any
especial nationality. We came at last into the plaza, now dignified
by the name of Portsmouth Square. It lies on the slant side of the
hill, and from a high pole in front of a long one-story adobe building
used as the Custom House, the American flag was flying. On the
lower side stood the Parker House—an ordinary frame house of about
sixty feet front—and towards its entrance we directed our course.

Our luggage was deposited on one of the rear porticos, and we
discharged the porters, after paying them two dollars each—a sum
so immense in comparison to the service rendered that there was no
longer any doubt of our having actually landed in California. There
were no lodgings to be had at the Parker House—not even a place
to unroll our blankets; but one of the proprietors accompanied us
across the plaza to the City Hotel, where we obtained a room with
two beds at $25 per week, meals being in addition $20 per week. I
asked the landlord whether he could send a porter for our trunks.
"There is none belonging to the house," said he; "every man is his
own porter here." I returned to the Parker House, shouldered a heavy
trunk, took a valise in my hand and carried them to my quarters, in the
teeth of the wind. Our room was in a sort of garret over the only
story of the hotel; two cots, evidently of California manufacture, and
covered only with a pair of blankets, two chairs, a rough table and a
small looking-glass, constituted the furniture. There was not space
enough between the bed and the bare rafters overhead, to sit upright,
and I gave myself a severe blow in rising the next morning without
the proper heed. Through a small roof-window of dim glass, I could
see the opposite shore of the bay, then partly hidden by the evening
fogs. The wind whistled around the eaves and rattled the tiles with a
cold, gusty sound, that would have imparted a dreary character to
the place, had I been in a mood to listen.

Many of the passengers began speculation at the moment of land-ing. The most ingenious and successful operation was made by a gentleman of New York, who took out fifteen hundred copies of The Tribune and other papers, which he disposed of in two hours, at one dollar a-piece! Hearing of this I bethough me about a dozen papers which I had used to fill up crevices in packing my valise. There was a newspaper merchant at the corner of the City Hotel, and to him I proposed the sale of them, asking him to name a price. "I shall want to make a good profit on the retail price," said he, "and can't give more than ten dollars for the lot." I was satisfied with the whole-sale price, which was a gain of just four thousand per cent!

I set out for a walk before dark and climbed a hill back of the town, passing a number of tents pitched in the hollows. The scattered houses spread out below me and the crowded shipping in the harbor, backed by a lofty line of mountains, made an imposing picture. The restless, feverish tide of life in that little spot, and the thought that what I then saw and was yet to see will hereafter fill one of the most marvellous pages of all history, rendered it singularly impressive. The feeling was not decreased on talking that evening with some of the old residents, (that is, of six months' standing,) and hearing their several experiences. Every new-comer in San Francisco is overtaken with a sense of complete bewilderment. The mind, however it may be prepared for an astonishing condition of affairs, cannot immediately push aside its old instincts of value and ideas of business, letting all past experience go for naught and casting all its faculties for action, intercourse with its fellows or advancement in any path of ambition, into shapes which it never before imagined. As in the turn of the dissolving views, there is a period when it wears neither the old nor the new phase, but the vanishing images of the one and the growing perceptions of the other are blended in painful and misty confusion. One knows not whether he is awake or in some wonderful dream. Never have I had so much difficulty in establishing, satisfactorily to my own sense, the reality of what I saw and heard.

I was forced to believe many things, which in my communications to The Tribune I was almost afraid to write, with any hope of their obtaining credence. It may be interesting to give here a few instances of the enormous and unnatural value put upon property at the time of my arrival.

The Parker House rented for $110,000 yearly, at least $60,000 of which was paid by gamblers, who held nearly all the second story. Adjoining it on the right was a canvas-tent fifteen by twenty-five feet, called "Eldorado," and occupied likewise by gamblers, which brought $40,000. On the opposite corner of the plaza, a building called the "Miner's Bank," used by Wright & Co., brokers, about half the size of a fire-engine house in New York, was held at a rent of $75,000. A mercantile house paid $40,000 rent for a one-story building of twenty feet front; the United States Hotel, $36,000; the Post-Office, $7,000, and so on to the end of the chapter. A friend of mine, who wished to find a place for a law-office, was shown a cellar in the earth, about twelve feet square and six deep, which he could have at $250 a month. One of the common soldiers at the battle of San Pasquale was reputed to be among the millionaires of the place, with an income of $50,000 *monthly.* A citizen of San Francisco died insolvent to the amount of $41,000 the previous Autumn. His administrators were delayed in settling his affairs, and his real estate advanced so rapidly in value meantime, that after his debts were paid his heirs had a yearly income of $40,000. These facts were indubitably attested; every one believed them, yet hearing them talked of daily, as matters of course, one at first could not help feeling as if he had been eating of "the insane root."

The prices paid for labor were in proportion to everything else. The carman of Mellus, Howard & Co. had a salary of $6,000 a year, and many others made from $15 to $20 daily. Servants were paid from $100 to $200 a month, but the wages of the rougher kinds of labor had fallen to about $8. Yet, notwithstanding the number of gold-seekers who were returning enfeebled and disheartened from the mines, it was difficult to obtain as many workmen as the forced growth of the city demanded. A gentleman who arrived in April told me he then found but thirty or forty houses; the population was then so scant that not more than twenty-five persons would be seen in the streets at any one time. Now, there were probably five hundred houses, tents and sheds, with a population, fixed and floating, of six thousand. People who had been absent six weeks came back and could scarcely recognize the place. Streets were regularly laid out, and already there were three piers at which small vessels could discharge. It was calculated that the town increased daily by from fifteen to thirty houses;

its skirts were rapidly approaching the summits of the three hills on which it is located.

A curious result of the extraordinary abundance of gold and the facility with which fortunes were acquired, struck me at the first glance. All business was transacted on so extensive a scale that the ordinary habits of solicitation and compliance on the one hand and stubborn cheapening on the other, seemed to be entirely forgotten. You enter a shop to buy something; the owner eyes you with perfect indifference, waiting for you to state your want; if you object to the price, you are at liberty to leave, for you need not expect to get it cheaper; he evidently cares little whether you buy it or not. One who has been some time in the country will lay down the money, without wasting words. The only exception I found to this rule was that of a sharp-faced Down-Easter just opening his stock, who was much distressed when his clerk charged me seventy-five cents for a coil of rope, intead of one dollar. This disregard for all the petty arts of money-making was really a refreshing feature of society. Another equally agreeable trait was the punctuality with which debts were paid, and the general confidence which men were obliged to place, perforce, in each other's honesty. Perhaps this latter fact was owing, in part, to the impossibility of protecting wealth, and consequent dependence on an honorable regard for the rights of others.

About the hour of twilight the wind fell; the sound of a gong called us to tea, which was served in the largest room of the hotel. The fare was abundant and of much better quality than we expected—better, in fact, than I was able to find there two months later. The fresh milk, butter and excellent beef of the country were real luxuries after our sea-fare. Thus braced against the fog and raw temperature, we sallied out for a night-view of San Francisco, then even more peculiar than its daylight look. Business was over about the usual hour, and then the harvest-time of the gamblers commenced. Every "hell" in the place, and I did not pretend to number them, was crowded, and immense sums were staked at the monte and faro tables. A boy of fifteen, in one place, won about $500, which he coolly pocketed and carried off. One of the gang we brought in the Panama won $1,500 in the course of the evening, and other lost $2,400. A fortunate miner made himself conspicuous by betting large piles of ounces on a single throw. His last stake of 100 oz. was lost, and I saw him the following morning dashing through the streets, trying to break his own neck or that of the magnificent *garañon* he bestode.

Walking through the town the next day, I was quite amazed to find a dozen persons busily employed in the street before the United States Hotel, digging up the earth with knives and crumbling it in their hands. They were actual gold-hunters, who obtained in this way about $5 a day. After blowing the fine dirt carefully in their hands, a few specks of gold were left, which they placed in a piece of white paper. A number of children were engaged in the same business, picking out the fine grains by applying to them the head of a pin, moistened in their mouths. I was told of a small boy having taken home $14 as the result of one day's labor. On climbing the hill to the Post Office I observed in places, where the wind had swept away the sand, several glittering dots of the real metal, but, like the Irishman who kicked the dollar out of his way, concluded to wait till I should reach the heap. The presence of gold in the streets was probably occasioned by the leakings from the miner's bags and the sweepings of stores; though it may also be, to a slight extent, native in the earth, particles having been found in the clay thrown up from a deep well.

The arrival of a steamer with a mail ran the usual excitement and activity of the town up to its highest possible notch. The little Post Office, half-way up the hill, was almost hidden from sight by the crowds that clustered around it. Mr. Moore, the new Postmaster, who was my fellow-traveler from New York, barred every door and window from the moment of his entrance, and with his sons and a few clerks, worked steadily for two days and two nights, till the distribution of twenty thousand letters was completed. Among the many persons I met, the day after landing, was Mr. T. Butler King, who had just returned from an expedition to the placers, in company with General Smith. Mr. Edwin Bryant, of Kentucky, and Mr. Durivage, of New Orleans, had arrived a few days previous, the former by way of the Great Salt Lake, and the latter by the northern provinces of Mexico and the Gila. I found the artist Osgood in a studio about eight feet square, with a head of Captain Sutter on his easel. He had given up gold-digging, after three months of successful labor among the mountains.

I could make no thorough acquaintance with San Francisco during this first visit. Lieutenant Beale, who held important Government dispatches for Colonel Frémont, made arrangements to leave for San José on the second morning, and offered me a seat on the back of one of his mules. Our fellow-passenger, Colonel Lyons, of Louisiana, joined us, completing the mystic number which travelers should be careful not to exceed. We made hasty tours through all the shops on Clay, Kearny, Washington and Montgomery streets, on the hunt of the proper equipments. Articles of clothing were cheaper than they had been or were afterwards; tolerable blankets could be had for $6 a pair; coarse flannel shirts, $3; Chilean spurs, with rowels two inches long, $5, and Mexican *sarapes,* of coarse texture but gay color, $10. We could find no saddle-bags in the town, and were necessitated to pack one of the mules. Among our camping materials were a large hatchet and plenty of rope for making lariats; in addition to which each of us carried a wicker flask slung over one shoulder. We laid aside our civilized attire, stuck long sheath-knives into our belts, put pistols into our pockets and holsters, and buckled on the immense spurs which jingled as they struck the ground at every step. Our "animals" were already in waiting; an *alazan,* the Californian term for a sorrel horse, a beautiful brown mule, two of a cream color and a dwarfish little fellow whose long forelock and shaggy mane gave him altogether an elfish character of cunning and mischief.

· · · ·

The City: Day and Night

A better idea of San Francisco, in the beginning of September, 1849, cannot be given than by the description of a single day. Supposing the visitor to have been long enough in the place to sleep on a hard plank and in spite of the attacks of innumerable fleas, he will be awakened at daylight by the noises of building, with which the hills are all alive. The air is temperate, and the invariable morning fog is just beginning to gather. By sunrise, which gleams hazily over the Coast Mountains across the Bay, the whole populace is up and at work. The wooden buildings unlock their doors, the canvas houses and tents throw back their front curtains, the lighters on the water are warped out from ship to ship; carts and porters are busy along the beach; and only the gaming-tables, thronged all night by the votaries of chance, are idle and deserted. The temperature is so fresh as to inspire an active

habit of body, and even without the stimulus of trade and speculation there would be a few sluggards at this season.

As early as half-past six the bells begin to sound to breakfast, and
for an hour thenceforth, their incessant clang and the braying of immense gongs drown all the hammers that are busy on a hundred roofs.
The hotels, restaurants and refectories of all kinds are already as
numerous as gaming-tables, and equally various in kind. The tables
d'hôte of the first class, (which charge $2 and upwards the meal,) are
abundantly supplied. There are others, with more simple and solid
fare, frequented by the large class who have their fortunes yet to
make. At the United States and California restaurants, on the plaza,
you may get an excellent beefsteak, scantily garnished with potatoes,
and a cup of good coffee or chocolate, for $1. Fresh beef, bread, po-
tatoes, and all provisions which will bear importation, are plenty; but
milk, fruit and vegetables are classed as luxuries, and fresh butter is
rarely heard of. On Montgomery street, and the vacant space fronting the water, venders of coffee, cakes and sweetmeats have
erected their stands, in order to tempt the appetite of sailors just arrived in port, or miners coming down from the mountains.

By nine o'clock the town is in the full flow of business. The streets
running down to the water, and Montgomery street which fronts the
Bay, are crowded with people, all in hurried motion. The variety of
characters and costumes is remarkable. Our own countrymen seem
to lose their local peculiarities in such a crowd, and it is by chance
epithets rather than by manner, that the New-Yorker is distinguished
from the Kentuckian, the Carolinian from the Down-Eastern, the
Virginian from the Texan. The German and Frenchman are most
easily recognized. Peruvians and Chileans go by in their brown
ponchos, and the sober Chinese, cool and impassive in the midst of
excitement, look out of the oblique corners of their long eyes at the
bustle, but are never tempted to venture from their own line of business. The eastern side of the plaza, in front of the Parker House and
a canvas hell called the Eldorado, are the general rendezvous of business and amusement—combining 'change, park, club-room and promenade all in one. There, everybody not constantly employed in one
spot, may be seen at some time of the day. The character of the groups
scattered along the plaza is oftentimes very interesting. In one place
are three or four speculators bargaining for lots, buying and selling

"fifty varas square" in towns, some of which are canvas and some only paper; in another, a company of miners, brown as leather, and rugged in features as in dress; in a third, perhaps, three or four naval officers speculating on the next cruise, or a knot of genteel gamblers, talking over the last night's operations.

The day advances. The mist which after sunrise hung low and heavy for an hour or two, has risen above the hills, and there will be two hours of pleasant sunshine before the wind sets in from the sea. The crowd in the streets is now wholly alive. Men dart hither and thither, as if possessed with a never-resting spirit. You speak to an acquaintance—a merchant, perhaps. He utters a few hurried words of greeting, while his eyes send keen glances on all sides of you; suddenly he catches sight of somebody in the crowd; he is off, and in the next five minutes has bought up half a cargo, sold a town lot at treble the sum he gave, and taken a share in some new and imposing speculation. It is impossible to witness this excess and dissipation of business, without feeling something of its influence. The very air is pregnant with the magnetism of bold, spirited, unwearied action, and he who but ventures into the outer circle of the whirlpool, is spinning, ere he has time for thought, in its dizzy vortex.

But see! the groups in the plaza suddenly scatter; the city surveyor jerks his pole out of the ground and leaps on a pile of boards; the venders of cakes and sweetmeats follow his example, and the place is cleared, just as a wild bull which has been racing down Kearny street makes his appearance. Two *vaqueros,* shouting and swinging their lariats, follow at a hot gallop; the dust flies as they dash across the plaza. One of them, in mid-career, hurls his lariat in the air. Mark how deftly the coil unwinds in its flying curve, and with what precision the noose falls over the bull's horns! The horse wheels as if on a pivot, and shoots off in an opposite line. He knows the length of the lariat to a hair, and the instant it is drawn taut, plants his feet firmly for the shock and throws his body forward. The bull is "brought up" with such force as to throw him off his legs. He lies stunned a moment, and then, rising heavily, makes another charge. But by this time the second *vaquero* has thrown a lariat around one of his hind legs, and thus checked on both sides, he is dragged off to slaughter.

The plaza is refilled as quickly as it was emptied, and the course of business is resumed. About twelve o'clock, a wind begins to blow from the north-west, sweeping with most violence through a gap between the hills, opening towards the Golden Gate. The bells and gongs begin to sound for dinner, and these two causes tend to lessen the crowd in the streets for business an hour or two. Two o'clock is the usual dinner-time for business men, but some of the old and successful merchants have adopted the fashionable hour of five. Where shall we dine today? The restaurants display their signs invitingly on all sides; we have choice of the United States, Tortoni's, the Alhambra, and many other equally classic resorts, but Delmonico's, like its distinguished original in New York, has the highest prices and the greatest variety of dishes. We go down to Kearny street to a two-story wooden house on the corner of Jackson. The lower story is a market; the walls are garnished with quarters of beef and mutton; a huge pile of Sandwich Island squashes fills one corner, and several cabbage-heads, valued at $2 each, show themselves in the window. We enter a little door at the end of the building, ascend a dark, narrow flight of steps and find ourselves in a long, low room, with ceiling and walls of white muslin and a floor covered with oil-cloth.

There are about twenty tables disposed in two rows, all of them so well filled that we have some difficulty in finding places. Taking up the written bill of fare, we find such items as the following:

Soups.		Entrees.	
Mock Turtle	$0 75	Fillet of Beef, mushroom	
St. Julien	1 00	sauce	1 75
Fish.		Veal Cutlets, breaded	1 00
Boiled Salmon Trout,		Mutton Chop	1 00
Anchovy sauce	1 75	Lobster Salad	2 00
Boiled.		Sirloin of Venison	1 50
Leg Mutton, caper sauce	1 00	Baked Macaroni	0 75
Corned Beef, Cabbage	1 00	Beef Tongue, sauce	
Ham and Tongues	0 75	piquante	1 00

So that, with but a moderate appetite, the dinner will cost us $5, if we are at all epicurean in our tastes. There are cries of "steward!" from all parts of the room—the word "waiter" is not considered sufficiently respectful, seeing that the waiter may have been a lawyer or merchant's clerk a few months before. The dishes look very small as they are placed on the table, but they are skilfully cooked and very palatable to men that have ridden in from the diggings. The appetite one acquires in California is something remarkable. For two months after my arrival, my sensations were like those of a famished wolf.

In the matter of dining, the tastes of all nations can be gratified here. There are French restaurants on the plaza and on Dupont street; an extensive German establishment on Pacific street; the *Fonda Peruana;* the Italian Confectionery; and three Chinese houses, denoted by their long three-cornered flags of yellow silk. The latter are much frequented by Americans, on account of their excellent cookery, and the fact that meals are $1 each, without regard to quantity. Kong-Sung's house is near the water; Whang-Tong's in Sacramento Street, and Tong-Ling's in Jackson street. There the grave Celestials serve up their chow-chow and curry, besides many genuine English dishes; their tea and coffee cannot be surpassed.

The afternoon is less noisy and active than the forenoon. Merchants keep within-doors, and the gambling-rooms are crowded with persons who step in to escape the wind and dust. The sky takes a cold gray cast, and the hills over the bay are barely visible in the dense, dusty air. Now and then a watcher, who has been stationed on the hill above Fort Montgomery, comes down and reports an inward-bound vessel, which occasions a little excitement among the boatmen and the merchants who are awaiting consignments. Towards sunset, the plaza is nearly deserted; the wind is merciless in its force, and a heavy overcoat is not found unpleasantly warm. As it grows dark, there is a lull, though occasional gusts blow down the hill and carry the dust of the city out among the shipping.

The appearance of San Francisco at night, from the water, is unlike anything I ever beheld. The houses are mostly of canvas, which is made transparent by the lamps within, and transforms them, in the darkness, to dwellings of solid light. Seated on the slopes of its three hills, the tents pitched among the chapparal to the very summits, it gleams like an amphitheatre of fire. Here and there shine out brilliant points, from the decoy-lamps of the gaming-houses; and through the indistinct murmur of the streets comes by fits the sound of music from their hot and crowded precincts. The picture has in it something unreal and fantastic; it impresses one like the cities of the magic lantern, which a motion of the hand can build or annihilate.

The only objects left for us to visit are the gaming-tables, whose day has just fairly dawned. We need not wander far in search of one.

Denison's Exchange, the Parker House and Eldorado stand side by side; across the way are the Verandah and Aguila de Oro; higher up the plaza the St. Charles and Bella Union; while dozens of second-rate establishments are scattered through the less frequented streets.

The greatest crowd is about the Eldorado; we find it difficult to effect an entrance. There are about eight tables in the room, all of which are thronged; copper-hued Kanakas, Mexicans rolled in their *sarapes* and Peruvians thrust through their ponchos, stand shoulder to shoulder with the brown and bearded American miners. The stakes are generally small, though when the bettor gets into "a streak of luck," as it is called, they are allowed to double until all is lost or the bank breaks. Along the end of the room is a spacious bar, supplied with all kinds of bad liquors, and in a sort of gallery, suspended under the ceiling, a female violinist tasks her talent and strength of muscle to minister to the excitement of play.

The Verandah, opposite, is smaller, but boasts an equal attraction in a musician who has a set of Pandean pipes fastened at his chin, a drum on his back, which he beats with sticks at his elbows, and cymbals in his hands. The piles of coin on the monte tables clink merrily to his playing, and the throng of spectators, jammed together in a sweltering mass, walk up to the bar between the tunes and drink out of sympathy with his dry and breathless throat. At the Aguila de Oro there is a full band of Ethopian serenaders, and at the other hells, violins, guitars or wheezy accordeons, as the case may be. The atmosphere of these places is rank with tobacco-smoke, and filled with a feverish, stifling heat, which communicates an unhealthy glow to the faces of the players.

We shall not be deterred from entering by the heat and smoke, or the motley characters into whose company we shall be thrown. There are rare chances here for seeing human nature in one of its most dark and exciting phases. Note the variety of expression in the faces gathered around this table! They are playing monte, the favorite game in California, since the chances are considered more equal and the opportunity of false play very slight. The dealer throws out his cards with a cool, nonchalant air; indeed, the gradual increase of the hollow square of dollars at his left hand is not calculated to disturb his equanimity. The two Mexicans in front, muffled in their dirty *sarapes,* put down their half-dollars and dollars and see them lost without changing a muscle. Gambling is a born habit with them, and they would lose thousands with the same indifference. Very different is the demeanor of the Americans who are playing; their good or ill luck is betrayed at once by involuntary exclamations and changes of countenance, unless the stake should be very large and absorbing, when their anxiety, though silent, may read with no less certainty. They have no power to resist the fascination of the game. Now counting their winnings by thousands, now dependent on the kindness of a friend for a few dollars to commence anew, they pass hour after hour in those hot, unwholesome dens. There is no appearance of arms, but let one of the players, impatient with his losses and maddened by the poisonous fluids he has drunk, threaten one of the profession, and there will be no scarcity of knives and revolvers.

There are other places, where gaming is carried on privately and to a more ruinous extent—rooms in the rear of the Parker House, in the City Hotel and other places, frequented only by the initiated. Here the stakes are almost unlimited, the players being men of wealth and apparent respectability. Frequently, in the absorbing interest of some desperate game the night goes by unheeded and morning breaks upon haggard faces and reckless hearts. Here are lost, in a few turns of a card or rolls of a ball, the product of fortunate ventures by sea or months of racking labor on land. How many men, maddened by continual losses, might exclaim in their blind vehemence of passion, on leaving these hells:

"Out, out, thou strumpet, Fortune! All you gods,
In general synod, take away her power;
Break all the spokes and felloes from her wheel,
And bowl the round knave down the hill of heaven,
As low as to the fiends!"

Four Months Later

Of all the marvellous phases of the history of the Present, the growth of San Francisco is the one which will most tax belief of the Future. Its parallel was never known, and shall never be beheld again. I speak only of what I saw with my own eyes.

When I landed there, a little more than four months before, I found a scattering town of tents and canvas houses, with a show of frame buildings on one or two streets, and a population of about six thousand. Now, on my last visit, I saw around me an actual metropolis, displaying street after street of well-built edifices, filled with an active and enterprising people and exhibiting every mark of permanent commercial prosperity. Then, the town was limited to the curves of the Bay fronting the anchorage and bottom of the hills. Now, it stretched to the topmost heights, followed the shore around point after point, and sending back a long arm through a gap in the hills, took hold of the Golden Gate and was building its warehouses on the open strait and almost fronting the blue horizon of the Pacific. Then, the gold-seeking sojourner lodged in muslin rooms and canvas garrets, with a philosophic lack of furniture, and ate his simple though substantial fare from pine boards. Now, lofty hotels, gaudy with verandas and balconies, were met with in all quarters, furnished with home luxury, and aristocratic restaurants presented daily their long bills of fare, rich with the choicest technicalities of the Parisian cuisine. Then, vessels were coming in day after day, to lie deserted and useless at their anchorage. Now scarce a day passed, but some cluster of sails bound *outward* through the Golden Gate, took their way to all corners of the Pacific. Like the magic seed of the Indian juggler, which grew, blossomed and bore fruit before the eyes of his spectators, San Francisco seemed to have accomplished in a day the growth of half a century.

When I first landed in California, bewildered and amazed by what seemed an unnatural standard of prices, I formed the opinion that there would be before long a great crash in speculation. Things, it appeared then, had reached the crisis, and it was pronounced impossible that they could remain stationary. This might have been a very natural idea at the time, but the subsequent course of affairs proved it to be incorrect. Lands, rents, goods and subsistence continued steadily to advance in cost, and as the credit system had been meanwhile prudently contracted, the character of the business done was the more real and substantial. Two or three years will pass, in all probability, before there is a positive abatement of the standard of prices. There will be fluctuations in the meantime, occasioning great gains and losses, but the fall in rents and real estate, when it comes, as it inevitably must in the course of two or three years, will not be so crushing as I at first imagined. I doubt whether it will seriously injure the commercial activity of the place. Prices will never fall to the same stand-

ard as in the Atlantic States. Fortunes will always be made by the
sober, intelligent, industrious, and energetic; but no one who is either
too careless, too spiritless or too ignorant to succeed at home, need
trouble himself about emigrating. The same general rule holds good,
as well here as elsewhere, and it is all the better for human nature
that it is so.

Not only was the heaviest part of the business conducted on cash
principles, but all rents, even to lodgings in hotels, were required to
be paid in advance. A single bowling-alley, in the basement story of
the Ward House—a new hotel on Portsmouth-Square—prepaid $5,000
monthly. The firm of Findley, Johnson & Co. sold their real estate,
purchased a year previous, for $20,000, at $300,000; $25,000 down,
and the rest in monthly instalments of $12,500. This was a fair speci-
men of the speculations daily made. Those on a lesser scale were frequently of a very amusing character, but the claims on one's astonishment were so constant, that the faculty soon wore out, and the most
unheard-of operations were looked upon as matters of course. Among
others that came under my observation, was one of a gentleman who
purchased a barrel of alum for $6, the price in New York being $9.
It happened to be the only alum in the place, and as there was a
demand for it shortly afterwards, he sold the barrel for $150. Another
purchased all the candle-wick to be found, at an average price of 40
cts. per lb., and sold it in a short time at $2.25 per lb. A friend of
mine expended $10,000 in purchasing barley, which in a week brought
$20,000. The greatest gains were still made by the gambling tables
and the eating-houses. Every device that art could suggest was used
to swell the custom of the former. The latter found abundant support
in the necessities of a large floating population, in addition to the
swarm of permanent residents.

For a month or two previous to this time, money had been very
scarce in the market, and from ten to fifteen per cent. monthly, was
paid, with the addition of good security. Notwithstanding the quantity
of coin brought into the country by emigrants, and the millions of
gold dust used as currency, the actual specie basis was very small
compared with the immense amount of business transacted. Nevertheless, I heard of nothing like a failure; the principal firms were
prompt in all their dealings, and the chivalry of Commerce—to use
a new phrase—was as faithfully observed as it could have been in the

old marts of Europe and America. The merchants had a 'Change and News-room, and were beginning to cooperate in their movements and consolidate their credit. A stock company which had built a long wharf at the foot of Sacramento-st. declared a dividend of ten per cent. within six weeks after the wharf was finished. During the muddy season, it was the only convenient place for landing goods, and as the cost of constructing it was enormous, so were likewise the charges for wharfage and storage.

There had been a vast improvement in the means of living since my previous visit to San Francisco. Several large hotels had been opened, which were equal in almost every respect to houses of the second class in the Atlantic cities. The Ward House, the Graham House, imported bodily from Baltimore, and the St. Francis Hotel, completely threw into the shade all former establishments. The rooms were furnished with comfort and even luxury, and the tables lacked few of the essentials of good living, according to a 'home' taste. The sleeping apartments of the St. Francis were the best in California. The cost of board and lodging was $150 per month—which was considered unusually cheap. A room at the Ward House cost $250 monthly, without board. The principal restaurants charged $35 a week for board, and there were lodging houses where a berth or "bunk"—one out of fifty in the same room—might be had for $6 a week. The model of these establishments—which were far from being "model lodging-houses"—was that of a ship. A number of staterooms, containing six berths each, ran around the sides of a large room, or cabin, where the lodgers resorted to read, write, smoke and drink at their leisure. The state-rooms were consequently filled with foul and unwholesome air, and the noises in the cabin prevented the passengers from sleeping, except between midnight and four o'clock.

The great want of San Francisco was society. Think of a city of thirty thousand inhabitants, peopled by men alone! The like of this was never seen before. Every man was his own housekeeper, doing, in many instances, his own sweeping, cooking, washing and mending. Many home-arts, learned rather by observation than experience, came conveniently into play. He who cannot make a bed, cook a beefsteak, or sew up his own rips and rents, is unfit to be a citizen of California. Nevertheless, since the town began to assume a permanent shape, very many of the comforts of life in the East were attainable. A family may now live there without suffering any material privations; and if every married man, who intends spending some time in California, would take his family with him, a social influence would soon be created to which we might look for the happiest results.

Towards the close of my stay, the city was as dismal a place as could well be imagined. The glimpse of bright, warm, serene weather passed away, leaving in its stead a raw, cheerless, southeast storm. The wind now and then blew a heavy gale, and the cold, steady fall of rain, was varied by claps of thunder and sudden blasts of hail. The mud in the streets became little short of fathomless, and it was with difficulty that the mules could drag their empty wagons through. A powerful London dray-horse, a very giant in harness, was the only animal able to pull a good load; and I was told that he earned his master $100 daily. I saw occasionally a company of Chinese workmen, carrying bricks and mortar, slung by ropes to long bamboo poles. The plank sidewalks, in the lower part of the city, ran along the brink of pools and quicksands, which the Street Inspector and his men vainly endeavored to fill by hauling cart-loads of chapparal and throwing sand on the top; in a day or two the gulf was as deep as ever.

The sidewalks, which were made at the cost of $5 per foot, bridged over the worst spots, but I was frequently obliged to go the whole length of a block in order to get on the other side. One could not walk any distance, without getting at least ankle-deep, and although the thermometer rarely sank below 50°, it was impossible to stand still for even a short time without a death-like chill taking hold of the feet. As a consequence of this, coughs and bronchial affections were innumerable. The universal custom of wearing the pantaloons inside the boots threatened to restore the knee-breeches of our grandfathers' times. Even women were obliged to shorten their skirts, and wear high-topped boots. The population seemed to be composed entirely of dismounted hussars. All this will be remedied when the city is two years older, and Portsmouth Square boasts a *pavé* as elegant as that on the dollar side of Broadway.

The severe weather occasioned a great deal of sickness, especially among those who led an exposed life. The city overflowed with people, and notwithstanding buildings were continually growing up like mushrooms, over night, hundreds who arrived were obliged to lodge in tents, with which the summits of the hills were covered. Fever-and-

ague and dysentery were the prevailing complaints, the great preval-
ence of which was owing undoubtedly to exposure and an irregular
habit of life. An association was formed to relieve those in actual want,
many of the wealthiest and most influential citizens taking an honorable part in the matter. Many instances of lamentable destitution were
by this means brought to light. Nearly all the hospitals of the place
were soon filled, and numbers went to the Sandwich Islands to recruit. The City Hospital, a large, well ventilated and regulated establishment, contained about fifty patients. The attending physician
described to me several cases of nearly hopeless lunacy which had
come under his care, some of them produced by disappointment and
ill-luck, and others by sudden increase of fortune. Poor human nature!

In the midst of the rains, we were greeted one morning with a
magnificent spectacle. The wind had blown furiously during the night,
with violent falls of rain, but the sun rose in a spotless sky, revealing
the Coast Mountains across the bay wrapped in snow half-way down
their sides. For two days they wore their dazzling crown, which could
be seen melting away hour by hour, from their ridges and cloven
ravines. This was the only snow I saw while in San Francisco; only
once did I notice any appearance of frost. The grass was green and
vigorous, and some of the more hardy plants in blossom; vegetables,
it is well known, flourish with equal luxuriance during the winter
season. At one of the restaurants, I was shown some remarkable specimens of the growth of California soil—potatoes, weighing from one
to five pounds each; beets and turnips eight inches in diameter, and
perfectly sweet and sound; and large, silver-skinned onions, whose
delicate flavor the most inveterate enemy of this honest vegetable
could not but have relished. A gentleman who visited the port of
Bodega, informed me that he saw in the garden of Capt. Smith, the
owner of the place, peavines which had produced their third crop
from the same root in one summer.

As the rains drove the deer and other animals down from the mountains, game of all kinds became abundant. Fat elks and splendid
black-tailed does hung at the doors of all the butcher-shops, and wild
geese, duck and brant, were brought into the city by the wagon-load.
"Grizzly bear steak," became a choice dish at the eating-houses; I had
the satisfaction one night of eating a slice of one that had weighed
eleven hundred pounds. The flesh was of a bright red color, very solid,

sweet, and nutritious; its flavor was preferable to that of the best pork. The large native hare, a specimen of which occasionally found its way to the restaurants, is nowise inferior to that of Europe. As an illustration of the money which might be spent in procuring a meal no better than an ordinary hotel-dinner at home, I may mention that a dinner for fifteen persons, to which I was invited, at the "Excelsior," cost the giver of it $225.

The effect of a growing prosperity and some little taste of luxury was readily seen in the appearance of the business community of San Francisco. The slouched felt hats gave way to narrow-brimmed black beavers; flannel shirts were laid aside, and white linen, though in-differently washed, appeared instead; dress and frock coats, of the fashion of the previous year in the Atlantic side, came forth from trunks and sea-chests; in short, a San Francisico merchant was almost as smooth and spruce in his outward appearance as a merchant any-where else. The hussar boot, however, was obliged to be worn, and a variation of the Mexican sombrero—a very convenient and becom-ing headpiece—came into fashion among the younger class.

The steamers which arrived at this time, brought large quantities of newspapers from all parts of the Atlantic States. The speculation which had been so successful at first, was completely overdone; there was a glut in the market, in consequence whereof newspapers came down to fifty and twenty-five cents apiece. The leading journals of New York, New Orleans and Boston were cried at every street-corner. The two papers established in the place issued editions "for the Atlan-tic Coast," at the sailing of every steamer for Panama. The offices were invaded by crowds of purchasers, and the slow hand-presses in use could not keep pace with the demand. The profits of these jour-nals were almost incredible, when contrasted with their size and the amount of their circulation. Neither of them failed to count their gains at the rate of $75,000 a year, clear profit.

There are some features of Society in California, which I have hitherto failed to touch upon in my narrative, but which deserve a passing notice before I take my final leave of that wonderful land. The direct effect of the state of things growing out of the discovery of the placers, was to develop new qualities and traits of character, not in single individuals, but in every individual of the entire com-munity—traits frequently most unlooked-for in those who exhibited

them in the most marked degree. Society, therefore, was for the time
cast into new forms, or, rather, deprived of any fixed form. A man,
on coming to California, could no more expect to retain his old nature
unchanged than he could retain in his lungs the air he had inhaled
on the Atlantic shore.

The most immediate and striking change which came upon the
greater portion of the emigrants was an increase of activity, and opportunity, of reckless and daring spirit. It was curious to see how men
hitherto noted for their prudence and caution took sudden leave of
those qualities, to all appearance, yet only prospered the more thereby.
Perhaps there was at bottom a vein of keen, shrewd calculation, which
directed their seemingly heedless movements; certain it is, at least,
that for a long time the rashest speculators were the most fortunate.
It was this fact, no doubt, that seemed so alarming to persons newly-
arrived, and gave rise to unnumbered predictions of the speedy and
ruinous crash of the whole business fabric of San Francisco. But nothing is more contagious than this spirit of daring and independent
action, and the most doleful prophets were, ere long, swallowed up in
the same whirlpool against which they had warned others.

The emigrants who arrive in California, very soon divide into two
distinct classes. About two-thirds, or possibly three-fourths of them are
active, hopeful and industrious. They feel this singular intoxication
of society, and go to work at something, no matter what, by which
they hope to thrive. The remaining portion see everything "through
a glass, darkly." Their first bright anticipations are unrealized; the
horrid winds of San Francisco during the dry season, chill and un-
nerve them; or, if they go to the placers, the severe labor and the ill
success of inexperienced hands, completes their disgust. They commit
a multitude of sins in the shape of curses upon every one who has
written or spoken favorably of California. Some of them return home
without having seen the country at all, and others, even if they obtain
profitable situations, labor without a will. It is no place for a slow,
an over-cautious, or a desponding man. The emigrant should be willing to work, not only at one business, but many, if need be; the grum-
bler or the idler had far better stay at home.

It cannot be denied that the very activity of California society
created a spirit of excitement which frequently led to dangerous excesses. The habits of the emigrants, never, even at home, very slow

and deliberate, branched into all kinds of wild offshoots, the necessary effect of the sudden glow and expansion which they experienced. Those who retained their health seemed to revel in an exuberance of animal spirits, which carried them with scarce a jar over barriers and obstacles that would have brought others to a full stand. There was something exceedingly hearty, cordial and encouraging in the character of social intercourse. The ordinary forms of courtesy were flung aside with a bluntness of good-fellowship infinitely preferable, under the circumstances. I was constantly reminded of the stories of Northern History—of the stout Vikings and Jarls who exulted in their very passions and made their heroes of those who were most jovial at the feast and most easily kindled with the rage of battle. Indeed, it required but little effort of the imagination to revive those iron ages, when the rugged gold-diggers, with their long hair and unshorn beards, were grouped around some mountain camp-fire, revelling in the ruddy light and giving full play to a mirth so powerful and profound that it would not have shamed the Berserkers.

The most common excesses into which the Californians run, are drinking and gambling, I say drinking, rather than drunkeness, for I saw very little of the latter. But a single case came under my observation while I was in the gold region. The man's friends took away his money and deposited it in the hands of the Alcalde, then tied him to a tree where they left him till he became sober. The practice of drinking, nevertheless, was widely prevalent, and its effects rendered more destructive by the large amount of bad liquor which was sent into the country. Gambling, in spite of a universal public sentiment against it, grew and flourished; the disappointment ruin of many emigrants were owing to its existence. The gamblers themselves were in many instances men who had led orderly and respectable lives at home. I have heard some of them frankly avow that nothing would induce them to acquaint their friends and families with the nature of their occupation; they would soon have enough, they said, and then they would wash their hands of the unclean stain, and go home to lead more honorable lives. But alas! it is not so easy to wash out the memory of self-degradation. If these men have in truth any sentiment of honor remaining, every coin of the wealth they have hoarded will awaken a shameful consciousness of the base and unmanly business by which it was obtained.

In spite, however, of all these dissipating and disorganizing influences, the main stock of society was sound, vigorous, and progressive. The rank shoots, while they might have slightly weakened the trunk, only showed the abundant life of the root. In short, without wishing to be understood as apologizing in any degree for the evils which existed, it was evident that had the Californians been more cool, grave and deliberate in their temperament—had they lacked the fiery energy and impulsive spirit which pushed them irresistibly forward—the dangers which surrounded them at the outset would have been far more imminent. Besides, this energy did not run at random; it was in the end directed by an enlightened experience, and that instinct of Right, which is the strength and security of a self-governed People. Hundreds of instances might be adduced to show that the worse passions of our nature were speedily developed in the air of California, but the one grand lesson of the settlement and organization of the country is of a character that ennobles the race.

The unanimity with which all united in this work—the frankness with which the old prejudices of sect and party were disclaimed—the freshly-awakened pride of country, which made every citizen jealously and disinterestedly anxious that she should acquit herself honorably in the eyes of the Nation at large—formed a spectacle which must claim our entire admiration. In view of the splendid future which is opening for California, it insures her a stable foundation on which to build the superstructure of her wealth and power.

After what has been said, it will appear natural that California should be the most democratic country in the world. The practical equality of all the members of a community, whatever might be the wealth, intelligence or profession of each, was never before thoroughly demonstrated. Dress was no gauge of respectability, and no honest occupation, however menial in its character, affected a man's standing. Lawyers, physicians and ex-professors dug cellars, drove ox-teams, sawed wood and carried luggage; while men who had been Army privates, sailors, cooks or day laborers were at the head of profitable establishments and not infrequently assisted in some of the minor details of Government. A man who would consider his fellow beneath him, on account of his appearance or occupation, would have had some difficulty in living peaceably in California. The security of the country is owing, in no small degree, to this plain, practical development of what the French reverence as an abstraction, under the name of Fraternité. To sum up all, in three words, LABOR IS RESPECT-ABLE: may it never be otherwise, while a grain of gold is left to glitter in California soil!

TO SAN FRANCISCO
VIA THE ISTHMUS OF PANAMA

by

JOSEPH W. GREGORY

As such a large proportion of the "Universal Yankee Nation," have a migratory tendency towards California at the present time, it has become a matter of no little interest to those persons about undertaking so important an affair as a journey thither, to ascertain not only that which will most conduce to their welfare on the route, but also what measures are needful, to guard against imposition and unnecessary delay.

Old travellers in the United States have found unforeseen vexations on this route, and it cannot therefore be expected that inexperienced persons without proper advice, will fare any better.

With a view of guiding *all* travellers to California by the way of the Isthmus, the following directions have been prepared, by one who has twice travelled this journey, and who asks favor for them only, for their *brevity* and *correctness*. Good health is essential to every one who desires success in California, and the saving of expense is no small object with most travellers. It is confidently believed that both results will be best attained by a strict adherence to the following suggestions.

From New York to Chagres, the route may be considered plain sailing, and we will commence with the anchorage off Chagres, which is usually from one to two miles distant. The Steam Ship Company

---

From *Gregory's Guide for California Travellers via the Isthmus of Panama*, the Black Vine Press, San Francisco.

provide for the landing of the passengers and their baggage, using the ship's quarter-boats for the former, and the launch of the Steamer *Orus* for the latter, conveying the whole to the *Orus,* which vessel lands the passengers on what is called the American side of the river. The captain of the *Orus* is paid by the Steam Ship for landing both passengers and baggage. Three or four taverns are kept at this landing by white men, one or two of whom are Americans.

After seeing your baggage safely landed from the *Orus,* your first objective should be to secure a good canoe—one holding four or five persons is the most preferable.

Then make your contract to convey yourself and baggage to Cruces, which will cost from thirty to forty dollars the trip, (six to eight dollars each person,) usually occupying three days, during which time your pleasure will be greatly enhanced, if you have been provident in supplying yourself with a sufficient stock of provisions.

The ranchos and huts on the river banks are poor "sights" for hungry travellers.

The sooner you set out with your canoe the better. If you leave about noon, you will find Gatson about ten miles up, a better place to remain over night than Chagres, and perhaps it is the best on the river.

Should you leave Chagres early in the morning, you may reach Vamos Vamos, about twenty miles distant before night. On the west bank is a rancho, containing two huts, called Blanquilla. This is about half way to Cruces.

The great secret of getting well up the river during the day, is to get off early in the morning, and be liberal to the men that work the canoe. You can coax, better than drive them. At the end of about two days you will reach Gorgona, where it is tempting to stay, but should you go on shore there, you will experience great difficulty when you are ready for a start, in getting your boatmen into their canoe again. This is their worst fault generally. From Gorgona to Cruces, it is about ten miles. At Gorgona, interested persons will advise you to take the road to Panama from that point. *Pay no attention to such advice,* for that road is totally impassable for nine months in the year.

Push on without delay to Cruces, and if you arrive there in the morning, you will hardly be able to get on the Panama road before the next morning. Meanwhile you can call at Funk's and Pleise's houses.

They forward baggage by mules to Panama. Ascertain their charge for sending it next morning, *but let no promises induce you to leave your baggage to be forwarded after you, but see it start at least.*

The above persons may ask ten or twelve dollars per hundred pounds, but plenty of natives can be had to carry it at the rate of seven to eight dollars per one hundred pounds. If you employ a native, it is necessary for you to have him sign an agreement, to fulfil his contract.

This you can get drawn in Spanish for twenty-five cents, to which you must make him sign his mark, binding him to deliver the baggage for the stipulated price, at Zacharisson Nelson & Co.'s office, Panama.

In two days you can walk to Panama and if desirable, keep your trunk and baggage in view the whole time, but I consider that quite unnecessary. Should you prefer riding, a mule would cost you from ten to sixteen dollars.

Arrival at Panama

On arrival at Panama, your first business is to ascertain from the Agents when the Steamer is to leave, and if you are to be delayed a week or more, it is advisable for four or five persons to engage a room, with a cot in it for each, and arrange for a supply of drinking water. All this will cost a dime a day for each person. Taking meals at Restaurants or Eating houses, a person may lodge in a good room, and thus live moderately at about three and a half dollars a week.

The day before the Steamer leaves, notice is posted up by the Agents of the hour that passengers are required to be at the Mole, in front of the Custom House.

Passengers are required to pay the expense of conveying themselves and their baggage to the Steamer.

Travellers in the Steamships between New York and Chagres, are of course much better provided, than on the Pacific Steamers.

Having the New York Markets to resort to, once in each month, makes a very essential difference. The Pacific Steamers are supplied with stores from New York, via Cape Horn, with the exception of such as are obtainable on the Pacific coast.

Private Stores

Steerage passengers will find one or two jars of preserves, and one or two pecks of dried fruit, (peaches or apples,) very acceptable. A few jars of pickles, and a few pounds of Milk, Soda, or Butter crackers, some Bologna Sausages and Cheese, a Ham and a piece of Smoked Beef, would not only prove very palatable and comfortable, but more agreeable in case of sea-sickness than Ship's fare.

The climate is too warm for butter to keep well. Gingerbread and fruit cake, sick or well, never comes amiss on the trip to Chagres, and would certainly prove welcome for two or three days on the Isthmus. For drinks, Limes can be had at houses on the Isthmus for lemonade, or if preferred, bottled ale and porter.

Take sufficient of coffee, tea, loaf sugar, &c., for five days' consumption in crossing the Isthmus, and should there be anything left of your stores on arriving at Panama, *anything* you have is preferable to tropical fruit, *which should be avoided* by all means.

A similar outfit of provisions is desirable for the steerage on the Pacific, and more so, for reasons before stated; each steerage passenger is provided with his own *plate, knife and fork, spoon, drinking-cup, mattress and pillow.*

During the delay, (always more or less at Panama,) persons who regard their health will avoid exposure or hard work in the sun, during the middle of the day. Perhaps more persons have died from imprudence in this respect than from any other cause. It is considered highly dangerous, and by many residents on the Isthmus as almost certain death, to drink ardent spirits after eating tropical fruit, as it produces fermentation in the bowels, which seems to defy the influence of all medical skill.

The use of milk should be avoided, in every form, while on the Isthmus. Numerous cases of distressing illness are known from its use.

Light clothing, such as is worn in the United States during the Summer months, is all sufficient for travelling purposes, from three days out of New York, to within five or six days short of San Francisco, after which, the usual warm clothing will be necessary.

In consequence of the great and bitter disappointment incurred by many persons, in being delayed for week and months in Panama, *it has become indispensably necessary,* for each person to be provided with a ticket for the Pacific Steamer, before leaving New York, which can be procured at the office of the Company, 54 South street, New York.

For want of this precaution, many have been compelled to wait at Panama, until they could send for a ticket to the above Office, *and some persons have been obliged to return for this object,* at a great sacrifice of both time and money. The expense of landing at San Francisco is borne by each passenger, the Steamer coming to anchor as near the city as the landing is safe and practicable.

This route to California, although more expensive than that by the way of Cape Horn, is by far the most desirable for those who can afford the additional outlay requisite, for many reasons; not the least of which is, the very great saving in time in making the trip, and the avoiding of a tedious and monotonous life on shipboard. The voyage by the way of Cape Horn will occupy on an average, five or six months, while by the Isthmus route, the trip is accomplished in as many weeks, and to most persons presents varied scenes of no ordinary pleasure. The voyage up the Chagres River, has been by some persons execrated in tolerably strong terms, not to say diabolical. As far as my own feelings were concerned, I must assert that I received the greatest pleasure and never beheld more magnificent scenery, or luxuriant vegetation, than I witnessed while upon this river. Nature here appears to have been most lavish in her efforts, and to have succeeded beyond her most sanguine expectations, and it would appear almost impossible that any, the most unimaginative being upon the earth, could here remain unmoved or find no pleasure in viewing her mighty works. All travellers however, do not think alike, and some so very difficult to please, complain even of the alligators *they heard of* on the river.

As my object however, is to present to future California travellers, clear and correct information concerning the Isthmus route, in as condensed a form as possible, as well as matters that if attended to, concern their personal comfort and will save outlay of money; any speculations foreign to such a purpose, would here be out of place. Besides, the press of the country has, for a long time past, through their numerous correspondents, given such varied and graphic descriptions of many points of interest on this route, that most persons of ordinary intelligence have become somewhat familiar with them.

•   •   •   •

After perusal of the foregoing, any practical man can before leaving home, estimate very nearly what his expenses will amount to by the time he lands in San Francisco. Some allowance for detention at Panama should be made, which you can easily estimate after learning from the Steam Ship Company in New York, on what day the Steamer will leave Panama.

As a matter of course, no prudent person will undertake so long a journey without making some provision in his calculations, for unforseen events, that may require some outlay beyond the estimate of his entire expenses. Any surplus of funds he may have on hand on his arrival at San Francisco, will not be found very burthensome, and he may feel quite sure, that his money will not trouble him long, if he remains, even for a little while, in a state of *masterly inactivity.*

Hoping that the foregoing remarks may prove serviceable, and a useful guide to the travelling public—

I remain

Their Humble Servant,

JOSEPH W. GREGORY,

Proprietor of Gregory's
California and New York Express.

THE FIRST
VIGILANCE COMMITTEE

by

JOSIAH ROYCE

NOT THE same judgment, by any means, can be passed upon the San Francisco vigilance committee of 1851 as upon the popular justice of the miners.

In some respects, to be sure, there is an unfortunate likeness. Both in the mines and in San Francisco carelessness had led to a destructive general license of mischief-makers. In both places the men of sense were forced at last to attend to their social duties. But in the mines there was, for a while, a far too general, a very absurd and wicked trust in lynch law as the best expression, under the circumstances, of the popular hatred of crime. San Francisco, as a community, never went so far as this. In that city lynch law was the expression of a pressing desire so to reform the social order that lynch law should no longer be necessary. What the success of these efforts was, we have to see from the facts.

The first great outburst of popular indignation at crime was that of February, 1851. On the 19th of February a merchant named Jansen was assaulted and robbed in his own shop by two men, who came in the evening, pretending to be customers. The crime, though not the first or the worst of its sort, seemed especially atrocious to the community, which chanced to be in a sensitive mood. The *Alta*, usually, in those days, a very sober and sensible paper, became for the moment

---

From *California from the Conquest in 1846 to the Second Vigilance Committee in San Francisco* by Josiah Royce. Houghton Mifflin Company, Boston, 1886.

a trifle over-excited. Nobody, says the editor, a day or two later, is secure, even in his own dwelling. And the ruffians, if arrested at all, are never punished. "How many murders have been committed in this city within a year! And who has been hung or punished for it? Nobody. How many men shot and stabbed, knocked down and bruised; and who has been punished for it? How many thefts and arsons, robberies, and crimes of a less note; and where are the perpetrators? Gentlemen at large, citizens, free to reenact their outrages." And so, finally: "We deprecate lynch law, but the outraged public," etc., etc.

Under these circumstances, the news that two men had been arrested as the perpetrators of this assault aroused the people to righteous indignation and to eloquence. One of these two men was soon said to be a certain rogue named Stuart, and notorious in the mines. On the 21st, the two men arrested were confronted with the wounded Jansen. The supposed Stuart he was said to have recognized at once as one of his assailants, and he had only a little doubt about the other prisoner. Accordingly when, on Saturday, the 22d, the two were to be brought up before the court in the city hall, for preliminary examination, the people collected, grew more and more excited, read copies of a well-written and rather foolish hand-bill (which called upon all good citizens to assemble on Sunday, at two o'clock, on the Plaza, for the sake of somehow ridding the community of its robbers and murderers), and so at last, with a shout, *"Now's the time!"* rushed towards and into the recorder's court room, in order to seize the prisoners. But a company of militia, the "Washington Guards," which had been called out, and was now on parade, ready to defend the officers of the law, entered the court-room just after the first of the mob had rushed in, cleared the room with fixed bayonets, and so saved the prisoners, who were then imprisoned in the not very secure basement of the city hall. The guards thus earned many hoots and hisses, insomuch that the wayward and still wholly disorganized crowd followed them home to their armory, challenged them to a fight, and were with difficulty persuaded at last to disperse.

About dusk that evening, a more sensible and dignified public meeting took place near the city hall, and was addressed by several speakers, among them Mr. Sam Brannan, the lion-hearted, a man always in love with shedding the blood of the wicked. A committee of prominent citizens, of whom he was one, was appointed by the public meeting to consider the situation, and also to assist the police in guarding the accused over night; and this committee's proceedings, after the greater meeting had adjourned, were also reported in the *Alta* of the next day. Mr. Brannan begged his fellow-members to take the chance now so kindly given them by fortune, and to try the prisoners themselves forthwith. He was tired of the law. He was "much surprised to hear people talk about grand juries, or recorders or mayors." He was "opposed to any farce in this business." Mr. Brannan's less enthusiastic fellows on the committee overruled him as to these somewhat immoral proposals; but they too were not free from excitement. Even the moderate and cautious Mr. Macondray, a prominent merchant, and one of the committee, declared that no court would dare to discharge these men; no lawyer would dare to plead their cause. But he very sensibly pointed out that a committee appointed by the sovereign people to guard prisoners could not well turn itself into a jury, and try them.

Now, however, one serious defect and danger about all this ardent and sincere popular indignation against the two prisoners lay in the fact that the supposed Stuart was really quite an innocent man, whose name was Burdue. He had been mistaken for the true assailant by poor Jansen, who was lying very seriously hurt with a concussion of the brain. The resemblance of the accused to the real criminal Stuart was indeed remarkable; but there were people in San Francisco who could on occasion identify the accused as an innocent man, unless the popular indignation at crime should forbid for the moment all defense of any supposed criminals.

Fortunately, however, the general sentiment of the wiser men of San Francisco favored giving the two accused a fair chance. And therefore, when on the next day the people assembled once more, a no less stern but much more sensible spirit prevailed than on the previous morning. Mr. William T. Coleman, later so noted in connection with both the great Vigilance Committees, came forward with a motion to appoint a committee to agree upon a plan of action, and this committee, having been chosen, reported that a judge and jury should be named, who should try the criminals at two o'clock the same day. This plan was submitted to the people, and adopted. The jury was appointed by popular consent. Great difficulty was found in getting a popular judge to serve; but at last one Mr. J. F. Spence was chosen, and two assistant judges were appointed. The chief actors in the subsequent trial were thus the result of some genuine reflection and of a careful choice, and the trial was therefore saved from becoming what the mob wished it to be,—a disorderly mock trial.

At two o'clock the popular court was complete master of the situation, and met in the district court room. Without any resistance from the officials this time, the prisoners were considered as subject to the jurisdiction of the new tribunal, although they were not removed from their cells. Two lawyers, prominent through many later years in California as attorneys, consented to defend the prisoners,—Judge Shattuck appearing for the supposed Stuart, Mr. Hall McAllister for the other; but counsel for the people was harder to find, regular attorneys declining, very naturally, to serve. Mr. Coleman at length undertook the work. The Jury were known men; and to Mr. R. S. Watson, their foreman, now of Milton, Mass., I am indebted for a very interesting oral account of the scene. Mr. Watson himself did not sympathize in any degree with the extravagance of the mob, and, as we shall see, his influence was ultimately used, with that of others, to save the prisoners. But the moment was one when the advice of cautious men was especially needed, and one may be glad that such were willing to serve.

The trial of the supposed Stuart took precedence, and, as we shall see, was the only act of the tribunal. The testimony, as the *Alta* shows, was of two sorts. Some of the witnesses declared themselves able to identify this man as one Stuart, somewhat notorious at Sacramento and in the mines as a most dangerous character, and several times proven guilty of theft and, they said, of worse. The other witnesses knew only that Jansen, who we remember was suffering ever since the assault from concussion of the brain, had said that this man looked so much like his own assailant that there could be little doubt about the identity. Judge Shattuck ably insisted upon the fact that, as the defense was the denial of this man's identity with the notorious Stuart, as well as with the assailant of Jansen, the cause of justice would demand some scrutiny of the prisoner's antecedents and life. Time was needed for this. And Judge Shattuck "had had no time to consult with the accused, to ascertain who were his friends and acquaintances, or to inquire in the case."

Under these circumstances, with a savage crowd in the court-room occasionally interrupting, and demanding the death of the prisoner, Judge Shattuck felt that his defense was somewhat hampered, and he begged the jury to remember the terrible responsibility of their position. He made some effort to get testimony to clear the prisoner, but the time allowed him was too short, and, as later appeared, the prisoner's few acquaintances, who, after all, were not exactly prominent citizens, were afraid to risk facing the popular tribunal and the mob, and were not easy to find that evening. Time wore away in wrangling about the case; the mob grew more and more impatient, and the counsel for the defense was frequently interrupted, and once or twice insulted. As Mr. Watson tells me, he himself was one of those on the jury most anxious to consider carefully the worth of Mr. Jansen's evidence, and he did not find it satisfying. For the injured man, lying in a stupor, had only been with difficulty aroused to view the prisoners. In the room had been, besides these prisoners, only poor Jansen's own friends. What thing more natural than that, under such circumstances, the man should reply, "Yes," when asked if these strangers were the man who had hurt him? When the jury at last retired, this doubtfulness, and in fact actual worthlessness, of the testimony in question was strongly insisted upon by the foreman and two others, and, although nine of the jury were ready to convict, these three held out firmly, through a long deliberation, and after many ballotings.

Much tumult, meanwhile, raged outside the court-room, and to some extent in it. The better class of citizens were urging the crowd to be patient; while the crowd were weary and disgusted to think that, now the beautifully simple machinery of popular justice was once set up, it somehow would not run smoothly, but was subject even to delays. During this time it was, and after ten o'clock at night, that Mr. E. S. Osgood learned that two men were accessible, and living down on "Long Wharf" (Commercial Street wharf), who could swear to the true identity of the prisoner, and to his whereabouts on the night of the assault. Before making an effort to go down in the thick darkness to the not very safe regions of Long Wharf, Mr. Osgood came forward in the courtroom, announced his purpose, and begged the court to be willing to wait for the new evidence, and to admit it when it should come. Some one present, as Mr. Osgood has told me, called out, asking him who he was; another thereupon shouted that this new-comer in court was well known to certain present as one Osgood, a responsible person; a third shouted: "No, I know who he is, one of those scoundrels that are trying to get their accomplice here off free"—and hereupon some angry discussion followed. Mr. Osgood gave his name and his business, but, as the *Alta* says, "the crowd refused to hear any further testimony." Yet Mr. Osgood set off in the darkness to find his witnesses, and, after some gloomy wanderings, he was successful. With some trouble he persuaded them to come with him to the court from their lodgings on Long Wharf. But before the return of the three, the case was for the time ended.

At nearly midnight, namely, the jury had returned to court, and the foreman had reported that they could not agree. Mr. Watson remembers well the unpleasant scene presented to himself and his fellow jurymen, with the weary and angry crowd all about, who began to call for the names of the disagreeing jurors, and to shout *"Hang them too!"*

But the scene was not to last long. The good citizens present were firm, the mob had diminished by reason of the lateness of the hour, the leaders insisted that the sovereign people, having referred the case to a jury, must abide by its decision, and the people were at last induced to disperse. One device to pacify them seems to have been a resort to that great medicine wherewith the American rids himsef of his dangerous social passions, just as the Aristotelian spectator of tragedy purges himself of his "Pity and Fear." This *Katharsis* namely is, with the American, political agitation. When Mr. Osgood returned with his witnesses, he found some of the recent heroes of popular justice loudly shouting: *"Hurrah for Weller!"* An impromptu political meeting had in fact just been taking place, and all the good citizens who were still out of bed were so interested in this new matter that Mr. Osgood with difficulty learned from them what had become of the prisoner. At last he heard that the popular tribunal had adjourned *sine die,* and that the prisoners had been left with the authorities for trial. And thus happily ended an affair in which the citizens of San Francisco had shown some of their worst as well as some of their best traits. A volunteer night patrol, organized by the merchants, thenceforth for a time aided the police force of the city, which was all this time, poorly trained, generally neglected, and ill-paid, getting its wages in depreciated city scrip.

But the great year of the popular tribunals was as yet only begun. The newspapers might hope that the city would escape the curse of popular justice, but the temper of the public made such escape impossible. One thing, however, was secured by the February outbreak; the public would be sure in time to learn from it the proper lesson as to the dangers of mere mob law. The supposed Stuart was some months later shown to be a rather weak, but, as to legal offenses, an innocent man. For the moment he escaped from San Francisco, only to fall a little later once more into trouble, in the interior, by reason of his singular resemblance to the redoubtable Stuart. From this trouble also he was released through evidence produced by the very San Franciscans who had been so near hanging him in February. The other prisoner accused of assault on Jansen was later convicted, and sentenced to the penitentiary, by a regular court. But he also was still later shown to be innocent, and was finally released. For the time, however, the mass of the citizens could not know how criminal might have proven the hasty methods of the 22d and 23d of February. When the committee of June was formed, with such men as the late foreman of the jury of February 23d in prominent places upon it, there was, however, a very decided effort made from the first to avoid every appearance of disorder. That the committee was needed at all resulted, as said, from the temper of the public mind, which, without some serious lesson in the troublesome work of popular justice, could not have been induced to forsake in any wise its over-confidence and its carelessness.

The first Vigilance Committee is rich in dramatic situations, but, after its first formation, its history shows little further that is novel in the way of socially important undertakings. Upon its early moments alone we shall dwell. Absolutely necessary, in order to distinguish it from the more disorderly and transient committees of the mines, would be, of course, a careful and sober organization. This it got, at the outset of its work, in June. What followed vindicated the good sense of the organization, but throws little new light on the ethics of popular justice.

The fire of May 4th had rendered the public more sensitive, discontented and suspicious than ever; but a genuine popular reform had not yet taken place. Reforms must have something to date from, and two or three minor popular excitements, produced by attempts at arson or by other crimes, were not sufficient for the purpose.

On Sunday, June 8, a very able letter appeared in the *Alta,* proposing the immediate formation of a Committee of Safety, and suggesting a plan for its operations. The plan as stated was admitted to be somewhat undigested, but was probably so strongly expressed chiefly for the sake of arousing popular attention. The committee of safety was to improve matters by boarding in time the vessels that arrived from Australia, and by refusing to let any doubtful characters land from them; while, as to the ruffians now in the city, ward committees of vigilance were arbitrarily to single them out and to warn them to leave the city within five days on pain of a "war of extermination," to be prosecuted against them. "Let us set about the work at once. It may be well to call a public meeting in the square, to organize and carry out these views. Without this, or some other similar plan, the evil cannot be remedied; and if there is not spirit enough amongst us to do it, why then in God's name let the city be burned, and our streets flow with the blood of murdered men."

The letter was throughout very well written. It is remarkable as not referring directly and openly to any one case before the public, and as not getting its inspiration from any one popular excitement or mob, and also as coming from one of the most cautious and conscientious of the jury at the recent trial of the false Stuart. Some of the writer's friends guessed at the authorship of the letter, and at breakfast at his restaurant, Sunday morning, he was accosted by several of them and asked about the matter. The *Alta* itself noticed the letter approvingly; and Mr. Watson had, as he said, "touched a train already laid." Others were on the point of a similar movement.

A few editorial and inspired articles in the *Alta,* on Monday and Tuesday, are the only public indications, during those days, that anything of importance was going on among the citizens interested in the new movement. The *Alta* of Wednesday, June 11, brings sufficient evidence, however, both of the movement and of its first consequences. The editor remarks, that morning, that mobs are indeed of no service in suppressing crime. But "the next affair of the kind will be of a different character, if we are correctly informed in regard to certain organizations of our citizens, which are now and have for several days been progressing. We understand that quite a large party banded themselves together at the California Engine House on Monday night, for the purpose of punishing incendiaries and other criminals." The organization of the committee had indeed been already provisionally perfected. Mr. Sam Brannan, with his wonted zeal, had offered them a room, and his offer had been accepted. Two taps on the engine-house bell were to call the committee together. The promptness of the work of the organization showed how many besides the anonymous correspondent of the *Alta* had had the thoughts to which he gave such vigorous expression. Prominent on the committee, besides the two already mentioned, were Mr. Wm. T. Coleman, Mr. Stephen Payran, Mr. S. E. Woodworth and many others.

But, as this same *Alta* of Wednesday learned even as it was going to press, the committee had no sooner organized than it had undertaken work. A thief, one Jenkins, a common ruffian of a very low type, had been detected Tuesday evening in the very act of burglary on Long Wharf, and, attempting to escape in a boat, was caught and brought back. At ten o'clock Tuesday night the members of the committee were called to their first appointed headquarters (near the corner of Sansome and Bush streets). For two hours the committee were engaged in examining the case, and at midnight Mr. Sam Brannan announced their verdict to the crowd assembled outside the rooms. The criminal, he said, was to be hanged in an hour or two on the Plaza. The execution took place at two. An attempt was made by the police on the Plaza to get Jenkins away from the committee, but the effort was hopeless, and the "old adobe," now so near its doom, did almost its last public service, before the June fire burned it down, in serving, through one of its projecting beams, as a gallows to hang Jenkins.

A time of feverish public excitement followed. The coroner's inquest implicated certain people as connected with the execution of Jenkins; but the committee, in a very dignified publication, declared all their members, of whom a complete list was given, equally implicated, and announced their firm intention to work for the purification of the city. This plain statement relieved the public mind. The committee was no merely secret organization; and its members were among the best-known men of the city. It plainly expressed the general sentiment. The question—why then could not this honest general sentiment have expressed itself before, in the selection of good and efficient officers?—now came too late. Once for all, only a glimpse of the terrible scenes of lynch law could make this public serious. And so the committee was indeed a necessity. Here, in fact, is one of the heretofore frequently mentioned cases where popular justice was not in itself sin, but was the confession of the past sin of the whole community.

The work during June, July, and August was both impressive and important. That it frightened the rogues, sent many of them away, and hanged three more besides Jenkins, is, as the reader now sees, the least of its merits. More important was the manifest sobriety and justice of the methods. The committee caught, tried, and hanged the true Stuart, who made at the last a full but untrustworthy confession. But by doing this piece of work the committee accomplished an act of justice to the poor fellow who had been mistaken for Stuart in February. He, namely, was now in jail in the interior, under sentence of death, all because of another consequence of his resemblance to Stuart. And the committee, when the truth had once become known, made every effort to save him and to set him free, and succeeded. Not mere vengeance, then, but justice, was the obvious motive of its acts.

In August the committee came nearly to an open collision with the authorities, who, at an unguarded moment, rescued from the rooms of the committee two of its condemned criminals, Whittaker and McKenzie. The committee, however, some days later, by a skillful and effective surprise, recaptured these two, and hanged them at once, all without more than the mere show of violence towards the police. Successively, then, the risk of an open fight with officers of the law was overcome. But the lesson of this was a serious one. Popular justice in San Francisco would, it was plain, involve fearful risks of an open collision between the officers and the people, and would be a great waste of social energy. Why not gain in future, through devotion to the duties of citizenship, what one thus in the end would have to struggle for in some way, perchance at the expense of much blood?

When the committee at last ceased its activity, this lesson was in everybody's mind. That the lesson was not more permanently taken to heart by San Francisco is indeed unfortunate. Too many of the citizens still felt themselves wanderers on the face of the earth. But at all events a good beginning had been made in righteousness.

THE WOMEN OF THE TOWN

by

ALBERT BENARD DE RUSSAILH

WHEN I first arrived here, there were only ten or twelve French women in San Francisco, but quite a number of American women had been here for some time, and were living in attractive houses with a certain amount of comfort and even luxury.

These all had come from New York, New Orleans, Washington, or Philadelphia and had the stiff carriage typical of women in those cities. Men would look hopefully at them in the streets, at least men who had just come to California, but they much preferred the French women, who had the charm of novelty. Americans were irresistibly attracted by their graceful walk, their supple and easy bearing, and charming freedom of manner, qualities, after all, only to be found in France; and they trooped after a French woman whenever she put her nose out of doors, as if they could never see enough of her. If the poor fellows had known what these women had been in Paris, how one could pick them up on the boulevards and have them for almost nothing, they might not have been so free with their offers of $500 or $600 a night. A little knowledge might have cooled them down a bit. But I'm sure the women were flattered by so much attention. Some of the first in the field made enough in a month to go home to France and live on their incomes; but many were not so lucky, and one still meets a few who have had a bad time and who are no better off financially than the day they stepped ashore. No doubt, they were blind to their own wrinkles and faded skins, and were too confident in their ability to deceive Americans regarding the dates on their birth certificates.

From the translation by Clarkson Crane published under the title *Last Adventure* by the Westgate Press, San Francisco, 1931.

Many ships have reached San Francisco during the past three or four months, and the number of women in town has greatly increased, but a woman is still sought after and earns a lot of money. Nearly all the saloons and gambling-houses employ French women. They lean on the bars, talking and laughing with the men, or sit at the card tables and attract players. Some of them walk about with trays of cigars hanging in front of them; others caterwaul for hours beside pianos, imagining they are singing like Madame Stoltz. Occasionally you find one who hides her real business and pretends to be a dressmaker or a milliner; but most of them are quite shameless, often scrawling their names and reception-hours in big letters on their doors. There is a certain Madame Cassini who runs a collar shop and claims to be able to predict the past, present, and future and anything else you like.

All in all, the women of easy virtue here earn a tremendous amount of money. This is approximately the tariff:

To sit with you near the bar or at a card table, a girl charges one ounce ($16) an evening. She has to do nothing save honor the table with her presence. This holds true for the girls selling cigars, when they sit with you. Remember they only work in the gambling-halls in the evening. They have their days to themselves and can then receive all the clients who had no chance during the night. Of course, they often must buy new dresses, and dresses are very expensive out here.

For anything more you have to pay a fabulous amount. Nearly all these women at home were streetwalkers of the cheapest sort. But out here, for only a few minutes, they ask a hundred times as much as they were used to getting in Paris. A whole night costs from $200 to $400.

You may find this incredible. Yet some women are quoted at even higher prices. I may add that the saloons and gambling houses that keep women are always crowded and are sure to succeed.

The famous beauties of San Francisco today are Marguet, Helene, Marie, Arthémise, Lucy, Emilie, Madame Mauger, Lucienne, Madame Weston, Eléonore, Madame St. Amand, Madame Meyer, Maria, Angéle, and others whose names I have forgotten.

There are also some honest women in San Francisco, but not very many.

[1852]

THE GOLD "SWINDLE"

by

THOMAS DE QUINCEY

IN THE case of California, the most painful feature at the outset was the torpor manifested by all the governments of Christendom as to a phenomenon that was leading their countrymen by wholesale into ruin. Helpless and ignorant as that army of children, which in an early stage of the Crusades set forward by land for Palestine; knowing as little as those children of the horrors that besieged the road, or of the disappointments that would seal its terminus, supposing it ever to be reached; from every quarter of Europe rushed the excited ploughman and artisan, as vultures on a day of battle to the supper of carrion: and not a word of warning or advice from their government.

On the continent this neglect had its palliation. Most governments were then too occupied by anxieties and agitation derived from the approaching future, or even by desperate convulsions derived from the present. But whither shall we look for the excuse of our own government? Some years ago, it was, by inconsiderate Radicals, made the duty of government to find work for the people. *That* was no part of their duty; nor *could* be; for it can be no duty to attempt impossibilities. But it *was* a part of their duty, officially, to publish remonstrances and cautions against general misapprehension of apparent openings, that too often were no real openings, for labor, and against a national delusion that for ninety-nine out of a hundred was sure to end in ruin. Two things government were bound to have done, viz., 1st, to have circulated a circumstantial account of the different routes to San Francisco, each with its separate distances assigned, and its

From *California and the Gold Mania*, the Colt Press, San Francisco, 1945.

separate varieties of inconceivable hardship; 2d, to have sent out a party of surveyors and mineralogists, with instructions to report from time to time, at short intervals, upon the real condition of the prospects before the gold-diggers, upon the comparative advantages of the several districts in California as yet explored, with these mineral views, and upon the kind of labors, and the kind of tools or other apparatus, that had any reasonable chance of success. Had this been done, some myriads of energetic and enterprising men, that have long since perished miserably, would have been still available for the public service. California, be its real wealth what it may, was a 'job;' a colossal job; and was worked as a job by a regular conspiracy of jobbers.

The root of this conspiracy lay and lies (in all senses *lies*) up and down the United States. It is no affront, nor intended as such, to the American Union or to Mr. Barnum, if I say that this gigantic republic (which, by the seventh census, just now in the course of publication, has actually extended its territorial compass in a space of ten years from about two millions of square miles, which it had in 1840, to three and a quarter millions of square miles which it had reached last midsummer) produces a race of Barnums on a pre-Adamite scale, corresponding in activity to its own enormous proportions. The idea of a Barnum does not at all pre-suppose an element of fraud. There are many honorable Barnums; but also there is a minority of fraudulent Barnums. All alike, good Barnums and bad Barnums, are characterized by Titantic energy, such as would tear into ribbons a little island like ours, but is able to pull fearlessly against a great bulk of a continent that the very moon finds it fatiguing to cross.

Now, it happened that the bad Barnums took charge of the California swindle. They stationed a first-rate liar in San Francisco, under whom, and accountable to whom, were several accomplished liars distributed all the way down to Panama, and thence to Chagres. All along the Atlantic seaboard, this gathering volley of lies and Californian 'notions' raced with the speed of gunpowder trains up to New York, in which vast metropolis (confounded amongst its seven hundred thousand citizens) burrowed the central bureau of the swindle. Thence in ten days these poetic hoaxes crossed over to a line of repeating liars posted in Liverpool and London, from which cities, of course, the lies ran by telegraph in a few hours over the European continent, and thence by Tartar expresses overland to Indus and the Ganges.

When the swindle got into regular working order, it was as good as a comedy to watch its mode of playing. The policy of the liars was to quarrel with each other, and cavil about straws, for the purpose of masking the subterranean wire of their fradulent concert. Liar No. 5, for instance, would observe carelessly in a Panama journal, that things were looking up at Sacramento, for (by the latest returns that could be depended on) the daily product of gold had now reached a million of dollars. Upon which No. 8 at Chagres would quote the paragraph into a local paper, and comment upon it thus with virtuous indigna: tion: 'Who or what this writer may be, with his daily million of dollars, we know not, and do not desire to know. But we warn the editor of that paper, that it is infamous to sport with the credulity of European emigrants. A million, indeed, daily! We, on the contrary, assert that the produce for the last three months, though steadily increasing, has never exceeded an average for half a million—and even *that* not to be depended on for more than nine days out of ten.' To him succeeds No. 10, who, after quoting No. 8, goes on thus: 'Some people are never content. To *our* thinking, half a million of dollars daily, divided amongst about fourteen hundred laborers, working only seven hours a day, is a fair enough remuneration, considering that no education is required, no training, and no capital. Two ounces of tobacco and a spade, with rather a large sack for bagging the gold, having a chain and padlock—such is the stock required for a beginner. In a week he will require more sacks and more padlocks; and in two months a roomy warehouse, with suitable cellars, for storing the gold until the fall, when the stoutest steamers sail. But, as we observed, some people are never content. A friend of ours, not twelve miles from San Francisco, in digging for potatoes, stumbled upon a hamper of gold that netted forty thousand dollars. And, behold, the next comer to that locality went off in dudgeon because, after two days' digging, he got nothing but excellent potatoes; whereas he ought to have reflected that our friend's golden discovery was a lucky chance, such as does not happen to the most hard-working man above once in three weeks.'

Then come furious controversies about blocks of gold embedded in quartz, and left at 'our office' for twenty-four hours, with liberty for the whole town to weigh and measure them. One editor affirms that the blocks weighed six quintals, and the quartz, if pulverized, would hardly fill three snuff-boxes. 'But,' says a second editor, 'the bore of our friend's nostrils is preter-naturally large; his pinch, being proportionable, averages three ounces; and three of his snuff-boxes make one horse-bucket. Six tons, does he say? I don't believe, at the outside, it reaches seven hundred weight.' Thereupon rejoins editor No. 1: 'The blockhead has mistaken a quintal for a ton; and thus makes us talk nonsense. Of course we shall always talk nonsense, when we talk in *his* words and not in our own. His wish was to undermine us: but so far from doing *that,* the knowing reader will perceive that he confirms our report, and a little enlarges it.'

Even in Scotland, as far north as Perth and Aberdeen, the incorporation of liars thought it might answer to suborn a youth, to all appearance an ingenuous youth, as repeating signalist in the guise of one writing home to his Scottish relations, with flourishing accounts of his success at the 'diggins.' Apparently he might have saved his postage, since the body of his letter represented him as having returned to Scotland, so that he might have reported his adventures by word of mouth. This letter was doctored so as to leave intentionally a very slight impression that even in California the course of life was chequered with good and evil. It had been found, perhaps, that other letters in more romantic keys had overleaped their own swindling purpose. The vivacious youth admitted frankly that on some days he got nothing, except, perhaps, a touch of catarrh. Such things were actually possible, viz., the getting nothing except a *soupçon* of catarrh, even in California. Finally, however, with all his candor, the repeating signalist left one great mystery unsolved. He had been getting nothing on some days; but still, after all these cloudy seasons had been allowed for, his gains had *averaged* from three to four guineas a day during the period of his stay. That being the case, one could not well understand what demon had led him ever to quit this garden of the Hesperides for Perth or Aberdeen, where no such golden apples grow either on the highroads, or even in gentlemen's 'policies,' beset with mastiff-dogs and policemen.

But why, or for what ultimate purpose, do I direct these satiric glances at the infant records of California, and the frauds by which she prospered? No doubt the period of her childhood, and of the battle which she had to fight at starting with an insufficient population, was shortened exceedingly and alleviated by unlimited lying. An altar she ought to raise, dedicated to the goddess of insolent mendacity, as the tutelary power under which she herself emerged into importance: this altar should be emblazoned upon the shield of her heraldic honors; this altar should stand amongst the quarterings on her coins. And it cannot be denied that a preliminary or heralding generation has perished in the process of clearing the way for that which is now in possession. What by perils of the sea, and the greater perils of the land route; what by 'plague, pestilence, and famine; by battle, and murder, and sudden death' (to quote our English Litany), within the precincts of the gold districts, probably not far from a quarter of a million are now sleeping in obscure graves that might have been saved by the interference of surveyors, guides, monitors—such as a benign and Christian government in Europe would assuredly have authorized officially.

But these things are not disputed; or only as a question of extent. The evil is confessed. Small or great, it is now over. War, it is true, and war of that ferocious character which usually takes place with the vindictive Indians apparently is now imminent; but this will be transitory, possibly favorable to peace and settlement, by absorbing the ruffianism of the state. And, in the meantime, the iniquity of the Lynch law is giving way, and thawing, as a higher civilization is mounting above the horizon. After a preliminary night of bloodshed and darkness, California will begin to take her place amongst the prosperous states of the American union.

[1853]

ON "LONG WHARF"

by

ALONZO DELANO

ALL THE WORLD have read of Babylon, of the Tower of Babel, and the confusion of tongues. Had the event, recorded in Holy Writ, occurred in the present day, instead of locating it in the now wastes of Asia I should have given it a local habitation on Central Wharf, Commercial Street, in San Francisco. Pass through Kearny Street, and look down through a portion of the town, which appears going out to sea to meet the shipping, in a sort of compromise between the land and old ocean. What a sea of heads, what a moving mass of human beings meets the view!

Most have read the passage of Bonaparte over the bridge of Lodi, when the Austrian cannon disputed his progress, and pictured to their mind the rush of men, and the vast slaughter through that narrow passage, in that desperate attempt. Were a cannon to be placed on Montgomery Street to defend it from such an inroad, the slaughter could not be less, and the sacrifice of human life would equal that of the passage of Lodi. It is like the waving of a field of corn in the breeze, a crowded mass of flesh and blood, one of the main arteries of the city. This is a congregation of all nations, creeds and tongues— English and Spanish, German, French, Chinese, Sandwich Islands, Indian, &c.—and in passing through, one hears their jargon at every corner, and sees the strange and peculiar costume of each nation; the flashy silk or muslin dresses of the embrowned Mexican señoritas— we can not call them pretty—bareheaded, or with a rich shawl carelessly thrown over their heads, which half hides a seeming Indian face; the sturdy German, with a heavy package nicely balanced on

From *Pen-Knife Sketches,* The Grabhorn Press, San Francisco, 1934.

her head, or the neat, tidy French and American belle, tripping along with a light step and joyous countenance; or, perchance, the plain, honest, good-natured face of the Kanaka girl, dressed in petticoats after no peculiar fashion, meets the gaze, and excites the wonder where all these women came from and what brought them here. Hand-carts, porters, drays, now and then a fine carriage, rattle over the plank pavement, adding confusion to the hubbub, in a sound of thunder, while at points along the wharf, the thimble-rigger, the French monte dealer, and low gamblers are gathering crowds around them, to practice upon the credulity of the unsophisticated. The pickpocket, the thief, of all grades, are in the crowd, & often, for want of other opportunity, a fight or excitement is got up to order, so that these light-fingered gentry can practice their vocation upon the idle lovers of pugilistic fun.

At corners of Montgomery, and Leidesdorff, and Sansome Streets, are musical gambling hells, where your loose change can be fiddled away on the turning of a card, and where your losses can be drowned, for an addlepate, in the flowing bowl. Rows, fights, and robberies are the order of the day, aye, and night, too, and to see sin and depravity in its most glaring colors, the seeker after such *pleasures* has only to walk from one end of Long Wharf to the other. An excitement can be got up at any moment by pretending to examine a quartz specimen, and instantly a man becomes the center of a wondering crowd. Still as a pedestrian elbows his way, at open spaces along the dock, you see crowds of sail boats and lighters alongside, discharging vegetables—the produce of California—cattle and sheep for the market, wool, coal, hay, &c., while numerous wholesale and retail shops of various kinds, restaurant and cigar divans, fill up the sum of human operations on this Great Babel of San Francisco.

Near the end of the wharf is Whitehall, the haven of wherrys. If you are looking around, as if in search of something, a trim red shirt is at your side, and a voice enquires, "A boat, sir? Carry you out and back for two dollars." Here, on both sides, are ships, barks, schooners, steamboats, and propellers, just off for Gold Bluff, Panama, Sacramento, Marysville, or Stockton, as you please; in fact, one may go to China, or eternity, for about the same price. For the one take a ship; for the other a steamboat, and in due time the port of destination will be reached. Take out papers for the one from the Customs House for the other at the monte table.

Among the incidents of Long Wharf life, deserving of notice, is a little hand-wagon with a tight box, labelled "Pure Water." This means just what it reads. There is no adulteration of salt, soda, soap, sulphur or suds. Get up at the peep of day, or look down at nine o'clock at night, in rain or shine, in hot or cold, and you will see that little cart of "pure water" moving along, drawn by a poor fellow with only one arm. Unobtrusive and modest in his demeanor, without a drop of hot-water aristocracy in his veins, the maimed water carrier pursues his daily rounds, and supplies his customers with the water they want during the day. At home, I should have asked what could a man with only one arm do in the land of gold, to gain his bread? What folly for such a man to go where two hands and a pick and shovel were necessary, and hardly obtain a living with both! Undismayed at such prospects, he resolved to strive with fortune, and win her smile with one arm, and among the hardy adventurers he sought the golden shore, and is not only earning an honest living but laying up money in his humble calling of dispensing one of the best gifts of God to his fellow laborers in San Francisco. Always be ready with a "bit" for the honest water carrier.

Such is a faint picture of the "confusion worse confounded" which greets the visitor to Long Wharf. Every day is like its fellow; no change, no cessation of the varied scenes which attract, amuse or pain. It is one of *the* business places of San Francisco, and every one who has had occasion to visit it, will recognize the sketch I give above.

MID-VICTORIAN BAD GIRL:
LOLA MONTEZ

by

OSCAR LEWIS

SOME CITIES, like some individuals, grow up too rapidly. San Francisco, more precocious than most, came close to skipping her childhood entirely. As early as 1853, old settlers were recalling the boisterous infancy of the city—a remote and half legendary period already four or five years in the past—and lamenting the fact that plank sidewalks and bathtubs and three-story brick buildings had taken the romance out of life. The turbulent camp of the Argonauts had gone conservative, and less than two years later its citizens were organizing a pioneer society. Newspapers pointed out that the city was as modern and safe and orderly as Boston, and scores of citizens had started patronizing the Chinese laundries and putting their money in the bank. The old devil-may-care spirit was gone; the proper attitude was one of easy cosmopolitanism combined with a slight but becoming ennui. By 1853, San Francisco had seen and heard practically everything.

But had it?

One brilliant morning in May of that year the Pacific Mail's new side-wheeler *Northerner* reached port after an uneventful run from Panama. She carried 275 bags of mail, and her passenger list included such important personages as William M. Gwin, Senator from the young state; Thomas O. Larkin, the Monterey merchant with a flair

From *Lola Montez: The Mid-Victorian Bad Girl in California* by Oscar Lewis. The Colt Press, San Francisco, 1938.

for diplomacy; Samuel Brannan, capitalist and ex-Mormon; a Congressman, an ex-Governor, and Patrick Purdy Hull, a personable young Irishman who edited one of the city's dailies. The passenger list, complete, was published in the papers next morning. Citizens glanced through it with mild curiosity. Travel to and from the States was already an old story; most solvent inhabitants made the trip as often as business or pleasure might demand it.

But eyes presently focused on the list and languid readers sat upright. "Lola Montez and companion," they read. And in parenthesis: "Countess of Landsfeld."

There was no need for the latter. Had the list read "Queen Victoria and Prince Albert" it would not have made a greater sensation. For Lola Montez was easily the most widely known and most thoroughly discussed young woman of her decade. San Franciscans well knew that she was world famous or, if one chose to put it that way, world notorious. Many did choose to put it that way, including the young woman herself, who often remarked plaintively, "I have always been notorious, never famous." A later writer called her "the international bad girl of the mid-Victorians," which remark would certainly have brought sharp reprisals from Lola herself had it been made in her time and within her hearing.

San Francisco was not so remote but that the outlines of her rocket-like career had preceded this startling appearance of her person. Born in Ireland and christened Maria Dolores Eliza Gilbert, she had become at fifteen the heroine of an elopement with an army officer, who had carried her off to India. Charming, headstrong, and uncommonly pretty, she had, all within a few months, disrupted the placid social life of the army post, set tongues wagging, flirted a bit, quarreled with her husband, and hurried back to England. There she remained for a short time in the background; then, in 1843, a new Spanish danseuse, by name Lola Montez, made her debut in London.

The *Morning Herald,* unimpressed by the unknown's ability as a dancer, commented on "the perfection of her Spanish beauty," and Maria Dolores Eliza Gilbert became permanently submerged in the new role.

There never was a question of her beauty. It made up, and more than made up, for her deficiencies as a dancer and later as an actress. Critics admitted that her talents were no more than ordinary, but they admitted it grudgingly and went on to devote the greater part of their reviews to enraptured descriptions of her face and figure. Anyone so lovely did not need to be an artist; it was enough that she allowed herself to be seen. In Paris, men smiled tolerantly at her dancing—and flocked to see her, both on and off the stage. She made important friends, and what is more, kept them. Her lively conversation, ready wit, and handsome eyes were remembered by everyone; all who wrote of her from first-hand knowledge made reference to them.

After her London and Paris debuts, events moved fast. By 1847, the mediocre dancer had attained international fame—and notoriety—as the mistress of King Ludwig of Bavaria. Within a year she had been made Countess of Landsfeld and had converted the elderly and infatuated king to the democratic ideas she had picked up in Paris. A few months more and she was forced to flee before the revolution that soon cost Ludwig his throne. In England again, still under thirty, she married an officer in the Life Guards, found herself arrested for bigamy and—positive proof of eminence—had the costume she wore at the trial described in the *Times*: a black silk dress, with a "close fitting black velvet jacket, a plain straw bonnet trimmed in blue, and a blue veil." She no doubt looked charming, for she got off lightly, suffering no greater inconvenience than the severing of her ties with the young guardsman,—a loss from which she recovered promptly.

The steamer that brought her to New York in 1851 was met by a committee of notables, while guns on adjacent forts boomed honorary salutes. The commotion, however, was not for the Countess but for a fellow passenger, the Polish patriot, Louis Kossuth. However, it is safe to guess that the beautiful dancer was not ignored; she was far too well-known. Famous or merely notorious, New York flocked to see her. It is said that during her stay she held open house while lines of the curious filed through her parlor and shook her hand, gladly paying a dollar a head for the privilege. The dancer who had kicked over a throne moved in the center of a circle of brilliant publicity while the whole nation followed her progress, from New York to Boston, to Philadelphia, to a dozen cities, winding up in New Orleans.

Where next? The question was not long debated. In the spring of '53, California was still Mecca for the footloose of half the world.

There was no advance publicity. In San Franicsco, celebrities were not announced; they merely arrived. Newspaper reporters met the steamers prepared for any sensation, and were seldom disappointed. Even the advent of Lola Montez was not beyond the capabilities of the young man from the *Herald*:

"This distinguished wonder," he began, "this world-bewildering puzzle, Marie de Landsfeld Heald (Heald was the name of the dispossessed young guardsman) has actually come to San Francisco, and her coming has acted like the application of fire to the combustible matter that creates public curiosity, excitement, or *furore*."

There was more in the same key, ending on this hospitable note: "Whether she comes as danseuse, authoress, politician, beauty, bluestocking or noble lady, she is welcomed—so she permit herself to be seen, admired, sung, courted and gone mad over here as elsewhere."

The *Northerner* had deposited an extremely well-advertised young woman in town, and the papers, no less than Lola herself, made the most of it. She arrived on Saturday morning; by Monday San Francisco's journals were filled with resumés of her career, along with announcements of her first public appearance. Tuesday's *Herald* stated that the demand was so great that seats for her opening performance were to be auctioned. Half the town gathered before the American Theatre at eleven the next morning. Bidding was so spirited that the first seat brought a premium of $65.00, the second $25.00, and so on down. Speculators did not fail to buy blocks of tickets; here if ever was a sure sell-out.

Lola's choice of role for her opening performance was not a very fortunate one. San Franciscans had packed the house to the doors out of curiosity to see one of the most celebrated beauties of her time; instead they saw a conscientious but uninspired Lady Teazle. But they forgot their disappointment when the Countess appeared between acts and thanked them in one of the pretty speeches she knew so well how to make, remembering to speak with the slight accent that became her Spanish origin. With the critics, it was the old story. They accepted the actress with pronounced reservations; for Lola herself there was nothing but praise. On her opening night she did not appear in her celebrated "Spider Dance," the fame of which, like that of her Bavarian episode, preceded her wherever she went. The dance, however, was announced for the second performance and the house was again jammed. Her play was "Yelva," but that was immaterial. The town was on hand to see the famous spiders shaken from the famous dress and the three-act drama was merely a prelude.

By present standards, the "Spider Dance" hardly deserved its reputation as an uncommonly sensational performance. It could not have been beautiful and it was certainly not scandalous. Nevertheless the performance, during which she simulated horror and whirling rapidly as she shook the whalebone and rubber spiders from her short dress and stamped on them, gave the dancer opportunity to display her talent for spirited pantomine. The dance always ended amid storms of applause that brought the Countess to the footlights, smiling and breathless, to thank her audience in one of her charming curtain speeches. The "Spider Dance," as she well knew, was her most effective instrument of popularity. Whenever interest began to cool or attendance to drop off the announcement of its revival could be depended on to fill the house again.

During the three weeks of her first San Francisco engagement Lola appeared in five plays. "A School for Scandal," "Yelva," "Maritana," "Charlotte Corday" and "Lola Montez in Bavaria." The latter, a badly written dramatization of her adventures in Munich, received unusual treatment from local critics. The theory was advanced that by appearing in the role, Lola the actress was doing less than justice to Lola the woman. The critic of the *Alta California* was particularly disturbed at this unusual form of self-slander. "History," he wrote, "pays her a higher compliment than her own play." This champion went on to argue that the real Lola Montez was not the spoiled and wayward court pet of the play but a dignified and resolute woman. "The play," he ended, "would deprive her of the . . . stronger attributes of a great woman's nature." A few days later he returned to the attack, presenting new arguments to prove that the actress was reprehensibly belittling her own place in history.

At any rate, "Lola Montez in Bavaria" was well liked and Lola's local popularity mounted to new levels. On the stage and off, she was easily the most conspicuous figure in the turbulent town. Everywhere interest centered on her charming person, her poodle-dog, her deftly made cigarettes, her incessant conversation—from which barbed wit and sarcasm were seldom excluded—and, curious contrast, her severely sober taste in dress.

From the moment of her arrival she projected herself into the life of the town, finding its atmosphere exactly to her liking. For it was her temperament to desire "the center of any storm as some minds love quietude." The day her engagement opened at the American chanced also to be the opening of the racing season at the new Pioneer Course, out near the Mission. In honor of the new favorite, one of the horses was rechristened "Lola Montez." The following Sunday the lady herself joined the procession streaming out the plank road to the racetrack, occupied a box in the grandstand and cheered delightedly as "Lola Montez" won the feature race. Afterwards she made her way through the milling crowd, presented a handsome blanket to her namesake and offered to ride the animal in an exhibition race.

But there were other theatres in town, and other actresses. The newcomer's preeminence did not go unchallenged. One of the rival houses, the San Francisco, was managed by J. Brutus Booth and Charles Chapman. Young Edwin Booth was a member of the company, as were Dr. Robinson and his children and the versatile and gifted Caroline Chapman. The company was energetic and resourceful, made up of seasoned troupers who knew local audiences like their own varied repertories. Lola's triumphs were a challenge they accepted with relish, for it gave them opportunity to use a weapon they had already employed effectively: satire.

But the actors at the San Francisco could not at once launch their counter-attack, and meantime the newcomer's fame continued to mount. By the middle of June her engagement was drawing to a close. Interest reached its height when she appeared in a benefit for the Volunteer Firemen's charity fund. Lola's presence assured a capacity house; $3500 was cleared for the fund.

Two evenings later at her final local appearance the firemen expressed their appreciation. The *Herald's* account suggests the spirit of the occasion.

"Lola had scarcely appeared on the stage when some of the enthusiastic firemen who filled the Parquette (the Howards and Empires were present in uniform) threw their hats up on the stage. She danced with great grace, keeping time with the castanets. . . . Upon the falling of the curtain she was called before it with great applause. She appeared, holding in her hand one of the firemen's caps filled with bouquets which she had picked up, and made a short address with a slightly foreign accent. She addressed herself to the audience and thanked them for their kind reception of her who did not merit it. She addressed herself to the firemen and said San Francisco could only become the great or greatest city it was destined to become by having the firemen to guard it; she would always remember them with pleasure and speak of them with praise in whatever land she might be; they had thrown her their hats, but she believed she also held their hearts. She addressed herself to the ladies, and recommended the firemen to their special favors; and withdrew amid universal applause, and three cheers from the firemen."

While the Countess was thus bringing her engagement to a close, members of the rival company were perfecting their campaign of ridicule. Warning of impending warfare was given by an announcement in the *Alta* stating that in addition to the regular performance (which chanced to be Edwin Booth in "Hamlet") Caroline Chapman was to appear in a sketch called "Lola Montez." The burlesque amused the audience and encouraged Miss Chapman to further efforts. At one of her performances Lola had appeared in a skit in which she took three parts; a few evenings later Miss Chapman put on a burlesque entitled "The Actress of All Work" and appeared in nine.

But these were merely experiments, designed to feel out the sentiment of the town toward satires on the distinguished Lola. The delight with which they were received encouraged the production of a longer and even more personal farce: "Who's Got The Countess?" This was written by Dr. Robinson, whose friendship for Lola did not prevent him from poking fun at her eccentricities. It was first played on Monday, June 20; the cast, of course, was headed by Caroline Chapman, in the role of "Mula, Countess of Bohemia." The piece was an immediate hit, for, though it had been hastily thrown together, it abounded in apt allusions immediately recognized by local theatregoers. Not only the Countess but all important members of the American company were lampooned. Miss Chapman had real opportunity to exercise her gift for mimicry and she scored a triumph by exaggerating Lola's mannerisms on and off the stage to the point of absurdity. The farce continued to play to crowded houses nightly for two weeks, an uncommonly long run for the period.

But the Countess was not without champions, particularly among the critics. The *Alta* admitted the popularity of the new farce and the cleverness of some of its allusions, and paid deserved tribute to the excellence of Caroline Chapman's work. The play itself was dismissed as "very miserably arranged . . . the dialogue lacking in wit, point, appropriateness and even common sense . . . and, to crown it all, bunglingly arranged in bad rhyme." On June 26, the *Herald* printed a letter condemning the piece on other grounds, terming it "an exceedingly coarse and vulgar attack on one who, whatever her faults and foibles may have been, has proved herself a noble-hearted and generous woman . . . and who little deserves . . . ridicule and scurrility." The play was pronounced a "vulgar misrepresentation of her manners and behavior, a ridiculous caricature of her person, and a coarse exaggeration of her pecularities . . . " The writer added: "If no gratitude is felt for her benevolence, good taste should have decreed at least that her name and character should not be publicly ridiculed and outraged in this community."

It is hardly likely that Lola took the farce with so much seriousness. She had many times proved herself able to fight her own battles, and she would hardly have hesitated to make reprisals had she considered herself unfairly treated. Moreover, her own engagement had drawn to a close and, whatever else might be said of it, the satire was advertising the tour of the interior towns on which she was about to embark.

There was still another reason why she ignored the play. Matters of far more importance were occupying her attention.

Lola was to open her tour with an engagement at Sacramento, beginning on the evening of July 5th. At daybreak on the morning of the 2nd she appeared at Mission Dolores and was married to her fellow-passenger of the *Northerner*, Pat Hull. The news focused the attention of the entire state on her. Hull, witty and attractive and then about thirty, was a popular figure about town, one of the owners of a local daily, the *Whig*. The Countess later remarked that she had married the Irishman because he could tell a story better than anyone she had ever met. An attempt to keep the wedding secret only partly succeeded. Several scores of citizens made that three-mile trek across the sandhills to be present.

Next day the *Golden Era* thus ended its account of the wedding: "The question, 'Who's Got the Countess?' we presume, is thus forever more put at rest." No such levity marred the dispatch of the local correspondent of the *Shasta Courier*:

"Lola Montez is married to a man of California! On the 3rd inst. this celebrated actress of unblemished virtue, the charming and peerless Madame Marie Elise Rosanna Dolores, Countess of Landsfeld, Baroness of Rosenthal, was united in the holy bonds of matrimony, at the holy church of the Mission by Father Flavel Fontaine, to Patrick Purdy Hull. It affords us the most exquisite happiness to inform our readers that the happy Mr. Hull is connected with the California press, being conductor of the San Francisco *Whig*. Of course he has immortalized himself. This is certainly a very great country. It is confidently asserted that Mr. and Mrs. Hull intend making the state their permanent residence, which announcement . . . we are frank to confess, fills our soul with emotions of sublime pleasure."

The newly immortalized Hull and his bride took the afternoon boat to Sacramento.

SAN FRANCISCO HARBOR

by

NANCY BUCKLEY

Tall ships, majestically fair,
In stately panoply,
With treasure for us, rich and rare,
Flash down our windy sea,
From Ports of Hundred Isles they sail,
Blown by the wind's cool breath,
Undaunted by the fiercest gale,
Or tangling nets of Death.

Where angry, storm-whipped waters meet
Each frenzied wind that comes
With wild tattoo and furious beat,
Like thunderous roll of drums;
Where, bright against the sky's blue-grey,
The silver sea-gulls fly;
Where green waves toss their feathery spray,
These gleaming sails pass by.

A thousand setting suns have blazed
On them their dazzling lights;
A thousand rising moons have gazed
At them through silent nights;
And now, where blows the western breeze
And leaps the snow-white foam,
At last, these welcome argosies
Are harbored safe at home.

NEVER BELOW
MONTGOMERY STREET

EDITOR, *The Pioneer,*   April 10, 1854

Mr. Editor,:—Some weeks since, I noticed in the *Herald* an article inquiring the cause of sudden deaths in San Francisco. I noted down on the spur of the moment the following brief remarks; but other engagements prevented my handing them in earlier for publication. As no other physician has in the mean time answered the article above alluded to, I will ask you to publish this, if in your opinion it will be of any service to the public.

The climate of this city, taken above Montgomery Street, is probably unequaled for salubrity by any other on the earth; but below Montgomery, as is well known, the atmosphere is impregnated with the malaria or miasma arising from the great quantity of decaying vegetable matter which has been constantly accumulating there for years. As far as my experience goes, not only do the sudden deaths almost invariably occur in the lower portions of the city, but by far the greater majority of all the deaths; and when they do not occur there, the causes of the disease can generally be traced to sleeping or working at night and early morning, below the old water line, which coursed, as will be recollected, along the line of Montgomery Street, or on the marshes and low grounds of our upper country, which, being annually overflowed, present a great deal of vegetable matter to decay. When a man, who has once been poisoned by malaria and whose constitution has become debilitated, is again infected by malaria, death often occurs almost instantaneously; and the same may be the case when the frame is much enfeebled by toil. In some of the low parts of England, laborers, who have lain down upon the ground to sleep, have often been known to die instantly. Many such instances from such causes, may be found recorded in McCulloch's Treatise on Intermittent Fevers. And so much do I, as a physician, fear the malaria of our low grounds, that I will never allow a patient to sleep below Montgomery Street if I can possibly avoid it.

J. B. Phinney, M.D.

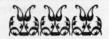

SUCH INELEGANT BUILDINGS

PROBABLY no city in this country can boast of buildings so substantial and thoroughly fireproof as those of San Francisco. Besides making the walls very thick, every care is taken to have the doors, window-shutters and roofs equally stout and incombustible; nor is this precaution at all surprising, when it is remembered that this city alone has lost more than twenty-five millions of dollars by fire.

The amount of money invested in this durable kind of improvement . . . is something over thirteen and a half millions of dollars—the number of buildings being six hundred and thirty-eight . . . It is a remarkable fact, however, that less than half of these improvements have been made with California gold. Ask the proprietors where they got the money which they have expended in the erection of these buildings, and they will tell you it came from the Atlantic States and from Europe. . . .

These buildings are erected upon the most eligible and convenient sites . . . and form what is properly termed about one-sixth of its superficies. Almost all of the residences or private dwellings are built of wood, and are very frail and inelegant. It is the intention, however, of a large number of the citizens to take down the wood and substitute brick or stone, as soon as they get able, if that is ever to be the case.

—Hinton Rowan Helper,
The Land of Gold
Baltimore, 1855

GENERAL SHERMAN
AND THE VIGILANTES OF '56

by

WILLIAM TECUMSEH SHERMAN

DURING the summer of 1856, in San Francisco, occurred one of those unhappy events, too common to new countries, in which I became involved in spite of myself.

William Neely Johnson was Governor of California, and resided at Sacramento City; General John E. Wool commanded the Department of California, having succeeded General Hitchcock, and had his headquarters at Benicia; and a Mr. Van Ness was mayor of the city. Politics had become a regular and profitable business, and politicians were more than suspected of being corrupt. It was reported and currently believed that the sheriff (Scannell) had been required to pay the Democratic Central Committee a hundred thousand dollars for his nomination, which was equivalent to an election, for an office of the nominal salary of twelve thousand dollars a year for four years. In the election all sorts of dishonesty were charged and believed, especially of "ballot-box stuffing," and too generally the better classes avoided the elections and dodged jury-duty, so that the affairs of the city government necessarily passed into the hands of a low set of professional politicians.

Among these was a man named James Casey, who edited a small paper, the printing office of which was in a room on the third floor of our banking-office. I hardly knew him by sight, and rarely if ever saw his paper; but one day Mr. Sather, of the excellent banking firm

From the *Memoirs of General William T. Sherman*, D. Appleton, New York, 1875.

of Drexel, Sather & Church, came to me, and called my attention to an article in Casey's paper so full of falsehood and malice, that we construed it as an effort to black-mail the banks generally. At that time we were all laboring to restore confidence, which had been so rudely shaken by the panic, and I went up-stairs, found Casey, and pointed out to him the objectionable nature of his article, told him plainly that I could not tolerate his attempt to print and circulate slanders in our building, and, if he repeated it, I would cause him and his press to be thrown out of the windows. He took the hint and moved to more friendly quarters. I mention this fact, to show my estimate of the man, who became a figure in the drama I am about to describe.

A respectable San Franciscan, James King of William, had been in 1853 a banker on his own account, but some time in 1854 he had closed out his business, and engaged with Adams & Co., as cashier. When this firm failed, he, in common with all the employés, was thrown out of employment, and had to look around for something else. He settled down to the publication of an evening paper, called the *Bulletin,* and, being a man of fine manners and address, he at once constituted himself the champion of society against the public and private characters whom he saw fit to arraign.

One evening of May, 1856, King published, in the *Bulletin,* copies of papers procured from New York, to show that Casey had once been sentenced to the State penitentiary at Sing Sing. Casey took mortal offense, and called at the *Bulletin* office, on the corner of Montgomery and Merchant Streets, where he found King, and violent words passed between them, resulting in Casey giving King notice that he would shoot him on sight. King remained in his office till about 5 or 6 P.M., when he started toward his home on Stockton Street, and, as he neared the corner of Washington, Casey approached him from the opposite direction, called to him, and began firing. King had on a short cloak, and in his breast-pocket a small pistol, which he did not use. One of Casey's shots struck him high up in the breast, from which he reeled, was caught by some passing friend, and carried into the express-office on the corner, where he was laid on the counter, and a surgeon sent for. Meantime, Casey escaped up Washington Street, went to the City Hall, and delivered himself to the sheriff (Scannell), who conveyed him to jail and locked him in a cell. Meantime, the news spread like wildfire, and all the city was in commotion, for King was very popular.

It so happened that, on the urgent solicitation of Van Winkle and of Governor Johnson, I had only a few days before agreed to accept the commission of major-general of the Second Division of Militia, embracing San Francisco. I had received the commission, but had not as yet formally accepted it, or even put myself in communication with the volunteer companies of the city.

After dinner, I went down-town to see what was going on; found that King had been removed to a room in the Metropolitan Block; that his life was in great peril; that Casey was safe in jail, and the sheriff had called to his assistance a *posse* of the city police, some citizens, and one of the militia companies. The people were gathered in groups on the streets, and the words "Vigilance Committee" were freely spoken, but I saw no signs of immediate violence.

The next morning I again went to the jail, and found all things quiet, but the militia had withdrawn. I then went to the City Hall, saw the mayor, Van Ness, and some of the city officials, agreed to do what I could to maintain order with such militia as were on hand, and then formally accepted the commission, and took the "oath." In 1851 (when I was not in California) there had been a Vigilance Committee, and it was understood that its organization still existed. All the newspapers took ground in favor of the Vigilance Committee, except the *Herald* (John Nugent, editor), and nearly all the best people favored that means of redress. I could see they were organizing, hiring rendezvous, collecting arms, etc., without concealment. It was soon manifest that the companies of volunteers would go with the "committee," and that the public authorities could not rely on them for aid or defense. Still, there were a good many citizens who contended that, if the civil authorities were properly sustained by the people at large, they could and would execute the law. But the papers inflamed the public mind, and the controversy spread to the country. About the third day after the shooting of King, Governor Johnson telegraphed me that he would be down in the evening boat, and asked me to meet him on arrival for consultation. We discussed the state of affairs fully; and Johnson, on learning that his particular friend, William T. Coleman, was the president of the Vigilante Committee, proposed to go and see him. *En route* we stopped at King's room, ascertained that he was slowly sinking, and could not live long; and then near midnight we walked to the Turnverein Hall, where the committee was known to be sitting in consultation.

The Governor knocked at the door, and on inquiry from inside— "Who's there?"—gave his name. After some delay we were admitted into a sort of vestibule, beyond which was a large hall, and we could hear the suppressed voices of a multitude. We were shown into a barroom to the right, when the Governor asked to see Coleman. The man left us, went into the main hall, and soon returned with Coleman, who was pale and agitated. After shaking hands all round, the Governor said, "Coleman, what the devil is the matter here?" Coleman said, "Governor, it is time this shooting on our streets should stop." The Governor replied, "I agree with you perfectly, and have come down from Sacramento to assist." Coleman rejoined that "the people were tired of it, and had no faith in the officers of the law." A general conversation then followed, in which it was admitted that King would die, and that Casey *must* be executed; but the manner of execution was the thing to be settled, Coleman contending that the people would do it without trusting the courts or the sheriff. Johnson then offered to be personally responsible that Casey should be safely guarded, and should be forthcoming for trial and execution at the proper time. I remember very well Johnson's assertion that he had no right to make these stipulations, and maybe no power to fulfill them; but he did it to save the city and state from the disgrace of a mob. Coleman disclaimed that the vigilance organization was a "mob," admitted that the proposition of the Governor was fair, and all he or any one should ask; and added, if we would wait a while, he would submit it to the council and bring back an answer.

We waited nearly an hour, and could hear the hum of voices in the hall, but no words, when Coleman came back, accompanied by a committee, of which I think the two brothers Arrington, Thomas Smiley the auctioneer, Seymour, Truett, and others, were members. The whole conversation was gone over again, and the Governor's proposition was positively agreed to, with this further condition, that the Vigilance Committee should send into the jail a small force of their own men, to make certain that Casey should not be carried off or allowed to escape.

The Governor, his brother William, Garrison, and I, then went up to the jail, where we found the sheriff and his *posse-comitatus* of police and citizens. These were styled the "Law-and-Order party," and some of them took offense that the Governor should have held communication with the "damned rebels," and several of them left the jail; but the sheriff seemed to agree with the Governor that what he had done was right and best.

Next day I was at the bank, as usual, when about noon the Governor called, and asked me to walk with him down-street.

He said he had just received a message from the Vigilance Committee to the effect that they were not bound by Coleman's promise not to do anything till the regular trial by jury should be had, etc. He was with reason furious, and asked me to go with him to Truett's store, over which the Executive Committee was said to be in session. We were admitted to a front-room up-stairs, and heard voices in the back-room. The Governor inquired for Coleman, but he was not forthcoming. Another of the committee, Seymour, met us, denied *in toto* the promise of the night before, and the Governor openly accused him of treachery and falsehood.

The quarrel became public, and the newspapers took it up, both parties turning on the Governor; one, the Vigilantes, denying the promise made by Coleman, their president; and the other, the "Law-and-Order party," refusing any further assistance, because Johnson had stooped to make terms with rebels. At all events, he was powerless, and had to let matters drift to a conclusion.

King died about Friday, May 20th, and the funeral was appointed for the next Sunday. Early on that day the Governor sent for me at my house. I found him on the roof of the International, from which we looked down on the whole city, and more especially the face of Telegraph Hill, which was already covered with a crowd of people, while others were moving toward the jail on Broadway. Parties of armed men, in good order, were marching by platoons in the same direction, and formed in line along Broadway, facing the jail-door. Soon a small party was seen to advance to this door, and knock; a parley ensued, the doors were opened, and Casey was led out. In a few minutes another prisoner was brought out, who proved to be Cora, a man who had once been tried for killing Richardson, the United States Marshal, when the jury disagreed, and he was awaiting a new trial. These prisoners were placed in carriages, and escorted by the armed force down to the rooms of the Vigilance Committee, through the principal streets of the city. The day was exceedingly beautiful, and the whole proceeding was orderly in the extreme. I was under the impression that Casey and Cora were hanged that same Sunday, but was probably in error; but in a very few days they were hanged by the neck—dead—suspended from beams projecting from the windows of the committee's rooms, without other trial than could be given in secret, and by night.

We all thought the matter had ended there, and accordingly the Governor returned to Sacramento in disgust, and I went about my business. But it soon became manifest that the Vigilance Committee had no intention to surrender the power thus usurped. They took a building on Clay Street, near Front, fortified it, employed guards and armed sentinels, sat in midnight council, issued writs of arrest and banishment, and utterly ignored all authority but their own. Governor Johnson, being again appealed to, concluded to go to work regularly, and telegraphed me about the 1st of June to meet him at General Wool's headquarters at Benicia that night. I went up, and we met at the hotel where General Wool was boarding. We discussed the state of the country generally, and I had agreed that if Wool would give us arms and ammunition out of the United States Arsenal at Benicia, and if Commodore Farragut, of the navy, commanding the navy-yard on Mare Island, would give us a ship, I would call out volunteers, and, when a sufficient number had responded, I would have the arms come down from Benicia in the ship, arm my men, take possession of a thirty-two-pound-gun battery at the Marine Hospital on Rincon Point, thence command a dispersion of the unlawfully-armed force of the Vigilance Committee, and arrest some of the leaders.

We played cards that night, carrying on a conversation, in which Wool insisted on a proclamation commanding the Vigilance Committee to disperse, etc., and he told us how he had on some occasion, as far back as 1814, suppressed a mutiny on the Northern frontier. I did not understand him to make any distinct promise of assistance that night, but he invited us to accompany him on an inspection of the arsenal the next day, which we did. On handling some rifled muskets in the arsenal storehouse he asked me how they would answer our purpose. I said they were the very things, and that we did not want cartridge boxes or belts, but that I would have the cartridges carried in the breeches-pockets, and the caps in the vest-pockets. I knew that there were stored in that arsenal four thousand muskets, for I recognized the boxes which we had carried out in the *Lexington* around Cape Horn in 1846.

Afterward, we all met at the quarters of Captain D. R. Jones of the army, and I saw the Secretary of State, D. F. Douglass, Esq., walk out with General Wool in earnest conversation, and this Secretary of State afterward asserted that Wool there and then promised us the arms and ammunition, provided the Governor would make his proclamation for the committee to disperse, and that I should afterward call out the militia, etc. On the way back to the hotel at Benicia, General Wool, Captain Callendar of the arsenal, and I, were walking side by side, and I was telling him (General Wool) that I would also need some ammunition for the thirty-two-pound guns then in position at Rincon Point, when Wool turned to Callendar and inquired, "Did I not order those guns to be brought away?" Callendar said: "Yes, General. I made a requisition on the quartermaster for transportation, but his schooner has been so busy that the guns are still there." Then said Wool: "Let them remain; we may have use for them." I therefrom inferred, of course, that it was all agreed to so far as he was concerned.

Soon after we had reached the hotel, we ordered a buggy, and Governor Johnson and I drove to Vallejo, six miles, crossed over to Mare Island, and walked up to the commandant's house, where we found Commodore Farragut and his family. We stated our business fairly, but the commodore answered very frankly that he had no authority, without orders from his department, to take any part in civil broils; he doubted the wisdom of the attempt; said he had no ship available except the *John Adams,* Captain Boutwell, and that she needed repairs. But he assented at last to the proposition to let the sloop *John Adams* drop down abreast of the city after certain repairs, to lie off there for *moral effect,* which afterward actually occurred.

We then returned to Benicia, and Wool's first question was, "What luck?" We answered, "Not much," and explained what Commodore Farragut could and would do, and that, instead of having a naval vessel, we would seize and use one of the Pacific Mail Company's steamers, lying at their dock in Benicia, to carry down to San Francisco the arms and munitions when the time came.

As the time was then near at hand for the arrival of the evening boats, we all walked down to the wharf together, where I told Johnson that he could not be too careful; that I had not heard General Wool make a positive promise of assistance. Upon this, Johnson called General Wool to one side, and we three drew together, Johnson said. "General Wool, General Sherman is very particular, and wants to know exactly what you propose to do." Wool answered. "I understand, Governor, that in the first place a writ of *habeas corpus* will be issued commanding the jailers of the Vigilance Committee to produce the body of some one of the prisoners held by them (which, of course, will be refused); that you then issue your proclamation commanding them to disperse, and failing this, you will call out the militia, and command General Sherman with it to suppress the Vigilance Committee as an unlawful body"; to which the Governor responded, "Yes." "Then," said Wool, "on General Sherman's making his requisition, approved by you, I will order the issue of the necessary arms and ammunition." I remember well that I said, emphatically: "That is all I want. Now, Governor, you may go ahead," We soon parted; Johnson and Douglas taking the boat to Sacramento, and I to San Francisco.

The Chief-Justice, Terry, came to San Francisco the next day, issued a writ of *habeas corpus* for the body of one Maloney, which writ was resisted, as we expected. The Governor then issued his proclamation, and I published my orders, dated June 4, 1855. The Quartermaster-General of the State, General Kibbe, also came to San Francisco, took an office in the City Hall, engaged several rooms for armories, and soon the men began to enroll into companies. In my general orders calling out the militia, I used the expression, "When a sufficient number of men are enrolled, arms and ammunition will be supplied." Some of the best men of the "Vigilantes" came to me and remonstrated, saying that collision would surely result; that it would be terrible, etc. All I could say in reply was, that it was for them to get out of the way. "Remove your fort; cease your midnight councils; and prevent your armed bodies from patrolling the streets." They inquired where I was to get arms, and I answered that I had them *certain*. But personally I went right along with my business at the bank, conscious that at any moment we might have trouble. Another committee of citizens, a conciliatory body, was formed to prevent collision if possible, and the newspapers boiled over with vehement vituperation. This second committee was composed of such men as Crockett, Ritchie, Thornton, Bailey Peyton, Foote, Donohue, Kelly, and others, a class of the most intelligent and wealthy men of the city, who earnestly and honestly desired to prevent bloodshed. They also came to me, and I told them that our men were enrolling very fast, and that, when I deemed the right moment had come, the Vigilance committee must disperse, else bloodshed and destruction of property would inevitably follow. They also had discovered that the better men of the Vigilance Committee itself were getting tired of the business, and thought that in the execution of Casey and Cora, and the banishment of a dozen or more rowdies, they had done enough, and were willing to stop. It was suggested that, if our Law-and-Order party would not arm, by a certain day near at hand the committee would disperse, and some of their leaders would submit to an indictment and trial by a jury of citizens, which they knew would acquit them of crime.

One day in the bank a man called me to the counter and said, "If you expect to get arms of General Wool, you will be mistaken, for I was at Benicia yesterday, and heard him say he would not give them." This person was known to me to be a man of truth, and I immediately wrote to General Wool a letter telling him what I had heard, and how any hesitation on his part would compromise me as a man of truth and honor; adding that I did not believe we should ever need the arms, but only the *promise* of them, for "the committee was letting down, and would soon disperse and submit to the law," etc. I further asked him to answer me categorically that very night, by the Stockton boat, which would pass Benicia on its way down about midnight, and I would sit up and wait for his answer. I did wait for his letter, but it did not come, and the next day I got a telegraphic dispatch from Governor Johnson, who, at Sacramento, had also heard of General Wool's "back-down," asking me to meet him again at Benecia that night.

I went up in the evening boat, and found General Wool's aide-de-camp, Captain Arnold, of the Army, on the wharf, with a letter in his hand, which he said was for me. I asked for it, but he said he knew its importance, and preferred we should go to General Wool's room together, and the general could hand it to me in person. We did go right up to General Wool's, who took the sealed parcel and laid it aside, saying that it was literally a copy of one he had sent to Governor Johnson, who would doubtless give me a copy; but I insisted that I had made a written communication, and was entitled to a written answer.

At that moment several gentlemen of the "Conciliation party," who had come up in the same steamer with me, asked for admission and came in. I recall the names of Crockett, Foote, Bailey Peyton, Judge Thornton, Donohue, etc., and the conversation became general, Wool trying to explain away the effect of our misunderstanding, taking good pains not to deny his promise made to me personally *on the wharf.* I renewed my application for the letter addressed to me, then lying on his table. On my statement of the case, Bailey Peyton said, "General Wool, I think General Sherman has a right to a written answer from you, for he is surely compromised." Upon this Wool handed me the letter.

I opened and read it, and it denied any promise of arms, but otherwise was extremely evasive and non-committal. I had heard of the arrival at the wharf of the Governor and party, and was expecting them at Wool's room, but, instead of stopping at the hotel where we were, they passed to another hotel on the block above. I went up and found there, in a room on the second floor over the bar-room, Governor Johnson, Chief-Justice Terry, and one or two others. All were talking furiously against Wool, denouncing him as a d—d liar, and not sparing the severest terms. I showed the Governor General Wool's letter to me, which he said was in effect the same as the one addressed to and received by him at Sacramento. He was so offended that he would not even call on General Wool, and said he would never again recognize him as an officer or gentleman. We discussed matters generally, and Judge Terry said that the Vigilance Committee were a set of d—d pork-merchants; that they were getting scared, and that General Wool was in collusion with them to bring the State into contempt.

About that time Crockett and his associates sent up their cards, but Terry and the more violent of the Governor's followers denounced them as no better than "Vigilantes," and wanted the Governor to refuse even to receive them. I explained that they were not "Vigilantes," that Judge Thornton was a "Law-and-Order" man, was one of the first to respond to the call of the sheriff, and that he actually went to the jail with his one arm the night we expected the first attempt at rescue, etc. Johnson then sent word for them to reduce their business to *writing*. They simply sent in a written request for an audience, and they were then promptly admitted.

After some general conversation, the Governor said he was prepared to hear them, when Mr. Crockett rose and made a prepared speech embracing a clear and fair statement of the condition of things in San Francisco, concluding with the assertion of the willingness of the committee to disband and submit to trial after a certain date not very remote. All the time Crockett was speaking, Terry sat with his hat on, drawn over his eyes, and with his feet on a table. As soon as Crockett was through, they were dismissed, and Johnson began to prepare a written answer. This was scratched, altered, and amended to suit the notions of his counselors, and at last copied and sent. This answer amounted to little or nothing. Seeing that we were powerless for good, and that violent counsels would prevail under the influence of Terry and others, I sat down at the table, and wrote my resignation, which Johnson accepted in a complimentary note on the spot, and at the same time he appointed to my place General Volney E. Howard, then present, a lawyer who had once been a member of Congress from Texas, and who was expected to drive the d—d pork-merchants into the bay at short notice.

I went soon after to General Wool's room, where I found Crockett and the rest of his party; told them that I was out of the fight, having resigned my commission; that I had neglected business that had been intrusted to me by my St. Louis partners; and that I would thenceforward mind my own business, and leave public affairs severely alone.

We all returned to San Francisco that night by the Stockton boat, and I never afterward had anything to do with politics in California, perfectly satisfied with that short experience. Johnson and Wool fought out their quarrel of veracity in the newspapers and on paper. But, in my opinion, there is not a shadow of doubt that General Wool did deliberately deceive us; that he had authority to issue arms, and that, had he adhered to his promise, we could have checked the committee before it became a fixed institution, and a part of the common law of California. Major-General Volney E. Howard came to San Francisco soon after; continued the organization of militia which I had begun; succeeded in getting a few arms from the country; but one day the Vigilance Committee sallied from their armories, captured the arms of the "Law-and-Order party," put some of their men into prison, while General Howard, with others, escaped to the country; after which the Vigilance Committee had it all their own way.

Subsequently, in July, 1856, they arrested Chief-Justice Terry, and tried him for stabbing one of their constables, but he managed to escape at night, and took refuge on the *John Adams*. In August, they hanged Hetherington and Brace in broad day-light, without any jury-trial; and, soon after, they quietly disbanded. As they controlled the press, they wrote their own history, and the world generally gives them the credit of having purged San Francisco of rowdies and roughs; but their success has given great stimulus to a dangerous principle, that would at any time justify the mob in seizing all the power of government; and who is to say that the Vigilance Committee may not be composed of the worst, instead of the best, elements of a community?

THE REMARKABLE WEATHER

IN AND ABOUT San Francisco it is rarely ever too cold or too hot; though the weather frequently changes, three or four times in a single day, from calm and warm to boisterous and cool, and from boisterous and cool to calm and warm again. In other places, where the days are intolerably close and sultry, it is necessary to have one or two blankets to sleep under at night. The remarkable aridity and unfruitfulness of the country at large, may be ascribed to the protracted drought of the summer which begins in April, and lasts until about the middle of November.

—Hinton Rowan Helper,
The Land of Gold

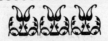

THE CITY BY THE SEA

by

GEORGE STERLING

At the end of our streets is sunrise;
At the end of our streets are spars;
At the end of our streets is sunset;
At the end of our streets—the stars.

Ever the winds of morning
Are cool from the flashing sea—
Flowing swift from our ocean,
Till the fog-dunes crumble and flee.

Slender spars in the offing,
Mast and yard in the slips—
How they tell on the azure
Of the sea-contending ships!

Homeward into the sunset
Still unwearied we go,
Till the northern hills are misty
With the amber of afterglow.

Stars that sink to our ocean,
Winds that visit our strand,
The heavens are your pathway,
Where is a gladder land!

At the end of our streets is sunrise;
At the end of our streets are spars;
At the end of our streets is sunset;
At the end of our streets—the stars.

THE TERRY-BRODERICK DUEL

by

BEN C. TRUMAN

AMONG the many duels in the early days of California none excited so much interest, and none had such an influence on politics and society, as the fatal meeting between David C. Broderick and David S. Terry. They were representative men. One was a United States Senator, and the other Chief-Justice of the Supreme Court of California. They were filling important niches in the history of the young State.

Moreover, no such political antagonism had existed since the days of Burr and Hamilton. The Republican Party was a healthy infant, and growing rapidly. The State was controlled by a two-winged Democracy. Gwin, Terry, Ashe, Brooks, Benham, and others worked the Lecompton wing, and Broderick, the friend of Stephen A. Douglas and an ardent opponent of the extension of slavery, was the soul of the anti-Lecompton wing. He and his followers occupied middle ground between nascent Republicanism and the Southern slave-Democracy. The friends of the Administration cherished a deep hatred for Broderick. With him out of the way, they might reunite the party on the old basis and control it. Broderick and his friends had thwarted the ambition of the "chivalry." After a desperate struggle he had secured a seat in the United States Senate, and had brought the haughty Gwin to terms. To retain his own seat in that body, Gwin had given the stonecutter a document pledging himself not to meddle with the official patronage of the Pacific coast. This document was known as the "scarlet letter." Broderick had said in a speech that

From *The Field of Honor* by Ben C. Truman. Fords, Howard & Hulbert, New York, 1884.

its writer ought to be as clearly marked for political ostracism as
Hester Prynne was socially marked by the initial on her breast. It was
a fatal letter. Politicians said that the man who had it in his possession
was doomed.

The immediate cause of the quarrel grew out of a speech made
by Judge Terry before the Lecompton Democratic State Convention
in Sacramento in 1859. He called Broderick an arch-traitor. He said:

"They (the anti-Lecomptonites) are the followers of one man, the
personal chattels of a single individual whom they are ashamed of.
They belong, heart, soul, body, and breeches, to David C. Broderick.
They are yet ashamed to acknowledge their master, and are called
themselves, aye, forsooth, Douglas Democrats, when it is known, well
known to them as to us, that the gallant Senator from Illinois, whose
voice has always been heard in the advocacy of Democratic principles,
who now is not disunited from the Democratic Party, has no affilia-
tion with them, no feeling in common with them. Mr. President and
gentlemen, I am mistaken in denying their right to claim Douglas
as a leader. Perhaps they do sail under the flag of Douglas; but it is
the banner of the Black Douglass, whose name is Frederick, not
Stephen."

Broderick read this speech while at breakfast in the International
Hotel, and grimly smiled. "I see," he remarked to D. W. Perley, a
lawyer and a friend of the Gwin faction "that Terry has been abusing
me. I now take back the remark that I once made that he is the only
honest judge on the Supreme bench. I was his friend when he was in
need of friends, for which I am sorry. Had the Vigilance Committee
disposed of him as they did of others, they would have done a righteous
act."

He alluded to Terry's arrest by the Vigilantes in August, 1856,
charged with cutting a man named Sterling A. Hopkins, in the attempt to free from arrest Reuben Maloney. Had Hopkins died, Terry
would probably have hanged. As it was, it took the strongest influence,
Masonic, press, and other, to save him from banishment.

Perley resented Broderick's remark. He professed to be a warm
friend of Judge Terry, and even went so far as to challenge the
Senator on his own account. His challenge was curtly declined with
the contemptuous remark, "Sir, I fight only with gentlemen of my
own position." Perley hurried off to Terry and repeated Broderick's

slighting remarks. The spark did not need fanning. It was already alight. The Judge wrote a letter of inquiry, to which Broderick returned the following reply:

"Friday Evening, September 9, 1859.

"Hon. D. S. Terry: Yours of this date has been received. The remarks made by me were occasioned by certain offensive allusions of yours concerning me, made in the Convention at Sacramento, and reported in the *Union* of the 25th of June. Upon the topic alluded to in your note of this date, my language, so far as my recollection serves me, was as follows: 'During Judge Terry's incarceration by the Vigilance Committee I paid two hundred dollars a week to support a newspaper in his (your) defence. I have also stated heretofore that I considered him (Judge Terry) the only honest man on the Supreme bench. But I take it all back.' You are the proper judge as to whether this language affords good ground for offence.

'I remain, etc.,

D. C. Broderick."

Judge Terry considered the Senator's remarks "fighting talk," and there was a resort to the code. Calhoun Benham, S. H. Brooks, and Thomas Hayes attended to his interests, and Joseph C. McKibben, David D. Colton, and Leonidas Haskell acted for Senator Broderick. As to the niceties of affairs of honor, the gentlemen who assisted Terry were much superior to Broderick's friends. McKibben was a Congressman, and probably had never before participated in a formal duel. D. D. Colton had been sheriff of Siskiyou and the hero of many rough-and-tumble fights incident to his office in those lawless days. Haskell was an every-day man, who dabbled in politics without neglecting his business. Benham, Brooks, and Hayes, on the contrary, had figured repeatedly on the field, the latter as principal on one or two occasions.

A meeting had been arranged for the 12th of September, at sunrise, near the boundary-lines of San Mateo and San Francisco counties. The principals and their friends were all on the ground, when the chief of police, Martin J. Burke, placed them under arrest.

They were brought before Police Justice H. P. Coon, and discharged on the ground that there had been no actual misdemeanor.

John A. McGlynn, a brother of a well-known Roman Catholic clergyman in New York; Andrew J. Butler, a brother of General B. F. Butler; and other friends of Broderick, had tried to dissuade him from fighting. He had listened to all their arguments, and had replied that his mind was made up—the duel could not be avoided with honor. He was quiet and composed, but inflexible.

It was thought that the arrest would stop further proceedings, but the principals were determined to have it out. The fact that a second meeting was to take place on the following morning was whispered to a few reporters under a promise of secrecy, and at midnight several vehicles left the city and drove toward the Laguna de la Merced, about ten or twelve miles from the city. Here the fight was to take place. It was cold, and the drivers frequently lost their way in the darkness. The breeze from the ocean cut like a knife.

As day broke a buggy was descried a short distance ahead, occupied, as we learned on overtaking it, by Henry Fritz, a confidential friend of Broderick. Notwithstanding his excessive corpulence, Fritz was blue with cold, and his teeth rattled like castanets. Another buggy, containing Dr. Hammond, Judge Terry's surgeon, was driven out of a small cañon. "All right," was the general exclamation; "we are on the track now." The doctor and Fritz laughed in concert. "We thought to throw you newspaper people off the scent," said the doctor, "but we find it is no use."

Other carriages were seen coming from different directions and skirting the lake. They all drew up at a rail fence which marked the boundaries of a milk ranch owned by one Davis, who rubbed his eyes in sleepy astonishment at such an irruption of visitors. There was not much conversation. One or two remarks were made, and a partisan of Terry's audibly whispered that Broderick might be carried dead from the field. Everybody seemed to feel that to one man, at least, that beautiful day was to be a day of death. Vaulting over the fence, the party went up a valley the centre of which had been selected as the scene of the encounter. Mr. Broderick had slept at the Lake House, near by, and with his friends was early on the ground. Judge

Terry and his friends were also prompt. About eighty spectators were present.

The seconds held a conference, and the pistols were examined and loaded. Judge Terry won the choice of weapons by the toss of a half-dollar. Mr. Hayes marked off the prescribed distance, ten paces, and warned spectators to get out of the line of fire. Meantime the respective seconds were busied about their principals. The Terry party were cool and collected, as became old hands at the business. Mr. Broderick's friends were apparently nervous and hesitating. One incident was not calculated to put the Senator in good heart. Mr. Haskell partly untied the Senator's cravat, and then walked off a few paces, wringing his hands as though overcome by his feelings. He then returned and removed the neckerchief.

Broderick was dressed in a long black surtout, and wore a soft wool hat drawn down over his brow. Terry was similarly attired. When the principals were placed, the punctilios of the code were observed. Calhoun Benham, Terry's chief second, approached Mr. Broderick, and passed his hands closely over his sides and chest, searching for concealed mail. Mr. McKibben made a similar examination of Terry, but he only touched his fingers to his waistcoat, bowed and withdrew. It has been thought that Mr. Benham's action irritated the Senator and impaired his poise. Before this Mr. Broderick had taken some coins from his vest-pocket and passed them to Mr. McKibben. Terry gave his loose change to Benham, who scattered it contemptuously on the sward. All things being in readiness, the pistols were cocked and their hair-triggers set by the seconds. They were then delivered to the combatants. It was observed at this time that Mr. Broderick appeared nervous and ill at ease. He repeatedly twitched the skirts of his surtout, as though they were in his way. He was also somewhat out of position, and Mr. McKibben corrected him. Broderick closely measured with his eye the ground between himself and Terry. Benham read the conditions of the meeting, and Mr. Colton followed with instructions as to the firing. He had won the word. Broderick was still nervous, but Terry stood firm and erect, a silhouette against the early morning light. The men held their weapons muzzle downward. A moment of painful silence ensued.

"Gentlemen," said Mr. Colton, in a clear voice, "are you ready?"

Both replied, but Broderick delayed a few seconds. He then said, "I am ready."

"Fire! One—" There was a report from the Senator's pistol. It was answered in a second by Terry's weapon. Broderick's pistol was discharged before he brought it to a level. This was probably caused by the fineness of the hair-trigger and his want of familiarity with that particular weapon. The bullet buried itself in the ground, two thirds of the distance between himself and his antagonist. It was a splendid line-shot, fallen short of its mark. Broderick had the reputation of being an expert with the pistol, and this result surprised those who knew his skill. With the crack of Terry's weapon Broderick winced, turned half round, and then made an effort to recover himself. "Hard hit," his friends murmured. These words were proved by his unavailing efforts to maintain an upright position. He drooped until finally he fell prone on the ground, with his pale face toward the sky. He was hard hit.

Juggling in the choice of weapons was openly charged in the newspapers. Bernard Lagoards, the armorer, a Frenchman, loaded Mr. Broderick's pistol, and Mr. Brooks charged the one intended for Judge Terry. The Judge had won the choice, and had chosen a weapon owned by R. Beard, a friend of Dr. Aylette, physician of the Insane Asylum at Stockton. They had been in the Doctor's possession two years. The armorer said that there was a difference in the pistols; that used by Senator Broderick carried the lightest bullet. He suggested that the usual mode in choosing weapons was to select those with which both parties were unfamiliar. He asked McKibben why he did not force his principal to use his (the armorer's) pistols. McKibben replied that Terry had won the choice, and the pistols were brought by his seconds. The armorer had never seen the pistols before, but maintained, in the presence of the seconds, that they were too light. He said that they could be discharged by a jar or jerk, and even went so far as to say that their hair-triggers might be so finely set that the breath of a strong-lunged man would discharge them.

The wounded Senator lay on the sward, with his head supported by his seconds, Colton and Haskell. His surgeon, Dr. Von Loehr, was nervous, and seemed uncertain how to act, and incapable of taking prompt measures. Mr. Broderick's life was ebbing away, and his face was pallid. Mr. Brooks, one of Terry's seconds, advanced, and, on behalf of his principal, tendered the services of his surgeon, Dr. Hammond.

"Yes, for God's sake," exclaimed McKibben, who was greatly excited, "send some one here, or Mr. Broderick will die where he lies!"

Dr. Hammond then came to Dr. Loehr's assistance, and cut away the wounded man's clothing, exposing his chest and the wound. It was a sorry sight. With every breath arterial blood spurted from the wound in bright jets and stained the fair skin. The group surrounding the fallen man shuddered. Strength of constitution, fortified by abstemious habits, might enable him to hold death off for a short time, but the brightness of the blood told that he was doomed. The ball entered the right breast between the second and third ribs, passing under the sternum, fracturing the edge, and then took a course over the heart, through the upper lobe of the left lung, striking the fifth rib on the left side, and proceeding upward, passed through the left armpit. Its tortuous course was remarkable, and the rending of the vitals must have been terrible. No wonder the Senator was unable to maintain an erect position for a second shot, and no wonder that he sank nerveless to the earth.

"Baker," said he, on his dying bed, to his fast friend, the orator, soldier, and statesman,—and they were the last words he spoke to him,—"Baker, I tried to stand firm when I was struck; but I could not. The blow blinded me."

As soon as Broderick fell, Davis, the owner of the ranch, who had been silently regarding the proceedings, started to his feet and shouted, "That is murder, by God!" He moved toward Terry, as though intending to assault him. He was intercepted by bystanders, who said that it was folly to provoke additional bloodshed. Davis brushed them aside, exclaiming, "I am Broderick's friend; I am not going to see him killed in that way. If you are men, you will join me in avenging his death."

"We know you are Mr. Broderick's friend, but we know as well that if you attack Terry there will be a general fight, and but few will get off this ground alive. Think a moment before you do this thing."

Luckily, this scene was not witnessed, nor the remarks overheard, by any of the Terry partisans, else there would have been a bloody conflict, whether their leader had been attacked or not. The milkman was quieted and sat himself down, breathing threatenings of slaughter.

Terry remained in his place. His arms were folded, and the muzzle of a pistol projected behind him. He stood erect, with face raised and an inquiring look, as though awaiting a demand for a second shot. His coolness and nerve were shown in the remark just after he delivered the fire: "The shot is not mortal; I have struck two inches to the right." Others say his words were, "Ah! I struck him a little too high."

Being assured of the helpless condition of his antagonist, he moved toward the carriages with his friends and then drove hastily to the city. He went to Stockton, where he owned a ranch, and quietly awaited events. Here he was arrested on the 23 day of September by two San Francisco police officers, brought to the city, and put under ten thousand dollars' bond.

Mr. Broderick was removed from the ground three quarters of an hour after he was shot, placed on a mattress in a spring wagon, and taken to the residence of his friend, Leonidas Haskell, at Black Point. He lingered in great pain until Friday, September 16, and expired at 9.20 in the morning. He did not speak much during his suffering. From his rent and torn breast no breath came without exertion. Words were agony. He felt, to use his own expression, as though a thousand-pound weight was pressing on his chest. But he did utter a sentiment which had great significance a few years after his death. "They have killed me," he said, "because I was opposed to slavery and a corrupt administration."

The death-bed scene was deeply affecting. The viaticum had been given by the priest, Father Maraschi. Around the couch, which had been drawn into the centre of the room, weeping friends were grouped—those who had honored and loved him in life, and were now assembled to witness, through their tears, the exit of that great soul that had won men and controlled councils. There were present Mr. and Mrs. Haskell, the Misses McDougall, Miss Cook, Colonel Edward D. Baker, ex-Governor McDougall, Hon. J. C. McKibben, General Colton, Hon. John Conness, Colonel A. J. Butler, John A. McGlynn, Elliott J. Moore, Herman Wohler, Moses Flannagan, and many others, prominent in social and political life, whom he had "grappled to his heart with hooks of steel." Governor McDougall stepped forward and closed the eyes that had looked their last.

Editors wrangled over the dead in a way that led to the belief that a feeling of self-interest had mingled with their sorrow. The *Times,* edited by C. A. Washburne, brother of E. B. Washburne, seemed to say, "See how much greater is my grief for the dead Senator than yours." Many expressions never uttered were credited to Broderick. Washburne was working in the interests of the Republican Party. The *Alta* and *Call* mourned without stint, while the *Bulletin* lost sight of individuals in considering the superior question of the *morale* of duelling. The *Herald* (Lecompton) had no tears for the fallen. It criticised only the mode of the killing, and patted Terry on the back. One of its articles brought out this reply:

"In the *Herald* this morning we are reported as saying, 'And if there was any advantage on either side it was surely with Mr. Broderick.' We have not made this statement, nor, at the same time, have we imputed any unfairness to Judge Terry or his seconds. Further, we have passed no judgment on the press and its peculiar views as to the unfortunate affair, our duty being simply to correct statements emanating either from the friends of Mr. Broderick or Mr. Terry not warranted by the facts. This we have done in all cases. The *Herald* of this morning contains the most serious misstatement we have yet seen. Mr. Broderick had *not* the choice of weapons, nor were his friends aware, until the publication of the *Herald,* that one weapon was easier on the trigger than the other. Had we believed there was any unfairness there could have been no meeting.

"Jos. C. McKibben,
"David D. Colton.
"San Francisco, September 16, 1859."

From the time that Broderick was wounded the whole city was in mourning. Every consideration was subordinate to anxiety as to his condition. His death was a public calamity. The remains were brought to the Union Hotel, corner of Kearny and Merchant streets, where they lay in state amid pyramids of flowers until Sunday, the 18th. Crowds of citizens awaited the body. Among others an old man walked up to the coffin, with hands crossed over his chest, whispering a prayer. He touched the forehead of the dead, and murmured, "God bless you! Your soul's in heaven! God bless you! California has this day lost her noblest son."

Then, reverently crossing himself, he walked slowly away. The incident is cited as an example of Broderick's peculiar power in creating a following aside from those who looked to him for patronage. This magnetic power was the bedrock of his political strength. He inspired affection other than that of mere gratitude.

The funeral took place at half-past one o'clock on Sunday afternoon. Before the procession moved, Colonel Edward D. Baker took a conspicuous place on the plaza, known as Portsmouth Square, opposite the hotel, and in the presence of a concourse that embraced nearly the entire adult population of the city pronounced a funeral oration. The beauty and magnificence of this tribute to a dead friend are historical. The orator's voice was heard far and wide, and those who crowded the streets leading to the plaza, for blocks away, caught his words distinctly. The peroration was as follows:

"But the last words must be spoken, and the imperious mandate of death must be fulfilled. O brave heart, we bear thee to thy rest; thus surrounded by tens of thousands we leave thee to the equal grave. As in life no other voice among us so rang its trumpet-blast upon the ear of freedom, so in death its echoes will reverberate amid our mountains and our valleys until truth and valor cease to appeal to the human heart.

"Good friend! True heart! Hail and farewell!"

THOSE RESTLESS
SAN FRANCISCANS

To ACQUAINT ourselves with the character of the speculators and business men in San Francisco would be a curious and interesting task. They are certainly the shrewdest rascals in the world, and a straight-forward, honest man, who acts upon principle and adheres to a legitimate system of dealing, can no more cope with them than he can fly. But nothwithstanding their shrewdness, and I might say, in some instances, their excellent business qualifications, they exhibit less method and system in their transactions than any class of traders I ever saw. Whatever they do is done in a helter-skelter, topsy-turvy sort of way, as if they had just fallen out of their element, and were scrambling to get back again. They never take time to do a thing well but are always bustling about in such a manner, that one would suppose they were making preparations for some calamitous emergency, rather than attending to the every day routine of an established occupation. This restless disposition is characteristic of the inhabitants of every part of the State. . . .

—Hinton Rowan Helper,
The Land of Gold

SAN FRANCISCO
IN THE 'FIFTIES

by

HUBERT HOWE BANCROFT

The People

To THE GREEKS, Delphi was the centre of the earth; to Jews and Christians, Jerusalem; to Californians, San Francisco.

Pastoral San Francisco was but a hamlet. Though a seaport, it had little to do with the sea, and was more like a cluster of houses in the country than a commercial town. The presidio maintained the dignity of government and war, and the mission the dignity of religion, so that for the traffickers at the cove little dignity remained or was required. Even when the galvanic shock of gold-discovery struck the place, it did not immediately assume large proportions, but rather stood stupefied for a moment before setting out on its broad pathway of progress.

Hence it was that during the winter of 1848-9 the place did not grow much, nor was it very large by the end of 1849. The principal buildings were clustered around the plaza, or Portsmouth square; brick structures were few, and there was not one really substantial building in the place. The greater part of the town consisted of tents and small shanties made out of packing-boxes, with some not very good houses of more pretentious construction. The few travelled streets were little better than mire during the rains, while the sidewalks were made of barrel staves and narrow pieces of board.

The autumn of 1850 saw quite a city-like settlement round Yerba

---

From *The Works of Hubert Howe Bancroft,* The History Co., San Francisco, 1888.

Buena cove. Prices of most necessities and some luxuries had come down within the reach of the masses, but were still high enough. Several new journals were started, such as the *Pacific News* and *Commercial Bulletin*. The El Dorado gambling house, from a canvas tent, had become a fine three-story brick building. The bay was noisy with steamers, many of which were transformed sailing boats, with old boilers which burst with the slightest provocation.

The fire of 1850 put an end to many irregularities. People then began to build in a more substantial manner. The fire of 1851, however, made a clean sweep of all that had been done, and the city began to assume a more regular appearance. Brick houses and planked streets took the place of the huddled huts and tents of the previous years. The bay was alive with shipping; by midsummer over a hundred steamers had entered and departed.

"Old things are passing away," sighed the meditative man, by old things referring to things two years old. The hills were being cut down and the hollows filled up. Montgomery street, which was the original high-water mark, was now in the heart of the city, and Sansome street, which had been filled up between Jackson and California streets, was the new water line. The water lots between Montgomery and Sansome were first piled, and then filled in. South of California, the steam excavator was busy scooping up the sand-hills, and dropping them into the low places along the border of the cove. A rail-track was laid on Battery street, along which cars were seen flying back and forth all day, dumping their loads into the water, the conductor, mounted on the foremost truck, lustily blowing his horn to give warning of approach.

The space bounded by Montgomery, Pacific, Jackson, and Kearny streets was, in the spring of 1851, a hollow filled with little wooden huts planted promiscuously, with numberless recess and fastnesses filled with Chileans—men, women, and children. The place was called Little Chile. The women appeared to be always washing, but the vocation of the men was a puzzle to the passers-by. Neither the scenery of the place nor its surroundings were very pleasant, particularly in hot weather. On one side was a slimy bog, and on the other rubbish heaps and sinks of offal. Notwithstanding, it was home to them, and from their filthy quarters they might be seen emerging on Sundays, the men washed and clean-shirted, and the women arrayed in smiling faces and bright-colored apparel. They could work and wallow patiently through the week provided they cold enjoy a little recreation and fresh air on Sunday. Whenever a vessel arrived from a home port, the camping ground presented a lively appearance. Round the chief hut or *tienda* lounged dirty men in parti-colored serapes and round-crowned straw hats, smoking drinking, and betting at monte. Most of these were either on their way to, or had lately returned from, the mines.

Walk Kearny street at night from California street to the Plaza. The shops are all closed, all but the saloons, mostly attended by a French or Spanish woman, and Cheap John auction stores, whose cries in husky voice and bad breath strive to roar above the jingling bells, before each door, where every one tries to ring down his neighbor. Passing along you step aside to avoid some reeling drunkard running into you, and as you approach the plaza, the blazing light from the thickly planted saloons glows in the thick, murky air without, and strains of mingled music from different bands fall upon the ear. Pouring in and out of temples dedicated to Bacchus and to Fortuna, are crowds of people of every hue, and tongue, and character under heaven.

But by 1853, an orderly, intelligent population was replacing the hurrying gold-seekers. Those who now purposed to make California their home, were resolved that the scum from eastern and European cities, and the convicts from the British penal colonies, should not be permitted to mar the fair prospects of the state, which sentiment led to popular tribunals, described in another volume.

Hundreds of Micawbers were always waiting for something, anything, to come along—waiting about the post-office, custom-house, and other federal and municipal free-soup houses; standing in auction rooms, and strolling down Long Wharf.

The country was filled with would-be great men—men who measured the greatness of their own worth by the fancied littleness of their neighbor. Every bosom beat high with aspirations. There was an indescribable stimulant in the business atmosphere, in mingling with men, not unlike that so often glorified in the physical, which chased away loneliness, generated excitement, stripped time of its monotony, and glued the heart of the adventurer forever to the soil.

Steamer Day

The signals on Telegraph Hill, semaphores that indicated ship arrivals to the town below, became so many and so intricate, and withal were so important to anxiously gazing expectants, that an enterprising lithographer conceived the idea of putting them on a chart where all could see and learn them. One night shortly after the publication of this chart, a newsboy sat in the top aloft of the theatre, cracking peanuts, and criticising the sons and daughters of Thespis, as they strutted their brief parts before him. Presently one rushed upon the stage with arms extended at right angles with his body, and exclaimed, "What means this my lord?" The boy who not only knew well the chart, but whose fancy was then revelling in the anticipated profits of his paper, cried out, "Side-wheel steamer!" The house, and the actor's arms, came down simultaneously. A story is like-wise told of a newly arrived emigrant across the plains, who, in applying this chart to the interpretation of the signals, mistook a windmill which stood near by for the arms of the tele-graph, and counting up the fans concluded that a fleet of clippers was coming in.

Twice or thrice a month the mail steamers, connecting San Francisco with New York by way of Panamá, departed and arrived. Both were peculiar and notable occasions.

It is difficult for one who has not lived it through to realize with what nervous pulsations these vessels were watched as they came and went. California was then well-nigh out of the world, beyond the pale of civilization, of Sabbath and home influence, of all the sweet memories and amenities that make life endurable. Her people were voluntary exiles, cut off from friends and all congenial society, doomed for a period to a life of self-abnegation and hard labor, and these days of steamer arrivals and departures were as links in the life-chain that was to bind the future to the past. The present went for nothing, or worse than nothing, perhaps; for it might be a nightmare, a horrible dream, a something to be blotted from the memory as soon as ended. When the steamer came in with passengers from home—the whole eastern seaboard, and west to the Missouri river, was then home to the expatriated of California—with perhaps friends on board, but above all with letters, what a flood of tender recol-lection rushed in upon the soul!

Therefore when the signal flag was unfurled, and the windmill looking indicator on Telegraph Hill stretched forth its long ungainly wooden arms and told the town of a steamer outside, a thrill went through the heart like that which Gabriel's trumpet sends into the fleshless bones of the dead. Some rushed to the hills; others mounted horses, and riding to the cliff, watched the little cloud of smoke under the skyline thicken and blacken; watched the vessel emerge as first the smoke-stack and spars, and then the hull appeared above the horizon; watched the little speck grow into a great leviathan, as lazily—oh! how lazily as it appeared to those on shore as well as those on board—it ploughed the sea and entered the Golden Gate; then returning watched the little boats as they put out from shore to board the monster—the quarantine officer's boat, perhaps, with the yellow flag, the Merchant's Exchange boat, and the express companies' boats; watched the white smoke from the steamer's gun curl up and float away in clouds, while the report reverbating through the streets roused the more abstracted occupants from their soul-absorbing work.

Then a stream of hacks, and wagons, and drays, and men on foot, hotel-runners, working-men, business-men, and loafers, set in toward the wharf. Proudly the great ship sweeps round the bay to the city front, as if conscious of the admiring gaze of the multitude; leisurely, and with majestic dignity, as if disdaining to make an exhibition of her strength. Now she stops her wheels, and yawns, and blows, and stretches her neck, after her fortnight's journey; then as she drops into her berth, the crowds on ship and shore begin their noisy jests and salutations. Hearts are there heavy with anxiety, waiting for tidings it may be which will affect their entire future; but on that sea of upturned faces you find no lowering clouds; the rippling waves are wreathed in smiles, and the stronger surges break into hilarity and badinage. Some are there to meet their friends, others from curiosity; some have climbed from small boats up the side of the vessel while she was approaching the wharf; others stand on the tops of piers, and when the ship is within a few feet leap on to the deck, where there is a scene of embracing, kissing, laughing, and crying, impossible to describe.

The passengers land and make their way to the hotels, when they luxuriate in a comfortable room, bath, and a table from which food once more seems palatable; clothes are taken from the trunk and put on, the creases in which mark the wearer as a new comer. Meanwhile lines begin to form at the post-office windows, although it may be twelve or twenty hours before the mails are ready for delivery. Thither congregate the anxiously expectant, the husband and father hungry for news from home, the lover with soft eyes and flushed cheek and tingling nerves, and in whose breast angels and imps alternately beat their tattoo as he waits to learn his fate; the rough miner, the merchant's clerk, the mechanic. Ah! never were letters so longed for or so prized. Alone in that motley crowd, for months without one word from home, the heart steeled to the world around them, deadened in that social Sahara, here was the only solace for heart-sickness, the only sustenance the soul would have perhaps for months to come.

Rapidly the lines lengthen, until perhaps five hundred persons are gathered there, having the appearance at a distance of a mob, but with the utmost order and regularity, each newcomer taking his place behind the last before him. There is no respect of persons, no crowding or josting; any attempt at unfairness is speedily put down by the omnipotent majority. The ragamuffin, who everyone knew never wrote or received a letter in his life, might take his stand beside the millionaire, and sell his place as opportunity offered, when near the window, to some one whose time was more valuable than money, which he frequently did for five, or ten, or twenty dollars. Some bring their stools and while away the time reading, smoking, and chewing. Eastern papers are sold by the newsboys, peripatetic cafés and liquor saloons walk about on French legs, and handcart hotels are rolled along the lines dispensing the ordinary edibles of the table. Finally, after long and tiresome waiting, the office window is opened and the line moves forward at the rate of a step in about three minutes.

Steamer-days, the day before the sailing of the steamer for the east, were the great tickings in social and commercial time. Bills were made to fall due on those days, letters must be written on that day, and collections and remittances made. Passengers must get ready, and if not before, they must secure their tickets. They were feverish, fidgety days. From morning till night collection clerks with a package of bills in one hand, and the mouth of a canvas coin-bag slung over the shoulder in the other, were rushing about the streets, and seldom was the office lamp extinguished before twelve or two o'clock.

On the morning of the sailing of the steamer, all work having been finished the day or evening previous, passengers go on board, attended by their friends to see them off. The idle and the curious of every caste and calibre likewise crowd the wharf and decks for an hour or two before the departure. Trunks are taken on board; the passengers, laden with packages of fruit, books, bottles, and boxes, find their respective places. In the cabin, the black bottle is frequently passed around, and the champagne made to flow freely. The forward part of the ship is filled with miners, going home with all the prestige of travel and adventure in strange lands. It is a matter of pride with many to be seen by their friends in their mining costume; so the bushy head and long beard are protected with care, and every hole in the battered hat, every patch in the woollen shirt, every dirt-stain on the greasy pantaloons, are regarded with hallowed affection. Thus appearing in his native village, with hints suggestive of secreted gold-dust, and inuendoes which seemed to say, "I could tell you a thing or two if I liked." "Perhaps John Robinson came back without his pile, and perhaps he didn't," the returned Californian is the hero of the hour.

It was common remark that more money went east in the steerage than in the cabin. Some carried buckskin bags of dust in their pockets, others in belts under their shirts, and guarded by an ominous-looking navy-revolver. Experience had made many shy of entrusting their hard earnings to banks and express companies, and freight on gold was high. Sometimes a party of two or three would put their fortunes in a carpet-bag, ten or twenty thousand dollars' worth of gold-dust, alternately guarding it, and never leaving it unwatched for a single instant during the whole voyage from San Francisco to New York, thereby saving in exchange the price of passage for each of them. Notwithstanding all their care, many returning miners were robbed by professional sharpers, who infested all the main avenues of travel, and followed their vocation regularly on the steamers between Aspinwall and New York.

Buying and Selling

If credits during the flush times were freely given, as a rule debts were promptly paid. Business was done upon honor. There was no law; away from the larger towns there were no pretensions in the way of tribunals for the collection of debts. Had there been such they would have received little patronage. If the debtor was ill and unable to work, why molest him? Poverty, there was none. When every rivulet and ravine yielded large returns to the application of pick and pan, he who was able to wield these implements could not be called poor. If the debtor was a rascal, and would not pay when he could, a knife would cut the difficulty, or a pistol-ball reach the wrong quicker than the law.

In the first flush of business upon the new American high-pressure principle, after gold had been discovered but before sufficient time had elapsed for cargoes to arrive from a distance, when money was plenty and prices had advanced in some instances a thousand per cent, the trick was to get goods, not to sell them. The two chief rival firms were Charles L. Ross, and Howard & Mellus, each of which kept a well-manned boat ready on the instant to shoot out toward the Golden Gate, on the approach of any merchant vessel, so as to forestall competitors in securing stock. To this end a sharp lookout was kept, as we may easily imagine, and every means adopted at once to catch the first view of the incoming vessels and blind the eyes of the others to the welcome sight. It happened one opaque, misty morning that the fog lifted for a moment only, just long enough for Ross' sentinel to see looming seaward a magnificent brig whose white sails in the vision seemed to fill the whole ocean. Ross and his crew were soon afloat, pulling hard in that direction. So was the rival boat, for the watchers had been watched, and such movements were well understood. The advantage, however, was with Ross, who beside having the start, knew where the vessel lay; and by pulling stoutly out of course and then escaping them in the fog, he threw his competitors off the scent, found the brig, crawled up the sides to the deck, and as coolly as possible after the fancy of Yankee traders, saluted the captain and opened negotiations. "What ye got?" demanded Ross. "Waal," the captain began, "there's some woolen shirts, a hundred and fifty or two hundred dozen—" "Stop a moment," exclaimed Ross who plainly heard the sound of oars approaching every moment nearer, "what'll you take for everything on board?" "Oh, I guess you are joking," simpered the skipper. "No,

I am not joking," said Ross, drawing from his pocket a handful of yellow gold. "What advance on your invoices will you take for all the merchandise in your ship?" The skipper pondered, not failing to notice the rapidly increasing noise of oars, this sharpwitted Boston captain; he pondered as he eyed the New York man thus met on this western side. It was a long proceeding, carefully collecting and laying in this cargo, in which twenty or more shippers were interested, and guiding it safely through divers-tempered winds, over 16,000 miles of ocean, to this very far-away port—it was a long proceeding to be disposed of summarily, for three months would have been a short time ordinarily in which to have sold the cargo. Three months; and fifty per cent. would have been regarded as a good round profit. "Come, captain, if you want to trade, and I take it that is what you are here for," said Ross, now growing a little nervous, "how much advance, and the money down?" The skipper looked him steadily in the eye, glanced significantly at Howard who was climbing up the side of the vessel, and answered slowly, "one hundred per cent." "I'll take it," Ross said. "This will bind the bargain," he added, as he passed over the handful of money. "And I'll make those woollen shirts pay for all the damned truck here," said the purchaser, as he regained his boat, swearing thus mildly not through lack of feeling, but because he was in training for a position as teacher in Wheeler's forth-coming Sabbath-school.

And the gentle Brannan, Sam; he learned to flaunt the Mormon's money bravely at the auctions. Sam delighted in auctions. Never was he so happy as when perched on a high box smoking a long cheroot, and sinking the small blade of his sharp knife into the soft pine. Gillespie was then at the head of the China trade, and the disposal of cargoes by auction was daily gaining favor. It saved so much trouble in the way of handling, and warehousing, and charging, and collecting, and prices were often better than when jobbed out.

One day, pursuant to notice, Gillespie put up a cargo of tea to sell. At the hour, there upon his box sat Sam, smoking, and spitting, and whittling, thinking perhaps of the extravagant price of wives in the market, and how much it would cost to people Zion at current rates; thinking of the temple to the living God which he was to rear in the wilderness; thinking of anything except lucre, and the price of tea. "Ten chests with the privilege," began Gillespie. "I will sell not less than ten chests, the purchaser to have the privilege of taking as much more at the price sold as he pleases." Around the open boxes merchants were blowing and crushing, and smelling and tasting; Sam sat serene. "And how much am I offered?" Gillespie went on. "Thirty-five cents, thirty-five; forty; and five; fifty; fifty-five cents I am offered; sixty. Are you all done gentlemen? Sixty cents, going; sixty cents, once; sixty cents, twice; third and last time—" "Sixty-one!" came from the top of the box. "Sixty-one, sixty-one cents, and sold. How much will take Mr. Brannan?" Now there was tea enough in that ship to give every grocer in town a good stock, and the bidders present had all so reckoned, and had deemed it folly running it up to a high price when they could just as well buy it low. The tea was then worth in the market one dollar and a quarter, or two dollars and a half, or five dollars, according as it was held and controlled. Brannan was the heaviest buyer there; he might take fifty chests out of the five hundred. So they reasoned, and were content that Sam, the ravenous, should first satisfy himself. Imagine, therefore their chagrin as in answer to the auctioneer's question, "How much will you take Mr. Brannan," they heard come from the top of the box, where the eyes were still bent on the continued whittling, in notes like the snarl of a coyote, "The whole damned concern!"

The prices of provisions were exceedingly unsteady, and those accustomed early in the morning to enter the markets with their baskets on their arms, for few delivered what they sold in those days, soon learned not to be surprised at anything in the way of prices. One day George Eggleston stood behind a box of fine fresh eggs talking with Bob Parker from whom he rented his stand when a customer came up. "How much are eggs?" "Six dollars." "What, a box?" "No, a dozen." "Give me a dozen." Something in the little trade struck Parker, who delighted in waggery, as a little ludicrous; probably it was the indifference with which the customer bought eggs, paying as cheerfully six dollars a dozen as six dollars a box. And the plot of a little joke instantly arose in his mind. "George," said he, when the customer had gone, "you will never make anything in this business if you don't keep better posted in prices." "How so?" demanded Eggleston. "Why, here you are selling eggs at six dollars a dozen, when the regular price everywhere is eighteen dollars," responded Parker. "But I know where I can get all I want at three dollars," said Eggleston. "That's it," replied Parker. "You haven't the business sense that tells a man how to make avail of his opportunities." Parker then turned to speak to a friend; but one ear was open to Eggleston's doings as a dapper little man of family stepped briskly up and began negotiations. "Hello, George, those are nice eggs; how do ye sell 'em." "Well," replied Eggleston, somewhat slowly and demurely, "eggs are a little up this morning; those are eighteen dollars a dozen." "All right," said the little man, "I'll take two dozen." And he laid down the thirty-six dollars far less grudgingly than the average Boston man would have given thirty-six cents for an equal quantity of the same commodity.

California gold largely increased the importation of silks, velvets, laces, jewelry, and other articles of luxury. It stimulated the building of houses, and carriages, the breeding of horses, but not the rearing of children; it increased the number of theatres, balls, parties, and concerts four fold, and advanced real estate values, and the prices of all commodities.

One day a man having 1,500 dozen eggs for sale, brought in by a coasting schooner, hailed a street merchandise-broker, of whom there were hundreds in those days, and insisted on his buying them, which the broker finally did, at 37½ cents a dozen. Right away the buyer began to sell at $4.50 a dozen, when the first seller exclaimed "What a fool I have been!" and securing the remainder at the last mentioned price, took them to Sacramento and sold them at $6 a dozen.

When tobacco was down, a man desirous of building a house on made ground tumbled in boxes of it, enough to form a foundation. Before the house was built tobacco was worth $1 a pound, more than a dozen such houses. Wanting a cross walk one threw in sacks of beans, which shortly after were worth thirty cents a pound.

Sickness was an expensive pastime in those days, and to indulge in some diseases was much more costly than in others. The fee-bill of the San Francisco medical society, organized June 22d, 1850, gives the prices for various visits and operations ranging from $16—one 'ounce,'—the lowest, to $1,000. A single visit was $32; a visit in regular attendance $32; for every hour detained $32 additional; advice $50 to $100; night visits an consulting physician $100; for various specified operations from $500 to $1,000.

Looking at the fleet of vessels at anchor in the harbor, one wondered how it was possible for three hundred thousand men to consume the cargoes of them all. But these three hundred thousand were equivalent to a million of mingled young and old, women, children, and men. Cities were to be built, farmes stocked, and mines developed, and all this required immense supplies and material. Little or nothing was then produced; even lumber for building, and vegetables and grain, were shipped from distant ports.

The captain of a vessel landing from a small boat, threw his valise upon the shore, and calling out to a ship's porter, "Carry that valise up to the hotel, my boy," pitched him a half dollar. Drawing back from the coin, which he had permitted to fall upon the ground, with an air of magnificent disgust, Jack drew from his pocket two half dollars, and throwing them over toward the captain, exclaimed as he turned upon his heel, "Carry it up yourself."

Some long-headed, leathery-brained Boston Yankee sent out shot. He had more shot than he could sell at home, and he had been told that there was considerable shooting among the miners; so he threw into a shipment a large consignment of shot. "Who wants shot in California!" exclaimed the consignee.

"Nobody," replied a broker.

"What'll ye give for 'em?"

"Don't want 'em."

"Didn't ask if you wanted them. I asked what you would give for them."

"Oh! ten or twenty cents a bag."

"They are yours at twenty cents."

The buyer then rubbed up his wits, and presently sold them at $4, to be run into revolver bullets. Then he bought a lot of tacks at ten cents a paper; for "what do people want of tacks who have no carpets?" he had asked. But when they began to tack up canvas houses, all those tacks went off lively at $2 a paper.

Of the firm of Priest, Lee and Company, at Sutter's Fort, was Christopher Taylor, who went from Oregon to San Francisco in 1848, on the brig *Henry,* which carried down produce, lumber, provisions, and passengers. In company with several Oregonians he proceeded up the Sacramento in the little vessel of Sutter and Hastings, arriving at Sutter's fort in September. There they hired a team to take them to Coloma, at which place they encamped. He whom Mr. Taylor called his partner went over to the middle branch, where he met friends whom he joined, and was soon making one or two hundred dollars a day. Being thus left alone, Taylor returned to the fort, arriving the 25th of September, and having in his pocket about twenty-five dollars. While considering in just what way he would make his fortune, his money being pretty well spent, he was accosted by his old friend Barton Lee. "Chris, what are you going to do?" "Well," said Taylor, "I think I shall go into business here." "You are just the man I want," returned Lee. "Come and dine with me."

Now either of these individuals had capital sufficient to pay a week's board; yet each thought the other possessed of abundance. Both, however, were enlightened before dinner was over. Lee had a little the advantage, as he had begun a large business by renting a room in the fort for a store, though he had nothing to put in it. For this he had promised to pay a rental of $100 a month; the first month's rent was still due. These interesting facts came out gradually between courses, as they might be told without affecting digestion.

"What do you think of it?" asked Lee after dinner. "I think I shall go into business," said Taylor. "Where is the stock to come from?" inquired Lee. "Do you know any one at San Francisco?" "No one," responded Taylor. "But we can get goods enough; we will buy them." There were at this time constantly arriving from the bay small sloops, laden with such goods as the miners required. Assuming the attitude of senior partner, although Lee had the room rented before him, Taylor said, "While I sweep out the store, you go down to the embarcadero and buy out the first vessel that arrives; buy everything on board." "But where will I get the money with which to pay for it all?" Lee wanted to know. "Leave that to me," replied Taylor. Lee did as he had been directed, and returned reporting the purchase of a cargo. "What does it consist of?" demanded Taylor. "Oregon bacon, flour, and boots and shoes," was the reply. "Exactly what we want," said Taylor. "About the pay—what arrangement did you make?" "Not any." "Well, in the morning say to him that his money is ready, and he shall have it as soon as the goods are landed." "That is all very well," said Lee, "but I would like to know what kind of a scrape I am getting into." "Does the captain drink?" "He soaks in it all the time." "All right; see that plenty of whiskey is always at hand; as fast as the cargo is discharged, send it to me, but do not let him take it out too rapidly; tell him our team is worked hard, and that we are so crowded we cannot stow it away faster."

All went on smoothly at the embarcadero. The master of the vessel thought Lee one of the best men he had ever met, exceedingly honest and truthful. Taylor handled himself lively about the store. He made trade brisk. Some of those in the crowd that was coming and going he knew; they and others wanted supplies. The goods as they arrived were not put into the store, but were piled up outside, thus making a grand display. Such large merchants must surely have large means, and good credit. The result of it all was the merchandise was sold as fast as delivered, and when the captain came for his money, the partners had enough to pay for the cargo, vessel, and all.

Duncan's Chinese salesrooms, thrown open the 5th of April, 1853, made a finer display of Oriental merchandise and curiosities than any similar establishment in Europe or America before or since. Spacious rooms, tastefully fitted up, were crowded with costly Asiatic goods, presenting the appearance more of a magnificent museum than a shop. The wealth and splendor of the Indies were spread out in tempting array for the benefit or ruin of purchasers—shawls from Thibet and Cashmere, silks embroidered by patient Hindoos, Chinese robes, ornaments in wood and ivory, work-boxes of Bombay, scented sandal-wood, grotesque carriages from Japan, porcelain ware, and paintings.

Beside the elaborately wrought silk and crape shawls, which were very popular at first, but which soon went out of fashion, the Chinese shops in San Francisco offered many curious articles. Carved ivory, representing animals, cities, pagodas, junks; puzzles, fans, chess and checker-men in wood and ivory; sandalwood roots twisted into peculiar shapes; gorgeous but flimsy silks, satins, and velvets; inlaid lacquered ware and china, silver filigree work, pictures, and a thousand other things, displaying the aesthetic shades in the minds of those half-civilized heathen.

Thus matters progressed. From a savage wilderness there soon emerged a settled community.

. . . . And Gambling

From the time of the gold discovery, which made all around of the roseate hue, there was an openness in all kinds of wickedness, a dash and abandon quite refreshing. Perhaps they play as heavily at the London gaming houses, and at the German springs, but the charm and freshness of unhackneyed nature is not there. In London, or even at the German springs, one would not often see a Sydney convict, a clergyman not three months from his preaching, a Harvard graduate, a Pennsylania farmer, and a New York newsboy all betting at the same table at the same time.

In California gambling there is little attempt at that quasi-respectability, or more plainly speaking, humbug, with which the lovers of a money hazard would fain gloss over their whist, chess, or horse-racing. It is the money men gamble for here, and they have no hesitation in saying so; hence, in a promiscuous assembly, each is attracted to such game as he fancies himself an adept in. The billiard-player gambles at pool, the card-sharper at poker, euchre, or old sledge, the lover of horses at racing, while the unskilled or indifferent lay down their gold at roulette, faro, or monte, notwithstanding in banking games the table has twenty or thirty per cent the advantage. The open-handed well-to-do Californian who flings his dollars around for the mere pleasure of seeing others scramble for them would call staking a few hundreds fun rather than gambling; but the individual earnest and constant at the tables, whatever the game or the amount staked, you may be sure is after 'blood,' as he himself would tell you.

The term gambler, in California, refers only to the professional, not being used in the abstract sense of one who gambles. The grocer deals out sugar and the gambler cards; he who buys a pound of sugar does not thereby become a grocer; neither is he who bets upon the cards, in California, called a gambler, that term being applied to a class *sui generis*. Wherever found, in the city or in the mines, one can almost always pick them out in a crowd. They are the best dressed men one meets; their pale, careworn, imperturbable faces wear an absent but by no means greedy air, and as they stand listlessly on the corner, or slowly and carelessly walk the street, by no means indifferent to a pretty female ankle, their calmly observant eyes, which are somewhat sunken in their sockets, seem to possess the faculty of looking through people while not looking at them, which habit was contracted at the gaming table.

The character of the typical gambler of the flush times is one of the queerest mixtures in human nature. His temperament is mercurial but non-volatilized; like quicksilver in cinnabar, its subtle vivacity is crystalized or massed in sulphur. Supreme self-command is his cardinal quality; yet, except when immersed in the intracacies of a game, his actions appear to be governed only by impulse and fancy. On the other hand his swiftest vengeance and cruellest butchery seem rather the result of policy than passion. His crimes are his profession's rather than his own. Confident with women, he is audacious with men. Prompt in action, expert, he is as ready to attack a dozen as one. He is never known to steal except at cards; and if caught cheating he either fights or blandly smiles his sin away, suffers the stakes to be raked down without a murmur, treats good-humoredly, and resumes the game unruffled. United with the coolest cunning is the coolest courage. He is as ready with his pistol as with his tooth-pick, but he never uses it unless he is right; then, he will kill a man as mercilessly as he would brush a fly from his immaculate linen.

Yet in his lonely disposition he is not quarrelsome, and never murders except professionally. He is a man to be feared, and in early times he was highly respected. He is all nerve, electrical in his organization, and depends wholly upon his own resources for justice and protection. He knows not fear; life to him is but a shuffle and a deal, in which the chances have already been calculated, and death at most is but the losing of the game—all matters of indifferent moment. In his disposition he is magnanimous; in his bearing noble; in his actions chivalrous. He will not do a mean thing; he discharges his pecuniary obligations with scrupulous exactitude, thus putting to shame the so-called English gentleman, and never disputes a bill. Desperate in an emergency, he is the foremost to brace peril; the most unselfish in suffering, and endures misfortune with heroic fortitude. He will fight for a friend as quickly as for himself, and share his last ounce with an unfortunate comrade. He will take every dollar from his victim should chance so order it, but he will as often give him back a portion should he stand in need of it. He has even been known to hand back money won from a simple-minded youth, with the advice not to indulge in play until he understands it better. Should a secret committee of some mining camp, seized with a spasm of moral reform, order him to leave the town, he receives the sentence with calm equanimity; should death be his portion he meets it with barbaric stoicism.

His pockets are always open, but his philanthropy knows no

formula; he will contribute to establish a church or a brothel, to support a Sunday-school or a swindle. He has his code of honor; but such things as orthodox conscience or conventional morality—he knows not and cares not what they are. In matters of justice he will act the unpopular part of advocate for a penniless horse thief, or falsely swear an alibi to save a friend. Over and over are told of them tales of the highest heroism; how one and another stood by some contemptible, ill-deserving, chance companion, knowing all the time that death was the penalty of chivalric devotion. Chance is his god, of whom he is a most faithful minister. Luck is his religion, and in it he is a firm believer and devotee. There is but one thing certain about it however, and that is, sooner or later it will change. To know when this point is reached is the sum of all knowledge.

In the practice of his profession, so long as his luck holds out good he never tires, and takes no rest. He accustoms himself to do without sleep, and if necessary can go for several days and nights without rest. He is a temperate man, being far too shrewd to benumb his faculties when he requires of them the keenest perception. Every now and then, while dealing his game, he orders drinks and cigars for his patrons, but sips sparingly from his own glass, as one puts on coal merely to prevent the fire from going out. He deals his game with the most perfect *sang froid,* and when undergoing the heaviest losses there is no trembling of fingers or change of expression in the colorless face, no twitching of muscles nor compression of lips; eye and manner maintain their cold indifference, and if compelled at last to announce his bankruptcy he does it with a smile such as never once before throughout the game lighted his impassive features. His views as to the common conduct of life are philosophic; in manner he is undemonstrative, and in speech reticent. In the practice of his profession he is bold in his operations, and fearless of consequences. His listless lounging and grave self-complacency contrast strongly with the fiery ebullitions of his surroundings. The restless emotion of the merchant and miner he regards with tranquil indifference. He interferes little in the affairs of others, is not specially skilled in matters of business, but he weighs and measures the character of those who play with him with the utmost nicety. He knows perfectly well whether one who draws a pistol or a knife means to use it; and on the instant takes measures accordingly. His brightly polished weapons are always at his elbow ready for immediate use, but he never touches them unless he deems it necessary, and then only to use them. He is studiously neat in his habits, and tends to foppishness in his costume. In the city his coat is of the latest cut, diamonds adorn his shirt, his high silk hat is black and glossy, and with a fancy-headed cane in a gloved hand he taps his closely-fitting well-polished boots. In the mines he sometimes affects the miner's dress, but his woollen shirt is gaily embroidered, and his slouched hat clean and graceful. A chain of gold specimens linked together is attached to a massive hunting watch, and massive rings of virgin gold and quartz encircle his soft white fingers. His sleek and well oiled hair is neatly brushed, his face closely shaven, leaving perhaps a mustache, but never whiskers long enough for exasperated losers to seize hold of. A fine cloth cloak is sometimes thrown loosely over the shoulder, and round the waist a bright scarlet silk sash supports his murderous weapons. When in funds he travels on a fat, sleek mule, with yellow buckskin gauntlets, broad-brimmed hat, and large silver spurs; if overtaken by adversity he walks.

The professional gambler seeks the best mines and the largest crowds. When gold begins to fail he migrates with the miners, following the diggers as the sea gull follows the pelican. Should the occupants of one camp become impecunious or disgusted and decline further play, he quietly packs up his tools, mounts his mule, and is off for another. Thus he may have to go for many days before he gets a game. In mountain towns his quarters may be a log cabin, with open broad fireplace, larger than the other cabins, but always occupying a central position. In tenting times his encampment was conspicuous for its ample accommodations, the whiteness of its canvas, and its gay trimmings.

It was in the larger cities, however, such as San Francisco, that this passion with the most unbridled license was displayed. In 1850 on two sides of the plaza were brick buildings devoted almost exclusively to gambling. There were the El Dorado, the Bella Union, the Rendez-vous, the Empire, the Parker House, and the Verandah. Here large halls were fitted up, some of them by companies formed in France, with oriental splendor. In one the ceiling, rich in fresco and gilt, was supported by glass pillars, pendant from which were great glass chandeliers. Around the walls were fine large paintings of nude female figures, and mirrors extending from floor to ceiling. Entering at night from the unlighted dismal street into an immense room lighted with dazzling brilliance, and loud with the mingled sound of musical instruments, the clink of coin and glasses, and the hum of human voices, was like passing from the dark depths to celestial brightness.

There were long rows of leather-covered mahogany tables on which were tempting spread out heaps of glittering gold and silver coin, nuggets, slugs, bars, and bags of dust, and where the votaries of chance might choose from every game known to the civilized gambling world.

With difficulty one elbowed one's way through the promiscuous crowd that here nightly congregated. There were men in black clothes, immaculate linen, and shining silk hats, merchants, lawyers, and doctors, Chileans, and Mexicans; Irish laborers, Negroes, and Chinamen, some crowded round the tables intently watching the games, others lounging about, smoking, chewing, spitting, drinking, swearing, now and then dropping a dollar, or a five, or ten, or twenty, or fifty-dollar piece, with real or well-feigned indifference as to the result. Now and then the games were momentarily interrupted by the crack of a pistol, and the loungers became a little demoralized as the ball whistled past their ears and lodged in the wall. If a man was killed or wounded he was taken out, but the nature of the affray was left to be learned from the morning papers, and in a few moments all was as before. Some of the saloons were open day and night, and paid enormous rents; six thousand dollars a month was paid for the El Dorado. There were also many private clubs or suites of rooms, where the players were more select and play ran higher. Nothing but gold coin was used in these places, and the stakes ran into the hundreds and thousands. A bet of any sum less than five dollars was regarded as contemptible. These rooms were often graced or disgraced by the presence of beautiful women, and sumptuous suppers were served, with the best of wines, all free to the patronizing visitors.

Like those of the pretty-waiter saloons and dance cellars of later times, the band may be an orchestra or regular musicians, a company of negro minstrels, a quartette of Mexican guitars, a piano, or if the room and counters be celestial, a Chinese scrape, squeak, and slam-bang.

Gambling from 1849 to 1852 was followed in San Francisco as a regular business, and there was no disgrace attached to the profession. Among the dealers of gambling games at that time were some of the most influential and talented citizens. But they were a transient race; they have gone forever. As a more refined civilization crept in and overwhelmed the low, the loose, and the vicious, gambling sank into disrepute. Law drove it behind locked doors and into windowless rooms. Then the gay gamblers of the olden time left the profession to a different class, and sought out new fields of distinction, perhaps in politics, law, or speculation.

"THE BEST BAD THINGS..."

I MAY not be a competent judge, but this much I will say, that I have seen purer liquors, better segars, finer tobacco, truer guns and pistols, larger dirks and bowie knives, and prettier courtezans, here in San Francisco, than in any other place I have ever visited; and it is my unbiased opinion that California can and does furnish the best bad things that are obtainable in America.

—Hinton Rowan Helper,
The Land of Gold

[1859]

TWENTY-FOUR YEARS AFTER

by

RICHARD HENRY DANA

On THE evening of Saturday, the 13th of August, 1859, the superb steamship *Golden Gate,* gay with crowds of passengers, and lighting the sea for miles around with the glare of her signal lights of red, green, and white, and brilliant with lighted saloons and state-rooms, bound up from the Isthmus of Panama, neared the entrance to San Francisco, the great centre of a world-wide commerce.

Miles out at sea, on the desolate rocks of the Farallones, gleamed the powerful rays of one of the most costly and effective light-houses in the world. As we drew in through the Golden Gate, another lighthouse met our eyes, and in the clear moonlight of the unbroken California summer we saw, on the right, a large fortification protecting the narrow entrance, and just before us the little island of Alcatraz confronted us,—one entire fortress. We bore round the point toward the old anchoring-ground of the hide ships, and there, covering the sand-hills and the valleys, stretching from the water's edge to the base of the great hills, and from the old Presidio to the Mission, flickering all over with lamps of its streets and houses, lay a city of one hundred thousand inhabitants. Clocks tolled the hour of midnight from its steeples, but the city was alive from the salute of our guns, spreading the news that the fortnightly steamer had come, bringing mails and passengers from the Atlantic world. Clipper ships of the largest size lay at anchor in the stream, or were girt to the wharves; and capacious high-pressure steamers, as large and showy as those of the Hudson or Mississippi, bodies of dazzling light, awaited delivery of our mails to take their courses up the Bay, stop-

---

From *Two Years Before the Mast,* Harper & Brothers, New York, 1840.

ping at Benicia and the United States Naval Station, and then up
the great tributaries—the Sacramento, San Joaquin, and Feather
Rivers—to the far inland cities of Sacramento, Stockton, and
Marysville.

The dock into which we drew, and the streets about it, were
densely crowded with express wagons and hand-carts to take luggage, coaches and cabs for passengers, and with men,—some looking
for friends among our hundreds of passengers,—agents of the press,
and a greater multitude eager for newspapers and verbal intelligence
from the great Atlantic and European world. Through this crowd I
made my way, along the well-built and well-lighted streets, as alive
as by day, where boys in high-keyed voices were already crying the
latest New York papers; and between one and two o'clock in the
morning found myself comfortably abed in a commodious room, in
the Oriental Hotel, which stood, as well as I could learn, on the
filled-up cove, and not far from the spot where we used to beach
our boats from the *Alert*.

Sunday, August 14th. When I awoke in the morning, and looked
from my window over the city of San Francisco, with its storehouses,
towers, and steeples; its court-houses, theatres, and hospitals; its daily
journals; its well-filled learned professions; its fortresses and light-
houses; its wharves and harbor, with their thousand-ton clipper
ships, more in number than London or Liverpool sheltered that day,
itself one of the capitals of the American Republic, and the sole
emporium of a new world, the awakened Pacific; when I looked
across the bay to the eastward, and beheld a beautiful town on the
fertile, wooded shores of the Contra Costa, and steamers, large and
small, the ferryboats to the Contra Costa, and capacious freighters
and passenger-carriers to all parts of the great bay and its tributaries,
with lines of their smoke in the horizon,—when I saw all these
things, and reflected on what I once was and saw here, and what
now surrounded me, I could scarcely keep my hold on reality at all,
or the genuineness of anything, and seemed to myself like one who
had moved in "worlds not realized."

I could not complain that I had not a choice of places of worship.
The Roman Catholics have an archbishop, a cathredral, and five or
six smaller churches, French, German, Spanish, and English; and
the Episcopalians a bishop, a cathedral, and three other churches;

the Methodists and Presbyterians have three or four each, and there are Congregationalists, Baptists, a Unitarian, and other societies. On my way to church, I met two classmates of mine at Harvard standing in a doorway, one a lawyer and the other a teacher, and made appointments for a future meeting. A little farther on I came upon another Harvard man, a fine scholar and wit, and full of cleverness and good-humor, who invited me to go to breakfast with him at the French house,—he was a bachelor, and a late riser on Sundays. I asked him to show me the way to Bishop Kip's church. He hesitated, looked a little confused, and admitted that he was not well up in certain classes of knowledge as in others, but by a desperate guess, pointed out a wooden building at the foot of the street, which any one might have seen could not be right, and which turned out to be an African Baptist meeting-house. But my friend had many capital points of character, and I owed much of the pleasure of my visit to his attentions.

The congregation at the Bishop's church was precisely like one you would meet in New York, Philadelphia, or Boston. To be sure the identity of the service makes one feel at once at home, but the people were alike, nearly all of the English race, though from all parts of the Union. The latest French bonnets were at the head of the chief pews, and business men at the foot. The music was without character, but there was an instructive sermon, and the church was full.

I found that there were no services at any of the Protestant churches in the afternoon. They have two services on Sunday: at 11 A.M., and after dark. The afternoon is spent at home, or in friendly visiting, or teaching of Sunday Schools, or other humane and social duties.

This is as much the practice with what at home are called the strictest denominations as with any others. Indeed, I found individuals, as well as public bodies, affected in a marked degree by a change of oceans and by California life. One Sunday afternoon I was surprised at receiving the card of a man whom I had last known, some fifteen years ago, as a strict and formal deacon of a Congregational Society in New England. He was a deacon still, in San Francisco, a leader in all pious works, devoted to his denomination and to total abstinence,—the same internally, but externally what a change! Gone was the downcast eye, the bated breath, the solemn, non-natural voice, the watchful gait, stepping as if he felt responsible for the balance of the moral universe! He walked with a stride, an uplifted open countenance, his face covered with beard, whiskers, and moustache, his voice strong and natural,—in short, he had put off the New England deacon and become a human being. In a visit of an hour I learned much from him about the religious societies, the moral reforms, the "Dashaways,"—total abstinence societies, which had taken strong hold on the younger and wilder parts of society,— and then of the Vigilance Committee, of which he had been a member, and of more secular points of interest.

In one of the parlors of the hotel, I saw a man of about sixty years of age, with his feet bandaged and resting in a chair, whom somebody addressed by the name of Lies. Lies! thought I, that must be the man who came across the country from Kentucky to Monterey while we lay there in the *Pilgrim* in 1835, and made a passage in the *Alert*, when he used to shoot with his rifle bottles hung from the topgallant studding-sail-boom-ends. He married the beautiful Doña Rosalia Vallejo, sister of Don Guadalupe. There were the old high features and sandy hair. I put my chair beside him, and began conversation, as any one may do in California. Yes, he was the Mr. Lies; and when I gave my name he professed at once to remember me, and spoke of my book. I found that almost—I might perhaps say quite—every American in California had read it; for when California "broke out," as the phrase is, in 1848, and so large a portion of the Anglo-Saxon race flocked to it, there was no book upon California but mine. Many who were on the coast at the time the book refers to, and afterwards read it, and remembered the *Pilgrim* and the *Alert*, thought they also remembered me. But perhaps more did remember me than I was inclined at first to believe, for the novelty of a collegian coming out before the mast had drawn more attention to me than I was aware of at the time.

Late in the afternoon, as there were vespers at the Roman Catholic churches, I went to that of Notre Dame des Victoires. The congregation was French, and a sermon in French was preached by an Abbé; the music was excellent, all things airy and tasteful, and making one feel as if in one of the chapels in Paris. The Cathedral of St. Mary, which I afterwards visited, where the Irish attended, was a contrast indeed, and more like one of our stifling Irish Catholic churches in Boston or New York, with intelligence in so small a proportion to the number of faces. During the three Sundays I was in San Francisco, I visited three of the Episcopal churches, and the Congregational, a Chinese Mission Chapel, and on the Sabbath (Saturday) a Jewish synagogue. The Jews are a wealthy and powerful class here. The Chinese, too, are numerous, and do a great part of the manual labor and small shop-keeping, and have some wealthy mercantile houses.

It is noticeable that European Continental fashions prevail generally in this city,—French cooking, lunch at noon, and dinner at the end of the day, with *cafe noir* after meals, and to a great extent the European Sunday, to all which emigrants from the United States and Great Britain seem to adapt themselves. Some dinners which were given to me at French restaurants were, it seemed to me,—a poor judge of such matters, to be sure,—as sumptuous and as good, in dishes and wines, as I have found in Paris. But I had a relish-maker which my friends at table did not suspect,—the remembrance of the forecastle dinners I ate here twenty-four years before.

August 17th. The customs of California are free; and any person who knows about my book speaks to me. The newspapers have announced the arrival of the veteran pioneer of all. I hardly walk out without meeting or making acquaintances. I have already been invited to deliver the anniversary oration before the Pioneer Society, to celebrate the settlement of San Francisco. Any man is qualified for election into this society who came to California before 1850. What moderns they are! I tell them of the time when Richardson's shanty of 1835—not his adobe house of 1836—was the only human habitation between the Mission and the Presidio, and when the vast bay, with all its tributaries and recesses, was a solitude,—and yet I am but little past forty years of age. They point out the place where Richardson's adobe house stood, and tell me that the first court and first council were convened in it, the first Protestant worship performed in it, and in it the first capital trial by the Vigilance Committee held. I am taken down to the wharves, by antiquaries of a ten or twelve years' range, to identify the two points, now known as Clark's and Rincon, which formed the little cove of Yerba Buena, where we used to beach our boats, now filled up and built upon. The island we called "Wood Island," where we spent the cold days and nights of December, in our launch, getting wood for our year's supply, is clean shorn of trees; and the bare rocks of Alcatraz Island, an entire fortress. I have looked at the city from the water, and at the water and islands from the city, but I can see nothing that recalls the times gone by, except the venerable Mission, the ruinous Presidio, the high hills in the rear of the town, and great stretches of the bay in all directions.

To-day I took a California horse of the old style,—the run, the loping gait,—and visited the Presidio. The walls stand as they did, with some changes made to accommodate a small garrison of United States troops. It has a noble situation, and I saw from it a clipper ship of the very largest class, coming through the Gate, under her fore-and-aft sails. Thence I rode to the Fort, now nearly finished, on the southern shore of the Gate, and made an inspection of it. It is very expensive and of the latest style. One of the engineers here is Custis Lee, who has just left West Point at the head of his class,— a son of Colonel Robert E. Lee, who distinguished himself in the Mexican War.

Another day I ride to the Mission Dolores. It has a strangely solitary aspect, enhanced by its surroundings of the most uncongenial, rapidly growing modernisms; the hoar of ages surrounded by the brightest, slightest, and rapidest of modern growths. Its old belfries still clanged with the discordant bells, and Mass was saying within, for it is used as a place of worship for the extreme south part of the city.

In one of my walks about the wharves, I found a pile of dry hides lying by the side of a vessel. Here was something to feelingly persuade me what I had been, to recall a past scarce credible to myself. I stood lost in reflection. What were these hides—what were they not?—to us, to me, a boy, twenty-fours years ago? These were our constant labor, our chief object, our almost habitual thought. They brought us out here, they kept us here, and it was only by getting them that we could escape from the coast and return to home and civilized life. If it had not been that I might be seen, I should have seized one, slung it over my head, walked off with it, and thrown it by the old toss—I do not believe yet a lost art—to the ground. How they called up to my mind the months of curing at San Diego,

the year and more of beach and surf work, and the steeving of the
ship for home! I was in a dream of San Diego, San Pedro,—with
its hill so steep for taking up goods, and its stones so hard to our bare
feet,—and the cliffs of San Juan!

All this, too, is no more! The entire hide-business is of the past,
and to the present inhabitants of California a dim tradition. The
gold discoveries drew off all men from the gathering or cure of
hides, the inflowing population made an end of the great droves
of cattle; and now not a vessel pursues the—I was about to say
dear—the dreary, once hated business of gathering hides upon the
coast, and the beach of San Diego is abandoned and its hide-houses
have disappeared. Meeting a respectable-looking citizen on the
wharf, I inquired of him how the hide-trade was carried on. "Oh,"
said he, "there is very little of it, and that is all here. The few that
are brought in are placed under sheds in winter, or left out on the
wharf in summer, and are loaded from the wharves into the vessels
alongside. They form parts of cargoes of other materials." I really
felt too much, at that instant, to express to him the cause of my
interest in the subject, and only added, "Then the old business of
trading up and down the coast and curing hides for cargoes is all
over?" "O yes, sir," said he, "those old times of the *Pilgrim* and *Alert*
and *California,* that we read about, are gone by."

III

THE CITY GROWS UP

INTRODUCTION

THE fifties, California's gold-rush decade, ended with no whimper; rather it set off a bang that sounded down the succeeding four decades in a series of rolling echoes.

This dramatic explosion was the discovery of the Comstock Lode in Nevada, which drew off California miners by the thousands to the fresh bonanza. California gold continued to be an enormously important part of the new state's economy, but the Comstock was the New Thing, and in the New West that was the important thing. Although the astonishing riches in Comstock silver had their effect upon San Francisco, particularly in the way of stock-trading, this volume will not report the discovery itself. The silver made some men enormously rich, and some of these men (when they are otherwise interesting), will appear in this Part III—William C. Ralston, for example. But the Comstock mines were only one of many influences upon the city that had suddenly begun to grow up.

Another influence, and a significant one at the beginning of the sixties was the imminence of the Civil War. Few doubted that in the end war would come, and the entire state of California was shadowed by the threat. Under this shadow many things happened; the Terry-Broderick duel whose story is told near the close of Part II is an example of the tensions that existed. Thomas Starr King, the great Unitarian preacher, arrived from Boston and gave some four years of his life to preserving California for the Union, practically killing himself in the effort, (he died exhausted at forty, and a statue of him now stands in the Capitol in Washington.) But the duel and Starr King's moving oratorical opposition were at least out in the open. Underground far more fantastic things were taking place among the rabid supporters of the South.

There was, for example, the conspiracy, developing out of the southern secret society known as The Knights of the Golden Circle, which was an outright attempt to take over California by capturing the Benicia Arsenal and the Presidio of San Francisco.

One of those active in the plot was Asbury Harpending, a Kentuckian in his early twenties who had come to the gold fields, made a fortune, and was ready for any kind of adventure that might help his South. In the first selection in Part III, Harpending himself tells the story of "The Plot that Failed" as he saw it from inside. The reader is welcome to speculate upon what might have happened if General Albert Sidney Johnston had not been the man of honor that he was; it is possible, even likely, that the whole course of the Civil War might have been altered if the Confederacy had had California's gold and the Comstock silver to draw upon. Harpending (who appears also later in Part III in a curiously different light), wrote his memoirs when he was an old man, but his participation in the effort to capture San Francisco was vivid in his mind and he tells the story dramatically and well.

Another episode whose echoes played an important part in the growth of both city and state was the Pony Express. In itself, the Pony Express was an unsuccessful venture. It operated for only eighteen months or so, and it lost its promoters something like a million dollars. Nevertheless it accomplished an all-important thing; the Pony pioneered the Central Route to California, demonstrated that it was practical, and, by so doing, swung Congress over to that belief. Further, the Pony was drama; his hoofs, pounding the trails that led through dangerous Indian country and over man-killing mountains and deserts, drummed the challenge of pioneering so loudly that all the world heard it. The courage and stamina of the Pony's riders gave America some tremendously good theatre; there was no resisting the excitement men felt when the Pony, flying over the prairie like "a belated fragrant of storm," as Mark Twain put it, carried mail from Missouri to California in only ten days. That was an accomplishment to thrill the most cynical. The Pony's run actually ended at Sacramento. But the first Pony came all the way down to San Francisco, aboard the steamer *Antelope* for those final eighty miles or so, and the city celebrated nobly as it should. The story here is from the old *Morning Call,* and the reader will perceive how strongly the reporter felt the drama of the occasion.

With the sudden wealth that continued to pour into San Francisco,

it is not surprising that the city developed, in its way, a kind of High
Society. It was an overblown, stuffy kind of Society, to be sure; what
else in a city so young and so newly rich? But the newspapers of the
time took it straight, printing page after page of solemn gush whenever a matron rich enough to be called social gave a levee or ball.
One newly arrived San Franciscan, Mark Twain, found himself
egregiously bored by the whole procedure, especially by the coyly
written accounts of what the good ladies wore to the dances and
dinners so scrupulously chronicled by the press. Twain, still very
much the frontier humorist and writing with the exaggeration that
both the frontier audience and his own temperament made inevitable,
was in fact so bored by the whole business that he sat down in his
Lick House bedroom-study and proceeded to give his imagination
rein in one of the wildest burlesques the Washoe Giant ever penned.
His "Lick House Ball" is included here so that it may help interpret,
by its hyperbole-run-riot, something of the pompous, even then more
than faintly ridiculous pretensions of what passed for Society at the
time.

By the end of the sixties, the greatest American enterprise yet
attempted was successfully concluded—the linking of the Atlantic
and Pacific by rail. Here again was high drama; the country had followed the progress of the rails as this was regularly reported; the
race between the Union Pacific, moving westward, and the Central
Pacific's Big Four (Hopkins, Huntington, Stanford and Crocker),
headed east, had been presented to Americans from coast to coast as
a regular feature in their newspapers, and the country was ready for
the great climax. This came early in May, 1869, when with due
pomp a tie of California laurel was put in place, the final golden
spike was driven, and the two engines were run ceremonially forward
and back over the point of juncture to symbolize the great achieve-
ment. New York, Philadelphia, Chicago, all celebrated the day, and
San Francisco outdid them all, as was natural, its citizens, not satisfied with their dancing in the streets, carrying through town a huge
transparency on which they had lettered "San Francisco Annexes the
United States!" I have chosen here, instead of an account of the
high jinks that went on in town, the moderately cool and precise
story of the joining of the rails at Promontory, Utah, as sent down

by telegraph to the *Alta Californian* where it appeared on May 12—perhaps in some sense as an anticlimax, though San Francisco was still eager for the exact details. By way of balance, I have included Bret Harte's verses, "What the Engines Said," which appeared a few weeks later in the *Overland Monthly* for June. Doubtless these are something shy of poetry, but their expression of what was uppermost in people's minds—Harte was always good at that—is worth recording here.

One of the fabulous men of this period was William Chapman Ralston, banker, builder, promoter on the grand scale. A man who saw everything at least twice life-size, Ralston moved through these years as the man who did more than any other to build San Francisco. When, for example, he decided to construct a hotel that would outshine any in America it seemed to him the most natural thing in the world to set up a furniture-factory to make that hotel's equipment. For the carpeting of the Palace, the famous New York firm of W. & J. Sloane installed a branch in San Francisco, and the store remains today one of the city's great establishments in its field. An impatient man when he knew he was right, Ralston brooked little interference with any of his schemes, and the next selection in this volume shows him in a typical action. What had happened was the Black Friday panic of 1869, when Jay Gould and James Fisk attempted to corner gold. President Grant would not listen to Ralston's desperate plea that his Bank of California be permitted to deposit gold bars with the San Francisco branch of the Mint, drawing gold coin against these so that the bank might meet any run. But Ralston was not a man to be thwarted, even by a President. The selection "Ralston Saves His Bank," taken from the late George D. Lyman's admirable book, *Ralston's Ring*, tells the story of one of the least known and most extraordinary defiances of the U. S. Government that ever took place—a nighttime raid on a United States mint, no less, boldly conducted by one of the biggest businessmen of his city. The reader will note, by the way, that Asbury Harpending turns up again in this account. He will appear once more in this Part III, as usual in a curious, off-beat role and as a participant in great affairs.

With business booming in spite of panics and temporary financial depressions, it is not surprising that the city's night life took on a sinister aspect. San Francisco, moreover, was a port, and throughout the world each great port develops its own means of taking a sailor-man's money away from him. Here the Barbary Coast fulfilled that function, at the same time providing certain kinds of entertainment for the gay blades of the town and certain sorts of employment for many of its less worthy citizens. Castigated from the pulpit, decried by the press, periodically the subject of shocked demands on the part of the city's women that it be closed down tight, the Barbary Coast went on flourishing in its wickedness, quite evidently because there was enough money in it so that those who held the political reins were eager to have it just as it was. I have chosen, as a description of the area, an account from *The Chronicle* in the autumn of 1869 when the Barbary Coast was at its worst and also its most prosperous. The professionally shocked reporter, while he conscientiously recorded all the vice he saw, plainly enjoyed himself as much as his paper intended its subscribers should when they read his story.

It is not always possible to divide a city's past neatly into precise periods, though it is always a temptation to try. In one way, however, the next selection does mark the end of an era in San Francisco.

The reader will bear in mind that the city's background had been from the beginning that of a never-never land in which, almost literally, anything might happen. The Sierra foothills had opened their treasure-house of gold. The Comstock had poured out its silver in a degree of richness wholly unbelievable before the Big Bonanza came in. The entire West, indeed, had become a place as incredibly rich as King Solomon's mines. Yes, you could credit the West with anything. Wherefore, when two mild-seeming, roughly dressed miners appeared in Ralston's bank in the spring of 1872 with a tale of a diamond discovery—and with a small canvas sack of diamonds as evidence—even bankers and men of business were ready to believe. Why not diamonds, after all? Why not indeed? They did believe, and because of their credulity there was perpetrated one of the most unikely hoaxes that ever took advantage of a ready-made will-to-believe. It involved Ralston and several of his business associates including Asbury Harpending (the reader will discover just how near tht center of the hoax Harpending must have been, too), and the ripples spread to New York, Washington and even to the Low Countries, where the world's great diamond-cutters shivered in apprehension, since it seemed that their trade might move to San

Francisco. Luckily, the public was not let in on the marvelous diamond mines. When the hoax blew up in their faces, Ralston and his colleagues sadly stood all the losses and tried to forget the whole thing. But the Great Diamond Hoax remains a characteristic fantasy of its time and place. And its inevitable collapse in its way wrote *finis* to the First Age of Faith in San Francisco. Men were still to attempt, and to accomplish, great things in their extraordinary city, but never again were they quite as naive. The Diamond Swindle moved San Francisco well on into its adolescence; after it, the city really began to grow up.

The rest of the world, moreover, began to make that discovery. San Francisco, it appeared, was worth visiting and worth writing about. Not all who came to observe and report liked the city; some found it still a crude town for all its size, its drive, its pretensions. One such was Anthony Trollope who came to have a look during an extended trip on which he wrote some twenty travel letters for the Liverpool *Weekly Mercury*. Trollope, doubtless uncomfortable in this brash New-World setting and longing for the established routines of his own England, was reasonably snippy about San Francisco, and his Letter covering the city, reprinted a few years ago by a local fine press, is quoted in this volume as "Nothing to See in San Francisco." It has interest, too, in another way, for its author was so obviously scandalized by the city's gambling in silver-mining stocks. To Trollope, the idea of a chambermaid in his hotel or a bootblack on the corner speculating in shares was horrifying, and he records with pious disapproval the "roaring herd" in the Exchange where such undignified transactions were carried on.

Still another sign of San Francisco's coming of age was symbolized, oddly, by a gentle madman.

During the 1860s and 1870s the best known figure in town was Joshua Abraham Norton, self-styled Emperor of the United States and Protector of Mexico. In many a city Emperor Norton would have been summarily clapped into jail. But San Franciscans, in their tolerance, were content to smile, to honor his "bonds," in amounts of twenty-five to fifty cents each, to feed him free, and even to permit him to publish his royal proclamations in the newspapers. Much has been written about Emperor Norton, but I have chosen an account by one of today's notable newspapermen, John Bruce, who tells the story in his book, *Gaudy Century*. The little Emperor died in 1880, and San Francisco showed that it possessed sufficient self-assurance to afford a foible when the members of the city's richest club took over the funeral and buried Norton I in the Masonic Cemetery. (When San Francisco's growth compelled the shifting of that grave-yard in 1934, the same club moved Norton's remains to a larger cemetery outside of town and reinterred the Emperor under a hand-some granite shaft.)

As a kind of postscript to this selection, I have included one of Emperor Norton's proclamations as it appeared in the Oakland *Daily News* across the bay from San Francisco, in 1869. It is inter-esting as a sample of the way the old man's mind worked. But it is doubly interesting because it "ordered" the Central Pacific Railroad Company to build a bridge across the Bay—and then, with the pleasantly cracked touch that the sad little Emperor gave to every-thing he did, specified that this bridge should continue into the Pacific, to those rocky mountain-tops that rise just a little above the sea, the Farralon Islands, inhabited even to this day only by seals, gulls, and those who maintain the lighthouse there.

San Francisco, then, moved on through the seventies fully con-scious that it was now a great city. Its ladies and gentlemen even appreciated—and bought—Art. To be sure, vice, corruption, crime were still common; the Barbary Coast still roared, and the amusingly miscalled Maiden Lane (true, it was then known as Morton Street) was a double row of cribs ruled by the magnificently named Iodoform Kate. But Culture was developing fast, and those who could afford it made considerable parade of their understanding in such matters. Those were the days of the anecdotal paintings, and in 1875 a San Francisco artist, Toby Rosenthal, was making himself a wonderful reputation with such canvases as "Love's Last Offering," "The Exile's Return" and the like. Commissioned by one of the city's wealthy merchants, Rosenthal then produced what he termed his Master-work, a painting titled "Elaine" in which he depicted the Lily Maid of Astolat, cold in death on her funeral barge, being ferried to Camelot. There was tremendous to-do about the picture. The mer-chant turned it down; another rich San Franciscan promptly snapped it up. "Elaine waltzes" were composed; it was said that Crown Prince

Wilhelm of Germany had fallen in love with the picture, and Society whispered, with a *frisson* of delighted horror, that the artist had actually obtained the corpse of a young girl from which to make his sketches, all for the sake of Truth in Art.

At any rate, at the height of the excitement, "Elaine" vanished. Exhibited at the corner of Iodoform Kate's domain and busy Kearny Street, the picture attracted visitors in the thousands. Then one night it disappeared; only the frame remained, ragged edges of canvas hanging from it. The story of the theft, the frantic headlines in the press, and the eventful recovery of "Elaine" will be found in this volume as Robert O'Brien, careful reporter of San Francisco's past, tells it in his book, *This Is San Francisco*. It carries its own moral and offers its own conclusion; a town that could be thrown into such a furor by a picture and its theft was obviously beginning to see itself as an adult in the company of cities.

In the autumn of 1875, a scant two months after "Billy" Ralston had gone for his swim in the bay and drowned, his Palace Hotel was officially opened with a public banquet to Lieutenant General Philip H. Sheridan. According to the reporter from the *Morning Call,* the scene beggared description, though in the immemorial way of reporters who make that statement he set out immediately to describe it. Actually the dinner was a reasonably impressive affair, with a menu, including fine French wines, that suggests the gustatory enthusiasm of its age. Much about the Palace had already found its way into the press, and the writer of the newspaper report—included here, complete with the menu and wine list—touched on the hotel's glories only incidentally; the city might be proud of its Palace in a way, but it had heard enough and more than enough of details. It had heard so much, in fact, that the hour was ripe for burlesque. No Mark Twain lived and wrote in San Francisco then, but there were those who were willing to try to emulate the Old Master in his trick of hyperbole-ad-absurdum. One such, pretending that his letter originated in the Hoboken, N. Y., *Democrat,* took a fling at it and his letter putting the Palace it its place with the rest of San Francisco, is reprinted here as a reminder that even in a city which took itself pretty seriously there were some who could poke fun at pomposity where they found it.

As the century wore on, more notable visitors came to San Francisco.

One was a phthisical Scot who nearly starved while he tried to write, and who found the raw fogs of the city very trying to his delicate chest. Altogether Robert Louis Stevenson spent no more than a few short months in California—in Monterey, in San Francisco and on his honeymoon with Fanny Vandegrift Osbourne up at Silverado on the slopes of Mt. St. Helena. But the city cherishes his memory nevertheless, wherefore I have included here his brief, joyous few paragraphs of what it was like to slide in an emigrant train down the slopes of the Sierra, through the great central valley, and into the city across the bay. I have followed this with Wallace Irwin's gentle sonnet written in 1898, four years after Stevenson's death, apropos the erection in San Francisco's Portsmouth Square of the Stevenson Fountain with the brave little galleon crowning the graven stone. Irwin, of course, knew San Francisco in his youth, and the reader will see that he knew Stevenson too, and understood the nature of the man and his indomitable courage.

Another distinguished visitor, bound on an errand of culture, arrived in San Francisco a few years later. This was Oscar Wilde, come to explain the nuances of art-appreciation to the ladies (a few gentlemen attended), in a series of lectures. One man who heard Wilde's talk was sword-sharp Ambrose Bierce who promptly went back to his desk at *The Wasp* and set down what he thought of the lecturer. The mildest thing Bierce could find to write was, "He had nothing to say, and he said it!" For the rest, the reader will find it in the selection "An Opulence of Twaddle" in which Bierce, after his relatively quiet beginning really lets himself go on the subject of the "intellectual jellyfish" who had the presumption to tell San Franciscans about art. The piece is perhaps a trifle heavy handed; the famous Town Crier could, and often did, pink his victims more neatly. But Bierce in a towering rage is a spectacle worth watching too, and here he is as obviously angry as he ever let himself get in print.

As the nineteenth century moved into its final quarter, life in San Francisco had taken on a kind of prosperous middle-class solidity that emphasized—indirectly but none the less surely—the general soundness of the city's businessmen. There had been the great mansions on Nob Hill, of course; the railroad men, Hopkins, Stanford, Huntington and Crocker, had built themselves impressive piles of marble or granite or neo-gothic scrollwork in wood; the silver kings a little later had done their best in brownstone brought around the Horn. But now, in the eighties, the modest fortunes were beginning to show. In street after street comfortable houses blossomed with bay windows—that characteristically San Franciscan architectural trick—built to catch all the sunlight possible where fogs are frequent. These were not mansions, but the dwellings of the respectably successful; overstuffed in the Victorian manner, no doubt, but the outward and visible evidence of money-in-the-bank. In them one found the prosperous storekeepers, the insurance men, the importers, the stock-brokers. The tenor of their lives was even, decent; their way was not the way of the very rich, but the way of the burgher who thought well of himself, of his business, his family and his city.

A few years ago the late Harriet Lane Levy, who grew up in just such a family and in just such a house, sat down in her old age and wrote the story of what life was like in those innocent days in her city. From her book, *920 O'Farrel Street,* I have taken a part of one chapter because nothing else in print so well reflects the *mores* of the decade and the city. As the reader will realize, it could not have been written at the time; there was needed the backward look, the passage of years, to mirror so faithfully a way of life more than half a century gone. But this piece does it beautifully, as the reader will discover.

It was at the very end of the eighties that young Rudyard Kipling arrived in San Francisco and set down, in a group of letters written to his paper in India, his impressions of the vigorous life he found there. He took pains to see a good deal of the city, to think about what he saw, and to relate it to the times in which he lived. His notes on the up-and-coming American Girl, as exemplified by the freshly pretty maids he met in San Francisco, read today almost like prophecy, and his comment upon the backstage political maneuvering and general corruptions of the time are both accurate and well considered. The cable cars astonished Kipling; so did the girl typist who quoted Theophile Gautier at him. He sat and suffered through some high-flown oratory at the Bohemian Club, but enjoyed the experience, especially the fine wines and good cigars with which he was regaled there. His remarks are lively, thoroughly Kiplingesque—his style was already well formed—and the reporting is easily better than average. Though he both liked the city and didn't like it, his correspondence provides a peephole, wider than most, into the San Francisco that was on the verge of moving on into the excited and exciting nineties.

A significant part of the nineties was the life of San Francisco's Chinatown. The first Chinese had made their way to California in the earliest days of the gold rush; San Francisco in those days was known to the Orientals by a term signifying "Golden Hills." In fact, as early as 1849 there were enough Chinese in the town so that an advisor was appointed to look after their interests; he was a young naval officer named Woodworth, son of that Samuel Woodworth who wrote "The Old Oaken Bucket." Throughout the gold-rush decade, the Chinese continued to come in; later, to help build his railroad, Charles Crocker imported Chinese laborers by the thousand to dig and drill in the mountains. Though a small proportion remained in the gold country to work over the mine dumps left by their less patient predecessors, most came down again to San Francisco where they found themselves compressed into what has ever since been the city's Chinatown. Their availability as cheap labor brought on riots, political squabbles, slogans such as "The Chinese Must Go!" and caused international complications that still trouble the world. Inevitably, the Chinese formed into business associations—tongs, as they were known—and as the Chinese began to prosper these grew more and more powerful. There were "tong wars" as a result, and here and there some more adroit Chinese succeeded in acquiring extraordinary wealth and influence through bribery and graft. Of these, the best known was "Little Pete," and I have selected for this volume Herbert Asbury's account of how "Little Pete," at last grown too big for his breeches, met his death at the hands of two fellow-Chineses as he sat in a barber's chair, for once without his bodyguard to protect him or a weapon within reach. Mr. Asbury tells the tale sparely and in vivid detail, and his account will remind more than one reader that the gangster type, betting high at the races, flashing big diamonds and treating himself to the best in lushly furnished apartments and appropriate young ladies, varies little from one era to another.

As the nineties drew to an end, there was one new excitement that eclipsed all others, in San Francisco as in the Atlantic Coast cities.

That was the war with Spain. It happened that the first American troops ever to leave the continent to fight in an American war sailed, not from an eastern port but from San Francisco—California's First Infantry on its way to the Philippines. On May 23, 1898, the regiment broke camp at the Presidio and marched to the steamer, *City of Peking,* to embark on its great adventure, and because San Francisco had never experienced such an emotional moment in all its history I have chosen a reporter's story purposely written to extract every possible drop of sentiment from the occasion. More than a little overwrought though it is, the account as it appeared in the *Call* next day unquestionably interprets the spirit of the citizens on that day when they lined Market Street to call their good-byes to the men in the khaki and broad-trimmed campaign hats of the time, and, because it does do this, it seemed well worth using for this volume.

Finally, with the century at its close, San Francisco produced a genuinely important novelist—its first, really, for Mark Twain, in spite of his brief apprenticeship in the city, was a San Franciscan only by courtesy.

This new man was Frank Norris, an intense, eager, sensitive youngster who was breaking new ground as a realist. His novel, *McTeague* was not published until just after the new century had begun, but the Polk Street setting was what Norris had seen and absorbed at the very end of the nineties. Here I have taken the first chapter of that remarkable novel, selecting it for its minutely exact descriptions of life in a shabby-genteel portion of a city that was already old enough to have its slightly run-down sections and also its confused McTeagues, part phony, part just plain puzzled by their inability to catch on to the rhythms of their time, men born just a little too late for their brute strength to be of use to them, bewildered in a kind of economy they could only half understand, yet bound to apply their undisciplined drives somehow. Norris was, in fact, San Francisco's First Writer, and it is appropriate enough that this Part III should close with this bit from his most original novel. It is bracketed, as the reader will observe, by two pieces of verse. One, "The Ballad of the Hyde Street Grip" by Gelett Burgess, celebrates the cable cars whose romance still lives in San Francisco as this is written, in spite of persistent attempts to eliminate it as an anachronism unsuited to modern transportation needs. The other, Wallace Irwin's "Telygraft Hill," shows one aspect, now long gone, of the hill which has been a lively part of the city's life from the days of its "Telegraph"—a semaphore which signaled the arrival of ships through the Gate an hour or more before the vessels rounded the tip of the peninsula and became visible downtown—on through its "slobby owld" period as the world's best spot to stretch washlines, its day as a parallel of New York's Greenwich Village, to its current manifestation as a site for modernistic apartment houses which have now almost shouldered the last French-bread-and-red-wine painter, poet and sculptor from its tower-crowned height.

Throughout this Part III, as the reader will realize, are scattered other verses and prose bits, each with its small contribution to the feel of the period covered, especially some excerpts from the column of Ambrose Bierce who saw to it that fools and rascals—and he defined both very broadly—felt the lash of his whip each week in one paper or another for twenty-odd years. Like the bits from the acid Hinton Helper in Part II, these are here to serve as notice that when all was not serene with San Francisco there was invariably someone to say so.

THE PLOT THAT FAILED

by

ASBURY HARPENDING

I HAD barely returned to San Francisco when the election of 1860 took place, resulting in the choice of Abraham Lincoln as President of the United States. All through the South this was accepted as the signal for a civil contest. The work of organization went ahead with feverish haste, and long before the inauguration of the new President the authority of the Federal Government was paralyzed in most of the slave states.

The attitude of California was of supreme moment, not understood, however, at the time. Had this isolated State on the Pacific joined the Confederacy, it would have complicated the problems of the war profoundly. With the city of San Francisco and its then impregnable fortifications in Confederate hands, the outward flow of gold, on which the Union cause depended in large measure, would have ceased as a stream of water is shut off by turning a faucet. It was the easiest thing in the world to open and maintain connection through savage Arizona into Texas, one of the strongholds of the South. It does not need a military expert to figure out what a vital advantage to the Confederacy the control of the Pacific would have proved.

History relates in a few brief words how the secession movement in San Francisco was extinguished by a wild outburst of patriotism. I am now going to tell for the first time the inside story of the well-planned effort to carry San Francisco, and with it California, out of the Union, and by what a narrow margin it finally failed of accomplishment.

From *The Great Diamond Hoax and Other Stirring Episodes in the Life of Asbury Harpending,* San Francisco, 1913.

I was young, hot-headed and filled with the bitter sectional feeling that was more intense in border states than in those farther north or south. I moved among my own people, got off all sorts of wild talk about spending that last dollar of my money, and my life if need be, to resist the tyrant's yoke, and was actually about to leave for my home in Kentucky when a quiet tip was given me that more important work was cut out for me where I was. My exaggerated wealth and irresponsible stories of my Mexican exploits had made me an actor in a great, silent drama despite my years and boyish look.

One afternoon I was told to be at the house of a well-known Southern sympathizer at nine in the evening. It was well apart from other buildings, with entrances from several directions. The gentle-man who owned it lived alone with only Asiatic attendants who understood little English and cared less for what was going on. When I arrived I was ushered into a large room where a number of gentlemen, most of them young but well established, were seated at a long table. I recognized among them leading men of San Francisco in various walks of life.

The spokesman, a great man of affairs, told me that I was trusted, that I had been selected as one to lead in an affair of great peril, an enterprise on which the future of the South might depend, and asked me if I were ready to risk life and fortune on the turn. I answered with an eagerness that satisfied my hearers and took an oath of which I have a copy:

"Having been brought to this room for the purpose of having a secret confided to me, and believing that to divulge such a secret would imperil the lives of certain Southern men as well as injure the cause of the South, I do solemnly swear in the name of the Southern States within whose limits I was born and reared, that I will never by word, sign, or deed hint at or divulge what I may hear tonight. Not to my dearest friend, not to the wife of my bosom, will I communicate the nature of the secret. I hold myself pledged by all I hold dear in heaven or on earth, by God and my country, by my honor as a Southern gentleman, to keep inviolate the trust reposed in me. I swear that no consideration of property or friendship shall influence my secrecy, and may I meet at the hands of those

I betray the vengeance due a traitor if I prove recreant to
this, my solemn obligation. So help me God as I prove true."

This oath was committed to memory by every member. Thus I
became one of a society of thirty men, pledged to carry California out
of the Union.

The Southern mind has a wonderful capacity for secret organization and for conducting operations on a vast scale behind the screen
of impenetrable mystery, and the operations of the Committee of
Thirty of which I now became a member demonstrated this trait.

The organization was simplicity itself. We were under the absolute
orders of a member whom we called "General". He called all meetings
by word of mouth, passed from member to member. Anything in the
way of writing was always burned before the meeting broke up. The
"General" received the large contributions in private, never drew a
check, settled all accounts in gold coin, and accounted only to himself for the expenditures.

Each member was responsible for organizing a fighting force of a
hundred men. This was not difficult. California at that time abounded
with reckless human material—veterans of the Mexican War, ex-
filibusters, ex-Indian fighters, all eager to engage in any undertaking
that promised adventure and profit. Each member selected a trusted
agent or captain devoted to the cause of the South. He then simply
told that agent to gather a body of picked men, that equipment and
pay for these men would be forthcoming. Nothing was said about
the nature of the service intended; the impression was given that
a filibustering expedition was in the wind. These various bands were
scattered in out-of-the-way places around San Francisco Bay, osten-
sibly engaged in wood cutting, fishing or the like but all waiting for
the word to act. Each member of the Committee kept his own counsel.
Only the General knew the locations of the various detachments.

Our plans were to paralyze all organized resistance by a series of
simultaneous attacks. The Federal army was little more than a shadow,
About two hundred soldiers were at Fort Point, less than a hundred
at Alcatraz, and a mere handful at Mare Island and at the Benicia
Arsenal where 30,000 stand of arms were stored. We proposed to carry
these strongholds by a night attack and also seize the arsenals of
the militia in San Francisco proper. With this abounding military
equipment we then proposed to organize an army of Southern
sympathizers sufficient in number to beat down any armed resistance.

All this may seem chimerical, but the reader may take my word that the opportunity was absolutely within our grasp. At least thirty per cent of the population was from the South. The large foreign element was either neutral or had Southern leanings. We had under discipline a fine body of fighting men, far more than enough to take the initial step with a certainty of success.

Moreover, those who might have offered effective resistance were lulled in fancied security or indifferent. In 1860 the ties that bound the Pacific to the government in Washington were nowhere very strong. The relationship, too, meant great loss to California; for all the immense tribute paid, the meager returns were a few public buildings and public works. Thousands were tired of being ruled from a distance of thousands of miles. The "Republic of the Pacific," which we intended to organize as a preliminary, would have been well received by many who, later, were among the most clamorous in supporting the Federal government.

By the middle of January, 1861, everything was in readiness. It remained only to strike the blow.

In January, 1861, General Albert Sidney Johnston had been placed in command of the Department of the Pacific.

Johnston was born in Kentucky but considered Texas his State. Thus he had a double bond of sympathy for the South. This was the man who had the fate of California in his hands. No one doubted the drift of his inclinations. At the same time, no one who knew the man and his exacting sense of honor doubted his absolute loyalty to any trust.

In all our deliberations, therefore, General Johnson figured only as a factor to be taken by surprise and subdued by force. We wished him well and hoped he might not suffer in what would be a brief struggle. No one dreamed for a moment that his integrity as commander of his military department could be tampered with.

One of the brilliant members of the early San Francisco Bar was Edmond Randolph, a man of rare talents and great personal charm. Born in Virginia, he was naturally an outspoken advocate of the South. He was one of our Committee, and on terms of social and professional intimacy with everyone of Southern leanings. He was on the closest terms with General Johnston, and there can be no doubt that, on his own motion and without authority from the Committee, he approached the General with some kind of questionable proposition. What happened at the interview no one knows, but Johnston's reply drove Randolph into a fury. He indulged in loose unbridled talk, told several of our Committee that he had seen Johnston and that the cause was lost, and otherwise in many ways exhibited an incredible indiscretion. No amount of warning could silence his unbalanced tongue.

This situation was discussed at several meetings, and finally it was decided that a committee of three should visit General Johnston in a social way, not to commit further folly by any intimation or suggestion but to gather, if possible, some serviceable hints for future use. To my joy, I was named one of the three.

I will never forget that meeting. We were ushered into the presence of General Johnston, a blond giant of a man with a mass of heavy yellow hair, little touched by age although he was nearing sixty. He had the nobility of bearing that marks a great leader, and it seemed to my youthful imagination that I was looking at a Hannibal or a Caesar come to life again.

He bade us courteously to be seated. Then, in a matter-of-fact, offhand way he said, "There is something I want to mention. I have heard foolish talk about a scheme to seize the strongholds of the government which are under my charge. Knowing this, I have prepared for emergencies, and I will defend the property of the United States with every resource at my command and with the last drop of blood in my body. If you wish, you may tell that to our Southern friends."

We sat there like a lot of petrified stone bottles. Then in an easy way he launched into a general conversation in which we joined as best we might. After an hour we departed. We had learned a lot, but not what we wished to know.

Of course, the foreknowledge and inflexible stand of General Johnston was a body blow. There was also another very disturbing factor —the Comstock Lode.

While we were deliberating, that marvelous mineral treasure-house began to open up new stores of wealth. Speculation was enormous. The opportunity for making money seemed without limit. Many of the Committee were deeply interested.

Now, it had been determined absolutely from the outset that our ambitions were to be bounded by the easily defended Sierra. We knew enough about strategy to understand that it would be simple madness to cross the mountains. That meant, of course, the abandonment of Nevada in our schemes.

This had been accepted with resignation when the great Comstock mines were thought to be played out. But when it became apparent, as it now had, that the surface of the Lode had barely been scratched and that secession might mean casting aside wealth beyond the dreams of avarice—well, patriotism and self-interest had a lively tussle. If Nevada, with its Comstock Lode, could have been carried out of the Union along with California, then I am almost certain that the story of those times would have been widely different. We certainly had the organized forces to carry out our plans.

But to extend the planning to Nevada was hopeless. And our meetings began to lack snap and enthusiasm. Just when we should have been active and resolute, something always hung fire.

The last night we met, the face of our "General" was careworn. After our customary repetition of the oath, he addressed the Committee. It was plain, he said, that the members were no longer of one mind. The time had now come for definite action, one way or another. He proposed to take a secret ballot that would be conclusive.

The word "Yes" was written on thirty slips of paper. The "No" was written on thirty more. These ballots were placed alongside a hat in a recess of the large room. Each member stepped forward, chose a slip and dropped it into the hat. "Yes" meant action; "No" meant disbandment. When all had voted our "General" took the hat, opened the ballots and tallied them. "I have to announce," he said, "that a majority have voted 'No'. I therefore direct that all our forces be dispersed, and I declare this Committee adjourned without delay!"

No another word was spoken. One by one the members departed. All I can say is that they kept their secret well.

Two days later, all the various armed bands had been paid off and dispersed. The "great conspiracy" if you wish to call it so, had vanished into the vast, silent limbo of the past.

Only the "General" knew the extent of the disbursements. My own impression is that they far exceeded a million dollars. I contributed $100,000 myself, which, of course, was an incident of the financial recklessness of youth.

THE FIRST PONY ARRIVES

(From the San Francisco *Bulletin*, April 14)

IT TOOK 75 ponies to make the trip from Missouri to California in 10½ days, but the last one—the little fellow who came down in the Sacramento boat this morning—had the vicarious glory of them all.

Upon him an enthusiastic crowd were disposed to shower all their compliments. He was the veritable Hippogriff who shoved a continent behind his hoofs so easily; who snuffed up sandy plains, sent lakes and mountains, prairies and forests, whizzing behind him like one great river rushing eastward; who left a wake like a clipper's, "carried a bone in his teeth," and sent his fame rippling off north and south as nothing has done before for years; who frightened whole tribes of Indians that thought it was an arrow whittled into a pony's shape that whizzed by; who made eagles and all swift-winged birds heartsick, and sent them into convention to devise measures to keep their reputation up; who crossed the railroad track, fifteen miles out of Sacramento, just as the cars had passed, and got into the City of the Plains just as the same cars arrived!

If we were Egyptians, and living several centuries ago, we should set up that Pony in the plaza today and all of us go a-worshipping him. But as we are not, but simple Californians, many of us spending four or five months getting here, all we could do was to go down and glorify him on his arrival this morning.

The boat waited for the Pony Express at Sacramento until 5 o'clock yesterday afternoon. The instant it arrived it came on board, and the *Antelope* put on all steam to accomplish an early trip.

Meanwhile at the theatres it had been announced that on the landing of the boat there would be ceremonies of reception, music, jollification, and some speeches. Possibly the last statement contributed to sending large portions of the people home; still, many determined to make a night of it and never mind the headache this morning. The California Band traveled up and down the streets, waking all the echoes, fetching out the boys, and making the night melodious. Bonfires were kindled here and there—on the Plaza, on the wharves, wherever there was an old tar-barrel to steal, a gathering of shavings, or a drygoods box to burn. The Monumental Fire Company's bell rang out a larger district-number than the city will know for several centuries to come; the Police, like Barkis, was willin', and the red-shirts as they came rushing to see where the fire was, got out their engines, joined the procession, lighted their torches, and would not go home until morning. A stranger would have thought the bay was on fire or a war proclaimed against the Naiads. The organized turn-out reached the foot of Broadway at midnight. With waltzes and Yankee Doodle, the airs of all the nations, and several improvised black-oak dances, the crowd's spirits were maintained until near one o'clock, when the *Antelope* came steaming down, wheeled, threw out her hawsers, was made fast, and the glorified Pony walked ashore.

The crowd cheered until their throats were sore; the band played as if they would crack their cheeks and lame their elbows for life; the boys stirred up their bonfires and the speech-makers studied their points. The procession re-formed, opened right and left, and the Pony, a bright bay when the torches flashed their light upon him but of the color of the crowd otherwise, paced gaily up to his stand. The line closed again, the band went ahead, the firemen followed with their machines, the centre of attraction, the Hippogriff, came next, and citizens fell in behind. There was only one lady on hand. As the pony trotted into line, she tore the ribbons from her bonnet and tied them around his neck.

All then moved up to the vicinity of the *Bulletin* offices and halted on Montgomery Street, just opposite the Pony Express. While the 25 letters that were brought were being distributed, the speech-makers were proceeding to uncork the bottles of their eloquence. Their friends said "Hear! Hear!" but the boys would leave it to the Pony. He considered a moment, eyed the ribbons about his neck, looked a bit sleepy, thought of his oats, and uttered a loud *neigh*. So the speeches were corked down again, the speech-makers tied comforters around their throats, the Dashaways cheered hoarsely, the ragtag-and-bobtail took something warm, the morning papers went to press, the crowd to bed, and the Pony to his stable.

The little fellow is in good condition this morning. The Committees had not begun to call upon him when we went to press, the Military had not been introduced, the Supervisors had not called a special meeting to vote him the freedom of the city.

Long live the Pony!

THE TIME THAT THE PONY MADE

The following, taken from the Way-bill of the Pony Express, shows the time made on the notable trip from St. Joseph to San Francisco:

Left St. Joseph, Mo.	6:30 P.M., on 3d April
Arrived Salt Lake City	6:30 P.M., on 9th "
Carson City	2:30 P.M., on 12th "
Strawberry Valley	4:35 A.M., on 13th "
Placerville	2:00 P.M., on 13th "
Sacramento	5:30 P.M., on 13th "
San Francisco	1:00 A.M., on 14th "

Those who have leisure may enjoy a comparison between the above and the following Schedule which was adopted before the Pony started. The Schedule allowed, to go from St. Joseph to—

Marysville	12 hours
Fort Kearney	31 "
Laramie	80 "
Bridger	108 "
Salt Lake	124 "
Camp Floyd	145 "
Carson City	188 "
Placerville	206 "
Sacramento	232 "
San Francisco	240 "

THE LICK HOUSE BALL

by

MARK TWAIN

E*ditors, The Golden Era:* I have received a letter from the land of
eternal summer—Washoe, you understand—requesting a short synop-
sis of the San Francisco fashions for reference.

There are ten note-paper pages of it. I read it all. For two hours
I worked along through it—spelling a word laboriously here and
there—figuring out sentences by main strength—getting three or four
of them corraled, all ragged and disjointed, and then skirmishing
around after the connection—two hours of unflagging labor, determination and blasphemy, unrewarded by one solitary shadow of a
suspicion of what the writer was trying to get through her head or
what she could possibly be up to—until I bore down upon the three
lines at the bottom of the last page, marked "P.S.," which contained
a request for information about the fashions here, and was the only
paragraph in the document wherein the light of reason glimmered.
All that went before it was driveling stupidity—all that the girl really
wished to say was in the postscript. It was not strange that I experienced a warm fellow-feeling for the dog that drank sixty gallons of
water to get a spoonful of mush in the bottom of the tank.

The young lady signs herself "Oenone." I am not acquainted with
her, but the respect, the deference which, as a white man and a
Christian, I naturally feel for members of her sex, impels me to take
no less pains in obliging her than were the circumstances different.

A fortunate occurrence has placed it in my power to furnish
Oenone with the very latest fashions: I refer to the great ball given

From *The Washoe Giant in San Francisco* by Mark Twain. By permission
of the publisher, George Fields, San Francisco, 1938.

me at the Lick House last Thursday night by a portion of the guests of that hotel, on the occasion of my promising to "let up" on Messrs. Jerome Rice, John B. Winters, Brooks, Mason, Charley Creed, Capt. Pease, and the other "billiard sharps" of the establishment.

It was a graceful acknowledgment of my proficiency in the beautiful science of billiards, as well as of the liberality I have shown in paying for about every game I ever played in the house.

I expect I have been rather hard upon those gentlemen, but it was no fault of mine—they courted their own destruction. As one of them expressed it, they "could not resist the temptation to tackle me"; and if they baited their hooks for a sardine and caught a whale, who is to blame? Possibly it will be a comfort to Capt. Pease to know that I don't blame him, anyhow; that there is no animosity whatever, and that I feel the same filial affection, the same kindly regard, etc., etc., just as if nothing had happened.

Oenone, (or Unknown, if it is all the same to you), the ball was a grand success. The Army was present and also the Navy. The nobility were represented by his Grace the Duke of Benicia, the Countess of San José, Lord Blessyou, Lord Geeminy, and many others whose titles and whose faces have passed from my memory. Owing to a press of imperial business, the Emperor Norton was unable to come.

The parlors were royally decorated, and the floors covered with a rich white carpet of mauve domestique, forty dollars a yard, imported from Massachusetts or the kingdom of New Jersey, I have forgotten which. The moment I entered I saw at a glance that this was the most extraordinary party ever given in San Francisco. I mentioned it to Benish (the very friendly, not to say familiar, relations existing between myself and his Grace the Duke of Benicia, permit of my addressing him in this way without impropriety) and he said he had never seen anything like it where he came from. He said there were more diamonds here than were displayed at the very creditable effort of the Messrs. Barron, recently. This remark revived in his breast a reminiscence of that ball. He observed that the evening before it came off, he visited all the jewelry shops in town for the purpose of leasing some diamonds for his wife, who had been invited; but others had gone before him and "cleaned out" (as the facetious nobleman expressed it) every establishment. There was but one shop where a diamond remained on hand; and even there, the proprietor was obliged to tell him—though it cost him pain to do it—that he only had a quart left, and they had already been engaged by the Duchess of Goat Island, who was going to the ball and could not do without them.

The memory of the incident affected the noble Benish almost to tears, and we pursued the theme no further. After this, we relapsed into a desultory conversation in French, in which I rather had the best of him; he appeared to have an idea that he could cypher out what I was driving at, whereas I had never expected to understand him in the first place.

But you are suffering for the fashions, Oenone. I have written such things before, but only by way of burlesquing the newspaper description of balls and dresses launched at the public every now and then by individuals who do not seem to know that writing fashion articles, like wet nursing, can only be done properly by women. A rightly constituted man ought to be above filching from the prerogatives of the other sex. As I have said, the fashion synopses heretofore written by myself, have been uncouth burlesques—extravagant paraphrases of the eloquence of female costume, as incomprehensible and as conflicting as Billy Birch's testimony in the case of the atrocious assassination of Erickson's bull by "Jonesy," with his infamous "stuffed club." But this time, since a lady requests it, I will choke down my distaste for such feminine employment, and write a faithful description of the queenly dresses worn at the Lick House party by several ladies whose tempers I think I can depend on. Thus:

Mrs. F. F. L. wore a superb toilette habillée of Chambry gauze; over this a charming Figaro jacket, made of mohair, or horse-hair, or something of that kind; over this again, a Raphael blouse of *cheveux de la reine,* trimmed round the bottom with lozenges formed of insertions, and around the top with bronchial troches; nothing could be more graceful than the contrast between the lozenges and the troches; over the blouse she wore a *robe de chambre* of regal magnificence, made of *Faille* silk and ornamented with macaroon (usually spelled "maccaroni") buttons set in black guipure. On the roof of her bonnet was a menagerie of rare and beautiful bugs and reptiles, and under the eaves thereof a counterfeit of the "early bird" whose specialty it hath been to work destruction upon such things since time began. To say that Mrs. L. was never more elaborately dressed in her life, would be to express an opinion within the range of possibility, at least—to say that she did or could look otherwise than charming, would be a deliberate departure from the truth.

Mrs. Wm. M. S. wore a gorgeous dress of silk bias, trimmed with tufts of ponceau feathers in the *Frondeur* style; elbowed sleeves made of chicories; plaited Swiss habit-shirt, composed of Valenciennes, *a la vielle,* embellished with a delicate nansook insertion scalloped at the edge; Lonjumeau jacket of maize-colored *Geralda,* set off with *bagnettes,* bayonets, clarinets, and one thing or another—beautiful. Rice-straw bonnet of Mechlin tulle, trimmed with devices cut out of sole-leather, representing aigrettes and arastras—or asters, whichever it is. Leather ornaments are becoming very fashionable in high society. I am told the Empress Eugenie dresses in buckskin now, altogether; so does Her Majesty the Queen of the Shoshones. It will be seen at a glance that Mrs. S's. costume upon this occasion was peculiarly suited to the serene dignity of her bearing.

Mrs. A. W. B. was arrayed in a sorrel organdy, trimmed with fustians and figaros, and canzou fichus, so disposed as to give a splendid effect without disturbing the general harmony of the dress. The body of the robe was of zero velvet, goffered, with a square pelerine of solferino *poil de chevre* amidships. The fan used by Mrs. B. was of real palm-leaf and cost four thousand dollars—the handle alone cost six bits. Her head dress was composed of a graceful cataract of white chantilly lace, surmounted by a few artificial worms, and butterflies and things, and a tasteful tarantula done in jet. It is impossible to conceive of anything more enchanting than this toilet— or the lady who wore it, either, for that matter.

Mrs. J. B. W. was dressed in a rich white satin, with a body composed of a gorgeously figured Mackinaw blanket, with five rows of ornamental brass buttons down the back. The dress was looped up at the side with several bows of No. 3 ribbon—yellow—displaying a skirt of cream-colored Valenciennes crocheted with pink crewel. The coiffure was simply a tall cone of brilliant field-flowers, upon the summit of which stood a glittering "golden beetle"—or, as we call him at home, a "straddle-bug." All who saw the beautiful Mrs. W. upon this occasion will agree that there was nothing wanting about her dress to make it attract attention in any community.

Mrs. F. was attired in an elegant Irish foulard of figured aqua-marine, or aqua fortis, or something of that kind with thirty-two perpendicular rows of tulle puffings formed of black zero velvets (Fahrenheit). Over this she wore a rich balmoral skirt—pekin stripe —looped up at the sides with clusters of field flowers, showing the handsome dress beneath. She also wore a white Figaro postillion pea-jacket, ornamented with a profusion of Gabriel bows of crimson silk. From her head depended tasteful garlands of fresh radishes. It being natural to look charming upon all occasions, she did so upon this, of course.

Miss B. wore an elegant goffered flounce, trimmed with a grenadine of *bouillonnee,* with a crinoline waistcoat to match; pardessus open behind, embroidered with paramattas of passementerie, and further ornamented at the shoulders with epaulettes of wheat-ears and string-beans; tulle hat, embellished with blue-bells, hash-bells, etc., with a frontispiece formed of a single magnificent cauliflower embedded in mashed potatoes. Thus attired Miss B. looked good enough to eat. I admit that the expression is not very refined, but when a man is hungry the similes he uses are apt to be suggested by his stomach.

It is hardly worth while to describe the costumes of the gentlemen, since, with the exception of a handsome uniform here and there (there were six naval Brigadier Generals present from the frigate *Lancaster*) they were all alike, and as usual, there was nothing worthy of particular notice in what they wore.

Oenone, I could furnish you with an accurate description of the costume of every lady who attended that party if it were safe to do it, but it isn't you know. Over in Washoe I generally say what I please about anybody and everybody, because my obliging fellow citizens have learned to put up with it; but here, common prudence teaches me to speak of those only who are slow to anger, when writing about ladies. I had rather lose my scalp, anyhow, than wound a lady's feelings.

But there is one thing you can rest assured of, Oenone: The pleasantest parties in the world are those given at the Lick House every now and then, and to which scarcely any save guests of the establishment are invited; and the ladies are handsomer, and dress with more taste and greater magnificence—but there come the children again. When that last invoice of fifteen hundred infants come around and get to romping about my door with the others, and hurrahing for their several favorite candidates for Governor (unaware that the election is over, poor little miscreants), I cannot write with such serene comfort as I do when they are asleep. Yet there is nothing I love so dearly as a clean, fat, healthy infant. I calculate to eat that whole tribe before I leave the Lick House.

Now, do you know, Oenone—however, I hear the stately tread of that inveterate chambermaid. She always finds this room in a state of chaos, and she always leaves it as trim as a parlor. But her instincts infallibly impel her to march in here just when I feel least like marching out. I do not know that I have ever begged permission to write "only a few moments longer"—never with my tongue, at any rate, although I may have *looked* it with my expressive glass eye. But she cares nothing for such spooney prayers. She is a soldier in the army of the household; she knows her duty, and she allows nothing to interfere with its rigid performance. She reminds me of U. S. Grant; she marches in her grand military way to the centre of the room, and comes to an "order arms" with her broom and her slop-bucket; then she bends on me a look of uncompromising determination, and I reluctantly haul down my flag. I abandon my position —I evacuate the premises—I retire in good order—I vamose the ranch. Because that look of hers says in plain, crisp language, "I don't want you here. If you are not gone in two minutes, I propose to move upon your works!" But I bear the chambermaid no animosity.

THE RAILS ARE JOINED

(From the *Alta Californian,* May 12)

PROMONTORY SUMMIT, GREAT SALT LAKE, May 10,:—Preparations for formally uniting the two grand divisions of the great trans-continental railway were all completed early this morning. Governor Stanford, with his friends from the Pacific Coast, were on the ground impatiently awaiting the arrival of the Directors of the Union Pacific from the East to commence the ceremony.

At 8:30, an engine, No. 119, with a palace and two passenger cars, and Vice-President Durant, Directors Duff and Dillon, General Casement, S. W. Coe, (Superintendent Pacific Union Express Company), Colonel Cogswell with five Companies of the Twenty-First U.S. Infantry, and several ladies and invited guests, arrived and hearty congratulations were exchanged between the representatives of the Eastern and Western sections of the Union. The day was clear and beautiful as the little gathering of less than one thousand people representing all classes from the humblest citizen to the highest civil and military authorities of every State from the Atlantic, Pacific, Canada and Mexico, met to enact the last scene in a mighty drama of peace, on a little grassy plain surrounded by green-clad hills, with the snow-clad summits of the Wasatch Mountains looking down on the placid blue waters of the inland sea of America in the distance. Occident and Orient, North and South, Saxon, Celt and Mongolian, each clad in his peculiar costume, mingled on common ground. All personal and sectional animosity, all distinctions of class, all prejudices of race and nationality were forgotten for the moment in the all-absorbing interest of the grand event of history and civilization about to take place.

The Honorable F. A. Trile from the State of Nevada presented a silver spike on behalf of the citizens of Nevada, with the remark:

"To the iron of the East and the gold of the West, Nevada adds her link of silver to span the continent and weld the irons." Governor A. K. P. Safford, on behalf of the State of Arizona, presented a spike composed of iron, gold, and silver, as an offering by Arizona, and said, "Ribbed with iron, clad in silver, and crowned with gold, Arizona presents her offering to the enterprise that has banded our continent and dictated a new pathway to commerce." The Honorable Leland Stanford responded.

At the conclusion of this part of the ceremony the crowd fell back at the request of General Casement, and Hart, the artist for the Union Pacific Company, photographed the scene, with the locomotives confronting one another, and the Chinese and Caucasian laborers completing the work.

It was announced that the last blow was to be struck. Every head was uncovered in reverential silence, and the Reverend Dr. Todd of Pittsfield, Massachusetts, offered up the following brief and deeply impressive invocation:

"Our Heavenly Father, in whom we live and move and have our being, we acknowledge Thee to be the God of the creation of the human mind, with its power and its successes. Now, on this beautiful day, in the presence of these lonely hills and golden summits, we render thanks that Thou hast by this means brought together the East and West and bound them together by this strong band of union. We implore Thee that Thou wilt bless this work of our hands which we have now completed—this monument of our labor—and that Thy blessing my rest upon it so long as the hills remain among which the ends have been joined together."

The magnificient tie of California laurel, with the commemorative plate of solid silver, was now brought forward and put in place, and Dr. Harkness, in behalf of the State of California, presented Governor Stanford with the gold spike with the following remarks:

"The last rail needed to complete the greatest railroad enterprise of the world is now about to be laid. The last spike needed to unite the Atlantic and the Pacific by a new line of travel and commerce is about to be driven to its place. To perform these acts the East and the West have come together. From California's mines of gold she has forged a spike, from her laurel woods she has hewn a tie, and by the hands of her citizens she offers them to become a part of the great highway which is about to unite her in closer fellowship with her sisters of the Atlantic. From her bosom was taken the first soil—let hers be the last tie and the last spike. With them accept the hopes and the wishes of her people that the success of your enterprise may not stay short of its brightest promises."

General Dodge, on behalf of the Union Pacific, then responded:

"Gentlemen, the great Benton prophesied that some day a granite statue of Columbus would be created on the highest peak of the Rocky Mountains, pointing westward, denoting this as the great route across the continent. You have made that prophecy today a fact. This is the way to India!"

Superintendent Coe, on behalf of the Pacific Union Express, then presented a sledge with which to drive in the last spike. Governor Stanford and Vice-President Durant now advanced, took in hand the sledge, and drove the last spike while the multitude stood silent. Edgar Mills of Sacramento, who was elected Chairman of the meeting, then announced that this great work was done, and that messages would be sent to President Grant and to the Associated Press. Then the silence of the multitude was broken and a great cheer went forth which, while it yet quivered on the gladdened air, was caught up by the willing lightning and borne to the uttermost ends of the earth. Cheer after cheer followed, for the Union, the Atlantic and Pacific States, the two Pacific Railroad Companies and their officers, and the President of the United States, and all was over.

After the junction of the two roads was completed, the guests adjourned to the palace car of the Union Pacific Railroad, which crossed the connecting point and then backed again, and Governor Stanford's car then passed over and back. The band of the Twenty-First then came up and played national airs, and toasts, sentiments, and speeches were the order of some hours.

(From the *Alta Californian*. May 12, 1869)

HUMBOLDT, MAY 11, 2 P.M., BY TELEGRAPH:—The special train conveying Governor Stanford, Assistant General Superintendent Corning, Judge Sanderson, Director March, Edgar Mills, Doctors Harkness and Smalley, and guests—Dennison, Conductor—which left Promontory Summit at 5 o'clock last evening, reached here at 2 p.m., having made twenty-one miles an hour, all stoppages included. The dust and heat coming over the Humboldt desert were terrific.

WHAT THE ENGINES SAID

by

BRET HARTE

What was it the Engines said,
Pilots touching—head to head
Facing on the single track,
Half a world behind each back!
This is what the Engines said,
Unreported and unread!

With a prefatory screech,
In a florid Western speech,
Said the Engine from the WEST:
"I am from Sierra's crest;
And, if altitude's a test,
Why, I reckon, it's confessed,
That I've done my level best."

Said the Engine from the EAST:
"They who work best talk the least.
S'pose you whistle down your brakes;
What you've done is no great shakes:
Pretty fair—but let our meeting
Be a different kind of greeting.
Let these folks, with champagne stuffing,
Not their Engines, do the *puffing*.

Listen! Where Atlantic beats
Shores of snow and Summer heats;
Where the Indian Autumn skies

Paint the woods with wampum dyes:
I have chased the flying sun.
Seeing all he looked upon—
Blessing all that he has blest—
Nursing in my iron breast
All his vivifying heat,
All his clouds about my crest;
And before my flying feet,
Every shadow must rereat.

Said the Western Engine, "Phew!"
And a long, low whistle blew.
"Come now, really that's the oddest
Talk for one so very modest—
You brag of your East! *You* do?
Why, *I* bring the East to *you!*
All the Orient—all Cathay—
Find through me the shortest way.
And the sun you follow here,
Rises in my hemisphere.
Really—if one must be rude—
Length, my friend, ain't longitude."

Said the Union: "Don't reflect, or
I'll run over some Director."
Said the Central: "I'm Pacific,
But when riled, I'm quite terrific.
Yet to-day, we shall not quarrel
Just to show these folks this moral,
How two Engines—in their vision—
Once have met without collision."

That is what the Engines said,
Unreported and unread.
Spoken slightly through the nose,
With a whistle at the close.

[1869]

RALSTON SAVES HIS BANK

by

GEORGE D. LYMAN

YOU'RE just the man I want to see," said Ralston, drawing Harpending into a chair near him. "If things go on as they are every bank in San Francisco will be closed by tomorrow afternoon. Not one of us can stand a half day's run, and all will go down in a heap. Then look out for hell in general to break loose. This will happen if I don't get a million dollars in coin in the vaults tonight. But I intend to get it, and want you and Maurice Doré to help."

Of late, Ralston's troubles had been multiplying at a terrific rate. No one could realize the hazardous conditions under which his bank had been operating. All known bonanzas had exhausted themselves; the Miners' Union had demanded a higher wage-scale; cheap Chinese labor had been excluded from Washoe; the great fire in the "Yellow Jacket" had wiped out the last promising streak of ore; Sutro had inflamed the working men against the Bank and had actually started his tunnel; the Union Mill & Mining Co. had been given up to rust; the Virginia & Truckee Railroad had nothing to haul. So much for his monetary source of supply. And in San Francisco expenditure had been doubling. Nor was that all.

Sometime since, Ralston had advanced Stanford and Huntington $3,000,000 with which to finish their railroad. Now that amount was a frozen asset. Lately, $2,000,000 had been sent out of San Francisco to finance some South American proposition. Thus, recently, $5,000,000 in gold had gone out of California. A good share of it had gone out of Ralston's bank, at any rate out of circulation.

From *Ralston's Ring* by George D. Lyman, copyright 1937 by Charles Scribner's Sons.

When, in July, 1869, Jay Gould had cornered "gold" and held the yellow metal at a huge premium and the gold coin in California had been drained eastward as through a sieve, Ralston was filled with fresh dread. Some mornings his bank doors opened with only $50,000 to $75,000 in coin in the vaults. If there was a run, never would he be able to withstand it. Yet, no matter how he was racked within, to the world at large Ralston had to present a light-hearted, debonair manner.

During all this time his only comfort lay in the bars of bullion, entrusted to his care, in the bank refinery. A terrible temptation it was to have gold in the raw, yet none available as coin to use over the counters. Worse still, owing to the fact that Ulysses S. Grant was just coming into his administration, the San Francisco branch of the United States Mint had been temporarily shut down. Strangely enough, President Grant had refused to allow local bankers to deposit gold bars with the San Francisco Assistant Treasurer and receive in return an equivalent in gold coin. Hard pressed as he was for funds, Ralston had brought all possible pressure to bear upon Grant but without results: like adamant the President stood between him and sufficient gold on his counters.

To Ralston it seemed ridiculous that he should find himself in such a plight when there was plenty of Comstock bullion in his possession and $14,000,000 in gold coin tucked away in the United States Sub-Treasury right in their very midst.

To Ralston it seemed like a legitimate transaction to deposit Comstock bullion in the Treasury and carry away an equivalent in gold coin. Not only was it legitimate, but under the prevailing circumstances imperative. And right was might. Ralston telegraphed this suggestion to President Grant. But there was no response. Innumerable times, at great expense, he wired the Bank of California's predicament: he was in the fringe of a "run", on the brink of failure.

As conditions became worse and panic and catastrophe stared him bleakly in the face, Ralston fairly burned up Western Union wires with his pleas for executive help. But President Grant remained obdurate. For some unaccountable reason he absolutely refused to sanction the exchange of bullion for coin or even to heed Ralston's cry of need. Yet right was might. And the fate of San Francisco trembled in the balance. A run spelled ruin to the Coast.

All the time, while the uneasy feeling on California Street was mounting, the strain had stained Ralston's face a crimson color and knitted the black brows above his troubled eyes. Nor could a canter on his favorite horse nor a plunge in the cold waters of the bay alleviate the load upon his shoulders.

It was on this day when tension was at its height that Asbury Harpending dropped into the bank and was ushered into Ralston's office. He, too, was feeling the financial pinch. He needed funds. He wanted to know something about the outlook. Most of all, he needed a tip or two, and he got it in no uncertain terms.

"Be at the bank at 1 o'clock—one tomorrow morning—and put on an old suit of clothes, for you will have plenty of hard work to do," Ralston said imperatively as Harpending got up to leave.

Shortly after midnight Doré and Harpending met by appointment. They were utterly mystified as to what Ralston wanted of them. Together they tramped through the deserted, dimly lighted streets. To them it seemed like old times in San Francisco—the times when footpads lurked in alleys—when blackjacks flourished in the dark— when a thud on the head was feared—and a splash in the bay followed. Warily they proceeded toward the Bank of California.

They found Ralston in his office with one of his trusted officials. Ralston was in the highest spirits. The spring of youth was in his step, but he counselled caution, no questions, and silence.

Noiselessly he led his mystified friends through darker downtown streets to the United States Sub-Treasury, then located on Montgomery Street between Sacramento and California. Through the shuttered windows a dim light shone. When within a few paces of the entrance Ralston called on his friends to halt. Alone, silently, he approached the door of the Sub-Treasury. To Harpending's and Doré's utter amazement and without challenge of any kind, they saw Ralston open the great bronze door. Whether he had used a key, tapped, or whispered a word, they could not tell. They watched him disapper over the threshold. Noiselessly they saw the door close behind him. Then they were alone on the street, gaping in open-mouthed astonishment.

How long they stood there they could not tell, but suddenly the door opened and Ralston emerged half-carrying, half dragging several heavy sacks.

"Take that to the bank," he ordered the dumbfounded duo, "the gentlemen there will give you something to bring back."

Away went Harpending and Doré, bent double with the heavy sacks on their backs.

The official at the bank received the sacks. He was gone for some time. At last he was back with several bars of Comstock bullion. These Harpending and Doré toted back to the Sub-Treasury. On the sidewalk they found Ralston, smilingly awaiting them with a fresh supply of bulky burlap bags. Over to Ralston they turned the bars and received in return the heavily laden sacks. Not a word passed between them.

Thus at dead of night, passing noiselessly to and fro, they transferred in actual weight, between Sub-Treasury and bank, nearly five tons of gold. From start to finish, from a physical standpoint, it was a heart-breaking, back-breaking job. Continually, Ralston spurred his friends on to greater effort. Work as they would they could not transfer as much gold as they needed, before dawn began to break. Harpending, young and athletic, had stood his end of the Herculean task well, but Maurice Doré, slight and of sedentary habit, was on the verge of collapse. Chest-foundered, he could not pull himself erect. But as long as the streets were wrapped in darkness, as long as Ralston needed them, the two held to their task. Gladly would these two friends have fallen in the street for Ralston. Gladly would they have died for him, had the banker exacted such a sacrifice. They were idolatrous in their devotion.

During all this time not a person had passed or interrupted them. Well Harpending and Doré knew that that was due to a pre-arrangement with the policemen on the beat. Even the law was ready and glad to connive with Ralston.

When the Bank of California opened next morning a rather ominous-looking crowd whose queues extended far down the street was in waiting. Lines began to form at the paying tellers' windows. Sure enough, the run was on. Ralston, gazing through the glass screen between his office and the bank proper, looked annoyed. Finally he could stand it no longer.

"Why are you making so many of our customers wait, on a busy day?" he grumbled to his head clerk. "Put more tellers on the windows and have your coin on hand."

More tellers appeared at the windows. More gold-laden trays were hustled up from bank vaults below. The crowd saw. Eyes bulged with amazement. The Bank of California had money to burn. The sight brought general relief. Quickly the news ran along California Street. The populace changed their minds. Abashed that they had ever doubted Billy Ralston, they slunk away to spread the good tidings throughout the city: there are trays and trays of gold on the counters of the Bank of California. Many doubters felt that they should go back to the bank and apologize to Ralston for entertaining any doubts.

When a serious run began on a neighboring bank, Ralston hurried to the spot, mounted a dry-goods box and addressed the crowd: "You are doing the bank and the city a great injustice," he chided, as if speaking to a roomful of naughty children. "The bank is absolutely sound, you need not wait here for a line-up. Bring your books to the Bank of California. We'll accomodate you with the cash."

Again abashed, the crowd slunk away. How could they doubt Billy Ralston?

Thus Ralston and Comstock bullion averted a tremendous panic. A crash, the consequences of which would have been State and coast-wide, had been averted by Ralston's bold front, and a nervy bluff backed by Comstock gold. The only trouble was Grant. What would he think of Ralston's defiance? Luckily three days later President Grant reversed himself and allowed gold to be exchanged at the Sub-Treasury for cash, which settled all anxiety.

But neither Mills nor Sharon, who were leading officers of the Bank, ever knew how Cashier Ralston gathered in nearly a million dollars after banking hours that day. All the satisfaction they ever got out of him was that a kind friend had come to the Bank's assistance. Ralston was locked within himself. There were times when a man could not tell all he knew or feared.

THE BARBARY COAST:

A CONTEMPORARY REPORT

T H E Barbary Coast! That mysterious region so much talked of; so seldom visited! Of which so much is heard, but little seen! That sink of moral pollution, whose reefs are strewn with human wrecks, and into whose vortex are constantly drifting barks of mortal life, while swiftly down the whirlpool of death go the sinking hulks of the murdered and the suicide! The Barbary Coast! The stamping ground of the Ranger, the last resort of the ruined *nymphe du pave,* the home of vice and harbor of destruction! The coast on which no gentle breezes blow, but where rages one wild sirocco of sin!

The main coast commences on Pacific street, near Montgomery, and follows the former through to Stockton. Various channels lead into it from the west ends of Kearny, Dupont and Stockton, while the broad roadstead of Jackson street stretches behind. It is indented by many bays and creeks, reeking with slime and filth and filled with noxious odors. Prominent among these are Bartlett alley, Dupont alley, Bull Run, Deadman's alley, Murder Point, Moketown, and others, which offer to the pilgrim on its shore scenes of wretchedness and pollution unparalled on this side of the great mountains. Night is the time to visit the coast. In the daytime it is dull and unattractive, seeming but a cesspool of rottenness, the air impregnated with smells more pungent than polite; but when night lets fall its dusky curtain the coast brightens into life and becomes the wild carnival of crime that has lain in lethargy during the sunny hours of day and now bursts forth with energy renewed by its siesta.

But come, the shades of night fall slowly around us, and with curiosity for a helmsman we will attempt a survey of the mysterious region. Up Washington to Kearny, and then turn to the right. Our

---

From the San Francisco *Chronicle,* November 28, 1869.

attention is attracted by a band playing before one of the most celebrated places of evening resort in our city, and also an outpost of the
"Coast."

Melodeons

Who has not heard of the "Bella Union?" Go to the farthest end
of our sage-brush in the mountain country, and you will meet some
antique miner of the primeval days who will tell, with glistening eye,
of the many queer sights he enjoyed at the ancient Bella Union.
The ancient Bella Union is no more. About eighteen months ago it
was torn down, and a new edifice marks its site; but the entertainment
has not changed with the architecture. We enter, and passing through
a large barroom find ourselves seated in a very pretty little theater,
surrounded with a circle of curtained private boxes, that resemble
so many pigeon holes. After giving the audience time to admire a
drop-curtain execrably painted, it is drawn up and exposes to view a
semi-circle of male and female performers seated on the stage; the
latter generally quite pretty and in no way diffident in displaying their
charms to the audience. Songs and dances of licentious and profane
character while away the hours of the evening, and all that can
pander to that morbid desire of the rabble for obscenity is served
in superior style.

If you have remained long enough below we will entrust ourselves
to a pigeon hole above. No sooner are you seated in the box than
the curtain drops on some broad farce and the orchestra prepares
for the interlude. But what is this? Don't be alarmed, my friend;
this is simply that pretty *danseuse* who performed the evolutions in
the hornpipe in the last act come to solicit the wherewithal to purchase a bottle of champagne. The request is a modest one, partaking
of the character of the fair petitioner. "Only $5; now don't be
stingy," is pouted persuasively. But you are stingy and the request
drops to a bottle of claret. "No?" Under the depressing influence of
your meanness it continues to drop until it at last reaches the humble
solicitation of "At least a whiskey straight."

In the next box are seated three or four young men of respectable
family connections, said respectable connections dozing away in their
residences on Rincon Hill and elsewhere under the hallucination
that their worthy scions are attending a levee of the Young Men's

Christian Association. How shocked they would be could they but see them as they sit there now, "playing particular smash," as they are pleased to term it, with the feminine attaches of the Bella Union. Well, night gives license to many strange things; but we won't moralize, although that pretty girl with the intellectual forehead that sits near one of the centers on the stage might tell you some very queer stories about some very worthy people, but she won't.

A "Free and Easy"

In the street again, shaping our course due west; Cheap Johns cry forth their wares on either side, while crowds of gaping humanity stand with mouth apart gazing upon them, listening to some story of blood, thunder and terror, that always terminates with "all for the small sum of one dollar." The Cheap John is an institution of western Kearny street, and rather a good one, for although he sells poor goods he receives poor pay, and a fair exchange is no robbery.

Now we commence to strike the flood tide of the Barbary Coast and smell its noxious vapors wafted towards us in company with the notes of bellowing trombone and wailing violin. On the opposite side, before we reach the Coast, is Brooks', and as it is a principal one, and therefore a type of the general melodeon business, we may as well drop in. Passing down a flight of stairs we find ourselves in a cellar filled with men sitting at tables covered with beer glasses, wrapped in a cloud of tobacco smoke, with all the effluvia of spilt beer and sawdust mixed, perfuming the murky place. One end of the cellar is partitioned off, with a raised alcove in the center, in which are gathered some eight or nine female performers. This is a free melodeon, unlike the Bella Union and its companion further down the street, the Pacific Theater, where admission is charged at the door. There are a number of them scattered over the city, all pandering to the most depraved taste of the low and vitiated. Bawdy songs and witticisms so obscene as to even meet with the disapprobation of the far from scrupulous audience are the order of the day, or rather night; while in behind the screen of boards orgies that may be imagined, but not described, hold sway. But honor where honor is due, truth where truth may mitigate a severe statement: Brooks' and places of its kin are low resorts that but afford pleasure to the vicious; but so far as the direct criminality of those in charge is concerned with regard to the stealing away of men's brains for the purpose of robbing their pockets, they are not guilty. They offer this vile species of entertainment, but outside of a wish to benefit the bar do not enter into the schemes of theft and murder that occur in the waiter-girl saloons.

Further up from Brooks' is the Thunderbolt Saloon, rendered famous by a recent tragedy. At present it labors under the depressing influence of that occurrence and does not thrive.

And now we enter the Moro of the Pacific coast. A perfect din of musical instruments, vocal music, the sound of dancers' feet, together with yell and curse, pour in from every quarter. A band playing popular airs occupies one corner; a large, "pretty waiter-girl" saloon, also with a band accompaniment, the other, while on the northeast side is a dance cellar that but recently achieved notoriety through a murder occurring on its steps—the Myers tragedy. The Barbary Coast is now fairly entered and henceforth it is plain sailing in this slough of moral pollution. On either side to the left the cellars are occupied by "pretty waiter-girl" saloons, having such enticing names as the "Dew-Drop-in," "Rosebud," "Tulip," "Occidental," etc. They do not extend far up the street, but cluster near the corner, leaving that portion of the coast above to the deeper sinks of vice.

A view of one will answer for the entire lot, of which there are a number on the principal thoroughfares of our city. No sooner do you enter than a nymph with the seraphic graces of a beer-pot glides up and invites you to a seat. If you seem reluctant, a gentle hand soothes down your coat-lapel, or possibly passes around your waist, until with gentle persuasion you take the proffered rest and proceed to imbibe. If from the country, the persuading system is highly effective, and, with the egotism of a male, you are willing to attribute all the movements of the fair one to admiration of your superior person. But you are laboring under a delusion, my friend; she is simply trying your pockets and testing your capacity to play the fool.

When seated, and "beer for two" called for, she will entertain you with any amount of small talk; but throughout, even with the older and more skillful ones, there is a certain restlessness of manner and quick suspicious movement of the eye that betokens thoughts and cogitations not in accordance with her winning smile. If she asks you to play a game of cards, as will very likely be the case, refuse point blank; also, if invited to play for champagne; but stop and listen to the music. For if the peculiar noise drummed out at the piano, accompanied by the wrangle of fiddle, clarionet and trombone, be music, surely a surfeit is provided. Quantity, not quality, appears to be the order of the day. The musicians of our city employed in these evening entertainments form a large number. They are chiefly tradesmen of the lighter branches of industry, and combine rehearsal and performance in the one effort of the evening.

Sometimes, though, a remnant of better days sits at the sorry instrument; and fingers that have done justice to Meyerbeer, Mozart and Beethoven wander listlessly through the strains of some popular air of the *canaille*. Frequently songs are introduced, and now and then, while strolling along the pavement, the higher notes of a rich soprano voice strikes on the ear, and we stop to listen; but, alas, they waver, fall, and become hoarse, showing the wreck and ruin of what at one time might have been the pride and pleasure of a happy and refined circle—now living monuments of the deformity that sin and sorrow have brought upon their owner.

Waiter Girls

The waiter girls have recently obtained an unenviable notoriety through crimes that have startled our community. Pretty waiter girls are an institution of the nineteenth century—differing materially from the rosy, buxom barmaid with whom our grandfathers, in the style of the antique gallant, were wont to pass the compliments of the evening as they took their pot of beer. The waiter girl may or may not be an improper character. Some get a percentage on the liquor they sell. This is nearly universally the case in the sale of champagne. But there are a number who offer neither virtues nor honesty of any description to mitigate the odium attached to their names.

These generally are in league (or, as the flash word has it, "cahoots") with the bar-tender and other attaches of the saloon.

A countryman whose pockets are weighted with the hard-earned wages of the harvest field, or winter in the redwoods, attends their levee. Word is passed that the visitor is "flush," and then, by a quiet, prearranged method, they proceed to "go through" him. Drink follows drink down his hot throat, while sense after sense departs from his head, disgusted with the base use he is making of his stomach. As the vile liquor takes effect, he becomes reckless and responds favorably to their request for champagne, etc. It takes but a short time to evaporate his "pile," and he again starts for the harvest field or redwoods, a sadder but not wiser man, for he will repeat the same performance when able.

In case the visitor gives evidence of plenty of money and is either exceedingly penurious, or excessively reckless about spending it, the well taught fingers of his female entertainer opens the pockets that a fool's generosity cannot and he is quickly relieved. Very often this operation is concluded with what is termed "putting a head on him," by the male muscularity of the establishment. In most cases, the man on the return of sobriety sighs at his folly, and thoroughly ashamed of the occurrence seeks to bury it in oblivion and it is soon forgotten, even by the few who saw it. In others, the victim applies to the police; but what can they do? The man acknowledges being drunk and but little reliance is to be placed on his statement; even after they have gone to the trouble of arresting the waitresses, it is a very difficult matter to prove the complicity of any of them.

On account of recent occurrences "doping" or drugging has received attention. Drugs are not used one half as much as they are said to be. In the first place, the liquor retailed at the bar is bad enough poison, without the assistance of any foreign substance; and then, again, drugging is rather a delicate matter.

More "doping" occurs at ordinary bars than at these "waiter-girl" saloons. The process of drugging an individual—and it is extensively used elsewhere in our city than on the "Barbary Coast"—is much as follows: A stranger comes into town with a plethoric wallet. Perhaps he has been already "spotted" by scoundrels, and it is, as termed in flash phrase, "a put-up job." By the way, it may here be remarked that the "flash" vernacular of the Pacific coast "roughs" differs materially from that of their Eastern brothers. The victim is taken from one saloon to another, even to places of amusement, by his treacherous companions, who, during the early part of the proceedings, spend their money even freer than the victim. But he has to pay for this liberality with immense interest. Ultimately the proper time and place are reached—drinks are called for, a wink to the bar-tender is given, and half an hour afterwards the worthy tester of our city's hospitality is found by the police in some alley, insensible or imbecile—*sans* money, *sans* watch, *sans* everything. Drugging places infest the Barbary shore, but they also exist in localities much less suspected.

There are several different drugs used in "doping". Snuff is given in beer and the juice of plug tobacco in some other liquors. If mixed drinks are called for, sulphate of morphine sometimes enter into their composition. In some cases drugging is entirely unnecessary and not resorted to, a peculiar course of drinks which the victim is persuaded to take answering the purpose. For instance: A glass of ale, followed by one of whiskey, then a glass of beer, succeeded by some strongly concocted mixed drink, will generally render one unaccustomed to the *abuse* of liquor insensible.

Barbary Coast "Rangers"

As it is Saturday night, and near the hour of twelve, we will have an excellent opportunity of seeing the Ranger Brigade. As we pass up the street to Stockton we meet them on every side, from the Colonel in command, who has stood on many a hard-contested field and travels strictly on his muscle, down to the lowest subaltern, who picks a pocket or robs a clothes line.

The chief men of the Ranger Brigade assume a flashy style of dress, prominent amongst which is a clean white shirt conspicuously exposed at the front. But the garment seems to sit ill on them and appears out of place. The rank and file dress most any way, but there is a certain stamp on their features with which Dame Nature has brevetted them all that is not to be mistaken. Do you see that middle aged, rather gentlemanly-looking individual wearing the coat of clerical cut that corresponds rather comically with his thick black mustache and lowering eyebrows, standing against the lamp-post talking with two others of more flashy dress and display? That is an officer high in command. He has been twice "across the bay;" once for manslaughter and once for some other crime, but each time through the influence of honorary members of the corps, (some of whom, by the way, occupy some rather prominent positions in our community, and who never cruise on the coast), has been pardoned out. The two individuals he is talking with are non-commissioned officers, who hang around the great men to do their dirty work. They have both enjoyed a residence at that popular sea-side resort, San Quentin. The Moro of the coast is a popular lounging place with them when off duty. That tall, dark man yonder does not belong to the brigade, but acts as a sort of independent scout. He knows the placid features of Judge Provines and has heard that gentleman deliver a sentence when he was an interested party. The force generally go well armed; and, although a city ordinance prohibits the carrying of concealed weapons, it is doubtful whether one of them could be "interviewed" by a policeman without the discovery of either revolver, knife, slingshot or brass knuckles on his person. As we proceed toward Stockton street the higher members of the brigade become scarce and are rarely met, while the rank and file throng the pave.

They are the roughest of the rough, and in the crowd through which we are now passing may be picked out representatives of every description of human villainy. The police know most of them and have them "spotted"—in other words, under their eye. But they are powerless to act against them, unless some breach of the public peace occurs. In Chicago this class is constantly being brought before the Police Court, charged with vagrancy and heavily fined, with the alternative allowed them of leaving the city within twenty-four hours. They generally choose the latter. If, after residing abroad for some time, they see fit to return, a "fly cop" notifies the regular force, and they are again arrested and put through the same course. This relieves the city of numbers of them. How this would work in San Francisco is hard to surmise.

And now we reach the scum of even the Barbary Coast, where every saloon is a den of crime and nearly every one has been the scene of some tragedy. Near here, between Stockton and Dupont, are the celebrated alleys of Bull Run, Dead Man and Moketown. The houses are all saloons and are filled with the very dregs of humanity. Oaths and curses that exhaust the most degrading exprssions of sin strike harshly on the ear. Ribald song and bawdy jest float through the polluted atmosphere with the squeal of fiddles and tumming of banjoes. Sometimes in the midst of the noise there is a shot, a curse, a shriek, a groan, and another hulk whirls down the dark whirlpool of death.

The dens are nearly all small and bear a striking resemblance to one another. A bar runs along one side, behind which stands a representative of the Ranger Brigade on duty. There is a bench or some chairs in the room where are seated some men and generally two or three females, who act as decoys, though to the eyes of the unaccustomed they would appear better to repel than to attract, so repulsive are their manners and appearance. In one end there generally is a curtained door. That curtain seems to say, "He who enters here may live to tell a tale." And so he may, but it will be one of sorrow; while if he does not a Coroner's inquest or an unknown corpse, found in the bay or on the street, will have to do it for him.

THE GREAT DIAMOND HOAX

by

JOSEPH HENRY JACKSON

WITH the Civil War over, the golden spike driven at Promontory Point, and the two seaboards joined by the new railroad, the Sixties gave way to the Seventies and a kind of recklessness hard to match in any other period. Gambling in mines came back with a rush. Only this time it was a matter of gambling with pieces of paper representing shares in a mine. Where men had once wagered their time, their health, even their lives, on the chance of finding a rich placer, a new vein, now they wagered their fortunes, big or little, on the rise and fall of mining stocks on the Exchange in San Francisco. The fever caught them all. Cooks, bell-boys, coachmen, and laundresses were buying and selling their small odd-lots while the big men sat back and managed the market. Mines were the fashion everywhere, and why not? Hadn't such men as William Chapman Ralston, George Hearst, Haggin, and a hundred others showed the way to millions? They had. And what was good enough for them was good enough for the little fellow, sequestering four-bit pieces from his wages to take a flyer on the Exchange.

Nor was this fever of speculation limited to California, though California and Nevada promotions furnished the basis for the stocks in which the people traded. France and Germany were at grips; London and New York were the world's great money centers. And both those great cities were arm-in-arm with San Francisco. Had not San Francisco demonstrated, time and again for two decades,

From *Anybody's Gold* by Joseph Henry Jackson. Copyright 1941 by Appleton Century Co. Reprinted by permission of the publishers, Appleton-Century-Crofts, Inc.

that the magnificent resources of the West had no end? Of course. It was a San Franciscan, Asbury Harpending, who opened the Seventies by floating in London, with the famous (some said infamous) Baron Grant, a new issue of stock in the mine known as the Mineral Hill. The shares were snapped up so fast that Harpending never really got over it; forty years later he was still marveling, in his memoirs, at the instantaneous success of the Mineral Hill flotation, out of which he and the Baron turned a profit of something over three hundred thousand pounds sterling.

In such periods of almost universal speculation there is one rule that invariably holds true. Sooner or later the men who manage and control the hysteria for their own ends wind up by catching it themselves. In San Francisco, in the Seventies, there was one classic example of precisely this law. The public did not suffer; due to the promoters' anxiety to keep all the profits, the biters were bitten, that was all. Earnestly and devotedly they had spread the message that the mines of the Far West constituted a glorious and inexhaustible source of mineral wealth, that there was no limit to what the investor might expect to find in them. Now they became the victims of their own hypnotic powers. What happened to them was known, after the bubble burst, as the Great Diamond Hoax. And because the Great Diamond Hoax could never have succeeded if it had not been for the two fabulous decades that preceded it, the story of that fantastic swindle is the perfect postscript to gold.

Mr. Asbury Harpending, highly successful San Francisco promoter and real estate operator, a friend and colleague of Ralston and a hundred other of the city's biggest men, had moved his office to London in 1871. Part of his reason was the Mineral Hill stock issue with which he and Baron Grant had had such an immediate success. Part of the reason, too, was Mr. Harpending's sudden realization that the Baron was inclined to ride the wave too recklessly. He had taken on another mine to float—this time a bad one which Harpending knew was bad. Harpending was out to stop him if possible.

The Baron, however, was not to be dissuaded, and this gave Harpending several things to think about. He subsidized a British financial paper and fought the Baron in its columns. He launched a private investigation into the affairs of the financial editor of the staid London *Times* whom he suspected of conniving, for his own profit, to forward the Baron's schemes. Harpending had these irons in the fire and a host of less important ones. He was in no mood to be interrupted when he received from his old friend, William Ralston of the Bank of California in San Francisco, a cable that was more like a letter; at the rates then in force, it had cost the sender something over $1,100.

The message was vague sometimes and at others astonishingly detailed. It told Harpending that somewhere in a remote section of the United States a vast diamond field had been discovered. The stones already turned up were of incalculable value, and more might be gathered in limitless quantities at very little expense. In this field the very ant-hills glittered with precious dust, and there was no doubt that it could be considered conservatively as a $50,000,000 proposition. Moreover the sender, Ralston, and a mining man named George D. Roberts whom Harpending knew, were in practical control. The message ended with an appeal to Harpending to come back to San Francisco as fast as he could get there and take on the job of general manager of the entire enterprise.

In his memoirs Harpending says that it seemed to him Ralston must be laboring under some strange delusion. He replied that his business in London made it neessary for him to stay where he was.

As far as Harpending was concerned, he writes, it might have ended there. But rumors began to get about. Financial men began to come to him and ask him what he knew about this discovery that W. C. Ralston was reported to have made; something about diamonds, wasn't it? Then no less astute a banker than the Baron Rothschild himself came to inquire. Harpending showed the Baron the cables he had had from Ralston, saying that while he had always had the greatest confidence in his friend he felt that somehow this time Mr. Ralston had been imposed upon and that it would all come to nothing. The Baron shook his head and told him not to be too sure. America had furnished the world with a few surprises already. It might have others in store. Then he went away.

At that moment one last cable arrived from San Francisco begging Harpending to come at once, even if he could stay only sixty days or, at the most, ninety. He turned for advice to an old friend, Alfred Rubery, a nephew of John Bright, with whom he had shared adventures in the old privateering days of the Civil War. And Rubery's advice decided him. It was nonsense to stay in London wondering what this was all about, Rubery said. The thing to do was to go back to San Francisco and find out. As for himself, he was bored to extinction with London and everything in it. He would be delighted to have such a good excuse to accompany Harpending to San Francisco. Maybe the two could stir things up again in the Far West as they had done half a dozen years earlier.

Harpending cabled Ralston that he and Rubery would make the trip as quickly as steamer and train could carry them. They arrived in San Francisco in May, 1872, ready to look at irrefutable proofs of the greatest diamond field in the world or to get back to London again as fast as they had come.

These were the facts spread before Harpending and his friend, Rubery, when they went down to see Mr. Ralston at the Bank of California:

A few months earlier two weather-beaten men, typical miners by their look, had come into the bank with a package they wanted put in a safe place. It was exceptionally valuable property, they said, and they would like to be sure it was well taken care of.

They were asked the nature of this property, and, after some hedging, they unrolled a bundle and displayed some stones which they said were uncut diamonds. Asked where they had found them they admitted that they had picked them up "in the desert." They would say no more, took their receipt, and left.

The secret leaked out, of course. The first man of importance to learn it was George D. Roberts, who found that one of the men, Philip Arnold, had done some prospecting for him some years before. Roberts insisted that Arnold and his partner, John Slack, come with him to meet Mr. Ralston. With Ralston at the time was William M. Lent; for some weeks only Ralston, Lent, and Roberts were let in on the find. At the meeting Arnold did the talking for his partner, Slack; it was Arnold, also, who handled all the negotiations afterward.

From Arnold and Slack the three financiers got the impression of two simple-minded old-timers, bewildered by their good luck. Yes, they had picked up these diamonds themselves, out in the desert, exact location unspecified. Arnold said vaguely that it was "a long way off." An interesting side-light here is that shortly after this meeting several groups of men were known to have departed quietly for Arizona looking for diamonds. It does not appear which of the three, Ralston, Lent, or Roberts, was responsible for sending out these scouting expeditions on his own, though it must have been one of them.

In any event, Arnold and Slack stuck to their determination not to reveal the location of their fields. Would they take in any others in order to help finance their venture? They were not eager, but eventually they were persuaded to part with a small interest in return for a hundred thousand dollars, which, they explained, they had to have in order to make sure of claims to the land surrounding their find. Ralston and his friends had at least got one foot inside the door to riches.

Here, however, the deal bogged down. Neither Arnold nor Slack could be persuaded to sell a further interest. In fact, they appeared to expect that the hundred thousand dollars would be turned over to them merely on the strength of their unsupported story. Ralston told them that he did not do business that way. Some one would have to see the diamond fields.

Arnold and Slack admitted that this was fair. After some thought they said they would conduct two men, no more, to the location of their claim; Ralston and Roberts might choose whom they pleased. But there was one proviso. At the point where Arnold and Slack would lead them off the beaten track, the two investigators must submit to being blindfolded for the duration of the trip into the desert. The same would hold true on the return trip. Ralston agreed for his fellow-promoters. The trip was made, and the investigators came back with more diamonds and enthusiastic reports of the ease with which they had been found. They had even a ruby or two. Ralston, Lent, and Roberts were sure they had hold of something big. It was at this point in the proceedings that Harpending and Rubery arrived in San Francisco.

The first thing Harpending wanted to do was to talk to Arnold and Slack. This was impossible; the men were out of town. Ralston told him why. It was a mattter of providing ample security for the hundred thousand they wanted from the banker.

Before Harpending's arrival, Arnold and Slack had made a proposal. The small package of diamonds in the bank's vault had been valued by such experts as were available in San Francisco at approximately $125,000, as nearly as rough stones could be figured. If the bankers did not feel this to be sufficient security, they, Arnold and Slack, would make another trip to their claims and bring back, as they put it, "a couple of million dollars' worth of stones." These they would hand over to Ralston's group as a guarantee of good faith. Ralston approved, and the men had left for their field. They were due to return any day now.

That put a different face on the matter. Harpending had to grant that two million dollars' worth of diamonds would be adequate security for a paltry hundred thousand in cash. More, he would very much like to look at two million dollars' worth of diamonds; it should be a sight worth seeing. As though it had been carefully timed, a telegram arrived at that moment from Arnold and Slack. They had reached Reno on their way back. Would Mr. Ralston, or some one he could trust, meet them at Lathrop to share in the heavy burden of responsibility? Harpending jumped at the chance. When the train pulled into Lathrop station, he boarded it and found his men without difficulty. Both were travel-stained and weather-beaten and looked extremely tired. Harpending sat down and Arnold began to tell him his story.

They had had a little trouble, Arnold said. They had luckily struck a spot which was enormously rich in stones, and selected enough to be worth, at their guess, about the two millions they had set out to get. These they had done up in two packages, one for each. On the way back they had been forced to build a raft in order to cross a river which was swollen with a sudden rain. This raft had been upset in the current, and they had very nearly lost both bundles of diamonds. One, indeed, had been swept into the water. They had thought of fishing for it, but since the remaining bundle must contain something like a million dollars in stones they had decided it would do. Harpending thought a million dollars' worth of diamonds ought to be fairly satisfactory, and when the two miners explained that they wanted to leave the train at Oakland in order to get some rest with friends, he scribbled them a receipt and took charge of the bundle. It must have seemed an eternity before the ferry reached the San Francisco shore where the Harpending carriage was waiting.

None of the group had been able to bear the thought of delaying their meeting as much as one day. They were assembled at Harpending's house, ready for him to arrive. Some one found a sheet and spread it on the billiard-table. Then Harpending cut the fastenings of the bundle, took hold of the lower corners of the sack, and upended it. Arnold and Slack's million dollars' worth of diamonds tumbled out on to the white cloth. This time there were still other rough stones mixed in with the diamonds. They had no trouble identifying them as emeralds and sapphires.

Matters moved quickly after that; Ralston and his friends were old hands at promotion and organization, and they went swiftly into their accustomed routine.

Arnold and Slack were called in and told that this business was too big for them. After some debate they agreed. Hundreds of millions would be made out of the new diamond fields; there could be no doubt about it. Even a small share would make them rich men, and they would have none of the trouble of financing that was bound to come with a promotion of such magnitude. Finally they said they would be content with a quarter share. Ralston and the rest congratulated them on their perspicacity, drew up the papers, and arranged for payment to them of cash sums amounting in all to something over $600,000 in return for three-quarters' interest. That took care of the two miners. The gems the syndicate held would be ample security for that much.

Next an outline of a corporation was sketched. Ralston, Lent, Roberts, and Harpending were owners of three-quarters of the property; the remainder would go to friends who deserved to be let in on such a good thing. The capital stock was set at $10,000,000, and the allotments of shares were defined. By way of letting the world know what they had, the syndicate then arranged for a display of the marvelous gems in a downtown office. The final step was to send a sample lot of stones to Tiffany's in New York for appraisal. If Tiffany agreed with the San Francisco experts, then a mining expert was to be found in New York and brought out to examine the fields. Arnold and Slack agreed to conduct this expert to the scene of their operations.

Harpending, as general manager, took the sample stones to New

York. His first move was to retain Samuel Barlow, a leader of the New York bar, as counsel. General B. F. Butler was also added to the corporation's legal staff. There were good reasons for this; General Butler was influential in Washington, and could aid the company materially in legislation needed to acquire the lands adjacent to the diamond fields. Then Mr. Tiffany was invited to meet with Harpending and his lawyers at Mr. Barlow's house to view the gems. There was no harm in making it a social occasion too while they were at it; the secret did not have to be kept any longer. Among those invited to the preview were General McClellan and Horace Greeley, who stood and watched while the great authority on precious stones sat down and allowed Harpending to open the treasure-sack.

Mr. Tiffany viewed the display gravely, sorted the stones into little heaps, held them up to the light. Then he spoke. In his memoirs, Asbury Harpending sets down his words. "Gentlemen," he said, "these are beyond question precious stones of enormous value. But before I give you an exact appraisement, I must submit them to my lapidary. I will report to you further in two days." Mr. Tiffany's lapidary was not quite as enthusiastic, though he did well enough. He said the stones that Mr. Harpending had brought would be worth $150,000. At that rate the total on hand would come to something like a million and a quarter or thereabouts. As general manager of the company, Mr. Harpending was satisfied. Only one step remained. They had to find a mining expert and take him to see the actual diamond fields. That part of it was easy. There was one man, Henry Janin, whose reputation was head and shoulders above all the rest. If he had any failing, it was on the side of conservatism; there had been complaints that Janin never took a chance. Manifestly he was the man they wanted. He agreed to make the examination for a fee of $2,500, all expenses, and the right to take up a thousand shares of stock at a price. It was not a low fee, all things considered, but with hundreds of millions practically in sight, Harpending was not one to boggle.

The party would have started for the diamond fields without further delay but for one minor difficulty. This was Arnold's restiveness. He had paper agreements, he said, but paper was not cash. So far, he and his partner had received a hundred thousand dollars. It seemed to him now that they ought to have another hundred thousand before revealing the location of the claims. He would be glad to let the amount remain in escrow pending Mr. Janin's report, but he did think that some such settlement as he suggested ought to be the next step. After some consideration, Harpending communicated with Ralston, back in San Francisco, who sent on the cash by telegraph. The important thing, he wired Harpending, was to get the expert out to the diamond fields and have the examination made. Harpending saw the point. He wasted no time in getting Janin, Rubery, Arnold, Slack, and himself, on a train headed West.

It was a long, hot, dusty ride out to Rawlins Springs in Wyoming Territory where Arnold said they must leave the train. There was one bit of confusion on the way which helped to pass the time. This was a telegram from George Roberts whose enthusiasm, now that Janin was hired and on the way, was too great to keep in check. His wire contained the information that he and a party of friends would leave San Francisco headed east and meet the Harpending party at Omaha, so that all might visit the great discovery together. Here Arnold flatly rebelled. He pointed out that this constant changing of arrangements was not good business, that he had fulfilled to the letter all his agreements, and that he expected the Ralston group to do the same. There were still obligations for the syndicate to meet, he said (which, from his viewpoint, was quite true), and until these were taken care of he did not wish to expose all the details of the great find to the world at large. Harpending perforce agreed with him, and wired Roberts and his fellow-enthusiasts to stay in San Francisco.

At Rawlins Springs the party rented the necessaary mules and horses, and struck off into the wilderness, led by Arnold and Slack. If they had expected to reach their goal quickly they were sorely disappointed. Arnold himself often seemed uncertain about his directions; sometimes the whole party would have to wait an hour or two while he climbed a high peak to find his landmarks. There were three days of this. On the fourth day, Arnold suggested the party remain in camp while he set out alone to "get his bearings." About noon he returned and said they might follow him. By evening they were encamped on the diamond fields they had heard so much about.

Next morning every one was up early and ready to begin the examination. The place to which Arnold had brought them was at an elevation of about seven thousand feet, so Harpending estimated. It was a gently sloping basin, comprising from thirty to forty acres of land, littered with rocks, through which a small stream ran. Arnold pointed out several ant-hills in which he had dug and found diamonds, and suggested that members of the party try these or any other places that took their fancy. In Rawlins Springs they had bought picks, pans, and shovels, and with these implements the party set to work, each member anxious to be the first to find a diamond. It was Rubery who won; within a few minutes the party heard him yell and joined him to see the rough stone he had uncovered. After that, all of them were lucky. For more than an hour they dug, turning up diamonds in profusion, many rubies, and a few sapphires and emeralds. Often jack-knives were sufficient to dig the gems from the mounds that sparkled with ruby and diamond dust. Harpending says in his memoirs that he and his friend Rubery felt "the intoxication that comes with sudden accession of boundless wealth."

The next day prospecting was resumed, Janin wandering farther afield than on the first day but finding diamonds wherever he went. He insisted upon taking a third day to extend his investigation, but at the end of that time he professed himself satisfied. He did point out, Harpending says, that the wise thing for the syndicate to do would be to see that it also had control of adjacent lands. He was assured that this would be taken care of; General Butler had been retained as counsel for that very purpose. On the fourth day they all spent their time staking off a wide stretch of country in all directions from the little basin in which the chief concentration of stones had been found. That was all that could be done. The next move was to get to civilization as soon as possible and start the wheels rolling. Slack and Rubery were left to guard the field, and the rest of the party headed back for the railroad.

Back in New York, Harpending set up an office, arranged with Baron Rothschild in London to handle the British end of the financing, kept in touch with Mr. Ralston who had insisted that the main office must be in San Francisco. The corporation was named The San Francisco and New York Mining and Commercial Company. Its powers were of the widest; it was not alone to engage in the business of mining and owning mines and their accessories, but also to engage in every class of commercial business including the preparation of precious stones for the market. It was this last point that had the widest repercussions. Those in the business deduced that it was the intention of the Company to move the great lapidary establishments of Amsterdam to the Pacific Coast. The news caused quite a flurry of excitement in the Low Countries.

The business of organization went on, Harpending keeping in constant touch with Ralston, who scorned ordinary correspondence and used the telegraph constantly. In San Francisco twenty-five friends of the Ralston group were permitted to subscribe for stock in the amount of $80,000 each, and this initial capital of $2,000,000 was paid in to the Company's account in the Bank of California. A stockholder's meeting was held and directors elected. New York was given two on the Board, Samuel P. Barlow, the Company's lawyer, and—for front—General George B. McClellan. One of the San Francisco members was the Rothschild representative for the Far West. There remained but one point to be settled. That was taken care of by a final payment of $300,000 to Arnold, who had a properly executed power of attorney to act for his partner, Slack. Finally, on July 30, 1872, the articles of incorporation were formally filed and the report of Mr. Janin was made public. Handsome offices were engaged, and David D. Colton was installed as General Manager. Mr. Harpending, as an owner, was glad to let Colton take over. On the wall of the office hung an enormous map showing the three-thousand-acre field with the relative positions of Discovery Claim, Ruby Gulch, Diamond Flat, and Sapphire Hollow. The plan was for the company to hold and work Discovery Claim. The other locations were to be placed as concessions on a basis of so much cash down and a royalty on the gems recovered.

The San Francisco newspapers had a high time with the story, now that it was out. Said the *Alta:* "The superintendent expressed the opinion that with twenty-five men he will be able to take out gems worth at least $1,000,000 a month. The stones will be brought to San Francisco and cut here."

The New York papers did even better, a contributor signing himself "Old Miner" writing, in the *Sun,* that the Company had in its possession a single gem larger than a pigeon's egg, of matchless purity of color and worth at a low estimate $500,000. Since he had not seen the map in Mr. Colton's office, "Old Miner" added that the great new diamond field was in Southeastern Arizona, which was not more than eight hundred miles too far to the south. The San Francisco *Bulletin* declared: "The implements used by the discoverers in extracting the diamonds were ordinary jack-knives. If so much wealth can be turned up by such primitive means, what might be accomplished by shovels and pickaxes? Little else is discussed in California Street but diamonds and rubies."

For three months San Francisco, New York, and London buzzed with talk about the new diamond fields. Fifteen *bona fide* offers were made by concessionaires who were anxious to pay as much as $200,000 down and return a royalty on gems to the amount of twenty per cent to the parent company. Three subsidiary diamond and ruby companies were organized, one of them placing on view a large reddish stone known as the "Staunton Ruby." Officials were deluged with letters asking to buy stock. Fortunately no one in the organization was willing to part with any. For on November 11, 1872, Mr. Lent, the President of the San Francisco and New York Mining and Commercial Company, received a message. It was from a small station in Wyoming and was signed by Clarence King, a geologist and engineer in the service of the United States Government. Mr. King stated, flatly and uncompromisingly, that the diamond fields were "salted," and that the entire affair was a colossal swindle from beginning to end.

Ralston and the rest must have felt in their bones that their dream was over. It had all been too good to be true anyhow. But they had to go through the motions. A committee was appointed and hastily sent to join King at the diamond fields. Mr. King was waiting for them, only too glad to show them what he had learned.

For one thing, the "ant hills" in which so many of the stones had been found—those dazzling mounds that had sparkled so with diamond dust and ruby powder—were not ant-hills at all but had been artfully constructed by human hands. At the base of each, holes had been poked with a stick, and at the bottom of each hole reposed a diamond, now and then a ruby or sapphire. No one had disturbed the ant-hills, perhaps because they looked so pretty gleaming in the sun, perhaps because there were so many diamonds to be picked up elsewhere. That is, no one had touched them until Mr.

King came along with his German assistant. They had done some kicking and poking and exposed the artificial nature of the mounds.

Another point the company investigators had missed was the presence of several stones—rubies and diamonds both—on the top of a large flat rock. They were pressed into crevices so that they would stay in place, which was puzzling to Mr. King and his helper. But the clincher had been a discovery the German made. Harpending, in his memoirs, reports his remarks verbatim, though he does not say how he learned the precise words the man used. The German had been working by himself, when all at once he stopped and called to Mr. King. "Look here, Mr. King," he had said. "This is the bulliest diamond field as ever was. Not only it produces diamonds, but it cuts them also!" King looked at what his helper held in his hand. It was a diamond, no doubt of it. Any one could see where the lapidary had worked on it.

The party returned to San Francisco, and on November 25th the general facts were given to the press. The Great Diamond Hoax was exposed, and two dozen rich and influential business men were the laughing stock of half the world.

There was nothing left but the dreary business of winding up the affairs of the San Francisco and New York Mining and Commercial Company.

Ralston's instant reaction was to see that none of the twenty-five men he had led into the scheme should suffer loss, and to this end he repaid them all their original investment, framing their receipts to hang on the wall of his office in the bank. The net loss of something close to three-quarters of a million dollars fell upon the chief owner-promoters—Ralston, Roberts, and Lent. There was an investigation, during which a private detective agency found that Arnold and Slack had made something like $50,000 in a mining deal in 1870; that Arnold had made two trips to Amsterdam and London to buy coarse stones, sailing each time from Halifax rather than from an American port; and that one of his London purchases had been a large quantity of the poorer grade South African stones known as "niggerheads." If there had been any doubt about it, a double confirmation arrived from London. The firm to which Baron Rothschild had submitted some of the sample diamonds for appraisal recognized them instantly as coming from the lot it had sold to the uncouth American. The firm was rather surprised to receive, shortly afterward, a photograph from a detective agency in the United States, but its manager was glad to identify the likeness as that of the same American, although since the purchase had been for cash he was unable to say whether or not the man's name was Arnold. That might have concluded the investigation but for the determination of Mr. Lent to follow Arnold on his own hook and see if he could not run him down.

It proved very simple. Arnold had gone back to his old home in Hardin County, Kentucky, bought a fine piece of land, a house, and a safe. He carried a good balance at the local bank, but it was common rumor that most of his wealth was kept in this strong box at home.

The rumor was confirmed when Mr. Lent of San Francisco arrived in Hardin County, hired a lawyer, and proceeded to file suit against Arnold for $350,000. Arnold's reply through the newspapers was vigorous, even abusive. He did not, he said, owe Mr. Lent or any one else a cent. He had half a million dollars in his safe, if anybody was interested. That money he had made by his arduous labors as a prospector and miner in the Far West, and this attempt to gain possession of it was no more and no less than a decent man might expect from a "shark from California," an outrage of the grossest sort. Further, this accusation that he had ever salted a claim was the purest fabrication. He had turned over to Mr. Lent's company a perfectly good diamond field; the report of Henry Janin proved its quality, as did the valuation put by Tiffany's of New York upon the stones he had extracted from it. If there had been any salting it had been done later; in fact, such skullduggery was about what one could expect from practically any "California scamp." Mr. Lent might put that in his pipe and smoke it. As for himself, he, Philip Arnold, would stand off the whole of California, if necessary in order to protect his rights, and he was certain that his fellow-Kentuckians would support his position.

Arnold understood his Hardin County and his friends. Even those who knew nothing about him declared themselves on his side as against the stranger from California where, as every one knew, any kind of jiggery-pokery could be put over. Mr. Lent was beaten even before his suit got under way. For some reason, never quite clear, however, Arnold indicated privately his willingness to compromise.

Harpending writes that he acted as go-between in the deal, and that in the end Arnold paid Lent $150,000 on consideration of immunity from further litigation. Whatever the arrangement, Arnold went his own way from that time forward. As it happened, he did not live long to enjoy his prosperity. Within a year he got into a shooting scrape which landed him in the hospital. He was on the way to recovery from a severe shoulder wound when pneumonia finished him.

As for Slack, Arnold's partner, he remains perhaps the greatest mystery in the whole affair. Always a silent man, preferring to let Arnold do the talking, he disappeared as silently as he played his part in the hoax. The last man to see him was Harpending's friend, Rubery, who had been left with him to guard the hundred-million-dollar claim in the mountains. When they were relieved of their watch they had gone together to the railway station at Rawlins Springs. Rubery left for San Francisco. Slack said he would wait for the eastbound train. Despite an active and prolonged search, nothing was ever heard of him again. More than one student has wondered how it came about, since Arnold and Slack had always represented themselves as partners, that all the profits turned up in Arnold's bank account and iron safe.

That was the Great Diamond Hoax, California's postcript to gold.

Shrewdly as Arnold handled his part in the affair, the swindle could never have succeeded if it had not been that even the smartest business men were half-blinded by the incredible wealth that had already been found in the new West. Diamonds, rubies, emeralds, and sapphires were not customarily found in the same fields; that was true. But who could tell about this vast western empire? As Baron Rothschild had said, America had produced many surprises already; why not another? Tiffany, after all, had said no more than that the stones shown him were diamonds. They were diamonds. The business Tiffany conducted was confined to cut gems; he and his local staff were no experts on uncut stones. Janin had the Tiffany report to go on. He was not concerned with the genuineness of the stones, nor with their quality; it was his affair only to check the presence of diamonds in the place where Arnold said they were. And they were there, plenty of them; Janin picked them out of the ground himself.

Nevertheless, the promoters had to take the ridicule. They had even to suffer the accusation that they had been in on the swindle, that even though they had sold no stock they were probably planning to do so in one gigantic operation. In London, the *Times* accused Harpending directly of acting in complicity with his friend Alfred Rubery to stage the entire diamond fraud. Rubery sued and recovered heavy damages. Harpending turned most of his holdings into cash, left California, and retired to his home state. Oddly enough it was Kentucky. Californias of a later generation had almost forgotten him when he returned to San Francisco in the first decade of this century to dispose of a mine he still owned on the Mother Lode and to write his account of the Great Diamond Hoax. To-day's reader may smile at his tart denial of the charge that the salting of the diamond claims was so crudely done that diamonds were even found in the crotches of the trees: "This," wrote Harpending, "was not true, for the very good reason that there were no trees there."

But—well, in 1944 some Harpending papers turned up in a stamp-dealer's cellar where they had been dumped after all stamps were cut off the old envelopes and deeds. Among them is a letter which should interest the reader of Harpending's memoirs or this narrative of the Great Diamond Hoax.

The letter is from one of the men involved, a friend of Harpending's and a confidant and associate of Ralston's in many deals. It is dated December 4, 1871, and the year is worth noting.

As the reader will recall, it was early in 1872 that Harpending received his first cable from Ralston begging him to come to San Francisco. It had been only a few days before this that the miners, Arnold and Slack had come to the Bank of California with their little sack of diamonds to be stowed safely in the vault. To put it differently, no one had heard of Arnold and Slack in connection with diamonds before the early spring of 1872. Or so Harpending indicates in his memoirs, and so the published accounts of the Diamond Hoax all agreed at the time. Certainly Ralston had had no knowledge of either man, or of diamonds in connection with them before that time.

Yet consider a line or two from this newly found letter to Harpending in London from his friend in San Francisco. After discussing other business affairs, including the Mineral Hill Mine, the writer says "Mrs. Arnold has been quite sick. Says Mr. A. was in Kentucky when she last heard from him, and that he would not return this winter." Clearly this friend of Harpending's knew a Mr. and Mrs. Arnold, the man being moreover, an Arnold from Kentucky. Where was "Mr. A." then? Perhaps discovering a fabulous diamond field in Wyoming? Well, perhaps. But there is one more sentence to this letter, written it must be remembered, in 1871, which was before any two miners named Arnold and Slack had ever turned up at the bank with their little canvas sack of trouble. That sentence, written to Harpending in London from his friend in San Francisco, reads "Can you send me one of the African rough diamonds?"

In the light of this, the student of the Great Diamond Hoax, and of Harpending's connection with it, may conclude to take a slightly different view from that presented by Harpending himself, in those memoirs written almost half a century later.

THE TOWN CRIER

Ambrose Bierce

IT IS WITH grim satisfaction that we record the destruction by fire of Bierstadt's celebrated picture of Yosemite Valley.

The painting has been a prolific parent of ten thousand abominations. We have had Yosemite in oils, in water colors, in crayon, in chalk and charcoal until in our very dreams we imagine ourselves falling from the summit of El Capitan or descending in spray from the Bridal Veil cataract. Besides, that picture has incited more unpleasant people to visit California than all our conspiring hotel-keepers could compel to return.

We are glad a blow has finally been struck at the root of immigration. If we can corral Hill's paintings and send East all the rest we may hope for peace. If not, we trust some daring spirit may be found to blow up the infernal Valley with Giant powder or glycerine soap.

[1875]

NOTHING TO SEE IN
SAN FRANCISCO

by

ANTHONY TROLLOPE

My WAY home from the Sandwich Islands to London took me to San Francisco, across the American continent, and New York,—whence I am now writing to you my last letter of this series. I had made this journey before, but had on that occasion reached California too late to visit the now world-famous valley of the Yo Semite, and the big pine trees which we call Wellingtonias. On this occasion I made the excursion, and will presently tell the story of the trip,—but I must first say a few words as to the town of San Francisco.

I do not know that in all my travels I ever visited a city less interesting to the normal tourist, who, as a rule, does not care to investigate the ways of trade or to employ himself in ascertaining how the people around him earn their bread. There is almost nothing to see in San Francisco that is worth seeing. There is a new park in which you may drive for six or seven miles on a well made road, and which, as a park for the use of a city, will, when completed, have many excellencies. There is also the biggest hotel in the world,—so the people of San Francisco say, which has cost a million sterling,—5 millions of dollars,—and is intended to swallow up all the other hotels. It was just finished but not opened when I was there. There is an inferior menagerie of wild beasts, and a place called the Cliff House to which strangers are taken to hear seals bark. Everything,—except hotel prices,—is dearer here than at any other large town I know; and the ordinary traveller has no peace left him either in

From *A Letter from Anthony Trollope*, the Colt Press, San Francisco, 1946.

public or private by touters who wish to persuade him to take this or the other railway route into the Eastern States.

There is always a perfectly cloudless sky over head unless when rain is falling in torrents, and perhaps no where in the world is there a more sudden change from heat to cold in the same day. I think I may say that strangers will generally desire to get out of San Francisco as quickly as they can, — unless indeed circumstances may have enabled them to enjoy the hospitality of the place. There is little or nothing to see, and life at the hotels is not comfortable. But the trade of the place and the way in which money is won and lost are alike marvellous. I found 10/a day to be about the lowest rate of wages paid to a man for any kind of work in the city, and the average wages of a housemaid who is, of course, found in everything but her clothes, to be over £70 per annum. All payments in California are made in coin, whereas in the other states of the Union except California, Oregon, and Nevada, monies are paid in depreciated notes,—so that the two dollars and a half per day which the labourer earns in San Francisco are as good as three and a quarter in New York. No doubt this high rate of pay is met by an equivalent in the high cost of many articles, such as clothing and rent; but it does not affect the price of food which to the labouring man is the one important item of expenditure. Consequently the labouring man in California has a position which I have not known him to achieve elsewhere.

In trade there is a speculative rashness which ought to ensure ruin according to our old world ideas, but which seems to be rewarded by very general success. The stranger may of course remember if he pleases that the millionaire who builds a mighty palace is seen and heard of and encountered at all corners, while the bankrupt will probably sink unseen into obscurity. But in San Francisco there is not much of bankruptcy; and when it does occur no one seems to be so little impressed as the bankrupt. There is a goodnature, a forbearance, and an easy giving of trust which to an old fashioned Englishman like myself seem to be most dangerous, but which I was assured there form the readiest mode of building up a great commercial community. The great commercial community is there, and I am not prepared to deny that it has been built after that fashion. If a young man there can make friends, and can establish a character for honesty to his friends and for smartness to the outside world, he can borrow almost any amount of money without security, for the purpose of establishing himself in business. The lender, if he feel sure that he will not be robbed by his protege, is willing to run the risk of unsuccessful speculation.

As we steamed into the Golden Horn (*sic*) the news reached us that about a month previously the leading bank in San Francisco, the bank of California, had "burst up" for some enormous amount of dollars, and that the manager, who was well known as one of the richest men and as perhaps the boldest speculator in the State, had been drowned on the day following. But we also heard that payments would be resumed in a few days; and payments were resumed before I left the city: that no one but the shareholders would lose a dollar, and that the shareholders were ready to go on with any amount of new capital; and that not a single bankruptcy in the whole community had been caused by this stoppage of the bank which had been extended for a period over a month! How came it to pass, I asked of course, that the collapse of so great a monetary enterprise as the bank of California should pass on without a general panic, at any rate in the city? Then I was assured that all those concerned were goodnatured, that everybody gave time,—that bills were renewed all round, and that in an hour or two it was understood that no one in San Francisco was to be asked for money just at that crisis. To me all this seemed to be wrong. I have always imagined that severity to bankrupt debtors,—that amount of severity which requires that a bankrupt shall really be a bankrupt,—is the best and indeed the only way of ensuring regularity in commerce and of preventing men from tossing up with other people's money in the confidence that they may win and cannot lose. But such doctrines are altogether out of date in California. The money of depositors was scattered broadcast through the mining speculations of the district, and no one was a bit the worse for it,—except the unfortunate gentleman who had been, perhaps happily, removed from a community which had trusted him long with implicit confidence, which still believed him to be an honest man, but which would hardly have known how to treat him had he survived. To add to the romance of the story it should be said that though this gentleman was drowned while bathing it seems to be certain that his death was accidental. It is stated that he was struck by apoplexy while in the water.

I was taken to visit the stock-brokers' Board in San Francisco,—

that is the room in which mining shares are bought and sold. The trader should understand that in California, and, still more, in the neighboring State of Nevada, gold and silver mining are now very lively. The stock-jobbing created by these mines is carried on in San Francisco and is a business as universally popular as was the buying and selling of railroad shares during our railway mania. Everybody is at it. The housemaid of whom I have spoken as earning £70 per annum, buys Consolidated Virginia or Ophir stock with that money; —or perhaps she prefers Chollar Potosi, or Best and Belcher, or Yellow Jacket, or Buckeye. She probably consults some gentleman of her accquaintance and no doubt in 19 cases out of 20 loses her money. But it is the thing to do, and she enjoys that charm which is the delectation of all gamblers. Of course in such a condition of things there are men who know how the wind is going to blow, who make the wind blow this way and that, who can raise the price of shares by fictitious purchases, and then sell, or depreciate them by fictitious sales and then buy. The housemaids and others go to the wall, while the knowing men build palaces and seem to be troubled by no seared consciences. In the mean time the brokers drive a roaring trade,—whether they purchase legitimately for others or speculate on their own account.

The Stock Exchange in London is I believe closed to strangers. The Bourse in Paris is open to the world and at a certain hour affords a scene to those who choose to go and look at it of wild noise, unintelligible action, and sometimes apparently of demoniac fury. The unitiated are unable to comprehend that the roaring herd in the pen beneath them are doing business. The Stock Exchange Board in San Francisco is not open to strangers, as it is in Paris, but may be visited with an order, and by the kindness of a friend I was admitted. Paris is more than six times as large as San Francisco; but the fury at San Francisco is even more demoniac than at Paris. I thought that the gentlemen employed were going to hit each other between the eyes, and that the apparent quarrels which I saw already demanded the interference of the police. But the uproarious throng were always obedient, after slight delays, to the ringing hammer of the Chairman and as each five minutes' period of internecine combat was brought to an end, I found that a vast number of mining shares had been bought and sold. Perhaps a visit to this Chamber, when the stockbrokers are at work between the hours of eleven and twelve, is of all sights in San Francisco, the one best worth seeing.

SAN FRANCISCO'S EMPEROR

by

JOHN BRUCE

W INTER darkness falls early in San Francisco when both fog and drizzle are difting along its seven hills. It is the Coastal Indians' "sad weather" when the weary creep into shelters. Aboriginal folk-lore says when chieftains die it is considered right that the night have a fog and rain drifting together. On such a night, San Francisco lost its only king, and its newspapers announced solemnly that the king was dead.

Norton I, Emperor of All America and Protector of Mexico Dei Gratia, was gone. In his pocket were a $2.50 gold piece, $3 in silver and a franc note of 1828. Police took him away from the corner of California and Dupont in a dead wagon that had not been hosed out for some time. He was dressed in his regimentals, with tarnished epaulettes. The withered flower was still in his lapel. The beaver hat with its bright feather cockade, the tri-colored umbrella and the knotted cane were tossed into the wagon before it drove away.

In January of 1880, Emperor Norton was dead after reigning with expert dignity for twenty-one years. His scrip had been honored without question; his proclamations were read and bowed to by thousands. He had always addressed the King of Prussia and Queen Victoria as "Dear Cousins," and suggested once that the Widow of Windsor might like to wed with him. He had been listed in the official City Directory as "Norton, Joshua (Emperor)." He had ordered the Republican and Democratic parties abolished as being incompatible. He had issued bonds and levied his own private taxes.

All this because the newspapers of San Francisco made him so. Emperor Norton was their creation. They had started him out in 1859, when he was just plain Joshua Abraham Norton, Character Number One. For years, they printed his proclamations and mentioned his social activities.

Now that the king was dead, the city decided that royalty should not lie in a pauper's grave. The Pacific Club (now Nob Hill's Pacific Union, most exclusive men's club in the city) took over. The richest men buried the poorest man.

In the undertaking parlor on lower O'Farrell Street, the Emperor lay in state for a day while 10,000 passed for a farewell look. Newspapers were lavish in their descriptions of the ceremonies. "The body lay in a wilderness of blooms," said the *Bulletin*.

When the Reverend W. L. Githens read the Episcopal service, a boys' choir sang "Nearer, My God, To Thee," and the congregation joined in the singing. Many wept. Part of San Francisco's tradition was being buried. The Pacific Club members bought the plot.

In 1849, Norton came to San Francisco with $40,000. By 1853 through speculations in foodstuffs, he was worth a quarter of a million and had constructed and was operating the first rice mill on the Pacific Coast. Then he tried to corner the rice market—and an unexpected arrival of rice-laden ships ruined him. He became a quiet eccentric, living alone in a cheap room.

In September of 1859, while the city's newspapers were shaking fists at each other over the Broderick-Terry duel, Editor Fitch of the *Bulletin* looked up one afternoon to see a man standing in the doorway of his small office. He had a piece of paper in his hand.

"I was wondering," the man said gently, "if you would care to publish this."

He placed the paper on the desk and without another word moved out. Fitch, already nicknamed the Deacon, looked at it later in the day when his deadline was passed. It read:

"At the peremptory request and desire of a large majority of the citizens of these United States, I, Joshua Norton, formerly of Algoa Bay, Cape of Good Hope, and now for the last nine years and ten months past of San Francisco,

California, declare and proclaim myself Emperor of these
United States; and in virtue of the authority thereby in me
vested, do hereby order and direct the representatives of
the different states of the Union to assemble in Musical Hall,
of this city, on the 1st day of February next, then and there
to make such alterations in the existing laws of the Union
as may ameliorate the evils under which the country is
laboring, and thereby cause confidence to exist, both at home
and abroad, in our stability and integrity.

Norton I.
Emperor of the United States."

Deacon Fitch had his moment of caprice. He printed it. Later,
defending his lapse of dignity, he said he considered the proclamation had a quality of relief in the midst of tension over the tragic
duel.

The announcement caused little notice, but Norton came back
to the *Bulletin* on October 12th, pleased and kindly intentioned.
He had a proclamation abolishing Congress because there was so
much fraud and corruption in public office that he thought it might
be well to start all over again. Fitch had another weak moment
and again published the Emperor's orders. This pleased His Majesty
so much that he proclaimed the *Bulletin* his official publication. He
came in soon with an order doing away with the State Supreme
Court because it had recently been reversing the lower courts.

By now, rude persons were beginning to laugh at the fellow a
serious-minded newspaper editor had created in a moment of caprice.
Particularly was he funny since he had donned a uniform. A newspaper or two ridiculed him and the Emperor had his official journal
publish his reply:

"Whereas, certain scurrilous and untrue articles, attacking
our right and propriety, have appeared in one or two insignificant papers of this city:

"Whereas, there are always portions of a community
whose taste can be pampered by low and improper articles:

"Therefore, I decree that the good sense and honesty of
purpose of the nation is not be insulted by such trash.

Norton I."

The Emperor, in his splendid uniform (which the general at

the Presidio had presented), took up the afternoon fashion promenade along Montgomery and Kearny Street, already a tradition in the city that was to thrive on traditions when times got hard. Gentlemen and their ladies made the *paseo* of the two main streets, dressed in their best, bowing and hat-lifting as they moved. To the young bloods it was also the cocktail route. The Emperor accepted the bows of his subjects with dignity. He had become an intimate reality. Newspapers accepted him as part of the fun of living in San Francisco. His scrip, printed by the famous printer, Charles A. Murdock, was now numbered serially, was signed, and bore the Emperor's picture. It was accepted without argument at its face value, four-bits (fifty cents). Each note carried a promise of 5 percent interest and was due in 1880. It is significant (if you are inclined to look at it that way) to note that all his bonds and scrip were payable in 1880—the year that he was to enter only eight days before dropping dead.

Saloons and restaurants liked the spirit of the thing. Norton ate where he pleased for twenty-one years; he never paid a cent; he offered one of his bonds for fifty cents if he felt generous. He marched into offices of the city's millionaires without bothering the secretaries outside. He always asked for a million or two, and it was proper to inform him that you were sorry but the Queen of Sheba or King Cole had been ahead of him, and would fifty cents be sufficient this time? It would.

He had any seat that was vacant at curtain time in the city's theaters. He paid no fare on the street cars. His clothing was furnished without cost by the best tailors (including the original Bullock & Jones), who announced by window cards that they were tailors by appointment to His Majesty. He made many walking sticks, some brought to him from the far ends of the earth.

Many years later, Robert Louis Stevenson, who loved San Francisco with all his generous heart, wrote about him in *The Wrecker*. He said:

" . . . . . In what other city would a harmless madman who supposed himself Emperor of the two Americas have been so fostered and encouraged? Where else would even the people of the streets have respected the poor soul's illusion? Where else would bankers and merchants have re-

ceived his visits, cashed his cheques, and submitted to his
small assessments? Where else would he have been suffered
to attend and address the exhibition days of schools and
colleges? Where else, in God's green earth, have taken his
pick of restaurants, ransacked the bill of fare, and departed scatheless? They tell me he was even an exacting
patron, threatening to withdraw his custom when dissatisfied; and I can believe it, for his face wore an expression
distinctly gastronomical . . . . "

As time went on and San Francisco took to its tender bosom the
strange, simple king, a blue book of the noblesse was kept by him.
Each loyal subject therein paid 50 cents on the first of the month,
a system something similar to tithing. Norton collected personally,
having no constable, and checked each off the book. One merchant,
who was away for eighteen months, cheerfully paid his nine dollars
upon return.

Occasionally the Emperor was permitted to inspect the troops at
the Presidio and the University of California cadets. Once he was
refused passage on the Sacramento boat. Norton had planned a trip
to the state capital to scold his legislators and was much annoyed.
He went to the *Alta California,* (at the time his official newspaper,
since Fitch's *Bulletin* had printed his last proclamation in small type
too near the classified advertisements), and complained. He ordered
a blockade order published, forbidding steamers up the river. The
steamship company didn't think it was funny at all. It was competing
now with the railroad. The company at once sent a life pass to the
Emperor—and the next day he boarded the steamer and refused to
return the salute of the mate at the gangplank.

One day, he saw a cartoon of himself in a store window, smashed
the window with his cane and strode away. The merchant apologized,
repaired the window at his own cost, and shortly after, when one of
Norton's dogs was impounded, paid the license fee to get him out.

Norton had two dogs, both of them almost as famous and as privi-
leged as their master—Lazarus and Bummer. When Bummer died
in 1865, the *Bulletin* carried a 500-word obituary, and Mark Twain
wrote a piece about him for the *Territorial Enterprise* in Virginia
City.

"That old Canine Celebrity of San Francisco," said the *Bulletin,* "surname Bummer, long petted and beloved by her citizens, is dead. It is generally known that he had been on the decline for some weeks past. He died as he had lived, open and above board, Bummer by name, bummer by nature, no more, no less . . . " There followed a sketch of Bummer's life, from his entrance into the city under the axle of a prairie schooner.

When Lazarus died, he got expert treatment, free, from a taxidermist, and ended up in a glass cage in a celebrated saloon on the Montgomery Street champagne route.

As he grew older, Norton became more and more peremptory with his tailors. Some of them let him wait and he complained in a letter to the supervisors. The *Bulletin,* no longer the official publication, bravely took chances of being charged with insult to the sovereign:

"His Majesty's full dress never-mention-'ems have lost their seat, and there is dangerous risk of the Empire being brought into contempt."

Norton stepped over to the *Examiner* and made it a member of his royal family. He then ordered printed:

"Whereas, the *Evening Bulletin* newspaper has been goosey enough to join proscriptive traitors against our Empire of the United States and Protectorate of Mexico:

"Therefore, we Norton I, Gratia Dei Emperor, do hereby fine the said *Bulletin* $2,000; the amount to be appropriated for our Royal Wardrobe."

All the papers, including the *Bulletin,* liked this and began to gang up on the supervisors, demanding they do something natty in the way of a uniform. Since this was hardly permissible by law, the supervisors dug into their own pockets and bought the old man a new suit.

Emperor Norton has remained San Francisco's Character Number One. Today, almost seventy years after his death, he is still occasional news. Sometimes a pioneer who was on his books remembers another story about him before following on to where we all—king and subject —go at last. Usually, the contradictions are reviewed. Although a king, Norton lived in a six-by-ten room in a lodging house, in what was hardly a bon-ton neighborhood. The sign over the door read, "Rooms, 25¢ and 50¢." Norton had one of the fifty-cent ones. It had a camp cot, a cane chair, a pitcher and bowl, nails on the walls for his clothing. Each evening before going to bed he gave the landlord fifty cents.

Many nights he played chess at the Mechanics' Institute, where the games (perhaps the very same ones) are still going on. He won often, a feat of skill, endurance and sagacity in this particular experts' arena where two world's champions have met defeat. Other nights he attended church festivals, theaters, musicals, lectures. He often entered debates and upheld his arguments intelligently and logically.

He was still a great favorite when 1880 came. Businessmen were accepting him at face value along with his tax levies. But his fateful year had arrived, and he dropped dead on a suitable night when the drizzle and fog were down.

So the city wished him a farewell amidst a great bank of flowers, did the sentimental thing because it pleased it to sweeten the sorrow of the parting.

Years later—1934—when a new and more materialistic city forgot its promise to its dead and removed all bodies from the old Masonic Cemetery where the Emperor had lain for fifty-four years, the Pacific Union Club once more took care of him.

When Norton I was unearthed, his redwood box was still intact but his body had not withstood time and those greedy creatures that live in the soil. The symbol of him, his uniform, was there, all except the wilted flower in his lapel.

At the new burial site in the great Woodlawn Cemetery, just across the county line, hundreds gathered to pay tribute again. The Municipal Band played and many spoke and Mayor Angelo Rossi placed a wreath on the tomb in behalf of the city. The 159th Infantry, Third Battalion, fired three volleys over the grave as it was filled in. The granite monument then placed at the head of the grave had chiseled upon its face:

Norton I

Emperor of the United States

and

Protector of Mexico.

Joshua A. Norton

1819-1880.

There are no quotation marks about any of these words.

BUILD THE BRIDGE!

WHEREAS, it is our pleasure to acquiesce in all means of civilization and population:

Now, therefore, we, Norton I, *Dei Gratia* Emperor of the United States and protector of Mexico, do order and direct first, that Oakland shall be the coast termination of the Central Pacific Railroad; secondly, that a suspension bridge be constructed from the improvements lately ordered by our royal decree at Oakland Point to Yerba Buena, from thence to the mountain range of Saucilleto (*sic*), and from thence to the Farallones, to be of sufficient strength and size for a railroad; and thirdly, the Central Pacific Railroad Company are charged with the carrying out of this work, for purposes that will hereafter appear. Whereof fail not under pain of death.

Given under our hand this 18th day of August, A.D. 1869.

NORTON I

From *Emperor Norton* by Allen Stanley Lane, by permission of The Caxton Printers, Ltd.

THE RAPE OF "ELAINE"

by

ROBERT O'BRIEN

MAIDEN LANE is a short street and a narrow one, with Kearny Street and Fred Solari's bar and grill at one end, and Stockton Street and Union Square at the other. Natives sometimes refer to the block nearer Union Square as "the upper block," and to the other one as "the lower block."

There is a Maiden Lane in London, and another in New York. Both are centuries older than this one, but it happens that a San Franciscan gets a wonderful feeling when he passes the window of John Wooster's optical shop, where the little flags of the radiometers spin in the sun, and rounds the corner of the Maiden Lane that meets Union Square. It is the feeling that now, in this quiet place, he can slow his stride, he can drift for a while, he has time to look at the puppies and the goldfish in the pet store window, and admire the flowers in a florist's shop. For him, a walk down that upper block is a five-minute vacation, a time to forget what's on his mind, to window-shop, to pass the time of day with the green boxwood, the privet and the coprosma that grow in sidewalk boxes.

Many years ago, when there was a murder a week on Kearny Street's Battle Row, and Spanish Kitty was the toast of the Barbary Coast, Maiden Lane was Morton Street and two blocks of depravity ruled by a lady known as Iodoform Kate. Compared to the cribs she operated, the worst dive in Pacific Street was as chaste as Southern Pacific waiting room. Harlots, naked from the waist up, sat in the crib windows and for a few pennies permitted passers-by to fondle their breasts. The rest they had to sell they sold for not much more, and Herbert Asbury says a hard-working girl on Morton Street entertained from eighty to a hundred customers a night. Respectable women caught slumming on Morton Street were upbraided from the crib windows for giving away the only thing an honest whore could market, and were driven from the alley by choruses of catcalls and jeers. Except for these infrequent intrusions, the residents of Morton Street were one big industrious family, obscene but happy, with a chicken in every pot and a red light over every door.

Paradoxically, the street's best story has nothing to do with the bawdy tarts of Iodoform Kate. Its heroine, indirectly at least, is Tennyson's Elaine, the Lily Maid of Astolat.

In 1875, a San Francisco boy named Toby E. Rosenthal was acquiring an international reputation as a painter. He was not a native of the city, but his father had brought him there as a child, and he had grown to adolescence on the slope of Telegraph Hill. The father now had a tailor shop crowded between a fruit stand and a laundry on Stockton Street, and the young man was over on the Continent. His paintings were anecdotal in subject, and photographic in treatment; he was a sort of Victorian Norman Rockwell.

On the strength of canvases with titles like *Love's Last Offering,* *Spring's Joys and Sorrow* and *The Exile's Return,* European critics were calling Rosenthal a genius, when Tiburcio Parrott, a wealthy San Francisco merchant, commissioned him to do a painting based on the lines from *Idylls of the King,*

> *And the dead steered by the dumb*
> *Went upward with the flood.*

It was to be a five-by-three oil painting illustrating the scene where the corpse of Elaine, dead of unrequited love for Lancelot, is ferried on a funeral barge to Camelot by her father's deaf-mute servant.

For some reason, the finished work did not please Parrott, and Rosenthal sold it for $3500 to another San Franciscan who dropped into his Munich studio one day, a Mrs. R. M. Johnson. Rosenthal proclaimed it his masterpiece, and back in San Francisco his hometown papers proudly played *Elaine* for all it was worth.

They carried feature stories on the artist's father, telling how, sitting cross-legged on his bench, he had stitched far into the night for years to earn the money to send his boy to the Royal Academy of

Munich. They reported breathlessly that Crown Prince Frederick William of Germany had fallen in love with *Elaine* and had offered Rosenthal $25,000 for the painting, but alas! it had already been sold to Mrs. Johnson. They told how Rosenthal had obtained the corpse of a young girl and propped it in position in his studio, and made the first sketches for *Elaine* from the dead model.

When they announced that Mrs. Johnson was going to exhibit *Elaine* in San Francisco, it gave the city its biggest thrill since Laura D. Fair had been acquitted of the murder of A. P. Crittenden three years before. Elaine Clubs were organized overnight. As fast as they could get them from the printer's, music stores sold hundreds of copies of *The Elaine Waltzes*, hastily composed in honor of the great art event. Booksellers frantically sent east for caseloads of *Idylls of the King*, as the demand for the poem which had inspired the masterpiece boomed it to top place on the best-seller list.

At the galleries of Snow & May, on the corner of Kearny and Morton Streets, the painting was unveiled March 30, 1875, a Tuesday. More than five thousand men, women and children, silent with awe and admiration, filed past *Elaine* that day and Wednesday and Thursday. Many of them, following advice given in the newspapers, were armed with opera glasses in order to detect and appreciate the minute details. Some were so moved by Elaine's sad fate and the melancholy gloom of the picture, they burst into tears and were led away weeping.

It was on Friday that the entire city, from the waterfront to the sand dunes, from North Beach to the Mission, staggered under the news that *Elaine* had been stolen—cut from its frame by vandals during the night. Excited San Franciscans read the headlines in the papers: "Alas! Elaine," mourned the *Daily Alta California*. Echoed the *Chronicle*, "Farewell, Sweet Sister!" They rushed out to tell the neighbors. Tongues wagged in Montgomery Street taprooms, in Market Street beer cellars, over Nob Hill tea tables and the backyard fences of Telegraph Hill.

Those who could hastened to the Morton Street corner to verify the report with their own eyes, and jammed the gallery to the doors. "The occasion seemed like a funeral, and the endless procession like a mournful cortege following some friend to the grave," said the *Chronicle*. "All spoke in hushed tones, and some ladies actually shed tears while looking on the empty frame . . . . The hands of ancient ladies were raised in holy horror . . . . "

Mrs. Johnson, the owner, received the news with sad but dignified calm. Contradicting a widespread rumor, she said she would offer no reward for the return of the painting, on grounds it would encourage wholesale robbery of other valuable works of art. But, she flashed, ordinary punishment was too good for the man who stole *Elaine*.

"He should either be hanged, drawn and quartered, or broken on the wheel," she said. "But, since those antique methods of punishment cannot be revived, I would have him scourged at the whipping post, after the manner of the baser criminals in Delaware."

Meanwhile, as the *Chronicle* dramatically put it, "that astute and energetic terror to evildoers, Police Captain I. W. Lees, had begun, at the very instant the loss became known, to revolve all the circumstances in the secret recesses of his busy brain."

Luckily for the Captain, an anonymous tipster reported seeing four sinister-looking characters standing in Morton Street outside Snow & May's basement window late the night of the crime. One had a scar on his face. Something in Captain Lees' busy brain clicked. "Scar, eh?" he mused. "That must be my old friend, Cut-Face Donahue." And, banking on this slender clue, he hatched some plans.

He and his men struck between two o'clock and four o'clock Sunday morning. At a Third street lodging-house, he picked up John Curran, James E. Allen and Tommy Wallace. Another member of the gang, James O'Neill, was routed out of bed in a Dupont Street brothel. Cut-Face Donahue, alias William Cloonan, was arrested in a house on lower Mission Street. After he had worked them over for a while, Captain Lees knew where the picture was—under the bedclothes in the back room of a shanty on Langton Street a South of Market alley. And that's where he found it, undamaged, wrapped in cotton cloth, sealed, and labeled, "Custom House Official Maps."

The news that *Elaine* had been recovered caused no less excitement than the report of its theft. The *Chronicle* put out a Sunday-morning extra and sold five thousand copies. Church-goers forgot the morning services and dashed to police headquarters to gaze at the famed painting. Announced the *Daily Alta California,* "A broad smile spread over the face of the community and caused a very perceptible sensation of pleasurable surprise and gratification as the news was heralded through the streets that 'Elaine is found! Elaine is found!' The news spread like the flame amid prairie grass, and, gathering as it advanced, blazed into fiery excitement."

When the painting was tacked back into its gilded frame and again placed on exhibition (guarded, this time, by two burly patrolmen), beside it hung a large photograph of the bearded man of the hour, Police Captain Lees.

Two months later, Allen, who had cut the canvas from the frame, Curran, his assistant, and Cut-Face Donahue, the brains behind the crime, started long prison terms at San Quentin. They confessed they had stolen *Elaine* in hopes of claiming a large reward, and never quite understood what all the commotion was about. It was Allen who put their disgust into words. "Hell," he sneered, "there's a little picture in the stores of a young hood nippin' a cigar from an old stiff who's lookin' in a window, that you can get for two-fifty. I'd rather have that than *Elaine* any day."

Maybe you would agree with him, and maybe you wouldn't, but you can find out the next time you're in Urbana, Illinois. That's where *Elaine* is now, on the wall of the art gallery of the University of Illinois.

THE TOWN CRIER

by

AMBROSE BIERCE

I*t is rumored in society circles that Mrs. William C. Ralston*
it about to contract a new matrimonial alliance.—Post
Respected author of this paragraph, we crave a word with you.
Sir, we venture to remind you that "to contract a new matrimonial
alliance" is simply "to marry again." Will you kindly state the existing objections to the latter expression, and point out the merits of
the former? The word "marry" is not, we hope, an immodest term.
We find it in all the dictionaries but in few of the newspapers—
never in the one which your talent deigns to adorn. The ingenuity
that you and the gentlemen who have the honor to labor in the same
literary field display in the invention of circumlocutory equivalents
for that word, is above and beyond all praise; but pardon us, we do
not quite perceive the necessity.

To "lead to the altar," to "join in the holy bonds of wedlock," to
"contract a matrimonial alliance," these are all sweet and pleasing
phrases. But as at present advised, and pending the better instruction
that it will doubtless be your pleasure to impart, we like the meaner
term too. But if you deem that objectionable, why don't you say
"nuptiate," you royal Bengal jackass?

FEEDING A LION
AT THE PALACE

(From the *Morning Call,* October 15)

THE leading citizens of San Francisco last night paid their respects to Lieutenant-General Philip H. Sheridan, U.S.A., at a public banquet given by them in honor of the gallant soldier. The event will be long remembered.

As a gathering of the social type, it eclipsed in grandeur, in princely magnificence, all previous assemblages of this character in this city. Two hundred of the foremost men of the community gathered around the illustrious military chieftain, and drank his health and bade him God speed for the gallant service he had rendered his country in its struggle for existence twelve years ago. The occasion was a fitting one, moreover to celebrate the opening of the Palace, the finest hotel on the face of the globe. The banquet, it is needless to add, under the direction of that prince of caterers, Warren Leland, has thrown into the shade all its predecessors in San Francisco.

The scene presented in the palatial dining hall beggars description. Three hundred brilliant gas jets illuminated the joyous surroundings, throwing a flood of light on the festive throng of black broadcloth and white neckties. The exquisite decoration of the banquet hall, with its long lines of cream-coloured columns, was still further embellished by an artistic draping of national colors at both ends and at the sides. Two long tables, running parallel to each other, extended the entire length of the hall, while a table at right angles to both occupied the upper end. At this were seated the principal guests of the evening. The brilliant array of new silverware, glittering glasses, fruit and flowers added further fascination to the scene. Meyers, the florist, exhibited the finest taste in his arrangement and disposition of the gems of the hothouse. On snowy rivers of tablecloth ran branches of green smilax in serpentine lines, trailing in most charming fashion around the bases of gilded tripods. The latter were placed at intervals along the tables, and supported baskets of the choicest tuberoses, camellias, tiger-lilies, heliotropes, variegated pinks, orange-blossoms and other bright colored flowers. The exhibition of pyramids of jellies and desserts enhanced the brilliance of the feast. Add to the picturesque effect of the tables, the rich and warm red Turkey carpets, the army of waiters in swallowtail coats and white Lisle-thread gloves, flitting noiselessly to and fro; the delightful music stealing in from a splendid military band playing in an antechamber, and a faint idea may be formed of the magnificence of the banquet scene.

The Bill of Fare was very neatly printed on white paper, folded in the fashionable style, and read as follows:

Huitres. *Chateau Yquem.*

Potage Royale. *Jerez.*

Hors d'Oeuvres d'Office: Saldade d'Anchois.
    Salade de Crevettes. *Vin du Rhin.*

Poisson: Filet de Sole a la Joinville.

Hors d'Oeuvres Chauds: Pate de Canard a la Perigueux.

Releve: Filet de Boeuf aux Champignons.
    Chateau Lafite.

Entree: Poulet Rosolio. *Chambertin*

Legumes: Artichauts a la Barigonie. Piments
    farcis. Pois Verts. Tomates Suitanes.

Punch a la Romaine. *Champagne.*

Rotis: Canards avec Confitures. Becassins
    Anglaises et Salade.

Patisseries: Pudding a la Diplomate. Meringues.
    Charlotte Moderne. Gelee au Maraschino.
    Glacees a la Napolitaine.

Pieces Montees: Nougat en Triomphe a la Jardiniere.
    Chateaux sur Roches Rustiques. Pagoda Chinoise.

Dessert: Fruits. Gateaux Assortis. Cafe.
    Cognac, Benedictine, Chartreuse.

The reader who has stumbled through the foregoing programme of eatables and vinous vehicles, expressed in fanciful French, when he understands that each dish was placed before the guests willy or nilly, may not think it a matter for astonishment that the process of absorption went gaily forward until near midnight. The plentiful flow of wine, in all the flavors considered palatable at dinner, together with the soothing influence of the finest brands of cigars, made it indeed possible to prolong indefinitely the feast of the gourmets; but in deference to the purpose of the banquet a halt was called on appetite. Three hours after a very long Grace had been pronounced, the guests leaned back in their chairs, whiffed aloft the incense of nicotine, and endeavored to digest the oratory which then began to effervesce. The regular toast list was not of extraordinary length, and the addresses were received with enthusiasm becoming the occasion. Among those who were toasted and responded were General Sheridan, Senator Sharon, and General La Grange, toastmaster being Governor Pacheco. The memory of William C. Ralston was drunk in silence, and the health of Governor Pacheco was received with cheers. Last, but not least, the health of the Palace Hotel Manager, Warren Leland, was responded to with much enthusiasm.

A VISITOR LOOKS AT RALSTON'S HOTEL

San Francisco, California
March 15

EDITOR THE HOBOKEN DEMOCRAT,
Hoboken, New Jersey.
Sir:

I am quartered at the Palace Hotel, one of the grandest hostelries in the United States.

The way I happen to be here is because Senator Sharon and my father used to be licked by the same schoolmaster in their native New England village and consequently were bosom friends. The Senator had known me from boyhood, in fact considered me a genius, and when I met him on Sansome Street, shortly after my arrival here, he shook me by the hand, took me to his hotel and instructed the clerk to give me the best room in the house, No. 24,999. He did so; and here I am, writing at an elevation above Mont Blanc, surrounded by clouds and looking from my window over a boundless expanse. This hotel is so wonderful that it merits a description.

It is built on a gigantic scale and is capable of containing one-fourth of the population of the city. It takes up an area of about 1,000 acres, and is fitted up, regardless of expense, with all the newest inventions. The blocks in the vestibule are of solid gold, and the railings on the stairs are silver-mounted. There are 150 beautiful clerks behind a solid rosewood counter a quarter of a mile in length, ornamented with silver. Each clerk has his hair parted in the middle, wears a diamond pin, and is exquisitely polite. They are so exceedingly

---

From the San Francisco *Chronicle*, April 2, 1877.

amiable and persuasive that they make you spend twice as much as you meant to, and make you feel satisfied with the most inferior accommodations.

There are 25,000 bellboys, one for each room, and numbered. They are located in a large basement room communicating with the office-boys' trap-doors. When a bell is rung by some impatient lodger in want of something, down goes the clerk's foot on a corresponding pedal and up shoots a bellboy. Sometimes a dozen rise so at once. He is put in a box, shut up in a pneumatic tube and whisked right into the room designated by the bell-dial. A door in the wall opens to receive him, an automatic clamp catches him by the coat-collar, and he is quietly dropped to the floor.

Going upstairs you would be astonished by the magnificent suites of parlors, miles in extent. In the ladies' grand parlor are stationed a fashionable dressmaker and man-milliners, who are in direct tele-graphic communication with Paris. The gentlemen's reading-rooms, lounging-rooms, smoking-rooms, bath-rooms, barber-rooms, billiard and private rooms for parties desiring privacy while dining and wining, are both numerous and elegant. Even the spittoons are made of gold. The elevators, 300 in number, half a mile up, are beautifully upholstered and fitted with every convenience to the traveler. The ladies' elevators have toilet tables and accessories, refreshment counters, full-length mirrors and sofas to recline on. The gentlemen's elevators have a bar and restaurant attached, and also a barber-shop run by the motive power of the elevator. Often a man's nose or ear is sliced off, but upon applying at the office you can get a new one which is probably better looking and more artistic.

Each single room or suite is supplied with faucets connecting with a pipe running from huge tanks on the roof, which contain different wines, brandies, sherries, ales, lager, liquor and bitters—also patent medicines. The flow from these tanks is registered in the office, so that the clerks can tell at any time what drinking is going on all over the house—also whether a man is drunk or sober. In the center of the hotel block is a hollow square occupied by a menagerie, a circus, an opera house and two theaters, one each for tragedy and comedy, which are kept open for the benefit of the guests, who are admitted free.

In the large dining hall, two acres square, 2,000 waiters dash about recklessly on skates. They are of all nationalties, and are required to be accomplished skaters. There is a circular railway on every floor to enable ladies and people in delicate health to visit each other while stopping at the hotel. A band of 250 pieces performs on top of the roof every evening, and at sunset a park of 100 pieces of cannon is fired off. The effect is grand. Every evening a celebrated aeronaut goes up in a balloon from the square in the middle of the hotel which is called the plaza.

It is astonishing that in such a vast caravansary so few people get hurt. Only about a dozen a day are killed. The hotel has its own undertaker and doctors and druggists. The arrangements for escape in case of fire or panic are ample. Hose and buckets are on every floor and in each room, ingeniously arranged in the ceiling, is a tank of water. By pulling a cord the room is flooded in a moment. To every floor, hanging from windows at intervals, is a thick rubber tube into which you jump and which lets you gently down until the fireman clasps you in his embrace and disengages you from the tube.

San Francisco is otherwise remarkable only for earthquakes, wind and dust, Chinese hoodlums, bar-rooms, pretty women and fast men. But you have read all about these, and since I have described the only wonder in San Francisco of which you have never heard, I will close. I leave for the Sandwich Islands on Tuesday.

ARRIVING IN SAN FRANCISCO

By

ROBERT LOUIS STEVENSON

WHEN I awoke next morning, I was puzzled for a while to know if it were day or night, for the illumination was unusual. I sat up at last, and found we were grading slowly downward through a long snowshed; and suddenly we shot into an open; and before we were swallowed into the next length of wooden tunnel, I had one glimpse of a huge pine-forested ravine upon my left, a foaming river, and a sky already coloured with fires of dawn. I am usually very calm over the displays of nature; but you will scarce believe how my heart leaped at this. It was like meeting one's wife. I had come home again—home from unsightly deserts to the green and habitable corners of the earth. Every spire of pine along the hill-top, every trouty pool along that mountain river, was more dear to me than a blood relation. Few people have praised God more happily than I did. And thenceforward, down by Blue Cañon, Alta, Dutch Flat, and all the old mining camps, through a sea of mountain forests, dropping thousands of feet toward the far sea-level as we went, not I only, but all the passengers on board, threw off their sense of dirt and heat and weariness, and bawled like schoolboys, and thronged with shining eyes upon the platform and became new creatures within and without. The sun no longer oppressed us with heat, it only shone laughingly along the mountain-side, until we were fain to laugh ourselves for glee. At every turn we could see farther into the land and our own happy futures. At every town the cocks were tossing their clear notes into the golden air, and

---

From *Travels and Essays* vol. 15, Charles Scribner's Sons, 1895.

crowing for the new day and the new country. For this was indeed our destination; this was "the good country" we had been going to so long.

By afternoon we were at Sacramento, the city of gardens in a plain of corn; and the next day before the dawn we were lying to upon the Oakland side of San Francisco Bay. The day was breaking as we crossed the ferry; the fog was rising over the citied hills of San Francisco; the bay was perfect—not a ripple, scarce a stain, upon its blue expanse; everything was waiting, breathless, for the sun. A spot of cloudy gold lit first upon the head of Tamalpais, and then widened downward on its shapely shoulder; the air seemed to awaken, and began to sparkle; and suddenly

"The tall hills Titan discovered,"

and the city of San Francisco, and the bay of gold and corn were lit from end to end with summer daylight.

AT THE STEVENSON FOUNTAIN

(Old Portsmouth Square, San Francisco)

By

WALLACE A. IRWIN

Perchance, from out the thousands passing by,—
The city's hopeless lotos-eaters these,
Blown by the four winds of the Seven Seas
From common want to common company,—
Perchance someone may lift his heavy eye
And smile with freshening memory when he sees
Those golden pennons bellying in the breeze
And spread for ports where fair adventures lie.

And O, that such a one might stay a space
And taste of sympathy, till to his ears
Might come the tale of him who knew the grace
To suffer sweetly through the bitter years,
To catch the smiles concealed in Fortune's face,
And draw contentment from a cup of tears!

AN OPULENCE OF TWADDLE

By

AMBROSE BIERCE

THAT sovereign of insufferables, Oscar Wilde, has ensued with his opulence of twaddle and his penury of sense. He has mounted his hind legs and blown crass vapidities through the bowel of his neck, to the capital edification of circumjacent fools and foolesses, fooling with their foolers. He has tossed off the top of his head and uttered himself in copious overflows of ghastly bosh. The ineffable dunce has nothing to say and says it—says it with a liberal embellishment of bad delivery, embroidering it with reasonless vulgarities of attitude, gesture and attire. There was never an impostor so hateful, a block-head so stupid, a crank so variously and offensively daft.

The limpid and spiritless vacuity of this intellectual jellyfish is in ludicrous contrast with the rude but robust mental activities he came to quicken and inspire. Not only has he no thoughts, but no thinker. His lecture is mere verbal ditch-water—meaningless, trite and without coherence. It lacks even the nastiness that exalts and refines his verse. Moreover, it is obviously his own; he had not even the energy and independence to steal it. And so, with a knowledge that would equip an idiot to dispute with a cast-iron dog, an eloquence to qualify him for the duties of caller on a hog-ranch, and an imagination adequate to the conception of a tomcat when fired by contemplation of a fiddle-string, this consummate and star-like youth, missing everywhere his heaven-appointed functions and offices, wanders about, posing as a statue of himself, and, like the sun-smitten image of Memnon, emitting meaningless murmurs in the blaze of women's eyes. He makes me tired.

From the *Wasp,* San Francisco, March 31, 1882.

And this gawky gowk has the divine effrontery to link his name with those of Swinburne, Rossetti and Morris—this dunghill he-hen would fly with eagles. He dares to set his tongue to the honored name of Keats. He is the leader, quoth'a, of a renaissance in art, this man who cannot draw—of a revival in letters, this man who cannot write! This littlest and looniest of a brotherhood of simpletons, whom the wicked wits of London, haling him from his obscurity, have crowned and crucified as King of the Cranks, has accepted the distinction in stupid good faith and our foolish people take him at his word. Mr. Wilde is pinnacled upon a dazzling eminence, but the earth still trembles to the dull thunder of the kicks that set him up.

THE BAY WINDOW

By

HARRIET LANE LEVY

FATHER sat at his ease in the bedroom bay window, looking down upon the street as from the balcony of a theater, approving the panorama like an old subscriber to the opera. Friends, walking along the sidewalk, looked up to wave a hand to him, or to make words with their lips. Along the block each bay window framed a face. Near the corner, at opposite sides of the bay window of their bedroom, old Grandpa Davis and old Grandma Davis stared into space, motionless, timeless, looking as though they had been recovered from the excavation of an ancient city. At her bedroom window, in the house next door to us toward the avenue, Mrs. Levison's fiddling fingers tapped the pane close to her thick dark face. Father's glance toward the avenue made an arc excluding her.

Father approved of O'Farrell Street, which to him was not the full stretch of its length, but the two blocks from Larkin Street to Van Ness Avenue on which friends and acquaintances had built their homes. He saw prestige and commercial value in the closeness of the 900 block to Van Ness Avenue, a block with a future. When San Francisco grew larger, someone would tear down the row of houses on the corner and build a handsome home, which would require our lot to increase its depth. O'Farrell Street represented a high peak in Father's life, the accumulation of savings sufficient for the building of a home for his wife "Yetta," his eldest daughter Addie, Polly, and me, in a new residence district of San Francisco. In like manner his business associates had saved and invested their capital, in a short

From *920 O'Farrell Street* by Harriet Lane Levy. Copyright 1937, 1947 by Harriet Lane Levy. By permission of Doubleday & Co., Inc.

time forgetting their old homes on the other side of Market Street. As "south of Market" lost in fashionable repute, their children denied them altogether.

O'Farrell Street was a dream come true, a dream which, if it never reached to the grandeur of Van Ness Avenue with mansions of the wealthy retired behind deep lawn and gilded iron fence, yet embodied a vision held and realized. O'Farrell Street proper was but one of the many parallel streets which moved out of Market Street, reclaiming unto themselves wastes of sand until they reached the avenue. Father spoke of our location as O'Farrell and Van Ness, and envisaged it as a corner, although the home of the Levisons and the fenced yard of the Toplitzes separated us from the corner of the avenue by sixty feet.

The 900 block had risen almost as a unit, one building going up after another in quick succession, a lot of sand transformed into residence and garden. The sand dunes at the corner on the farther side of the avenue, which abruptly halted the march of O'Farrell Street westward and which, upon windy afternoons, sent fine sand into our hair and eyes, did not diminish Father's appreciation. In a city where sand dunes rolled from Van Ness to the ocean, our sand dune was a plausible termination.

The houses on the north side of O'Farrell acquired variation by the swell of a bay window, or the color of a painted surface. All buildings gave out a fine assurance of permanence. Father approved of the block not only for its location, but for the honesty of its construction to which he had been witness. It was a solid street; the sidewalks were without dip or break. The planked street, held together by thirty-penny spikes, resisted the iron shoes of the heavy dray horses. Houses, sidewalks, street were of the best wood provided by the most reliable contractors, guaranteed perfect; and Father knew our house to be the most substantial. O'Farrell Street, to the senses, was solid as a cube. When I turned the corner, my heart quickened at the sight of our white house springing forth from the drabness of its neighbors. To me its white paint was as marble.

Permanent as the house was the small street garden. If the bloom was pinched, and if the fence offered superfluous defense to plants that never yielded a bouquet, we felt no lack. In the shadowed strip

of ground, running along the side of the house beside the row of
nipped primroses, chives grew for Father. On Sunday mornings he
came down the backway with plate and knife, and cut off a handful
for his breakfast. He stopped a moment in the garden to look up
and down the street, or to crumple a leaf of lemon verbena or myrtle
and inhale its odor. How pleasant to own a garden with an iron
fence, and to walk upon the graveled walk around the center plot.
Ours was the only garden with a graveled walk. Occasionally a
hummingbird flew into the garden, stabbed its single blossom, and
was off almost too quickly to register.

The south side of 900 broke away from the ordered arrangement
of the north side. Small groups of narrow bay-windowed houses
served as rented homes to small families. Near the corner of Polk
Street stood the cow barn of old man Waller, to which the anemic
children of the neighborhood, glass in hand, hurried in the early
morning hours to receive "warm milk fresh from the cow." At night
small boys rang the door-bells of the wild-eyed old man and scattered before he answered. The block ended with the store at the
corner, where household wants were supplied by Hink, the ashen-
haired grocer with bleached eyelashes, who never smiled, but gave
honest weight.

The occupants of the south side of O'Farrell were negligible
to us. We identified them vaguely as "the people across the street."
When they walked down their steps on Sunday morning, our minds
registered only "going to church." Their entrance into their homes
through the street door, which their keys unlocked, awoke no curiosity
regarding their identity or occupation within their homes. Our eyes
swept over them, across Polk Street, recovering sight only with the
handsome Fuller house, at the corner, which led the succession of
aristocratic residences on the block below.

Between the private life of 920 O'Farrell and the street a bay
window offered unbroken communication. From the darker rooms
we made frequent visits to the window to catch a breath of sunlight, or pick a bit of news to carry back to the family. If the bell
rang, we leaned out of the window to discover who was at the
door below, and darted back again within the minute, ready to act
upon our discovery. Mother paused a moment in the bay between

forays upon dust and disorder. If she sighted a threatening visitor, she calculated the likelihood of having been observed and gave quick instructions to Maggie Doyle, the maid of all work.

Mother warned us to keep an eye out and report if we saw two men approaching with portfolios. They might come any day. Days passed with no sign of them. Then one morning when I was standing at the window I saw two men, each with a large black book in his hand, climb the steps of the Lessings; not the Joseph Lessings, our neighbors, but the S. S. Lessings, farther down the block. I flew to the back of the house, down the backstairs, into the kitchen.

"They're coming!" I gasped.

"Who is coming?" Mother asked, irritated at my excitement.

"The assessors."

What the Assyrians had been to the Babylonians, and the Persians to the Assyrians, what the Huns had been to Rome, and the Indians to the American colonists, the assessors were to us. The assessors were the deputies of the city administration who appraised the value of household and personal effects for purposes of taxation. From house to house they went, extracting data after battles with the tenants. Sometimes they were fine men; that meant that they were easy-going, and susceptible to blandishment. But they were more likely to be mean fellows, unyielding to persuasion. Uncertainty invested their coming with excitement and fear. To me the mission of the assessor was to uncover, to seize, to consume. I felt that no secret was secure from his eagle eye. He could see through mattresses and closet doors. When he appeared, standards were reversed; pride of ownership shrank into fear of detection. He poised a pencil and fate hung trembling upon admission. All codes of polite convention were abrogated; the questions he asked about purchases and prices were those gentlemen never asked. His coming was catastrophic.

"The assesors!" I cried to Mother again.

Even as I spoke the word, fires kindled on the hilltops—signals that flamed alarm from tribe to tribe. Sister Polly at the piano, sister Addie in her bedroom, Maggie Doyle in the basement washroom, caught the warning and hurried to join the defense. Furs, velvet coats, feather neckpieces were gathered from closets and rushed into old canvas-covered trunks. Silver soup ladle, sugar bowl, and napkin rings were thrust behind red braided pillow shams. The diamond rings vanished from Mother's fingers to hallowed places beneath her bodice.

"The table cover," Mother commanded, and Maggie Doyle swept from the dining-room table the richly appliquéd garnet plush cover.

We dismantled as the locust eats. In a few minutes everything that made for opulence had been removed, and the rooms were reduced, as far as possible, to a semblance of shabbiness and poverty. The bell rang, and Mother answered.

"We are the assessors," one of the deputies announced.

Mother's face lit with interest. "Come right in," she said and, quickly walking past the parlor doors, led them with embracing hospitality into the chill of the darkened dining room.

"Be seated, gentlemen," she said and sat down herself as if in anticipation of a pleasant disclosure.

Then the drama began, a contest between the not too clever political agents, conscientious but not overzealous, and little Mother, determined to admit only where denial was useless, and to fight to the death when there was a chance for escape. The assessors spread their opened books upon the bare table. One rose and opened the folding doors leading into the music room. Mother followed.

"Square piano? Ah, a Steinway."

"Brought from the old house," Mother agreed helpfully.

The assessor's serching eye dropped to the Axminster carpet.

"We are hoping to get a new one as soon as we can afford it," Mother said, as if in answer to a criticism of its shabbiness.

"Any jewelry, diamonds?" he asked as they returned to the dining room.

"Diamonds?" Mother laughed heartily. "One is lucky to have shoes this year."

The assessors chuckled. They would have been helpless before the miracle had she confessed her brooch and earrings. And so they moved on from room to room, Mother growing younger and gayer, parrying questions with lightness and humor. So might Lady Macbeth have beguiled the gentle Duncan.

She tried to avoid entrance into the parlor, but the assessor turned the knob and entered. The shutters were tightly closed, the shades drawn, the tables devoid of ornament. The tall mirrors, dismantled of terra-cotta and bisque figures, wore a strange austerity. But more than removal of decoration would have been needed to make the assessors visualize the dilapidation and decay that Mother sought to project.

"That's a handsome set of furniture," said the assessor.

"Is?" asked Mother archly. "Was, fifteen years ago."

Altogether it was a gay encounter, made up of question and retort, short pauses, and hearty laughter. It ended in the tinkle of glasses.

"You will have a little something?"

They would; and returned to the dining room. The day was hot and many flights of steps lay before them. From the locked cupboard Mother brought forth the stately decanter, realizing with a pang, as she told Father that night, that the decanter was of embossed silver, and the bottles of Bohemian glass. But the eyes of the men were upon the contents and they were no longer officials of the government.

"To your health, madam," they said, rising.

"To yours, gentlemen," Mother responded and, having won at every point, she drank in hearty friendliness.

There was more laughter as they stood talking on the front steps. Then the door closed.

I ran out to Mother. "What happened, what happened?"

"Call Maggie Doyle. Those steps were never washed this morning," Mother said.

I returned to the window in time to see the assessors disappear into the Lessing house, to the accompaniment of small boys of the neighborhood, standing at the foot of the steps, their lips glued to their harmonicas.

There was no activity of the street unheralded and unaccompanied by melody. Every instrument—violin, trombone, even bagpipes—importuned the tender heart or, lacking instrument, the unassisted voice sent forth its plea on a curve of song. A youthful yodel unexpectedly roughened into, "Rags, bottles, and sacks" and, above the seat of a disheveled, lumpy buckboard, eager black eyes smiled up at us insinuatingly from a gaunt bearded face. Twice a week two stalwart beggars, hatless, coatless, one offering a wooden peg, the other an empty sleeve, took their stand on the sidewalk opposite our house, and together discharged at our window the lusty chords of "Die Wacht am Rhein." If we delayed our response, "Lieb Vaterland, magst ruhig sein" was suggested softly, like a secret confidence, and we accepted it as a valid argument for a contribution.

Every Monday morning a hale old Frenchman zigzagged up the street, leisurely swinging from a sidewalk to sidewalk, an old broadbrimmed felt hat hanging from his hand. Sometimes he walked in silence, smiling reminiscently, as if his path lay among open fields; then he stopped unpredictably, and addressed to the sky the full content of the "Marseillaise." Like a call for volunteers, "Le jour de gloire est arrivé" displaced the air. He picked up a coin as if it were a bouquet, and bowed acknowledgment of our tribute to France.

A low circling monotone of song, "Any old knives to grind, any old knives to grind," approached and passed before we caught sight of the long, bony back of the grinder, deeply arched under his wheel, as he plodded toward the avenue, ring a bell softly.

But beyond all the music of the street the melodies of the hand organ made appeal, stirring obscure founts of feeling. Every Sunday for twenty years the organ-grinder lifted the straps from his shoulders, folded his legs at the edge of the sidewalk between 920 and 922, raised his large brown eyes, emptied of recognition or petition, and turning the crank of his organ in the same slow circle, released his changeless repertoire. No matter where I was, in the back bedroom or kitchen, no matter what I was doing, the melodies of *Il Trovatore* penetrated the walls, arresting my thoughts and my hands. The music rippled over the mind to an ancient shore, reminding me of some unremembered, unfulfilled promise, haunting me with the questions, "Don't you know? Can't you remember?" until disquiet impelled my feet to the front window to seek reassurance from the familiar figure below. We never spoke to him, but before the hammer had hit the anvil a dozen strokes, Mother sent Maggie Doyle down to the street with a dime which sentiment never enlarged to fifteen cents nor surfeit ever reduced to five. Father grew into the portliness of the prosperous merchant, and the beard of the organ-grinder grizzled with age, but every Sunday Father opened his window, even when it rained, so as not to miss the "Anvil Chorus." Twenty years were too short to exhaust Father's love for *Il Trovatore*. Sung on the grand opera stage by Kellogg and Carey, clanged by the band in Golden Gate Park, or tinned from a street organ, it stirred Father's tenderness and retouched some dream.

These solicitations of the heart were all in the history of the day, as spontaneous as the crowds moving up to the cathedral at the corner of the avenue for mass, the butcher boy leaping from his cart with a blood-soaked brown-paper parcel, or the baker drawing out from his wagon cupboard trays of twistbread, or round, plump loaves of rye.

But a doctor's buggy, stopping at a house, was another matter. Illness spread excitement like a social celebration. "He is there again!" Polly called, and Addie and I hurried to the window in time to catch sight of the coattails of Dr. Hartman hurrying up the steps of the Simons'. A single call piqued curiosity, a second awoke concern; but a protracted visit disrupted our meal, and fed conjecture for a day. Dr. Hartman's carriage, waiting an hour each morning at the door of the handsome Mrs. Simon, weeks after her recovery from typhoid, was a subject not be exhausted in one household, but to be settled in conference. If a young graduate drove a carriage and pair, or was driven in a coupé like Dr. Levi Lane, Mother mocked the artifice.

The best of the offerings of the street was the unheralded presence during the night of a two-storied wooden house beneath my window moving slowly toward the avenue. Beheld in the dim light, it moved with a fabled unreality. An old house, lifted from its native foundations, adventuring toward a new location, wore a half-tipsy, dislocated look not unnatural to so fantastic an experience. Through its uncurtained windows it appealed self-consciously, disclaiming responsibility for the unbecoming situation in which it found itself.

"See what they persuaded me to do at my age," it seemed to say. I felt embarrassed for the old house, compelled to leave familiar ground for some more fashionable neighborhood, where, in spite of its fresh coat of paint, it would not be permitted to forget its history.

A windless accomplished the transit; a single horse circling in continuous motion wound the rope, stepping over it at each turn until roughly called to a halt. If the creaking old wood and the harsh command of men awoke me, I drew a deep breath to help the

poor tired horse pull the house over the ever-shifting rollers before
I fell asleep again.

At nine o'clock every morning the men of O'Farrell Street left
their homes for their places of business downtown; dressed in brushed
broadcloth and polished high hats, they departed soberly as to a
funeral. The door of each house opened and let out the owner who
took the steps firmly, and, arriving at the sidewalk, turned slowly
eastward toward town. A man had not walked many yards before
he was overtaken by a friend coming from the avenue. Together
they walked with matched steps down the street.

All the men were united by the place and circumstances of their
birth. They had come to America from villages in Germany, and
had worked themselves up from small stores in the interior of
California to businesses in San Francisco.

From the bedroom window we watched them, foreseeing the interruptions to their march. The initial heat of a political argument
halted their first advance. Another six yards and they stopped again
to face each other and twist a protesting hand. The full stop came
at the corner of Polk Street, where gestures were fully unsheathed
and fingers touched the chest and swung out into the air. If Father
was walking with Mr. Levison, our neighbor, we could measure by the
dislocation of his stovepipe the degree of his failure to convince the
stubborn Republican that Grover Cleveland was the greatest President
in American history.

Compared to the unabashed enjoyment of the private affairs of
a whole block, the experience of a single family within its own walls
was astringent living. Puffing up the steps of 916 with the package-
laden, fat Mrs. Lessing; stepping delicately from the hired victoria
with the pretty daughter of the Nathans; or arriving from Frankfort
with the new German cousin of the Davises and her basket trunk,
we lived spaciously. One glimpse was all we needed. We knew how to
spread it over areas of participation.

One morning I looked out of the window and saw three women
in black crossing the street and making for our house. The black
extended beyond their bodies, down their sides, flapping brokenly
like mortuary wings. They came as one, borne upon us not by the
wind, but by the current of an inner purpose. I was afraid of them,
although I knew the mission of three Jewish women, coming together

on a morning visit, to be a merciful one. I knew that they were our itinerant associated charities outward bound to relieve a private need.

I called Mother. She quickly exchanged her purple wrapper for a dress, sought her purse, and went down the stairs to receive them.

The Eureka Benevolent Society ministered to avowed poverty; but no public channel existed to the concealed distress, which must be discovered by a friend, whispered to another and another, creating a trio of benevolence which would move upon the land, knocking upon the door with a stern compulsion to charity.

When Mother entered the dining room they had just alighted, three large, black shapes austere and imposing. They unfolded their tale in orderly procedure. One introduced the grievous story, a second elaborated upon it, the third drew it to a conclusion, deepened in value by threefold affirmation. The tale was told under the breath, with lids lowered against the knowledge which they were obliged to divulge. Occasionally eyes sought eyes for corroboration, in reproach of life. Then they sat in silence, resting the case, having asked for nothing. Mother left the room, returning with the purse already in her pocket, and offered her contribution which was appropriated, though apparently unperceived.

"A nice day," Mother said as she opened the street door, letting in the sunshine.

But the trio refused the message of the sun. In sustained gloom they descended our steps, and ascended those of our neighbor.

The south side of the 800 block held a story. I walked along it with delight, my interest concentrated upon the large double residence in the middle of the block which gave balanced grandeur to the whole neighborhood. It was the home of John Mackay, king of Consolidated Virginia, the mine that, at the turn of a shovel, had converted a poor miner into a multi-millionaire. Daily I passed Jewish homes before which my spirit automatically drew back; the Friedenthals sat upon my heart heavily; the proud obscured the sun. Not so the home of John Mackay. The Mackay house swept away all small barriers; it trailed clouds of glory from the mining centers of Nevada; it broke life into claims and stakes and tips and noble gamblers and inexhaustible outpourings of gold. It brought to our doors the Comstock Lode and Virginia City.

The broad staircase, leading to the entrance, was high and the time required to climb and descend it provided moments for satisfying observation. What matter that the street door closed upon the curious; the outside offered enough. The steps democratically descended to the sidewalk, and young girls ran up and down them, swinging into the street with easy stride. Could a prophetic eye have seen in them a future Italian princess and a Vanderbilt of New York, it would have remained permanently glued to the entrance door. The occupants of the house and their friends filled their roles like characters in a novel; carriages stood constantly before the door, barouche, coupé, and high stanhope. Wooden coachmen sat in aristocratic immobility, footmen sprang like acrobats from their seats to hand out the ladies of the house. The solid silver-mounted harnesses clinked with the very tinkle I had read about in novels of the titled. The horses *were* bays, their flanks *did* shine. On the night of a ball the elite of the city stepped, if they were women, or sprang, if they were men, from their carriages to a crimson velvet carpet, which glowed from the street to the entrance door. However, better than all this confirmation of imagined pageantry, more enlarging to experience, extending horizons to the limitless unknown, was the daily arrival of the milkman and the delivery into the house of huge cans of milk for the Mackays' daily bath. Beside such witness to fabled treasure, diamonds were pebbles, golden dinner service, plate.

I told myself that it was not the flourish of wealth but the romance of the triumphal passage from mining cabin to a city mansion that commanded my obeisance, and I made an effort to resist the argument for importance offered by the display of private parade. Before a victoria with a single driver it was easy to retain my assurance; but coachman and footman, clad in colored livery, rigid above a closed coupé, scattered my identity. At the approach of a plum-colored livery, the forehead of my spirit brushed the sidewalk.

SAN FRANCISCO BAY

by

JOAQUIN MILLER

How fair is San Francisco Bay
When golden stars consort and when
The moon pours silver paths for men,
And care walks by the other way!
Huge ships, black-bellied, lie below
Broad, yellow flags from silken Chind,
Round, blood-red banners from Nippon,
Like to her sun at sudden dawn—
Brave battleships as white as snow,
With bannered stars tossed to the wind,
Warm as a kiss when love is kind.

[1889]

RUDYARD KIPLING IN
SAN FRANCISCO

He Arrives in the City

"Serene, indifferent of fate,
  Thou sittest at the western gate,
  Thou seest the white seas fold their tents,
  Oh warder of two Continents.
  Thou drawest all things small and great
  To thee beside the Western Gate."

THIS is what Bret Harte has written of the great city of San Francisco, and for the past fortnight I have been wondering what made him do it. There is neither serenity nor indifference to be found in these parts; and evil would it be for the Continent whose wardship were intrusted to so reckless a guardian. Behold me pitched neck-and-crop from twenty days of the High Seas, into the whirl of California, deprived of any guidance, and left to draw my own conclusions. Protect me from the wrath of an outraged community of these letters be ever read by American eyes. San Francisco is a mad city—inhabited for the most part by perfectly insane people whose women are of a remarkable beauty. When the "City of Peking" steamed through the Golden Gate I saw with great joy that the block-house which guarded the mouth of the "finest harbour in the world, Sir," could be silenced by two gunboats from Hong Kong with safety, comfort and despatch.

Then a reporter leaped aboard, and ere I could gasp held me in his toils. He pumped me exhaustively while I was getting ashore,

From *Rudyard Kipling's Letters from San Francisco*, the Colt Press, San Francisco, 1949.

demanding, of all things in the world, news about Indian journalism. It is an awful thing to enter a new land with a new lie on your lips. I spoke the truth to the evil-minded Custom-house man who turned my most sacred raiment on a floor composed of stable-refuse and pine-splinters; but the reporter overwhelmed me not so much by his poignant audacity as his beautiful ignorance. I am sorry now that I did not tell him more lies as I passed into a city of three hundred thousand white men! Think of it! Three hundred thousand white men and women gathered in one spot, walking upon real pavements in front of real plate-glass windowed shops, and talking something that was not very different from English. It was only when I had tangled myself up in a hopeless maze of small wooden houses, dust, street-refuse, and children who play with empty kerosene tins, that I discovered the difference of speech.

"You want to go to the Palace Hotel?" said an affable youth on a dray. "What in hell are doing here, then? This is about the lowest place in the city. Go six blocks north to corner of Geary and Market; then walk around till you strike corner of Gutter and Sixteenth, and that brings you there."

I do not vouch for the literal accuracy of these directions, quoting but from a disordered memory.

"Amen," I said. "But who am I that I should strike the corners of such as you name? Peradventure they be gentlemen of repute, and might hit back. Bring it down to dots, my son."

I thought he would have smitten me, but he didn't. He explained that no one ever used the word "street," and that every one was supposed to know how the streets run; for sometimes the names were upon the lamps and sometimes they weren't. Fortified with these directions I proceeded till I found a mighty street full of sumptuous buildings four or five stories high, but paved with rude cobble stones in the fashion of the Year One. A cable-car without any visible means of support slid stealthily behind me and nearly struck me in the back. A hundred yards further there was a slight commotion in the street—a gathering together of three or four—and something that glittered as it moved very swiftly. A ponderous Irish gentleman with priest's cords in his hat and a small nickel-plated badge on his fat bosom emerged from the knot, supporting a Chinaman who had been stabbed in the eye and was bleeding like a pig. The bystanders went their ways, and the Chinaman, assisted by the policeman, his own. Of course this was none of my business, but I rather wanted to know what had happended to the gentleman who had dealt the stab. It said a great deal for the excellence of the municipal arrangements of the town that a surging crowd did not at once block the street to see what was going forward. I was the sixth man and the last who assisted at the performance, and my curiosity was six times the greatest. Indeed, I felt ashamed of showing it.

There were no more incidents till I reached the Palace Hotel, a seven-storied warren of humanity with a thousand rooms in it. All the travel-books will tell you about hotel arrangements in this country. They should be seen to be appreciated. Understand clearly— and this letter is written after a thousand miles of experiences— that money will not buy you service in the West.

When the hotel clerk—the man who awards your room to you and who is supposed to give you information—when that resplendent individual stoops to attend to your wants, he does so whistling or humming, or picking his teeth, or pauses to converse with someone he knows. These performances, I gather, are to impress upon you that he is a free man and your equal. From his general appearance and the size of his diamonds he ought to be your superior. There is no necessity for this swaggering, self-consciousness of freedom. Business is business, and the man who is paid to attend to a man might reasonably devote his whole attention to the job.

In a vast marble-paved hall under the glare of an electric light sat forty or fifty men; and for their use and amusement were provided spittoons of infinite capacity and generous gape. Most of the men wore frock-coats and top-hats,—the things that we in India put on at a wedding breakfast if we possessed them,—but they all spat. They spat on principle. The spittoons were on the staircases, in each bedroom—yea, and in chambers even more sacred than these. They chased one into retirement, but they blossomed in chiefest splendour round the Bar, and they were all used, every reeking one of 'em. Just before I began to feel deathly sick, another reporter grappled me. What he wanted to know was the precise area of India in square miles. I referred him to Whittaker. He had never heard of Whittaker. He wanted it from my own mouth, and I would not tell him. Then he swerved off, like the other man, to details of journalism in our own country. I ventured to suggest that the interior economy of a paper most concerned people who worked it. "That's the very thing that interests us," he said. "Have you got reporters anything like our reporters on Indian news papers?" "We have not," I said, and suppressed the "thank God" rising to my lips. "Why haven't you?" said he. "Because they would die," I said. It was exactly like talking to a child—a very rude little child. He would begin almost every sentence with: "Now tell me something about India," and would turn aimlessly from one question to another without the least continuity. I was not angry, but keenly interested. The man was a revelation to me. To his questions I returned answers mendacious and evasive. After all, it really did not matter what I said. He could not understand. I can only hope and pray that none of the readers of the "Pioneer" will ever see that portentous interview. The man made me out to be an idiot several sizes more drivelling than my destiny intended, and the rankness of his ignorance managed to distort the few poor facts with which I supplied him into large and elaborate lies. Then thought I: "The matter of American journalism shall be looked into later on. At present I will enjoy myself."

No man rose to tell me what were the lions of the place. No one volunteered any sort of conveyance. I was absolutely alone in this big city of white folks. By instinct I sought refreshment and came upon a bar-room, full of bad Salon pictures, in which men with hats on the backs of their heads were wolfing food from a counter. It was the institution of the "Free Lunch" that I had struck. You paid for a drink and got as much as you wanted to eat. For something less than a rupee a day a man can feed himself sumptuously in San Francisco, even though he be bankrupt. Remember this if ever you are stranded in these parts.

Later, I began a vast but unsystematic exploration of the streets. I asked for no names. It was enough that the pavements were full of white men and women, the streets clanging with traffic, and that the restful roar of a great city rang in my ears. The cable-cars glided to all points of the compass. I took them one by one till I could go no farther. San Francisco has been pitched down on the sand-bunkers of the Bikaneer desert. About one-fourth of it is ground reclaimed from the sea—any old-timer will tell you all about that. The remainder is ragged, unthrifty sand-hills, pegged down by houses.

From an English point of view there has not been the least attempt at grading those hills, and indeed you might as well try to grade the hillocks of Sind. The cable-cars have for all practical purposes made San Francisco a dead level. They take no count of rise or fall, but slide equably on their appointed courses from one end to the other of a six-mile street. They turn corners almost at right angles; cross other lines, and, for aught I know, may run up the sides of houses. There is no visible agency of their flight; but once in a while you shall pass a five-storied building, humming with machinery that winds up an everlasting wire-cable, and the initiated will tell you that here is the mechanism. I gave up asking questions. If it pleases Providence to make a car run up and down a slit in the ground for many miles, and if for two-pence-halfpenny I can ride in that car, why shall I seek the reasons of the miracle?

Rather let me look out of the windows till the shops give place to thousands and thousands of little houses made of wood—each house just big enough for a man and his family. Let me watch the people in the cars, and try to find out in what manner they differ from us, their ancestors. They delude themselves into the belief that they talk English,—"the" English,—and I have already been pitied for speaking with "an English accent." The man who pitied me spoke, so far as I was concerned, the language of thieves. And they all do. Where we put the accent forward, they throw it back, and vice versa; where we use the long "a," they use the short; and words so simple as to be past mistaking, they pronounce somewhere up in the dome of their heads. How do these things happen? Oliver Wendell Holmes says that Yankee schoolmarms, the cider, and the salt codfish of the Eastern States are responsible for what he calls a nasal accent. A Hindu is a Hindu and a brother to the man who knows his vernacular; and a Frenchman is French because he speaks his own language; but the American has no language. He is dialect, slang, provincialism, accent, and so forth. Now that I have heard their voices, all the beauty of Bret Harte is being ruined for me, because I find myself catching through the roll of his rhythmical prose the cadence of his peculiar fatherland. Get an American lady to read to you "How Santa Claus came to Simpson's Bar," and see how much is, under her tongue, left of the beauty of the original.

But I am sorry for Bret Harte. It happened this way. A reporter asked me what I thought of the city, and I made answer suavely that it was hallowed ground to me because of Bret Harte. That was true. "Well," said the reporter, "Bret Hart claims California, but California don't Claim Bret Harte. He's been so long in England that he's quite English. Have you seen our cracker-factories and the new offices of the Examiner?" He could not understand that to the outside world the city was worth a great deal less than the man.

He Meets a Bunco-Steerer

Night fell over the Pacific, and the white sea-fog whipped through the streets, dimming the splendours of the electric lights. It is the use of this city, her men and women, to parade between the hours of eight and ten a certain street, called Kearny Street, where the finest shops are situated. Here the click of heels on the pavement is loudest, here the lights are brightest, and here the thunder of the traffic is most overwhelming. I watched Young California and saw that it was at least expensively dressed, cheerful in manner, and self-asserting in conversation. Also the women are very fair. The maidens were of generous build, large, well-groomed, and attired in raiment that even to my inexperienced eyes must have cost much. Kearny Street, at nine o'clock, levels all distinctions of rank as impartially as the grave. Again and again I loitered at the heels of a couple of resplendent beings, only to overhear, when expected the level voice of culture, the staccato "Sez he, Sez I," that is the mark of the white servant-girl all the world over.

This was depressing because, in spite of all that goes to the contrary, fine feathers ought to make fine birds. There was wealth—unlimited wealth—in the streets, but not an accent that would not have been dear at fifty cents. Wherefore, revolving in my mind that these folk were barbarians, I was presently enlightened and made aware that they also were the heirs of all the ages, and civilized after all. There appeared before me an affable stranger of prepossessing appearance, with a blue and an innocent eye. Addressing me by name, he claimed to have met me in New York at the Windsor, and to this claim I gave a qualified assent. I did not remember the fact, but since he was so certain of it, why then—I waited developments. "And what did you think of Indiana when you came through?" was the next question. It revealed the mystery of previous acquaintance,

and one or two other things. With reprehensible carelessness, my
friend of the light-blue eye had looked up the name of his victim
in the hotel register and read "India" for Indiana. He could not
imagine an Englishman coming through the States from West to
East instead of by the regularly ordained route. My fear was that in
his delight at finding me so responsive he would make remarks about
New York and the Windsor which I could not understand. And
indeed, he adventured in this direction once or twice, asking me
what I thought of such and such streets, which, from his tone, I
gathered were anything but respectable. It is trying to talk unknown
New York in almost unknown San Francisco. But my friend was
merciful. He protested that I was one after his own heart, and
pressed upon me rare and curious drinks at more than one bar. These
drinks I accepted with gratitude, as also the cigars with which his
pockets were stored. He would show me the Life of the City. Having
no desire to watch a weary old play again, I evaded the offer, and
received in lieu of the Devil's instruction much coarse flattery.
Curiously constituted is the soul of man. Knowing how and where
this man lied; waiting idly for the finale; I was distinctly conscious,
as he bubbled compliments in my ear, of soft thrills of gratified pride.
I was wise, quoth he, anybody could see that with half an eye; saga-
cious; versed in the affairs of the world; an acquaintance to be
desired; one who had tasted the cup of Life with discretion. All this
pleased me, and in a measure numbed the suspicion that was thoroughly aroused. Eventually the blue-eyed one discovered, nay insisted,
that I had a taste for cards (this was clumsily worked in, but it was
my fault, in that I met him half-way, and allowed him no chance
of good acting). Hereupon, I laid my head to one side, and simulated unholy wisdom, quoting odds and ends of poker-talk, all
ludicrously misapplied. My friend kept his countenance admirably;
and well he might, for five minutes later we arrived, always by the
purest of chances, at a place where we could play cards, and also
frivol with Louisiana State Lottery tickets. Would I play? "Nay,"
said I, "for to me cards have neither meaning nor continuity; but let
us assume that I am going to play. How would you and your friends
get to work? Would you play a straight game, or make me drunk, or
—well, the fact is I'm a newspaper man, and I'd be much obliged if
you'd let me know something about bunco-steering." My blue-eyed

friend cursed me by his gods,—the Right and the Left Bower; he even cursed the very good cigars he had given me. But, the storm over, he quieted down and explained. I apologised for causing him to waste an evening, and we spent a very pleasant time together. Inaccuracy, provincialism, and a too hasty rushing to conclusions were the rocks that he had split on; but he got his revenge when he said: "How would I play with you? From all the poppycock (Anglice: bosh), you talked about poker, I'd ha' played a straight game and skinned you. I wouldn't have taken the trouble to make you drunk. You never knew anything of the game; but the way I was mistaken in you makes me sick." He glared at me as though I had done him an injury. To-day I know how it is that, year after year, week after week, the bunco-steerer, who is the confidence-trick and card-sharper man of other climes, secures his prey. He slavers them over with flattery, as the snake slavers the rabbit. The incident depressed me because it showed I had left the innocent East far behind, and was come to a country where a man must look out for himself. The very hotel bristled with notices about keeping my door locked, and depositing my valuables in a safe. The white man in a lump is bad.

He Looks at Liquor and Politics

This brings me by natural sequence to the great drink question. As you know, of course, the American does not drink at meals as a sensible man should. Indeed, he has no meals. He stuffs for ten minutes thrice a day. Also he has no decent notions about the sun being over the yard-arm or below the horizon. He pours his vanity into himself at unholy hours, and indeed he can hardly help it. You have no notion of what "treating" means on the Western slope. It is more than an institution; it is a religion, though men tell me that it is nothing to what it was. Take a very common instance. At 10:30 a.m. a man is smitten with desire for stimulants. He is in the company of two friends. All three adjourn to the nearest bar,—seldom more than twenty yards away,—and take three straight whiskies. They talk for two minutes. The second and third man then treat in order; thus each walks into the street, two of them the poorer by three goes of whiskey under their belt and one with two more liquors than he wanted. It is not etiquette yet to refuse a treat. The result is peculiar. I have never yet, I confess, seen a drunken man in the streets, but

I have heard more about drunkenness among white men, and seen more decent men above or below themselves with drink, than I care to think about. And the vice runs up into all sorts of circles and societies. Never was I more astonished than at one pleasant dinner party to hear a pair of pretty lips say casually of a gentleman friend then under discussion, "He was drunk." The fact was merely stated without emotion. That was what startled me. But the climate of California deals kindly with excess, and treacherously covers up its traces. A man neither bloats nor shrivels in this dry air. He continues with the false bloom of health upon his cheeks, an equable eye, a firm mouth, and a steady hand till a day of reckoning arrives, and suddenly breaking up about the head, he dies, and his friends speak his epitaph accordingly. Why people who in most cases cannot hold their liquor should play with it so recklessly I leave others to decide. This unhappy state of affairs has, however, produced one good result which I will confide to you. In the heart of the business quarter, where banks and bankers are thickest, and telegraph wires most numerous, stands a semi-subterranean bar tended by a German with long blond locks and a crystalline eye. Go thither softly, treading on the tips of your toes, and ask him for a Button Punch. 'Twill take ten minutes to brew, but the result is the highest and noblest product of the age. No man but one knows what is in it. I have a theory it is compounded of the shavings of cherubs' wings, the glory of a tropical dawn, the red clouds of sunset, and fragments of lost epics by dead masters. But try you for yourselves, and pause a while to bless me, who am always mindful of the truest interests of my brethren.

But enough of the stale spilth of bar-rooms. Turn now to the august spectacle of a Government of the people, by the people, for the people, as it is understood in the city of San Francisco. Professor Bryce's book will tell you that every American citizen over twenty-one years of age possesses a vote. He may not know how to run his own business, control his wife, or instill reverence into his children, may be pauper, half-crazed with drink, bankrupt, dissolute, or merely a born fool; but he has a vote. If he likes, he can be voting most of his time—voting for his State Governor, his municipal officers, local option, sewage contracts, or anything else of which he has no special knowledge.

Once every four years he votes for a new President. In his spare moments he votes for his own judges—the men who shall give him justice. These are dependent on popular favor for re-election inasmuch as they are but chosen for a term of years—two or three, I believe. Such a position is manifestly best calculated to create an independent and unprejudiced administrator. Now this mass of persons who vote is divided into two parties—Republican and Democrat. They are both agreed in thinking that the other party is running creation (which is America) into red flame. Also the Democrat as a party drinks more than the Republican, and when drunk may be heard to talk about a thing called the Tariff, which he does not understand, but which he conceives to be the bulwark of the country or else the surest power for its destruction. Sometimes he says one thing and sometimes another, in order to contradict the Republican, who is always contradicting himself. And this is a true and lucid account of the forepart of American politics. The behind-part is otherwise.

Since every man has a vote and may vote on every conceivable thing, it follows that there exist certain wise men who understand the art of buying up votes retail, and vending them wholesale to whoever wants them most urgently. Now an American engaged in making a home for himself has not time to vote for turn-cocks and district attorneys and cattle of that kind, but the unemployed have much time because they are always on hand somewhere in the streets. They are called "the boys", and form a peculiar class. The boys are young men; inexpert in war, unskilled in labour; who have neither killed a man, lifted cattle, or dug a well. In plain English, they are just the men who can always be trusted to rally round any cause that has a glass of liquor for a visible heart. They wait—they are on hand—; and in being on hand lies the crown and the glory of American politics. The wise man is he who, keeping a liquor-saloon and judiciously dispensing drinks, knows how to retain within arm's reach a block of men who will vote for or against anything under the canopy of Heaven. Not every saloon-keeper can do this. It demands careful study of city politics, tact, the power of conciliation, and infinite resources of anecdote to amuse and keep the crowd together night after night, till the saloon becomes a salon. Above all, the liquor side of the scheme must not be worked for immediate profit. The boys who drink so freely will ultimately pay their host a thousand-fold. An Irishman, and an Irishman preeminently, knows how to work such a saloon parliament. Observe for a moment the plan of operations. The rank and file are treated to drink and a little money—and they vote. He who controls ten votes receives a proportionate reward; the dispenser of a thousand votes is worthy of reverence, and so the chain runs on till we reach the most successful worker of public saloons—the man most skilful in keeping his items together and using them when required. Such a man governs the city as absolutely as a king. And you would know where the gain comes in? The whole of the public offices of a city (with the exception of a very few where special technical skill is required) are short-term offices distributed according to "political" leanings. What would you have? A big city requires many officials. Each office carries a salary, and influence worth twice the pay. The offices are for the representatives of the men who keep together and are on hand to vote. The Commissioner of Sewage, let us say, is a gentleman who has been elected to his office by a Republican vote. He knows little and cares less about sewage, but he has sense enough to man the pumping-works and the street-sweeping-machines with the gentlemen who elected him. The Commissioner of Police has been helped to his post very largely by the influence of the boys at such and such a saloon. He may be the guardian of city morals, but he is not going to allow his subordinates to enforce early closing or abstention from gambling in that saloon. Most offices are limited to four years, consequently he is a fool who does not make his office pay him while he is in it.

The only people who suffer by this happy arrangement are, in fact, the people who devised the lovely system. And they suffer because they are Americans. Let us explain. As you know, every big city here holds at least one big foreign vote—generally Irish, frequently German. In San Francisco, the gathering place of the races, there is a distinct Italian vote to be considered, but the Irish vote is more important. For this reason the Irishman does not kill himself with overwork. He is made for the cheery dispensing of liquors, for everlasting blarney, and possesses a wonderfully keen appreciation of the weaknesses of lesser human nature. Also he has no sort of conscience, and only one strong conviction—that of deep-rooted hatred toward England. He keeps to the streets, he is on hand, he votes joyously, spending days lavishly,—and time is the American's dearest commodity. Behold the glorious result. To-day the city of San Francisco is governed by the Irish vote and the Irish influence, under the rule of a gentleman whose sight is impaired, and who requires a man to lead him about the streets. He is called officially "Boss Buckley," and unofficially the "Blind White Devil." I have before me now the record of his amiable career in black and white. It occupies four columns of small print, and perhaps you would think it disgraceful. Summarized, it is as follows: Boss Buckley, by tact and deep knowledge of the seamy side of the city, won himself a following of voters. He sought no office himself, or rarely: but as his following increased he sold their services to the highest bidder, himself taking toll of the revenues of every office. He controlled the Democratic party in the city of San Francisco. The people appoint their own judges. Boss Buckley's people appointed judges. These judges naturally were Boss Buckley's property. I have been to dinner parties and heard educated men, not concerned with politics, telling stories one to another of "justice," both civil and criminal, being bought with a price from the hands of these judges. Such tales they told without heat, as men recording facts. Contracts for road-mending, public buildings, and the like, are under the control of Boss Buckley, because the men whom Buckley's following sent to the City Council adjudicate on these contracts; and on each and every one of these contracts Boss Buckley levies his percentage for himself and his allies.

The Republican party in San Francisco also have their boss. He is not so great a genius as Boss Buckley, but I decline to believe that he is any whit more virtuous. He has a smaller number of votes at his command.

He Visits the Bohemian Club

There are no princes in America, at least with crowns on their heads; but a generous-minded member of some royal family received my letter of introduction. Ere the day closed I was a member of two clubs and booked for many engagements to dinner and party. Now this prince, upon whose financial operations be continual increase, had no reason, nor had the others, to put himself out for the sake of one Briton more or less; but he rested not till he had accomplished all in my behalf that a mother could think of for her debutante daughter. Do you know the Bohemian Club of San Francisco? They say its fame extends over the world. It was created somewhat on the line of the Savage by men who wrote or drew things, and it has blossomed into most unrepublican luxury. The ruler of the place is an owl—an owl standing upon a skull and cross-bones, showing forth grimly the wisdom of the man of letters and the end of his hopes for immortality. The owl stands on the staircase, a statue four feet high, is carved in the woodwork, flutters on the frescoed ceilings, is stamped on the note paper, and hangs on the walls. He is an Ancient and Honorable Bird. Under his wing 'twas my privilege to meet with white men whose lives were not chained down to routine of toil, who wrote magazine articles instead of reading them hurriedly in the pauses of office-work, who painted pictures instead of contenting themselves with cheap etchings picked up at another man's sale of effects. Mine were all the rights of social intercourse that India, stony-hearted step-mother of Collectors, has swindled us out of. Treading soft carpets and breathing the incense of superior cigars, I wandered from room to room studying the paintings in which the members of the club had caricatured themselves, their associates, and their aims. There was a slick French audacity about the workmanship of these men of toil unbending that went straight to the heart of the beholder. And yet it was not altogether French. A dry grimness of treatment, almost Dutch, marked the difference. The men painted as they spoke—with certainty. The club indulges in revelries which it calls "jinks", high and low, at intervals; and each of these gatherings is faithfully portrayed in oils by hands that know their business. In this club were no amateurs spoiling canvas because they fancied they could handle oils without knowledge of shadows or anatomy—no gentleman of leisure ruining the temper of publishers and an already ruined market with attempts to write "because everybody writes something these days." My hosts were working, or had worked, for their daily bread with pen or paint, and their talk for the most part was of the shop shoppy—that is to say, delightful. They extended a large hand of welcome and were as brethren, and I did homage to the Owl and listened to their talk. An Indian Club about Christmas-time will yield, if properly worked, an abundant harvest of queer tales; but at a gathering of Americans from the uttermost ends of their own continent the tales are larger, thicker, more spinous, and even more azure than any Indian variety. Tales of the War I heard told by an ex-officer of the South over his evening drink to a Colonel of the Northern army; my introducer, who had served as a trooper in the Northern Horse, throwing in emendations from time to time.

Other voices followed with equally wondrous tales of riata-throwing in Mexico or Arizona, of gambling at army posts in Texas, of newspaper wars waged in godless Chicago, of deaths sudden and violent in Montana and Dakota, of the loves of half-breed maidens in the South, and fantastic huntings for gold in myterious Alaska. Above all, they told the story of the building of old San Francisco, when the "finest collection of humanity on God's earth, Sir, started this town, and the water come up to the foot of Montgomery Street." Very terrible were some of the tales, grimly humorous the others, and the men in broadcloth and fine linen who told them had played their parts in them.

"And now and again when things got too bad they would toll the city bell, and the Vigilance Committee turned out and hanged the suspicious characters. A man didn't begin to be suspected in those days till had committed at least one unprovoked murder," said a calm-eyed, portly old gentleman. I looked at the pictures around me, the noiseless, neat-uniformed waiter behind me, the oak-ribbed ceiling above, the velvety carpet beneath. It was hard to realize that even twenty years ago you could see a man hanged with great pomp.

They bore me to a banquet in honour of a brave Lieutenant, Carlin, of the "Vandalia," who stuck by his ship in the great cyclone at Apia and comported himself as an officer should. On that occasion I heard oratory with the roundest "o's"; and devoured a dinner the memory of which will descend with me into the hungry grave. There were about forty speeches delivered; and not one of them was average or ordinary. It was my first introduction to the American Eagle screaming for all it was worth. The Lieutenant's heroism served as a peg from which the silver-tongued ones turned themselves loose and kicked. They ransacked the clouds of sunset, the thunderbolts of Heaven, the deeps of Hell, and the splendours of the Resurrection, for tropes and metaphors, and hurled the result at the head of the guest of the evening. Never since the morning stars sang together for joy, I learned, had an amazed creation witnessed such superhuman bravery as that displayed by the American navy in the Samoa cyclone. Till earth rotted in the phophorescent star-and-stripe slime of a decayed universe that God-like gallantry would not be forgotten. I grieve that I cannot give the exact words. My attempt at reproducing their spirit is pale and inadequate. I sat bewildered on a coruscating Niagara of—blatherumskite. It was magnificient—it was stupendous; and I was conscious of a wicked desire to hide my face in a napkin and grin. Then, according to rule, they produced their dead, and across the snowy tablecloths dragged the corpse of every man slain in the Civil War, and hurled defiance at "our natural enemy" (England, so please you!) "with her chain of fortresses across the world." Thereafter they glorified their nation afresh, from the beginning, in case any detail should have been overlooked, and that made me uncomfortable for their sakes. How in the world can a white man, a Sahib of our blood, stand up and plaster praise on his own country? He can think as highly as he likes, but his open-mouthed vehemence of adoration struck me almost as indelicate. My hosts talked for rather more than three hours, and at the end seemed ready for three hours more. But when the Lieutenant—such a big, brave, gentle giant!— rose to his feet, he delivered what seemed to me as the speech of the evening. I remember nearly the whole of it, and it ran something in this way: "Gentlemen—it's very good of you to give me this dinner and to tell me all these pretty things, but what I want you to understand—the fact is—what we want and what we ought to get at once is a navy—more ships—lots of 'em—" Then we howled the top of the roof off, and I, for one, fell in love with Carlin on the spot. *Wallah!* He was a man.

The Prince among merchants bade me take no heed to the warlike sentiments of some of the old Generals. "The sky-rockets are thrown in for effect," quoth he, "and whenever we get on our hind legs we always express a desire to chaw up England. It's a sort of family affair."

And indeed, when you come to think of it, there is no other country for the American public speaker to trample upon.

France has Germany; we have Russia; for Italy, Austria is provided; and the humblest Pathan possesses an ancestral enemy. Only America stands out of the racket; and therefore, to be in fashion, makes a sand-bag of the mother-country; and bangs her when occasion requires. "The chain of fortresses" man, a fascinating talker, explained to me after the affair that he was compelled to blow off steam. Everybody expected it. When we had chanted "The Star Spangled Banner" not more than eight times, we adjourned. America is a very great country, but it is not yet Heaven with electric lights and plush fitting, as the speakers professed to believe. My listening mind went back to the politicians in the saloon who wasted no time in talking about freedom, but quietly made arrangements to impose their will on the citizens. "The Judge is a great man; but give thy presents to the Clerk," as the proverb saith.

He Meets the Ladies

I am hopelessly in love with about eight American maidens—all perfectly delightful till the next one comes into the room. O-Toyo was a darling, but she lacked several things; conversation, for one. You cannot live on giggles. She shall remain unmoved at Nagasaki while I roast a battered heart before the shrine of a big Kentucky blonde who had for a nurse, when she was little, a negro "mammy." By consequence she had welded on to Californian beauty, Paris dresses, Eastern culture, Europe trips, and wild Western originality, the queer dreamy superstitions of the negro quarters, and the result is soul-shattering. And she is but one of many stars. Item, a maiden who believes in education and possesses it, with a few hundred thousand dollars to boot, and a taste for slumming. Item, the leader of a sort of informal salon where girls congregate, read papers, and daringly discuss metaphysical problems and candy—a sloe-eyed, black-browed, imperious maiden. Item, a very small maiden, absolutely without reverence, who can in one swift sentence trample upon and leave gasping half a dozen young men. Item, a millionairess, burdened with her money, lonely, caustic, with a tongue keen as a sword, yearning for a sphere, but chained up to the rock of her vast possessions. Item, a typewriter-maiden earning her own bread in this big city, because she doesn't think a girl ought to be a burden on her parents. She quotes Theophile Gautier, and moves through the world manfully, much respected, for all her twenty inexperienced summers. Item, a woman from Cloudland who has no history in the past, but is discreetly of the present, and strives for the confidences of male humanity on the grounds of "sympathy." (This is not altogether a new type.) Item, a girl in a "dive" blessed with a Greek head and eyes that seem to speak all that is best and sweetest in the world. But woe is me!—she has no ideas in this world or the next, beyond the consumption of beer (a commission on each bottle), and protests that she sings the songs allotted to her nightly with no more than the vaguest notion of their meaning.

Sweet and comely are the maidens of Devonshire; delicate and of gracious seeming those who live in the pleasant places of London; fascinating for all their demureness the damsels of France clinging closely to their mothers, and with large eyes wondering at the wicked world; excellent in her own place and to those who understand her is the Anglo-Indian "spin" in her second season; but the girls of America are above and beyond them all. They are clever; they can talk. Yea, it is said that they think. Certainly they have an appearance of so doing. They are original, and look you between the brows as a sister might look at her brother. They are instructed in the folly and vanity of the male mind, for they have associated with "the boys" from babyhood, and can discerningly minister to both vices, or pleasantly snub the possessor. They possess, moreover, a life among themselves, independent of masculine associations. They have societies and clubs and unlimited tea-fights where all the guests are girls. They are self-possessed without parting with any tenderness that is their sex-right; they understand; they can take care of themselves; they are superbly independent. When you ask them what makes them so charming, they say: "It is because we are better educated than your girls and we are more sensible in regard to men. We have good times all around, but we aren't taught to regard every man as a possible husband. Nor is he expected to marry the first girl he calls on regularly." Yes, they have good times, their freedom is large, and they do not abuse it. They can go driving with young men, and receive visits from young men to an extent that would make an English mother wink with horror; and neither driver nor drivee have a thought beyond the enjoyment of a good time. As certain also of their own poets have said:—

"Man is fire and woman is tow,
And the Devil he comes and begins to blow."

In America the tow is soaked in a solution that makes it fireproof, in absolute liberty and large knowledge; consequently accidents do not exceed the regular percentage arranged by the Devil for each class and climate under the skies. But the freedom of the young girl has its drawbacks. She is—I say it with all reluctance—irreverent, from her forty-dollar bonnet to the buckles in her eighteen-dollar shoes. She talks flippantly to her parents and men old enough to be her grandfather. She has a prescriptive right to the society of the Man who Arrives. The parents admit it. This is sometimes embarrassing, especially when you call on a man and his wife for the sake of information; the one being a merchant of varied knowledge, the other a woman of the world. In five minutes your host has vanished. In another five his wife has followed him, and you are left with a very charming maiden doubtless, but certainly not the person you came to see. She chatters and you grin; but you leave with a very strong impression of a wasted morning. This has been my experience once or twice. I have even said as pointedly as I dared to a man: "I came to see you." "You'd better see me in my office, then. The house belongs to my women-folk—to my daughter, that is to say." He spoke the truth. The American of wealth is owned by his family. They exploit him for bullion, and sometimes it seems to me that his lot is a lonely one. The women get the ha'-pence; the kicks are all his own. Nothing is too good for an American's daughter (I speak here of the moneyed classes). The girls take every gift as a matter of course. Yet they develop greatly when a catastrophe arrives and the man of many millions goes up or down and his daughters take to stenography or type-writing. I have heard many tales of heroism from the lips of girls who counted the principals among their friends. The crash came; Mamie or Hattie or Sadie gave up their maid, their carriages and candy, and with a No. 2 Remington and a stout heart set about earning their daily bread.

"And did I drop her from the list of my friends? No, sir," said a scarlet-lipped vision in white lace. "That might happen to me any day."

It may be this sense of possible disaster in the air that makes San Franciscan society go with so captivating a rush and whirl. Recklessness is in the air. I can't explain where it comes from, but there it is. The roaring winds off the Pacific make you drunk to begin with. The aggressive luxury on all sides helps out the intoxication, and you spin for ever "down the ringing groves of change" (there is no small change, by the way, west of the Rockies) as long as money lasts. They make greatly and they spend lavishly; not only the rich but the artisans, who pay nearly five pounds for a suit of clothes and for other luxuries in proportion. The young men rejoice in the days of their youth. They gamble, yacht, race, enjoy prize-fights and cock-fights—the one openly, the other in secret—they establish luxurious clubs; they break themselves over horse-flesh and—other things; and they are instant in quarrel. At twenty they are experienced in business; and embark in vast enterprises, take partners as experienced as themselves, and go to pieces with as much splendour as their neighbours. Remember that the men who stocked California in the Fifties were physically, and as far as regards certain tough virtues, the pick of the earth. The inept and the weakly died en route or went under in the days of construction. To this nucleus were added all the races of the Continent—French, Italian, German, and of course, the Jew. The result you shall see in large-boned, deep-chested, delicate-handed women, and long, elastic, well-built boys. It needs no little golden badge swinging from his watch-chain to mark the Native Son of the Golden West—the country-bred of California. Him I love because he is devoid of fear, carries himself like a man, and has a heart as big as his boots. I fancy, too, he knows how to enjoy the blessings of life that his world so abundantly bestows upon him.

And what more remains to tell? I cannot write connectedly, because I am in love with all those girls aforesaid and some others who do not appear in the invoice. The type-writer girl is an institution of which the comic papers make much capital, but she is vastly convenient. She and a companion rent a room in a business quarter, and copy manuscript at the rate of six annas a page. Only a woman can manage a type-writing machine, because she has served apprenticeship to the sewing machine. She can earn as much as a hundred dollars a month, and professes to regard this form of bread-winning as her natural destiny. But oh how she hates it in her heart of hearts! When I had got over the surprise of doing business and trying to give orders to a young woman of coldly clerkly aspect, intrenched behind gold-rimmed spectacles, I made inquiries concerning the pleasures of this independence. They liked it—indeed, they did. 'Twas the natural fate of almost all girls,—the recognised custom in America, —and I was a barbarian not to see it in that light.

"Well, and after?" said I. "What happens?"

"We work for our bread."

"And then what do you expect?"

"Then we shall work for our bread."

"Till you die?"

"Ye-es—unless—"

"Unless what? A man works till he dies."

"So shall we." This without enthusiasm—"I suppose."

Said the partner of the firm audaciously: "Sometimes we marry our employers—at least that's what the newspapers say."

The hand banged on half a dozen of the keys at once. "Yes, I don't care. I hate it—I hate it—I hate it, and you needn't look so!"

The senior partner was regarding the rebel with grave-eyed reproach.

"I thought you did," said I. "I don't suppose American girls are much different from English ones in instinct."

"Isn't it Theophile Gautier who says that the only differences between country and country lie in the slang and the uniform of the police?"

Now in the name of all the Gods at once, what is one to say to a young lady (who in England would be a Person) who earns her own bread, and very naturally hates the employ, and slings out-of-the-way quotations at your head? That one falls in love with her goes without saying; but that is not enough.

A mission should be established.

THE TOWN CRIER

Ambrose Bierce

"*I sing not with the minstrels*
Who have learned the art of song;
I sing that my heart's happy
As a bird the bright day long."
                    —M. W. S. in the *Pacific*
        If less your heart were happy
        The better were your song;
        I'm going to the minstrels—
        By-by. Ta-ta. So long.
                    —A. B.

Stanford and Huntington, so long at outs,
Kissed and made up. If you have any doubts
Dismiss them, for I saw them do it, man;
And then—why, then I clutched my purse and ran!

A morning paper says three unclaimed gold watches are in the hands of the police, and that it is not definitely known who stole them. It is definitely known who will steal them.

TONG CHIEF: "LITTLE PETE"

by

HERBERT ASBURY

THE greatest and most successful of Chinatown's tong chieftains was Fung Jing Toy, better known as Little Pete, who was head of the Sum Yops and in control of other tongs with which the Sum Yops were allied. For nearly ten years he was the most powerful Chinaman on the Pacific Coast, and although it is doubtful if he ever swung a hatchet or fired a pistol, he was responsible for the deaths of no fewer than fifty men. He had a fair command of English, which he acquired at American night-schools, but if the stories told about him are true, he could neither read nor speak Chinese and employed an interpreter to assist him in communicating with many of his henchmen. He lived with his wife and two children on the third floor of a three-storey building at Washington Street and Waverly Place, from the balcony of which, as a boy of ten, he had watched the great fight between the Suey Sings and the Kwong Docks in 1875. He slept in a windowless room behind a barred and bolted door, on either side of which was chained a vicious dog. During his waking hours he wore a coat of chain mail, and inside his hat was a thin sheet of steel curved to fit his head. He employed a bodyguard of three white men, and when he went abroad, one walked beside him, and another in front, while the third brought up the rear. And prowling within call were half a dozen of his own *boo how doy*, heavily armed. Also, where Little Pete went he was accompanied by a trusted servant bearing his jewel-case and toilet articles, for the tong leader was a great dandy, and much concerned about his appearance. He

---

possessed many diamond rings, a dozen handsomely engraved gold watches, and half a score of gold and platinum match-boxes set with diamonds and other precious stones. He changed his jewelry several times daily and never wore a suit, though he had forty, two days in succession. Two hours each morning he spent combing, brushing, and oiling his long and glossy queue, of which he was inordinately proud. In his leisure time he played upon the zither, listened to the music of his crickets, or wrote comedies, which were translated into Chinese and performed at the Jackson Street Theatre. He owned the playhouse and never had any trouble getting his pieces produced.

Little Pete was five years old when his father, a merchant, brought him to San Francisco from Canton. He began his career as an errand-boy for a Chinese shoe-manufacturer, and during his late teens peddled slippers from house to house in Chinatown. When he was about twenty-one years old, he embarked upon the only honest business venture of his adult life—a shoe-factory under the firm name of J. C. Peters & Company. Soon afterwards, attracted by the profits in vice, he became interested in gambling houses and opium dens and also entered the slave trade in partnership with Kwan Leung and the latter's wife Fon Suey, a noted procuress. Backed by the Sum Yop tong, of which he gained complete control before his twenty-fifth birthday, he soon enlarged his activities. Instead of buying girls, he began to steal them, particularly from dealers and crib-owners who were members of the Sue Yop tong, one of the most powerful organizations in Chinatown. He also interfered in other Sue Yop enterprises, and the two tongs were soon engaged in one of the bitterest and bloodiest of all the wars of Chinatown. During the early stages of this conflict Little Pete overreached himself. He forgot that in the final analysis vice in Chinatown existed only upon the sufferance of the white authorities. When one of his killers was arrested and placed on trial for the murder of a Sue Yop man in 1887, Little Pete boldly tried to bribe the jurors, the District Attorney, and everyone else connected with the prosecution. He was promptly clapped into jail, later convicted of attempted bribery, and sent to San Quentin Prison for five years.

When Little Pete was released, he again assumed his position as head of the Sum Yops and fanned into flame the embers of the war with the Sue Yops, which had subsided during his incarceration. He also strengthened his position by retaining as counsel for the Sum Yops an influential criminal lawyer, Thomas D. Riordan, and by forming an alliance with Christopher A. Buckley, the famous blind political boss of San Francisco, whom Little Pete called the Blind White Devil. With Buckley's support, Little Pete was soon the undisputed king of Chinatown. Every form of vice, and almost every form of legitimate business as well, paid him tribute. If the owners of gambling houses, opium dens, or brothels refused to pay, their establishments were immediately closed by the white police—and reopened a few days later with Little Pete's men in charge. The girls in all of the cribs operated by Little Pete and his associates were supplied with counterfeit half-dollars, which they gave as change to drunken men.

Little Pete's income from his various enterprises must have been enormous, but he was not satisfied. He looked around for new sources of revenue and became greatly interested in the possibilities of horse racing. Early in the spring of 1896 he became a familiar figure in the betting rings of the Bay District and Ingleside tracks and soon attracted attention by the size of his bets. He regularly wagered eight thousand dollars a day, and he never lost. Within two months he had won a hundred thousand dollars, and the stewards of the Pacific Coast Jockey Club began to believe that there might be some connection between Little Pete's streak of luck and the sudden epidemic of sick horses and bungling rides by hitherto skillful jockeys. Private detectives followed several riders to the office of J. C. Peters & Company, and further investigation disclosed the fact that Little Pete was not only paying the jockeys to lose races, but was bribing trainers and stablemen to poison horses against which he wished to wager. As a result of the inquiry Jockeys Jerry Chorn and Young Chevalier were ruled off the turf for life, while Jockey Arthur Hinrichs and Dow Williams, who had been Lucky Baldwin's trainer, were barred from the two tracks which Little Pete honored with his operations. Nothing could be done to Little Pete, who retired to Chinatown with a substantial addition to his fortune.

Little Pete's star, however, was setting. He had become so rapacious that the Sue Yops determined, once and for all, to end his reign. They invited twelve other tongs, all of which had felt the weight of Little Pete's heavy hand, to join them in a war of extermination against the Sum Yops, and a formidable force of *boo how doy* took the field. A price of three thousand dollars was placed upon Little Pete's head, probably the largest sum that the tongs have ever offered for the death of an enemy. For weeks the hatchetmen of the allies kept close upon the trail of the chieftain of the Sum Yops, as did many free-lance professional killers, all eager to win the amount, which to them meant an old age of luxury in China. But none could pierce the wall of white bodyguards and *boo how doy* with which Little Pete had surrounded himself.

In January 1897 there arrived in San Francisco two young Chinamen, Lem Jung and Chew Tin Gop, who had been prospecting in the mountains near Baker City, Oregon. They had accumulated a small fortune and had come to San Francisco to see the sights of Chinatown, after which they intended to return to China. They were members of the Suey Sing tong, now allied with the enemies of the Sum Yops, but they were men of peace. Neither had ever handled a hatchet or fired a pistol or participated in a tong fight. They knew nothing of Little Pete, and first learned of his villainies, and of the money that would be paid to his slayer, from their cousin Lem Jok Lep, who represented the Suey Sings on the board of strategy that had been created by the allied tongs to devise means of eradicating the Sum Yops. With rising indignation Lem Jung and Chew Tin Gop listened to Lem Jok Lep's recital of the many indignities which Little Pete had heaped upon the heads of their tong brothers.

"There is no reason," said Lem Jung, "why we should not earn this money. I myself shall kill this man."

With no experience in fighting, and with scarcely any plan of campaign, these young men rushed in where the bravest hatchetmen had trodden with the utmost caution. On the evening of January 23, 1897, which was the Chinese New Year's Eve, Lem Jung and Chew Tin Gop walked calmly into a barber-shop on the ground floor of Little Pete's building at Waverly Place and Washington Street. There they found Little Pete bending over with his head under a faucet, while the barber wetted his hair preparatory to plaiting it into a queue. Every circumstance favored the assassins. Little Pete had left his apartment in a hurry, accompanied by only one of his bodyguard. And this man he had sent out to buy a paper only a few minutes before Lem Jung and Chew Tin Gop entered the shop. For the moment Little Pete was defenseless. Chew Tin Gop remained near the door on guard while Lem Jung quickly stepped forward, caught Little Pete by the hair, brushed the barber aside, and shoved the muzzle of a heavy revolver down the back of the tong leader's neck, inside the coat of mail. He pulled the trigger, and Little Pete fell to the floor dead, with five bullets in his spine. The murderers escaped, received their money, and fled to Portland, where they were received as heroes. Eventually they took ship to China. The police arrested four Chinese, Chin Poy, Wing Sing, Won Lung, and Won Chung, who had been found loitering near the barbershop. On each were found revolvers, knives, and hatchets. Wing Sing and Chin Poy were brought to trial for the murder, but were acquitted.

The death of Little Pete demoralized the Sum Yops, and the *boo how doy* of the Sue Yops and their allies promptly began a slaughter, which ended only upon the intervention of the Emperor Kwang Hsu of China, to whom Thomas Riordan, attorney for Little Pete and the Sum Yops, cabled for help. The emperor called into consultation the great Chinese statesman Li Hung Chang.

"The matter has been attended to," said Li Hung Chang. "I have cast into prison all relatives of the Sue Yops in China, and have cabled to California that their heads will be chopped off if another Sum Yop is killed in San Francisco."

And in far-away America the war ended with startling suddenness, and the Sue Yops and the Sum Yops signed a treaty of peace which has never been violated.

The spirit of Little Pete ascended to his ancestors in a blaze of magnificence, though perhaps without proper sustenance, for his funeral was probably the most spectacular ever held in San Francisco. A cortége more than a mile long followed the body to the grave, and the air rang with the report of firecrackers, the "windy chaos" created by three Chinese bands, and the crackling of rattles swung by black-gowned priests. Scores of hacks had been rented for the occasion, and a dozen express wagons hauled the baked meats and the rice and the cases of gin and tea which had been provided that the spirit of the tong chieftain might refresh itself before beginning the long flight to heaven. But at the cemetery a company of hoodlums fell upon the cortége, routed the mourners, and feasted upon the funeral viands.

OFF TO THE PHILIPPINES

(From the San Francisco *Call,* May 24)

PERHAPS San Francisco is not easily stimulated to an outward show of enthusiam. But yesterday it was aroused, not to clamor and tumult but to the tender emotion which finds expression in farewell spoken brokenly, in the tear which none tries to conceal. A wave of patriotic fervor swept the community, thrilling every heart. The men of the First California were on their way to war. People lined the streets to pay them, as they passed, the tribute of a flower, a hand-clasp, a warm "God bless you!"

It was not my privilege to see the men leave camp but only to watch the throng at Third and Market Streets. No idle curiosity had collected that throng. I was proud to be one of it, and to realize that in all the hearts there was a single sentiment—only the desire to honor the soldiers, to let them know how they were loved of the people from among whom they go, and how the flags they bear held high the colors we all love.

Bold and brave, they had answered the call of their country, eager to go whither needs must be to meet, across a dreary stretch of water and under a tropic sun, a foreign and merciless foe. They had not stopped to think of the danger; the flag had been threatened; it was enough. So yesterday, when these gallant young soldiers were march-ing to war, the citizens turned out to see them go, and saw them through misty eyes.

Long before the time for the First to appear, the corner at which they were turn from Market into Third was crowded as it had never been before. From every window faces were peering, and the waving Stars and Stripes filled the air with radiance. There was no degree of impatience save when the streetcars showed inclination to force a passage or some vandal driver attempted to break into the press.

Then the bodily strength of the indignant crowd intervened with a firmness little short of violence. There was a large proportion of women in the gathering, and this was to have been expected. They gave color and character to the vast assemblage. The shadow of the Red Cross fell upon the massed people. The noble workers who by this emblem signify the devotion which has brought so much comfort, looked out from their headquarters, cheering and waving.

From above, at regular intervals, a cannon at the top of the Spreckels Building boomed. It told that the men had left camp, that they were coming. There was a sound of bugles from the waterfront. Now and then there would be a round of cheering. But it was not a noisy occasion. The emotion which held possession of men and women was not one that impelled to shouting.

Then there passed over the thousands standing there a murmur as though each spoke to his neighbor. Someone had caught the note of the bugle or the faint tap of the distant drum. The clatter of hoofs announced the mounted ecsort. Then came the tramp, tramp, a rattle of arms, hats off, and a round of cheers. The boys of the First were near. On they came, buoyant as for a holiday, erect and proud as beseemed heroes.Their weapons were burnished, their eyes aglow with a tender light. Perhaps in this demonstration there was to them a revelation. They must have felt elated and happy, albeit leaving home and all they loved, for they were in the midst of friends. There was no possibility of precise military order. There is nothing in the tactical manual which permits a stranger to clasp the hand of a man in the ranks. It is even outside of rules for a gray-haired mother to rush forward to kiss the bonny son her country is taking from her, and for her to kiss the other boys near him must be reckoned a further transgression. There is no official provision for adding flowers to the equipment of a soldier in heavy marching order. Yet all these things were done and none tried to prevent.

Boom! The cannon from its dizzy height had sent its salute again, and a wreath of smoke floated hazily off into the sky.

A woman marched by the side of her husband. She bore his rifle, he carried their child in his strong arms, and ever and again he stooped over so that their lips met. It was a picture to touch all, and it was one of many pictures. The people seemed swayed by a strange dual impulse of mingled sadness and joy. They were sorry to see the boys go, yet gloried in their going. They were conscious of a desire to call them back, but a greater desire to cheer them on. Even the women, sobbing in the arms of brother, sweetheart, or husband, had no word of reproach, nor tried to make harder the last hours ashore. Through all their tears there shone a pride that theirs had been the men so quick to answer when the summons reached them.

Coming down Market Street the soldiers had marched in fours and with the precision of veterans, but they could do it no longer. The press became so great that it was with difficulty two kept abreast and progress was made in single file. When at any moment a girl is likely to break into the ranks, when countless thousands are anxious to get so near as to deliver a message face to face, when the tender of a bouquet is an incident marking almost every drum beat, confusion arises. The drum of one company was actually silenced for a space. The drummer was captured by an army of young women who kissed him till he blushed rosy red and went on his way embarrassed but blissful, timing his taps to his heart beats and giving a sample of double-quick time. And thus they went by, showered with good wishes, laden with gifts, knowing they went from a city which loved them well.

There was one thought not given words, but it must have been in every mind. It must have been this thought which cast a somber tinge over all the glitter and made the sunshine less brilliant, the shadow more pronounced. Some in the companies going past so blithely would never come back. They knew the chance of battle when they accepted it. They were going forward without fear and without regret, but those who witnessed their going wondered if the city, so proudly sending them forth, confident in their valor, was in after time to have the chance to extend a greeting. When I noticed men ordinarily stern and perhaps selfish, looking on while tears of which they were not ashamed rolled down their cheeks, when ladies whom society knows waved all the flags they could grasp, I realized that all stood on a plane of equality. No lines were drawn. Some soldiers, perhaps, had none near of kin nor bound by personal tie to bid them adieu, but the adieus were for them. Patriotism is a heritage all may share and it creates a blood bond.

The pageant was magnificent, not as an array of military splendor but as an exhibition of the spirit animating the public. It is not mine to explain the detail, but rather as one of thousands to express some measure of the impression the boys of the First made upon those who arose early that they might hedge the path of the outgoing with bloom and cheer the soldiers with fraternal hail, a token of gratitude and encouragement.

In this manner did San Francisco make its farewells to the First. Now the *Peking* swings at anchor in the stream, prepared to take them beyond our ken. What fortune may await no man can tell, but that it may be fair fortune the people of this city hope.

When next these boys shall march here may it be up Market Street, not down, in each bronzed face the happiness of victory, while bells ring and cannon thunder a mighty jubilation, that crowned with honor our boys are home again.

BALLAD OF THE
HYDE STREET GRIP

by

GELETT BURGESS

Oh, the rain is slanting sharply, and the Norther's blowing cold,
When the cable strands are loosened she is nasty hard to hold;
There's little time for sitting down and little time for gab,
For the bumper guards the crossing, and you'd best be keeping tab!
Two-and-twenty "let-go's" every double trip—
It takes a bit of doing on the Hyde Street Grip!

Throw her off at Powell street, let her go at Post,
Watch her well at Geary and at Sutter, when you coast,
Easy at the Power House, have a care at Clay,
Sacramento, Washington, Jackson, all the way!
Drop the rope at Union, never make a slip—
The lever keeps you busy on the Hyde Street Grip!

Foot-brake, wheel-brake, slot-brake and gong,
You've got to keep 'em working, or you'll be going wrong!
Rush her on the crossing, catch her on the rise,
Easy round the corners, when the dust is in your eyes!
And the bell will always stop you, if you hit her up a clip—
You are apt to earn your wages, on the Hyde Street Grip!

North Beach to Tenderloin, over Russian Hill,
The grades are something giddy and the curves are fit to kill!
All the way to Market Street, climbing up the slope,
Down upon the other side, hanging to the rope;

But the sight of San Francisco as you take the lurching dip!
There is plenty of excitement, on the Hyde Street Grip!

Oh, the lights are in the Mission and the ships are in the Bay;
And Tamalpais is looming from the Gate across the way;
The Presidio trees are waving and the hills are growing brown!
And the driving fog is harried from the Ocean to the town!
How the pulleys slap and rattle! How the cables hum and whip!
Oh, they sing a gallant chorus on the Hyde Street Grip!

When the Orpheum is closing and the crowd is on the way,
The conductor's punch is ringing and the dummy's light and gay;
But the wait upon the table by the Beach is dark and still—
Just the swashing of the surges on the shore below the mill;
And the flash of Angel Island breaks across the channel rip,
And the hush of midnight falls upon the Hyde Street Grip!

[1899]

PARLOR ON POLK STREET

by

FRANK NORRIS

IT WAS Sunday, and, according to his custom on that day, Mc-Teague took his dinner at two in the afternoon at the car conductor's coffee-joint on Polk Street. He had a thick gray soup; heavy, under-done meat, very hot, on a cold plate; two kinds of vegetables; and a sort of suet pudding, full of strong butter and sugar. On his way back to his office, one block above, he stopped at Joe Frenna's saloon and bought a pitcher of steam beer. It was his habit to leave the pitcher there on his way to dinner.

Once in his office, or, as he called it on his signboard, "Dental Parlors," he took off his coat and shoes, unbuttoned his vest, and having crammed his little stove full of coke, lay back in his operating chair at the bay window, reading the paper, drinking his beer, and smoking his huge porcelain pipe while his food digested; crop-full, stupid, and warm. By and by, gorged with steam beer, and overcome by the heat of the room, the cheap tobacco, and the effects of his heavy meal, he dropped off to sleep. Late in the afternoon his canary bird, in its gilt cage just over his head, began to sing. He woke slowly, finished the rest of his beer—very flat and stale by this time—and taking down his concertina from the book-case, where in week days it kept the company of seven volumes of "Allen's Practical Dentist," played upon it some half-dozen very mournful airs.

McTeague looked forward to these Sunday afternoons as a period of relaxation and enjoyment. He invariably spent them in the same fashion. These were his only pleasures—to eat, to smoke, to sleep, and to play upon his concertina.

From *McTeague* by Frank Norris. Copyright 1899 by Doubleday & Co., Inc.

The six lugubrious airs that he knew always carried him back to the time when he was a car-boy at the Big Dipper Mine in Placer County, ten years before. He remembered the years he had spent there trundling the heavy cars of ore in and out of the tunnel under the direction of his father. For thirteen days of each fortnight his father was a steady, hard-working shift-boss of the mine. Every other Sunday he became an irresponsible animal, a beast, a brute, crazy with alcohol.

McTeague remembered his mother, too, who, with the help of the Chinaman, cooked for forty miners. She was an overworked drudge, fiery and energetic for all that, filled with the one idea of having her son rise in life and enter a profession. The chance had come at last when the father died, corroded with alcohol, collapsing in a few hours. Two or three years later a traveling dentist visited the mine and put up his tent near the bunk-house. He was more or less of a charlatan, but he fired Mrs. McTeague's ambition, and young McTeague went away with him to learn his profession. He had learnt it after a fashion, mostly by watching the charlatan operate. He had read many of the necessary books, but he was too hopelessly stupid to get much benefit from them.

Then one day at San Francisco had come the news of his mother's death; she had left him some money—not much, but enough to set him up in business; so he had cut loose from the charlatan and had opened his "Dental Parlors" on Polk Street, an "accommodation street" of small shops in the residence quarter of the town. Here he had slowly collected a clientele of butcher boys, shop girls, drug clerks, and car conductors. He made but few acquaintances. Polk Street called him the "Doctor" and spoke of his enormous strength. For McTeague was a young giant, carrying his huge shock of blond hair six feet three inches from the ground; moving his immense limbs, heavy with ropes of muscle, slowly, ponderously. His hands were enormous, red, and covered with a fell of stiff yellow hair; they were hard as wooden mallets, strong as vises, the hands of the old-time car-boy. Often he dispensed with forceps and extracted a refractory tooth with his thumb and finger. His head was square-cut, angular; the jaw salient, like that of the carnivora.

McTeague's mind was as his body, heavy, slow to act, sluggish. Yet there was nothing vicious about the man. Altogether he suggested the draught horse, immensely strong, stupid, docile, obedient.

When he opened his "Dental Parlors," he felt that his life was a success, that he could hope for nothing better. In spite of the name, there was but one room. It was a corner room on the second floor over the branch post-office, and faced the street. McTeague made it do for a bedroom as well, sleeping on the big bed-lounge against the wall opposite the window. There was a washstand behind the screen in the corner where he manufactured his moulds. In the round bay window were his operating chair, his dental engine, and the movable rack on which he laid out his instruments. Three chairs, a bargain at the second-hand store, ranged themselves against the wall with military precision underneath a steel engraving of the court of Lorenzo de' Medici, which he had bought because there were a great many figures in it for the money. Over the bed-lounge hung a rifle manufacturer's advertisement calendar which he never used. The other ornaments were a small marble-topped centre table covered with back numbers of "The American System of Dentistry," a stone pug dog sitting before the little stove, and a thermometer. A stand of shelves occupied one corner, filled with the seven volumes of "Allen's Practical Dentist." On the top shelf McTeague kept his concertina and a bag of bird seed for the canary. The whole place exhaled a mingled odor of bedding, creosote, and ether.

But for one thing, McTeague would have been perfectly contented. Just outside his window was his signboard—a modest affair—that read: "Doctor McTeague. Dental Parlors. Gas Given"; but that was all. It was his ambition, his dream, to have projecting from that corner window a huge gilded tooth, a molar with enormous prongs, something gorgeous and attractive. He would have it some day, on that he was resolved; but as yet such a thing was far beyond his means.

When he had finished the last of his beer, McTeague slowly wiped his lips and huge yellow mustache with the side of his hand. Bull-like, he heaved himself laboriously up, and, going to the window, stood looking down into the street.

The street never failed to interest him. It was one of those cross streets peculiar to Western cities, situated in the heart of the residence quarter, but occupied by small tradespeople who lived in the rooms above their shops. There were corner drug stores with huge jars of red, yellow, and green liquids in their windows, very brave and gay; stationers' stores, where illustrated weeklies were tacked upon bulletin boards; barber shops with cigar stands in their vestibules; sad-looking plumbers' offices; cheap restaurants, in whose windows one saw piles of unopened oysters weighted down by cubes of ice, and china pigs and cows knee deep in layers of white beans. At one end of the street McTeague could see the huge power-house of the cable line. Immediately opposite him was a great market; while farther on, over the chimney stacks of the intervening houses, the glass roof of some huge public baths glittered like crystal in the afternoon sun. Underneath him the branch post-office was opening its doors, as was its custom between two and three o'clock on Sunday afternoons. An acrid odor of ink rose upward to him. Occasionally a cable car passed, trundling heavily, with a strident whirring of jostled glass windows.

On week days the street was very lively. It woke to its work about seven o'clock, at the time when the newsboys made their appearance together with the day laborers. The laborers went trudging past in a straggling file—plumbers' apprentices, their pockets stuffed with sections of lead pipe, tweezers, and pliers; carpenters, carrying nothing but their little pasteboard lunch baskets painted to imitate leather; gangs of street workers, their overalls soiled with yellow clay, their picks and long-handled shovels over their shoulders; plasterers, spotted with lime from head to foot. This little army of workers, tramping steadily in one direction, met and mingled with other toilers of a different description—conductors and "swing men" of the cable company going on duty; heavy-eyed night clerks from the drug stores on their way home to sleep; roundsmen returning to the precinct police station to make their night report, and Chinese market gardeners teetering past under their heavy baskets. The cable cars began to fill up; all along the street could be seen the shop keepers taking down their shutters.

Between seven and eight the street breakfasted. Now and then a waiter from one of the cheap restaurants crossed from one sidewalk to the other, balancing on one palm a tray covered with a napkin. Everywhere was the smell of coffee and of frying steaks. A little later, following in the path of the day laborers, came the clerks and shop girls, dressed with a certain cheap smartness, always in a hurry, glancing apprehensively at the power-house clock. Their employers followed an hour or so later—on the cable cars for the most part—whiskered gentlemen with huge stomachs, reading the morning papers with great gravity; bank cashiers and insurance clerks with flowers in their buttonholes.

At the same time the school children invaded the street, filling the air with a clamor of shrill voices, stopping at the stationers' shops, or idling a moment in the doorways of the candy stores. For over half an hour they held possession of the sidewalks, then suddenly disappeared, leaving behind one or two stragglers who hurried along with great strides of their little thin legs, very anxious and preoccupied.

Towards eleven o'clock the ladies from the great avenue a block above Polk Street made their appearance, promenading the sidewalks leisurely, deliberately. They were at their morning's marketing. They were handsome women, beautifully dressed. They knew by name their butchers and grocers and vegetable men. From his window McTeague saw them in front of the stalls, gloved and veiled and daintily shod, the subservient provision-men at their elbows, scribbling hastily in the order books. They all seemed to know one another, these grand ladies from the fashionable avenue. Meetings took place here and there; a conversation was begun; others arrived; groups were formed; little impromptu receptions were held before the chopping blocks of butchers' stalls, or on the sidewalk, around boxes of berries and fruit.

From noon to evening the population of the street was of a mixed character. The street was busiest at that time; a vast and prolonged murmur arose—the mingled shuffling of feet, the rattle of wheels, the heavy trundling of cable cars. At four o'clock the school children once more swarmed the sidewalks, again disappearing with surprising suddenness. At six the great homeward march commenced; the cars were crowded, the laborers thronged the sidewalks, the newsboys chanted the evening papers. Then all at once the street fell quiet; hardly a soul was in sight; the sidewalks were deserted. It was supper hour. Evening began; and one by one a multitude of lights, from the demoniac glare of the druggists' windows to the dazzling blue whiteness of the electric globes, grew thick from street corner to street corner. Once more the street was crowded. Now there was no thought but for amusement. The cable cars were loaded with theatre-goers

—men in high hats and young girls in furred opera cloaks. On the sidewalks were groups and couples—the plumbers' apprentices, the girls of the ribbon counters, the little families that lived on the second stories over their shops, the dressmakers, the small doctors, the harness makers—all the various inhabitants of the street were abroad, strolling idly from shop window to shop window, taking the air after the day's work. Groups of girls collected on the corners, talking and laughing very loud, making remarks upon the young men that passed them. The *tamale* men appeared. A band of Salvationists began to sing before a saloon.

Then, little by little, Polk Street dropped back to solitude. Eleven o'clock struck from the power-house clock. Lights were extinguished. At one o'clock the cable stopped, leaving an abrupt silence in the air. All at once it seemed very still. The only noises were the occasional footfalls of a policeman and the persistent calling of ducks and geese in the closed market. The street was asleep.

Day after day, McTeague saw the same panorama unroll itself. The bay window of his "Dental Parlors" was for him a point of vantage from which he watched the world go past.

On Sundays, however, all was changed. As he stood in the bay window, after finishing his beer, wiping his lips, and looking out into the street, McTeague was conscious of the difference. Nearly all the stores were closed. No wagons passed. A few people hurried up and down the sidewalks, dressed in cheap Sunday finery. A cable car went by; on the outside seats were a party of returning picnickers. The mother, the father, a young man, and a young girl, and three children. The two older people held empty lunch baskets in their laps, while the bands of the children's hats were stuck full of oak leaves. The girl carried a huge bunch of wilting poppies and wild flowers.

As the car approached McTeague's window the young man got up and swung himself off the platform, waving good-bye to the party. Suddenly McTeague recognized him.

"There's Marcus Schouler," he muttered behind his mustache.

Marcus Schouler was the dentist's one intimate friend. The acquaintance had begun at the car conductors' coffee-joint, where the two occupied the same table and met at every meal. Then they made the discovery that they both lived in the same flat, Marcus occupying a room on the floor above McTeague. On different occasions Mc-

Teague had treated Marcus for an ulcerated tooth and had refused
to accept payment. Soon it came to be an understood thing between
them. They were "pals."

McTeague, listening, heard Marcus go up-stairs to his room above.
In a few minutes his door opened again. McTeague knew that he
had come out into the hall and was leaning over the banisters.

"Oh, Mac!" he called. McTeague came to his door.

"Hullo! 's that you, Mark?"

"Sure," answered Marcus. "Come on up."

"You come on down."

"No, come on up."

"Oh, you come on down."

"Oh, you lazy duck!" retorted Marcus, coming down the stairs.

"Been out to the Cliff House on a picnic," he explained as he sat
down on the bed-lounge, "with my uncle and his people—the Sieppes,
you know. By damn! it was hot," he suddenly vociferated. "Just look
at that! Just look at that!" he cried, dragging at his limp collar.
"That's the third one since morning; it is—it is, for a fact—and you
got your stove going." He began to tell about the picnic, talking very
loud and fast, gesturing furiously, very excited over trivial details.
Marcus could not talk without getting excited.

"You ought t'have seen, y'ought t'have seen. I tell you, it was outa
sight. It was; it was, for a fact."

"Yes, yes," answered McTeague, bewildered, trying to follow. "Yes,
that's so."

In recounting a certain dispute with an awkward bicyclist, in which
it appeared he had become involved, Marcus quivered with rage.
" 'Say that again,' says I to um. 'Just say that once more, and' "—
here a rolling explosion of oaths—" 'you'll go back to the city in the
Morgue wagon. Ain't I got a right to cross a street even, I'd like to
know, without being run down—what? I say it's outrageous. I'd a
knifed him in another minute. It was an outrage. I say it was an
outrage."

"Sure it was," McTeague hastened to reply. "Sure, sure."

"Oh, and we had an accident," shouted the other, suddenly off on
another tack. "It was awful. Trina was in the swing there—that's my
cousin Trina, you know who I mean—and she fell out. By damn! I
thought she'd killed herself; struck her face on a rock and knocked

out a front tooth. It's a wonder she didn't kill herself. It *is* a wonder; it is, for a fact. Ain't it, now? Huh? Ain't it? Y'ought t'have seen."

McTeague had a vague idea that Marcus Schouler was stuck on his cousin Trina. They "kept company" a good deal; Marcus took dinner with the Sieppes every Saturday evening at their home at B Street station, across the bay, and Sunday afternoons he and the family usually made little excursions into the suburbs. McTeague began to wonder dimly how it was that on this occasion Marcus had not gone home with his cousin. As sometimes happens, Marcus furnished the explanation upon the instant.

"I promised a duck up here on the avenue I'd call for his dog at four this afternoon."

Marcus was Old Grannis's assistant in a little dog hospital that the latter had opened in a sort of alley just off Polk Street, some four blocks above. Old Grannis lived in one of the back rooms of McTeague's flat. He was an Englishman and an expert dog surgeon, but Marcus Schouler was a bungler in the profession. His father had been a veterinary surgeon who had kept a livery stable near by, on California Street, and Marcus's knowledge of the diseases of domestic animals had been picked up in a haphazard way, much after the manner of McTeague's education. Somehow he managed to impress Old Grannis, a gentle, simple-minded old man, with a sense of his fitness, bewildering him with a torrent of empty phrases that he delivered with fierce gestures and with a manner of the greatest conviction.

"You'd better come along with me, Mac," observed Marcus. "We'll get the duck's dog, and then we'll take a little walk, huh? You got nothun to do. Come along."

McTeague went out with him, and the two friends proceeded up to the avenue to the house where the dog was to be found. It was a huge mansion-like place, set in an enormous garden that occupied a whole third of the block; and while Marcus tramped up the front steps and rang the doorbell boldly to show his independence, McTeague remained below on the sidewalk, gazing stupidly at the curtained windows, the marble steps, and the bronze griffins, troubled and a little confused by all this massive luxury.

After they had taken the dog to the hospital and had left him to whimper behind the wire netting, they returned to Polk Street and had a glass of beer in the back room of Joe Frenna's corner grocery.

Ever since they had left the huge mansion on the avenue, Marcus had been attacking the capitalists, a class which he pretended to execrate. It was a pose which he often assumed, certain of impressing the dentist. Marcus had picked up a few half-truths of political economy—it was impossible to say where—and as soon as the two had settled themselves to their beer in Frenna's back room he took up the theme of the labor question. He discussed it at the top of his voice, vociferating, shaking his fists, exciting himself with his own noise. He was continually making use of the stock phrases of the professional politician—phrases he had caught at some of the ward "rallies" and "ratification meetings." These rolled off his tongue with incredible emphasis, appearing at every turn of his conversation— "Outraged constituencies," "cause of labor," "wage earners," "opinions biased by personal interests," "eyes blinded by party prejudice." McTeague listened to him, awe-struck.

"There's where the evil lies," Marcus would cry. "The masses must learn self-control; it stands to reason. Look at the figures, look at the figures. Decrease the number of wage earners and you increase wages, don't you? don't you?"

Absolutely stupid, and understanding never a word, McTeague would answer:

"Yes, yes, that's it—self control—that's the word."

"It's the capitalists that's ruining the cause of labor," shouted Marcus, banging the table with his fist till the beer glasses danced; "white-livered drones, traitors, with their livers white as snow, eatun the bread of widows and orphuns; there's where the evil lies."

Stupefied with his clamor, McTeague answered, wagging his head:

"Yes, that's it; I think it's their livers."

Suddenly Marcus fell calm again, forgetting his pose all in an instant.

"Say, Mac, I told my cousin Trina to come around and see you about that tooth of hers. She'll be in to-morrow, I guess."

TELYGRAFT HILL

by

WALLACE IRWIN

O Telygraft Hill she sits mighty and fine,
Like a praty that's planted on ind,
And she's bannered wid washin's from manny a line,
Which flutther and dance in the wind.
O th' goats and th' chickens av Telygraft Hill
They prosper all grand and serene,
For when there's short pickin' on Telygraft Hill
They feed their swate sowls on the scene.

For the Irish they live on the top av it,
And the Dagos they live on the base av it,
And every tin can in the knowledge av man,
Is scattered all over the face av it,
Av Telygraft Hill, Telygraft Hill,
Nobby owld, slobby owld Telygraft Hill.

O Telygraft Hill she sits proud as a queen
And the docks lie below in the glare
And th' bay runs beyant 'er all purple and green
Wid th' ginger-bread island out there,
And the ferry boats toot at owld Telygraft Hill,
And th' Hill it don't care if they do
While the Bradys and Caseys av Telygraft Hill
Joost sit there enj'yin' the view.

For the Irish they live on the top av it,
And the Dagos they live on the base av it,

And every tin can in the knowledge av man,
Is scattered all over the face av it,
Av Telygraft Hill, Telygraft Hill,
Nobby owld, slobby owld Telygraft Hill.

Sure Telygraft Hill has a castle from Wales
Which was built by a local creator.
He made it av bed-slats wid hammer and nails
Like a scene in a stylish the-ay-ter.
There's rats in the castle o'Telgraft Hill,
But it frowns wid an air of its own
For it's runnin' th' bloof that owld Telegraft Hill
Is a sthrong-howld of morther and shtone.

For the Irish they live on the top av it,
And the Dagos they live on the base av it,
And every tin can in the knowledge of man,
Is scattered all over the face av it,
Av Telygraft Hill, Telygraft Hill,
Nobby owld, slobby owld Telygraft Hill.

And Telygraft Hill has an iligant lot
Of shanties and shacks, Hivin knows!
An' they're hangin' on tight to the jumpin-off spot
Be the grace av th' Saints and their toes;
And th' la-ads that are livin' on Telygraft Hill
Prefer to remain where they're at,
For they'd not trade a hen-roost on Telygraft Hill
For a mansion below on the flat.

For the Irish they live on the top av it,
And the Dagos they live on the base av it,
And every tin can in the knowledge av man,
Is scattered all over the face of it,
Av Telygraft Hill, Telygraft Hill,
Nobby owld, slobby owld Telygraft Hill.

PART IV

CITY OF OUR TIMES

INTRODUCTION

I N SPITE of the mystics who prophesied, in San Francisco as elsewhere, that with the end of the century there would also arrive the
end of the world, the city turned its corner safely enough and the
twentieth century began.

As was natural, some overlap might have been observed. George
Sterling's poem, with which this Part IV opens, though it was
written a bit later nevertheless expresses the transitional period
perfectly. With its faint flavor of rose-leaves and romance, it recalls
the nineties; older San Franciscans still quote its "cool, grey city"
refrain with the instinctive knowledge that Sterling had the right
feel for it. But he is also voicing a truth when he notes the essentially
westward orientation of the port, and the city at the continent's end;
he saw very clearly that the Winds of the Future blew toward San
Francisco, and said so; his poet's sensibility guided him aright.

Another kind of overlapping was to be detected in the holdover of
the do-as-you-please types, men who disregarded law as though it
simply did not exist and went about their business as they saw fit,
as men had done only a brief half-century earlier in the search for
gold. Some of these observed a few of the outward forms of law, at
least sufficiently so that they avoided direct brushes with its officers.
Others were overtly engaged in banditry and the devil take the
hindmost.

In the early 1900s San Francisco Bay, particularly at its upper end
where the Sacramento and San Joaquin Rivers merged with tidewater, was famous for its oyster beds. By nature these were difficult
for their lawful owners to protect; indeed at the time there was more
than a little debate about the validity of the owner principle itself
when it came to underwater possession. The field was ideal for extra-
legal enterprise, and a whole system of piracy grew up in which a
bold enough individual might pull dollars almost out of nowhere

if he was willing to take his chance on defying the law. After all, an oyster was an oyster; sacked and delivered at any one of half a hundred wharves along the East Bay front or in San Francisco, who was to say exactly whence it came? Jack London's half-reportorial, half-fictional account, "A Raid on the Oyster Pirates," shows beautifully this early twentieth-century phase of banditry, and I have chosen it for this reason as well as for its physical reflection of one of the city's fringes that was then as wild as though it had been a hundred instead of a mere dozen or so miles distant from the city's down town offices.

Complementing this violent sort of reminder of the city's brash past was the more innocent daring of the self-consciously defiant artist groups—young men and women many of whom posessed considerable talent but who felt the need to show their contempt for mere money-grubbing by meeting to discuss Literature and kindred subjects in restaurants that made them at home. Chief of these, in the first few years of the 1900s, was "Papa" Coppa's, where young writers, painters, composers and their friends invited their souls in the fumes of garlic and acid red wine, covered Coppa's walls with extravagant caricatures, mottoes and symbolic paintings, and (when well-to-do "slummers" began to discover the restaurant), sat by themselves in their own corner and did their best to live up to the bourgeois idea of what artists and writers ought to look like. It may have been at Coppa's that Gelett Burgess, only a year or two earlier, thought of the lines about the Purple Cow which dogged the unfortunate man the rest of his life, and it was certainly in that comfortable, easy-going atmosphere that Will Irwin, Ernest Peixotto, Porter Garnett and many another made their first tentative approaches to their careers. At any rate, Papa Coppa, though he loved and helped his artist-writer patrons, extending them credit, permitting them to decorate his walls and argue half the night over a single bottle of cheap wine, was not unaware that the tourist also played a part in his profits, and he developed many dishes which, though they were beyond the purses of his Bohemian younger clients, brought better heeled gourmets to sample his menu. One such was his *Chicken Portolá a là Coppa,* baked in a sealed coconut shell, and for its reflection of a time when its good food gave San Francisco the reputation it still holds, Coppa's own recipe for that dish is included here.

The old Coppa's, pictures and all, was soon to be destroyed when the city shook and burned in four dreadful days, but the recipe is still a pleasant echo of an era when more people found time to eat well, drink well, and be—that old-fashioned word—gay.

San Francisco's earthquake, in the early morning of April 18, 1906, and the fire that followed it, were really what ended the old century and began the new.

Reporters, poets and novelists did their level best, at the time and afterward, to put that catastrophe into words; an entire literature of the Quake and Fire may be found on reference library shelves. For almost half a century, too, San Franciscans dated events by "before the fire," and "after the fire," eschewing the word "earthquake" as though this aspect of the calamity had never been.

That habit of speech has gradually been forgotten; the visitor today may speak openly of The Earthquake, as San Franciscans themselves do now. And it remains the most significant episode in the city's history since the discovery of gold. For this reason I have selected several pieces of prose and verse relating to the great disaster, purposely rejecting the often repeated bits of folklore—the great Caruso's solemn oath never to visit such a dangerous city again, and such matters—and, instead, selecting excerpts that will, on the one hand, describe the occurrence and on the other, show the city's reactions.

For sheer, vivid description of the shocking abruptness of the quake I have found no better prose piece than the bit I have selected from Kathryn Hulme's novel, *We Lived as Children.* Here are the quake and the following fire as seen through the eyes of a child, which viewpoint gives the events added poignancy as the reader will discover. Along with this is the high-keyed first report, printed next day by three of San Francisco's newspapers which combined forces and issued a joint edition from the presses of the Oakland *Tribune* across the Bay; it provides the immediate, half-stunned reaction of a group of newspapermen who knew they had to get the story into print somehow, and do it fast. A slightly later reaction, highly charged with emotion and warmly flavored with courage, shows in the verses of "The Damndest Finest Ruins," written by one of the city's businessmen who felt he must put into words the pride San

Franciscans still felt in their city when it was no more than embers and rubble.

Two days later, at the other edge of the continent, a San Franciscan sat at his desk in the New York *Sun,* read the dispatches from the Pacific Coast and, at his editor's request, wrote at white heat the story of the San Francisco he had known, the San Francisco that was now gone. Will Irwin's "The City That Was" became in its way a kind of classic, and was published later in that year in a small book, here reprinted in its entirety excepting for a few more or less private reminiscences which mean little now. When Irwin wrote his piece it was still too early to say how the city would face up to the emergency after the first shock had worn away, but a set of light stanzas, "Barriers Burned," expresses on the level of humorous verse the spirit that animated citizens when they set about rebuilding their San Francisco. Charles K. Field—a cousin of Eugene—who wrote the poem, commented in verse more than once upon the fire; many still quote with glee his quatrain in reply to the pastors who solemnly preached that through the great disaster San Francisco had only been punished for its sins. Learning that a good friend's liquor warehouse had come through intact, Field observed,

> *If, as they say, God spanked the town*
> *For being over-frisky,*
> *Why did He burn His churches down*
> *And spare Hotaling's whiskey?*

Only a little later, in his novel, *The Heart Line,* Gelett Burgess spoke his admiration for the city that had accomplished such miracles of reconstruction, and I have taken just a single brief paragraph from that novel as a quick glimpse of one San Franciscan's honest feeling about his city as it rose from its ashes.

Now, with the quake and fire in the past, San Francisco moved into its new phase, an adulthood in which there were still mixed happy recollections of its youth. Kathryn Forbes in *Mama's Bank Account,* remembered not only Mama but a city, still raw from its fearful experience, that was nevertheless able to exercise a powerful pull on those who had come to know it. In the chapter I have chosen here, the reader will see how the city drew back even those who had determined to leave, and will also understand, perhaps, something of how thoroughly San Francisco had become a melting pot for people from everywhere. This same thread runs through the selections immediately succeeding—Stewart Edward White's loving testimonial to the old Chinese houseboys who became integral parts of the families they served; Lemuel De Bra's dramatic short-story of the city's Chinatown, (chosen for an O. Henry Memorial Award volume when it was first published in the 1920s); Charles Caldwell Dobie's "The Gift," in which still another facet of San Francisco, the life of the middle-European worker in the 1930's, is affectionately depicted. And in "No More Sad Thoughts" George Mardikian, long one of the city's leading restaurateurs, pays tribute to the (to him) astonishing lightheartedness he found in San Francisco when he arrived as a very young man from an Armenia in which the fears and hatreds of an old time still dampened every man's existence. Loving all America, as he found himself doing, Mardikian nevertheless deplored certain of its eating habits and, among these, one of the least happy was the average American's notion of a potato salad. In the preface to his cookbook, "Dinner at Omar Khayyam's" from which I have taken this excerpt, he therefore sets down detailed instructions on how a decent potato salad should be made, and I have included this as well, for the excellent reason that the result is quite as good as he says it will be.

As the reader has discovered by this time, San Francisco is a good many kinds of city. Among other things it has, in its time, had its share of crime, from the days of the Rush when, as historian H. H. Bancroft frankly said, the town was drunk with gold, down through the heyday of its sordid Barbary Coast and to such episodes of violence as the sudden taking-off of the flashy tong boss Little Pete. A collection such as this, therefore, would hardly be properly rounded out unless it included a straight-out account of one of its more sensational murders. Here I have chosen to use Alfred Meyers' " 'Boss Missy': The Case of Rosetta Baker," taken from a group of cases in the volume, *San Francisco Murders*. It has special interest for several reasons; it reflects the city's life in the confused 1930s, the depression era when social lines that had begun to break down in the feverish 1920s were almost entirely wiped out for the time being; the case (except in the view of Mr. Meyers who has studied it carefully and come to an opinion which the editor shares), was never really solved; and it shows the way in which an emotional stereotype —in this case the cliché that "an old Chinese servant could never do such a thing"—may influence an entire group of newspapers and therefore the city's populace in general. At the end of a trial filled with unexplained loose ends and an exceptional array of grotesqueries of one sort or another, the elderly Chinese who had protested so violently that he had not killed his "Boss Missy," sailed for his native land carrying with him the secret of his mistress' death—if he knew it. The reader, under Mr. Meyers' expert guidance, may make up his own mind about what Liu Fook knew, or didn't. Meantime he will have had a good look at still another aspect of San Francisco and its people.

Three selections remain. One, Stanton A. Coblentz's admirable sonnet "From the Golden Gate Bridge," is here partly because it is a thoughtful poem as well as a good one, and partly because in a book about a city famous for its two great bridges at least one of them should be recognized, and the great span that takes the Golden Gate in one tremendous leap is the more dramatic of the two. "Sun on Fisherman's Wharf," which is part of a chapter from the novel, *Fiddler's Green,* by Ernest K. Gann, is included because in addition to its deft handling it concerns another well-known feature of San Francisco. Visitors in unfailing numbers take time to see The Wharf, a small gateway to the bay and the Pacific beyond; they have been told that it is picturesque and so it is, though much of it is self-consciously so with its tourist bait of hand-painted sea shells and such. Nevertheless the true quality of The Wharf comes through; if it stays stubbornly picturesque in spite of everything, this is because it exists for a sound reason. Behind the façade of sidewalk crab kettles and gaping tourists, The Wharf itself is there because the fishing boats are, and these latter with their pink and blue trim and their furled sails—nowadays diesel power is taking over more and more—represent an economic actuality, the thousands of tons of fish they bring in each year. Mr. Gann knows The Wharf; a novelist part time, he is also the owner of a fishing vessel and a contributor to his city's fish economy like the other owners whose chunky, sturdy boats lie alongside his in the little basin. And, as this bit from his novel will demonstrate, his novelist's eye and ear have caught the look and sound of the little group whose portraits he paints here—

not the fisherman but men of another kind, whose lives are no more
than tangent to The Wharf and its business, yet are part of the
city too.

Finally in these times it is often the newspaper writer rather than
the professed Literary Man who best catches the atmosphere, the
"feel," the tone-of-voice, so to say, of his own city. That is why I
have chosen to round off this collection with some excerpts from a
book by the San Francisco columnist, Herb Caen. Some fifteen years
ago when Caen came down as a young man from a town in California's great Valley to snap up trifles unconsidered by others and
make a daily odds-and-ends newspaper column of them, he christened San Francisco, (with perhaps a lingering recollection of
Manhattan's O. Henry at the back of his mind), Baghdad-By-The-
Bay, and the city has been this to him ever since. There is little of
its color, its romance, its lively vigor, its frequent absurdities, that
he has missed, and when he gathered up and reworked some of his
columns a year or so ago, bringing together enough of them to make
a book, it was not surprising to find that it read, as someone observed
at the time, like a love letter to San Francisco. It is with this affec-
tionate, kaleidoscopic, somewhat haphazard but always warmhearted
view of a great and greatly-loved city that this volume comes to
its end.

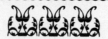

THE COOL, GREY CITY
OF LOVE

by

GEORGE STERLING

Tho I die on a distant strand,
And they give me a grave in that land,
Yet carry me back to my own city!
Carry me back to her grace and pity!
For I think I could not rest
Afar from her mighty breast.
She is fairer than others are
Whom they sing the beauty of.
Her heart is a song and a star—
My cool, grey city of love.

Tho they tear the rose from her brow,
To her is ever my vow;
Ever to her I give my duty—
First in rapture and first in beauty,
Wayward, passionate, brave,
Glad of the life God gave.
The sea-winds are her kiss,
And the sea-gull is her dove;
Cleanly and strong she is—
My cool, grey city of love.

The winds of the Future wait
At the iron walls of her Gate,
And the western ocean breaks in thunder,

And the western stars go slowly under,
And her gaze is ever West
In the dream of her young unrest.
Her sea is a voice that calls,
And her star a voice above,
And her wind a voice on her walls—
My cool, grey city of love.

Tho they stay her feet at the dance,
In her is the far romance.
Under the rain of winter falling,
Vine and rose will await recalling.
Tho the dark be cold and blind,
Yet her sea-fog's touch is kind,
And her mightier caress
Is joy and the pain thereof;
And great is thy tenderness,
O cool, grey city of love!

[1900]

A RAID ON THE
OYSTER PIRATES

by

JACK LONDON

OF THE fish patrolmen under whom we served at various times, Charley Le Grant and I were agreed, I think, that Neil Partington was the best. He was neither dishonest nor cowardly; and while he demanded strict obedience when we were under his orders, at the same time our relations were those of easy comradeship, and he permitted us a freedom to which we were ordinarily unaccustomed, as the present story will show.

Neil's family lived in Oakland, which is on the Lower Bay, not more than six miles across the water from San Francisco. One day, while scouting among the Chinese shrimp-catchers of Point Pedro, he received word that his wife was very ill; and within the hour the *Reindeer* was bowling along for Oakland, with a stiff northwest breeze astern. We ran up the Oakland Estuary and came to anchor, and in the days that followed, while Neil was ashore, we tightened up the *Reindeer's* rigging, overhauled the ballast, scraped down, and put the sloop into thorough shape.

This done, time hung heavy on our hands. Neil's wife was dangerously ill, and the outlook was a week's lie-over, awaiting the crisis. Charley and I roamed the docks, wondering what we should do, and so came upon the oyster fleet lying at the Oakland City Wharf. In the main they were trim, natty boats, made for speed and bad weather, and we sat down on the stringer-piece of the dock to study them.

From *Tales of the Fish Patrol*. By permission of Mrs. Charmian K. London.

"A good catch, I guess," Charley said, pointing to the heaps of oysters, assorted in three sizes, which lay upon their decks.

Pedlers were backing their wagons to the edge of the wharf, and from the bargaining and chaffering that went on, I managed to learn the selling price of the oysters.

"That boat must have at least two hundred dollars' worth aboard," I calculated. "I wonder how long it took to get the load?"

"Three or four days," Charley answered. "Not bad wages for two men—twenty-five dollars a day apiece."

The boat we were discussing, the *Ghost*, lay directly beneath us. Two men composed its crew. One was a squat, broad-shouldered fellow with remarkably long and gorilla-like arms, while the other was tall and well proportioned, with clear blue eyes and a mat of straight black hair. So unusual and striking was this combination of hair and eyes that Charley and I remained somewhat longer than we intended.

And it was well that we did. A stout, elderly man, with the dress and carriage of a successful merchant, came up and stood beside us, looking down upon the deck of the *Ghost*. He appeared angry, and the longer he looked the angrier he grew.

"Those are my oysters," he said at last. "I know they are my oysters. You raided my beds last night and robbed me of them."

The tall man and the short man on the *Ghost* looked up.

"Hello, Taft," the short man said, with insolent familiarity. (Among the bayfarers he had gained the nickname of "The Centipede" on account of his long arms.) "Hello, Taft," he repeated, with the same touch of insolence. "Wot 'r you growlin' about now?"

"Those are my oysters—that's what I said. You've stolen them from my beds."

"Yer mighty wise, an't ye?" was the Centipede's sneering reply. "S'pose you can tell your oysters wherever you see 'em?"

"Now, in my experience," broke in the tall man, "oysters is oysters wherever you find 'em, an' they're pretty much alike all the Bay over, and the world over, too, for that matter. We're not wantin' to quarrel with you, Mr. Taft, but we jes' wish you wouldn't insinuate that them oysters is yours an' that we're thieves an' robbers till you can prove the goods."

"I know they're mine; I'd stake my life on it!" Mr. Taft snorted.

"Prove it," challenged the tall man, who we afterward learned was known as "The Porpoise" because of his wonderful swimming abilities.

Mr. Taft shrugged his shoulders helplessly. Of course he could not prove the oysters to be his, no matter how certain he might be.

"I'd give a thousand dollars to have you men behind the bars!" he cried. "I'll give fifty dollars a head for your arrest and conviction, all of you!"

A roar of laughter went up from the different boats, for the rest of the pirates had been listening to the discussion.

"There's more money in oysters," the Porpoise remarked dryly.

Mr. Taft turned impatiently on his heel and walked away. From out of the corner of his eye, Charley noted the way he went. Several minutes later, when he had disappeared around a corner, Charley rose lazily to his feet. I followed him, and we sauntered off in the opposite direction to that taken by Mr. Taft.

"Come on! Lively!" Charley whispered, when we passed from the view of the oyster fleet.

Our course was changed at once, and we dodged around corners and raced up and down side-streets till Mr. Taft's generous form loomed up ahead of us.

"I'm going to interview him about that reward," Charley explained, as we rapidly overhauled the oyster-bed owner. "Neil will be delayed here for a week, and you and I might as well be doing something in the meantime. What do you say?"

"Of course, of course," Mr. Taft said, when Charley had introduced himself and explained his errand. "Those thieves are robbing me of thousands of dollars every year, and I shall be glad to break them up at any price,—yes, sir, at any price. As I said, I'll give fifty dollars a head, and call it cheap at that. They've robbed my beds, torn down my signs, terrorized my watchmen, and last year killed one of them. Couldn't prove it. All done in the blackness of night. All I had was a dead watchman and no evidence. The detectives could do nothing. Nobody has been able to do anything with those men. We have never succeeded in arresting one of them. So I say, Mr.— What did you say your name was?"

"Le Grant," Charley answered.

"So I say, Mr. Le Grant, I am deeply obliged to you for the

assistance you offer. And I shall be glad, most glad, sir, to cooperate with you in every way. My watchmen and boats are at your disposal. Come and see me at the San Francisco offices any time, or telephone at my expense. And don't be afraid of spending money. I'll foot your expenses, whatever they are, so long as they are within reason. The situation is growing desperate, and something must be done to determine whether I or that band of ruffians own those oyster beds."

"Now we'll see Neil," Charley said, when he had seen Mr. Taft upon his train to San Francisco.

Not only did Neil Partington interpose no obstacle to our adventure, but he proved to be of greatest assistance. Charley and I knew nothing of the oyster industry, while his head was an encyclopaedia of facts concerning it. Also, within an hour or so, he was able to bring to us a Greek boy of seventeen or eighteen who knew thoroughly well the ins and outs of oyster piracy.

At this point I may as well explain that we of the fish patrol were free lances in a way. While Neil Partington, who was a patrolman proper, received a regular salary, Charley and I, being merely deputies, received only what we earned—that is to say, a certain percentage of the fines imposed on convicted violators of the fish laws. Also, any rewards that chanced our way were ours. We offered to share with Partington whatever we should get from Mr. Taft, but the patrolman would not hear of it. He was only too happy, he said, to do a good turn for us, who had done so many for him.

We held a long council of war, and mapped out the following line of action. Our faces were unfamiliar on the Lower Bay, but as the *Reindeer* was well known as a fish-patrol sloop, the Greek boy, whose name was Nicholas, and I were to sail some innocent-looking craft down to Asparagus Island and join the oyster pirates' fleet. Here, according to Nicholas's description of the beds and the manner of raiding, it was possible for us to catch the pirates in the act of stealing oysters, and at the same time to get them in our power. Charley was to be on the shore, with Mr. Taft's watchmen and a posse of constables, to help us at the right time.

"I know just the boat," Neil said, at the conclusion of the discussion, "a crazy old sloop that's lying over at Tiburon. You and Nicholas can go over by the ferry, charter it for a song, and sail direct for the beds."

"Good luck be with you, boys," he said at parting, two days later. "Remember, they are dangerous men, so be careful."

Nicholas and I succeeded in chartering the sloop very cheaply; and between laughs, while getting up sail, we agreed that she was even crazier and older than she had been described. She was a big, flat-bottomed, square-sterned craft, sloop-rigged, with a sprung mast, slack rigging, dilapidated sails, and rotten running-gear, clumsy to handle and uncertain in bringing about, and she smelled vilely of coal tar, with which strange stuff she had been smeared from stem to stern and from cabin-roof to centreboard. And to cap it all, *Coal Tar Maggie* was printed in great white letters the whole length of either side.

It was an uneventful though laughable run from Tiburon to Asparagus Island where we arrived in the afternoon of the following day. The oyster pirates, a fleet of a dozen sloops, were lying at anchor on what was known as the "Deserted Beds." The *Coal Tar Maggie* came sloshing into their midst with a light breeze astern, and they crowded on deck to see us. Nicholas and I had caught the spirit of the crazy craft, and we handled her in most lubberly fashion.

"Wot is it?" some one called.

"Name it 'n' ye kin have it!" called another.

"I swan naow, ef it ain't the old Ark itself!" mimicked the Centipede from the deck of the *Ghost*.

"Hey! Ahoy there, clipper ship!" another wag shouted "wot's yer port?"

We took no notice of the joking, but acted, after the manner of greenhorns, as though the *Coal Tar Maggie* required our undivided attention. I rounded her well to windward of the *Ghost*, and Nicholas ran for'ard to drop the anchor. To all appearances it was a bungle, the way the chain tangled and kept the anchor from reaching the bottom. And to all appearances Nicholas and I were terribly excited as we strove to clear it. At any rate, we quite deceived the pirates, who took huge delight in our predicament.

But the chain remained tangled, and amid all kinds of mocking advice we drifted down upon and fouled the *Ghost*, whose bowsprit poked square through our mainsail and ripped a hole in it as big as a barn door. The Centipede and the Porpoise doubled up on the cabin in paroxysms of laughter, and left us to get clear as best we could. This, with much unseamanlike performance, we succeeded in doing, and likewise in clearing the anchor-chain, of which we let out about three hundred feet. With only ten feet of water under us, this would permit the *Coal Tar Maggie* to swing in a circle six hundred feet in diameter, in which circle she would be able to foul at least half the fleet.

The oyster pirates lay snugly together at short hawsers, the weather being fine, and they protested loudly at our ignorance in putting out such an unwarranted length of anchor-chain. And not only did they protest, for they made us heave it in again, all but thirty feet.

Having sufficiently impressed them with our general lubberliness, Nicholas and I went below to congratulate ourselves and to cook supper. Hardly had we finished the meal and washed the dishes, when a skiff ground against the *Coal Tar Maggie's* side, and heavy feet trampled on deck. Then the Centipede's brutal face appeared in the companionway, and he descended into the cabin, followed by the Porpoise. Before they could seat themselves on a bunk, another skiff came alongside, and another, and another, till the whole fleet was represented by the gathering in the cabin.

"Where'd you swipe the old tub?" asked a squat and hairy man, with cruel eyes and Mexican features.

"Didn't swipe it," Nicholas answered, meeting them on their own ground and encouraging the idea that we had stolen the *Coal Tar Maggie*. "And if we did, what of it?"

"Well, I don't admire your taste, that's all," sneered he of the Mexican features. "I'd rot on the beach first before I'd take a tub that couldn't get out of its own way."

"How were we to know till we tried her?" Nicholas asked, so innocently as to cause a laugh. "And how do you get the oysters?" he hurried on. "We want a load of them; that's what we came for, a load of oysters."

"What d'ye want 'em for?" demanded the Porpoise.

"Oh, to give away to our friends, of course," Nicholas retorted. "That's what you do with yours, I suppose."

This started another laugh, and as our visitors grew more genial we could see that they had not the slightest suspicion of our identity or purpose.

"Didn't I see you on the dock in Oakland the other day?" the Centipede asked suddenly of me.

"Yep," I answered boldly, taking the bull by the horns. "I was watching you fellows and figuring out whether we'd go oystering or not. It's a pretty good business, I calculate, and so we're going in for it. That is," I hastened to add, "if you fellows don't mind."

"I'll tell you one thing, which ain't two things," he replied, "and that is you'll have to hump yerself an' get a better boat. We won't stand to be disgraced by any such box as this. Understand?"

"Sure," I said. "Soon as we sell some oysters we'll outfit in style."

"And if you show yerself square an' the right sort," he went on, "why, you kin run with us. But if you don't" (here his voice became stern and menacing), "why, it'll be the sickest day of yer life. Understand?"

"Sure," I said.

After that and more warning and advice of similar nature, the conversation became general, and we learned that the beds were to be raided that very night. As they got into their boats, after an hour's stay, we were invited to join them in the raid with the assurance of "the more the merrier."

"Did you notice that short, Mexican-looking chap?" Nicholas asked, when they had departed to their various sloops. "He's Barchi, of the Sporting Life Gang, and the fellow that came with him is Skilling. They're both out now on five thousand dollars' bail."

I had heard of the Sporting Life Gang before, a crowd of hoodlums and criminals that terrorized the lower quarters of Oakland, and two-thirds of which were usually to be found in state's prison for crimes that ranged from perjury and ballot-box stuffing to murder.

"They are not regular oyster pirates," Nicholas continued. "They've just come down for the lark and to make a few dollars. But we'll have to watch out for them."

We sat in the cockpit and discussed the details of our plan till eleven o'clock had passed, when we heard the rattle of an oar in a boat from the direction of the *Ghost*. We hauled up our own skiff, tossed in a few sacks, and rowed over. There we found all the skiffs assembling, it being the intention to raid the beds in a body.

To my surprise, I found barely a foot of water where we had dropped anchor in ten feet. It was the big June run-out of the full moon, and as the ebb had yet an hour and a half to run, I knew that our anchorage would be dry ground before slack water.

Mr. Taft's beds were three miles away, and for a long time we rowed silently in the wake of the other boats, once in a while grounding and our oar blades constantly striking bottom. At last we came upon soft mud covered with not more than two inches of water— not enough to float the boats. But the pirates at once were over the side, and by pushing and pulling on the flat-bottomed skiffs, we moved steadily along.

The full moon was partly obscured by high-flying clouds, but the pirates went their way with the familiarity born of long practice. After half a mile of the mud, we came upon a deep channel, up which we rowed, with dead oyster shoals looming high and dry on either side. At last we reached the picking grounds. Two men, on one of the shoals, hailed us and warned us off. But the Centipede, the Porpoise, Barchi, and Skilling took the lead, and followed by the rest of us, at least thirty men in half as many boats, rowed right up to the watchmen.

"You'd better slide outa this here," Barchi said threateningly, "or we'll fill you so full of holes you wouldn't float in molasses."

The watchmen wisely retreated before so overwhelming a force, and rowed their boat along the channel toward where the shore should be. Besides, it was in the plan for them to retreat.

We hauled the noses of the boats up on the shore side of a big shoal, and all hands, with sacks, spread out and began picking. Every now and again the clouds thinned before the face of the moon, and we could see the big oysters quite distinctly. In almost no time sacks were filled and carried back to the boats, where fresh ones were obtained. Nicholas and I returned often and anxiously to the boats with our little loads, but always found some one of the pirates coming or going.

"Never mind," he said; "no hurry. As they pick farther and farther away, it will take too long to carry to the boats. Then they'll stand the full sacks on end and pick them up when the tide comes in and the skiffs will float to them."

Fully half an hour went by, and the tide had begun to flood, when this came to pass. Leaving the pirates at their work, we stole back to the boats. One by one, and noiselessly, we shoved them off and made them fast in an awkward flotilla. Just as we were shoving off the last skiff, our own, one of the men came upon us. It was Barchi. His quick eye took in the situation at a glance, and he sprang for us; but we went clear with a mighty shove, and he was left floundering in the water over his head. As soon as he got back to the shoal he raised his voice and gave the alarm.

We rowed with all our strength, but it was slow going with so many boats in tow. A pistol cracked from the shoal, a second, and a third; then a regular fusillade began. The bullets spat and spat all about us; but thick clouds had covered the moon, and in the dim darkness it was no more than random firing. It was only by chance that we could be hit.

"Wish we had a little steam launch," I panted.

"I'd just as soon the moon stayed hidden," Nicholas panted back.

It was slow work, but every stroke carried us farther away from the shoal and nearer the shore, till at last the shooting died down, and when the moon did come out we were too far away to be in danger. Not long afterward we answered a shoreward hail, and two Whitehall boats, each pulled by three pairs of oars, darted up to us. Charley's welcome face bent over to us, and he gripped us by the hands while he cried "Oh, you joys! You joys! Both of you!"

When the flotilla had been landed, Nicholas and I and a watchman rowed out in one of the Whitehalls, with Charley in the sternsheets. Two other Whitehalls followed us, and as the moon now shone brightly, we easily made out the oyster pirates on their lonely shoal. As we drew closer, they fired a rattling volley from their revolvers, and we promptly retreated beyond range.

"Lot of time," Charley said. "The flood is setting in fast, and by the time it's up to their necks there won't be any fight left in them."

So we lay on our oars and waited for the tide to do its work. This was the predicament of the pirates: because of the big run-out, the tide was now rushing back like a millrace, and it was impossible for the strongest swimmer in the world to make against it in the three miles to the sloops. Between the pirates and the shore were we, precluding escape in that direction. On the other hand, the water was rising rapidly over the shoals, and it was only a question of a few hours when it would be over their heads.

It was beautifully calm, and in the brilliant white moonlight we watched them through our night glasses and told Charley of the voyage of the *Coal Tar Maggie*. One o'clock came, and two o'clock, and the pirates were clustering on the highest shoal, waist-deep in water.

"Now this illustrates the value of imagination," Charley was saying "Taft has been trying for years to get them, but he went at it with bull strength and failed. Now we used our heads . . . "

Just then I heard a scarcely audible gurgle of water, and holding up my hand for silence, I turned and pointed to a ripple slowly widening out in a growing circle. It was not more than fifty feet from us. We kept perfectly quiet and waited. After a minute the water broke six feet away and a black head and white shoulder showed in the moonlight. With a snort of surprise and of suddenly expelled breath, the head and shoulder went down.

We pulled ahead several strokes and drifted with the current. Four pairs of eyes searched the surface of the water, but never another ripple showed, and never another glimpse did we catch of the black head and white shoulder.

"It's the Porpoise," Nicholas said. "It would take broad daylight for us to catch him."

At a quarter to three the pirates gave their first sign of weakening. We heard cries for help, in the unmistakable voice of the Centipede, and this time, on rowing closer, we were not fired upon. The Centipede was in a truly perilous plight. Only the heads and shoulders of his fellow-marauders showed above the water as they braced themselves against the current, while his feet were off the bottom and they were supporting him.

"Now, lads," Charley said briskly, "we have got you, and you can't get away. If you cut up rough, we'll have to leave you alone and the water will finish you. But if you're good, we'll take you aboard, one at a time, and you'll be saved. What do you say?"

"Ay," they chorused hoarsely between their chattering teeth.

"Then one man at a time, and the short men first."

The Centipede was the first to be pulled aboard, and he came willingly, though he objected when the constable put the handcuffs on him. Barchi was next hauled in, quite meek and resigned from his soaking. When we had ten in our boat we drew back, and the second Whitehall was loaded. The third Whitehall recieved nine prisoners only—a catch of twenty-nine in all.

"You didn't get the Porpoise," the Centipede said exultantly, as though his escape materially diminished our success.

Charley laughed. "But we saw him just the same, a-snorting for shore like a puffing pig."

It was a mild and shivering band of pirates that we marched up the beach to the oyster house. In answer to Charley's knock, the door was flung open, and a pleasant wave of warm air rushed out upon us.

"You can dry your clothes here, lads, and get some hot coffee," Charley announced, as they filed in.

And there, sitting ruefully by the fire, with a steaming mug in his hand, was the Porpoise. With one accord Nicholas and I looked at Charley. He laughed gleefully.

"That comes of imagination," he said. "When you see a thing, you've got to see it all around, or what's the good of seeing it all? I saw the beach, so I left a couple of constables behind to keep an eye on it. That's all."

CHICKEN PORTOLÁ

A LÁ COPPA

Clarence E. Edwords

in *Bohemian San Francisco*

TAKE a fresh cocoanut and cut off the top, removing nearly all of the meat.

Put together three tablespoons of chopped cocoanut meat and two ears of fresh corn, taken from the cob. Slice two onions into four tablespoonsfuls of olive oil, together with a tablespoonful of diced bacon fried in olive oil, add one chopped green pepper, half a dozen tomatoes stewed with salt and pepper, one clove of garlic, and cook all together until it thickens.

Strain this into the corn and cocoanut and add one spring chicken cut in four pieces. Put this mixture into the shell of the cocoanut, using the cut-off top as a cover, and close tightly with a covering of flour-paste around the jointure to keep in the flavors.

Put the cocoanut into the a pan with water in it, and set in the oven, well heated, for one-hour, basting frequently to prevent the cocoanut from burning.

A bare recital of the terms of the recipe cannot bring to the uninitiated even a suspicion of the delightful aroma that comes from the cocoanut when the top is lifted, nor can it give the slightest idea of the delicacy of the savor arising from the combination of the cocoanut with the young chicken.

By permission of Paul Elder & Co., Publisher.

EARTHQUAKE AND FIRE

by

KATHRYN HULME

CHANDELIERS shattered through the house as we snatched at clothes laid out in order for the picnic. We were all in the same room without knowing how we got there. The shocks threw us against the wall, back on the bed. Buzz whimpered, his sweater on backwards. Never mind, never mind. Jen had tears rolling down her cheeks, no sound of crying. My teeth chattered, I clenched my jaw, nothing could stop anything. A far grumble of earth roared to nearness, under the house, under our feet. Timber creaked and crockery pitched off pantry shelves. A crack opened in the wall and spread under our gaze like a vein down to the slats beneath the plaster.

Hurry, hurry, said mother.

We fled down the hall past lurching pictures, stopped in terror as the Alaskan harpoons fell from the antler prongs. We clung together at the head of the stairs watching them wave and twist while the doorframe made a ripping noise. Then mother led the way. She snatched up the picnic hamper as we ran through the door.

We stood dazed in the middle of the street. Neighbors in nightgowns yelled: *No, there! WHERE?—The vacant lot—live wires.* We got across just as a telephone pole tumbled, pulling with it a loop of deadly wire. Mother moaned: Oh, oh! as it writhed where our feet had been. We clutched mother speechlessly while the second and third shocks came, feeling her knees shaking under her skirt. The ground rocked. Our own sobs were lost in the shrieks of those still running toward the open space. An underground roar came with

---

Reprinted from *We Lived as Children* by Kathryn Hulme, by permission of Alfred A. Knopf, Inc. Copyright 1938 by Kathryn Hulme.

each temblor; it didn't seem safe to stand on earth, but there was no place to go.

A sharp twist nearly flung us to the ground, then the rocking stopped. We stared at each other unable to recognize the faces we saw. We stared at the rising sun; even that looked gray and drained with fright like the faces around us. We stood with legs apart waiting for another shock, ears strained for the rumbling. Only sounds of loosened bricks rattling down roofs, crashes of glass, and a queer indrawn sobbing all around us. A little shake came, almost more awful than the twisters because no sound came with it, a quiet tremor like nerves after a convulsion. Then someone said in an everyday voice: It's all over.

We saw Dr. Sonntag embracing his Lena, crying: Gott verdanke, Gott verdanke! He wore only gray wool underdrawers and a striped shirt, but it didn't seem funny. Mr. Percy in pajamas and straw hat came up to mother and said: In another second I was going to come and get you, and we had a sense of a man looking out for us. Mother asked in the smallest voice I ever heard from her: Do you think it's all over? I should say it is, said Mr. Percy; why, that first quake lasted nearly two minutes. He stamped the ground with his carpet slippers and said scornfully: That's all this old earth is capable of in one day. We felt much better. A man would know. Presently his eye fell on the picnic hamper, he stood back in amazement. Say, he said, you folks look as though you'd planned on this. He acted aggrieved. You might have let a neighbor in on the secret, he said. Then he went around telling everyone that we knew the earthquake was coming, we even packed a picnic lunch for it. He brought the first smiles and walked off like a hero, saying: I'm going to get my clothes.

We'll sit down and wait awhile, mother said; Buzz, you spread out the coats. No, I know, we'll all help, she said, pretending not to notice his shaking hands. Jen was white, but her hands were steady. We sat close together, the thumping of the heart and the trembling seemed less with our bodies touching. I was the only one with a peculiarity unshared. My teeth chattered so I felt I ought to apologize.

I ca-a-n't m-m-m-ake them st-st-stop, I tried to say.

Buzz, hearing such sounds, lifted his head from mother's lap and looked with interest at my chattering jaw. Gee whizz, ma, he said, she'll knock out all her teeth.

After a while it was fun looking around seeing what people had snatched up in their dash from houses. One woman held a Bohemian glass bowl—But no food in it, Jen remarked like an observant house-keeper. When we looked over the birdcages, both parrot and canary, the clocks, bed pillows, and coal-scuttles our neighbors had picked up, nothing anyone could eat, we felt quite superior about mother's choice of picnic hamper. Also, we were properly dressed. We began making fun of the half-clads. Mother had to hush us, but she did it with encouraging pats as if to say: I'll be with you in a minute just as soon as I'm sure . . . while her eyes searched the overcast sky like an anxious mariner's.

The vacant lot where we sat was the end of civilization. Behind us rolled grassy fields lifting finally to Twin Peaks. The Statue of Liberty hill was nearer, beginning almost in our backyard. Only the hills looked as if nothing had happened. Our street was scattered with shingles and stair railings, chimneys and window-panes, and one house three doors down from us had had an entire side wall taken off so that it was like looking into a large-scale dollhouse, kitchen, dining-room, and parlor downstairs, bedrooms above with a brass bedstead hanging over the open edge—Clinging by its castors, mother said, and for some reason made my brother remember our cat.

Alfred! He raised up. One of us was missing. I'm going to get Alfred, he said.

Mother said: I'll go, and started to rise.

Buzz had been listening to the men ordering their women-folk about. He fixed mother with a look. You stay here, ma—there were tears in his eyes he was so frightened to go back to the house alone— I can get Alfred quicker, he said, he answers my whistle.

Mother held him. Is it all right, do you think? she asked Mr. Short, the wholesale grocer whose family camped next to us.

Sure, it's all over, said Mr. Short, let the kid go, it'll do him good. But say, sonny, he said to Buzz, steer wide around those wires, they haven't cut the current yet.

Don't go in the house, dear, just stand in the backyard and whistle, mother said. Buzz kissed her the way he'd seen the men do and walked toward the house, his half-laced leggings flapping.

Mother's eyes went out after him like guiding hands. We saw him go into the narrow alley that led to the backyard. He didn't look much taller than the calla lilies.

Fine son you've got there, Mr. Short said to mother; that's what I like to see. He had three daughters. Mother answered him without taking her eyes from the empty alleyway. We heard a thin whistle. I thought jealously: I wouldn't have been able to whistle with these chattering teeth . . . then we felt it, a tremor that started the noises again in all the houses. Before we got to our feet the shock reached its peak, splitting and crashing. Mr. Short held mother. The brass bed fell off the floor edge of the unfinished house.

You can't, you can't, he yelled. Just as mother broke away, Buzz came round the corner of the house, vomiting violently every few steps, the cat dragging from his clenched arm. The earthquake was over by the time he reached us.

Jen took the cat, and mother took Buzz. None of us said anything on account of his face. It had been the end of the world to him there alone in the yard. When he could speak he told us the back stairs had come off the house. They fell off, ma, he stuttered. The kitchen door looked so funny all alone. Alfred was scared to death. The red claw-marks showed he still had blood in his body.

I'd have been terribly scared, I chattered.

Oh, you, a girl, Buzz said, and mother held him over while he retched again.

The militia moved into the cow hollows beyond the end of our street. We watched their white tents go up in rows. The flag they hoisted disappointed us a little; it wouldn't float on the breeze, because there was no breeze. The heavy atmosphere hung with a dangerous stillness as if waiting. We didn't realize for a long time that the murk we saw in one corner of the sky was smoke.

A horse cab appeared at the foot of our street. We watched it wind up the hill round the wreckage bringing Mr. Percy's sister back to the parent home. As the cabby deposited his fare and turned his horse, he shouted to us: The whole town's a-burning'. He waved his whip and drove down the hill to get more refugees.

Fire! We had been so absorbed in our own block-length world

we had almost forgotten the rest of the city. Refugees, ruins, burst gas mains, fire, fire, fire. The words flashed through our group from man to man. We heard mother repeat each one in a whisper. Bucket brigades, martial law, ten thousand refugees, twenty thousand, it went beyond our scope. Jen knew about some of it, but Buzz and I couldn't get beyond the word *fire*. We shivered with excitement. The biggest fire we'd ever seen was when a row of three flats burned down. The whole city, Buzz murmured, his feverish eyes lifting to the hill, picking his seat for the sight.

His fever increased so that we couldn't go up the hill that night with the neighbors. We went back to the house early and mother put him to bed. Dr. Sonntag had gone downtown to help with the injured; mother had no one to turn to for help. She sat beside his bed changing the wet packs.

What do you think it is? Jen whispered, and when mother whispered back: I don't know, I don't know, there was such despair in her voice that I forgot the look of the house, the twisted chandeliers, bricks on the carpet, and broken glass everywhere, and sat beside the bed.

It was all right as long as there was daylight, but none of us liked it when dark came on with Buzz shouting in a delirium all about his birthday picnic and wanting to go to Golden Gate Park. The order had come that not even a match could be struck in a house, the militia was there to enforce it. Two soldiers with muskets were parading up and down the street watching all windows.

When it was too dark to read the thermometer, mother kept her hand on my brother's forehead. I thought of the flashlight my father owned, it was the first time I had thought of him that day. It was the first whole day I could remember when I had not gone after him in my thought.

I think he'll reach the crisis soon, mother whispered, it's a fast fever. She said *fast fever* in two gasps. Buzz had passed beyond delirium his dead quiet was worse than his shouting. I can't trust my hand, mother said. Jen, what do you think?

A movement, then Jen's small voice: He feels hot, mother.

I heard mother stand up. A voice like a general's came out of the dark. Run quickly, she said to me, pull down all the shades, every shade in the front of the house, *I'm going to see that thermometer.*

I stumbled down the hall, my heart pounding—us against the American army, us against the American army. The parlor, then mother's front bedroom—the shades came down with such loud clicks I thought the whole street would hear.

Back in Buzz's room mother had a tiny night light lit, a wick floating in a tumbler of oil. Buzz's face looked like a pomegranate on the pillow. He didn't know the thermometer was in his mouth. Mother waited, watching the clock; her shadow on the wall went over a crack so that it looked as if she were split in two. She removed the theremometer and held it over the light. The footsteps thumping up the front stairs sounded like a whole regiment. A soldier bumped cursing through the door just as mother's lips said: One hundred and four.

Whaddya doin' with that light? *Put it out,* the soldier roared, and poked his musket toward mother. His body was part of his shadow going up to the ceiling. Mother looked as though she came only to his knees when she stood in front of him blocking the way.

My boy is sick, I must have a light. She said it like knives grinding on a whetstone. Then she broke down and Jen and I cried with her. The soldier dropped his musket with such a clatter we all cringed.

Lemme see him, the soldier said. He tramped over to the bed, his buckles and brass buttons shining in the light. He put his hand on my brother's forehead. What the thermometer say? he growled. Mother stopped crying and told him. Keep him covered, see? He's outa it now, he's sleepin', he aint dead. Mother asked: Are you sure? Do you know? *Know?* snapped the soldier. Say, lady I doctored enough fevers in the Philippines to burn up a house. He picked up his gun, turned on mother as if he was going to shoot her. Put them other two kids to bed, he ordered, and get some sleep yourself. you're all right tonight, see, the fire's on Nob Hill blowin' toward the Gate. He saluted and went clanking down the stairs. We dragged a double mattress into Buzz's room. A soldier had given us orders.

Next morning wasn't like a beginning of day, there was a tired light. Sheets still hanging from our clothesline in the backyard were covered with bits of charred paper. Jen and I ran outside to look, we had slept in our clothes and did not have to dress.

Ashes and charred bits were falling from the sky, coming so

slowly they looked motionless in the air. The particles didn't seem of earth, you could imagine something high up in the sky had been on fire the night before.

It's a big fire, Jen said, and wet her fingers to see if there was any wind.

Neighbors were climbing the hill behind our house. They went up single file carrying small bundles. Around the base of the statue was a crowd of people who had come up from the Mission district. We ran back to the house with the news.

Buzz was gnawing cold chicken, looking as if he had never had a sick day in his life. He was dressed in extra sweaters and mother had put a cape over his shoulders and pulled the pointed hood over his head. She was rolling up bedding by the front door. Jen and I carried down food from the pantry. All together it made such a load that mother said we'd have to have a horse if we had to leave in a hurry. She was trying to be casual so Buzz wouldn't run up another fever of fright. She really didn't need to worry. The prospect of no more houses excited us.

I know just where we can camp, Buzz said, that old quarry half-way up Twin Peaks. I argued for a place nearer Sutro Forest so we could find mushrooms when our store food was eaten. We almost came to blows while mother was tying a twenty-dollar gold piece in a handkerchief and pinning it to her corset. Don't squabble, we're not burned out *yet,* she said.

Not yet . . . we started toward the hill with the last of the strag-glers, hearing those words on all sides. Buzz and I scrambled ahead as if the fire might go out and there would be nothing to see from the hill. We had promised mother we would wait for her near the top. She came up with Jen faster than any of the others, she didn't have to put her hands down and come on all fours over the steep places. She'll be good, camping, Buzz said.

The fire was so big we couldn't think of it as a fire at first. There was no beginning or end, it spread over the downtown district from Mission to the Golden Gate in such a wide arc we had to turn our heads to see it all. It was too big even for Buzz; he sat like the rest of us, staring.

The children stayed near their parents, listening to the naming of relatives' houses that were in the path of the flames. Every family had its roll-call, ours was the mill and grandmother's house. Buzz said he could see through the smoke to the Potrero waterfront. I see the gasworks opposite the mill, he said. Mother gave a start when he said gasworks.

Do you think father is over there? Jen whispered. Mother looked hard through the distant smoke, seeing him running back and forth across the roof of the mill laying wet sacks, shouting to men below to hand up more. Your father is always where there's danger, she said. But wool won't burn, ma, Buzz assured her. No, dear, she said so no one else could hear, but gas tanks can explode.

A man, a stranger from the other side of the hill, said: They'll dynamite, try to stop it jumping Van Ness Avenue.

Dynamite. Buzz and I looked at each other in an explosion of glances.

And grandma's house, Jen said.

Our grandmother's house was five blocks up the hill from Van Ness Avenue. We couldn't see it from where we were, a smaller hill below us got in the way, but we could imagine grandmother holding the fort until flames ran up the vine trellises into her bedroom window. She'd have all her yellow perils up in her room comforting them as if they were her own sons although probably the Chinese cook would break away. He had a family in Chinatown, a picture bride he had bought and had had shipped over to him by one of the regular agencies.

Well, the Barbary Coast's gone, someone said, look at that, will you? The flames were brightest where the man pointed, as if a lot of boxwood had suddenly caught. We couldn't understand why our neighbors were so elated.

Thank God for that.

It's the only thing that could have cleaned that sink.

I thought from mother's silence that she felt as we did, she had been with us that time. Father's chauffeur had been sent to take us all for a ride; we had made the round of the Embarcadero, looking at the ships from every country in the world, the foreign flags and sailors smoking long pipes with painted china bowls, then suddenly we had swung into Pacific Street, the Barbary Coast, and mother crying out: *Tim, not here, not here, the children,* while he grinned back at her and said: Won't hurt 'em, they're too young, and drove up the narrow street past dance-halls with carved wood statues of naked women holding up the front portals. We watched the brighter burning with regret.

There was too much to watch and always the dynamiting to wait for. Every now and again I looked from the fire to us, sitting on a hill in the middle of a morning watching a city burn. A man put out his hand, caught bits of drifting char, and said: San Francisco, Queen of the Golden Gate, and blew it off his hand with a look on his face that made me think of my father, casual when you knew he wasn't feeling so. We had it in our hair, bits of San Francisco, black scraps of wallpaper, drifting ash of business files, maybe some of it from the stacks of gold-backs that had been burned up in banks. It was exciting to guess where it might have come from but I knew I must not guess aloud. The grown-ups were acting as though they were at a funeral.

I thought the dynamiting would relieve the sadness, but it didn't. Buildings went up in air, dropping apart in fragments that showered down like fireworks. Each time it happened there was a comment.

There goes the Phelan Building.

That's the Crocker Bank, oh, my God.

A superb skyrocket flew high from a bed of fire and turned into a parachute of embers.

Spreckels, the dead voice said, and scraps of ash fell off the shaking heads of those who couldn't speak.

Mother's tears dropped in her lap. She couldn't look at the exploding buildings the way we children did. Men around us were crying like mother, not because they had a business down there or money in the melting bank vaults, they didn't mention those; but because it was their background being blown up.

It's going to jump the firebreak anyhow, a voice said.

A wind began to blow in from the Bay. Smoke pointed the direction of it, inland toward our hills. People from the Mission district started down their side of the hill to fetch the belongings which, like us, they had left piled by front doors.

It's blowing away from the waterfront, Jen said, bringing father again to our thoughts. Perhaps over there on the other side of the smoke he was watching the new direction of the fire, thinking of us. I knew instinctively that we would see him that night, though when I looked at the flames that separated us I didn't see how he would get through.

By afternoon the fire had spread to the Mission. There were still dozens of blocks of houses between the foot of our hill and the flames, but we could smell the smoke now.

If it gets as far as Mission Dolores, Mr. Percy said, then we're goners. Mother motioned him to sit down beside her. They started talking together.

Only one place, one place, we heard mother say.

Not Golden Gate Park, thousands there, danger of pestilence, Mr. Percy said.

No, no, the hills, mother whispered. It was a plot. We saw them move closer so none of the others could overhear. Mr. Percy listened to mother with admiration. We felt proud of her; she had a plan no man had thought of. He asked her a question and we heard her say: The children will know that. She beckoned to us.

When were you children last at the reservoir? she whispered.

Jen said: Not for months—but Buzz and I began to tremble. It was such an unexpected question. Only a week ago we had been playing round that forbidden place in the hollow below Twin Peaks. We had climbed over the barbed wire surrounding the open reservoir and had had a terrible experience. I caught a stern look from Mr. Percy, no use to tell a lie.

Last week, I answered.

Was there much water in it? mother asked. Buzz looked off toward the fire.

A little, I said, not very much.

But how much? mother insisted.

I could think only of one way to describe the depth. I said: Well, it's not over a child's head. Buzz paled.

Are you sure? How do you know? Mr. Percy asked.

Buzz felt there was no hope left; the tassel on the top of his hood shook as he said: Because I fell in.

Mother's laugh bewildered us. I thought they'd know, she said to Mr. Percy, and he laughed too. We were sent off without a scolding. The low-toned conversation continued, we couldn't catch any more words. The Short family was sitting near by, augmented by relatives from downtown. We could see that mother was being careful that they should not overhear her plan.

As the fire moved closer other families on the hill were making plans too, drawing apart, whispering, and writing down lists of provisions. Buzz and I walked around pretending to be searching better viewpoints for the fire. Within an hour we knew where every family in the neighborhood was planning to run if the fire broke over the hill, except our own.

Mother watched now with measuring eyes, getting opinions from the men as to whether it would reach the base of the hill during the night. Mr. Percy and his sister stood with her, a close three guarding a secret from the rabble that had been streaming up the hill all morning. I could see there were quite a few people one wouldn't want to live with in a cave for several days.

That night mother told us. We had gone back to the wrecked house where the baskets of food were hidden. We were sitting on the front porch with slices of my brother's birthday cake in our hands, dropping crumbs and not caring. Mother looked reckless and wild with her hair blown and no plate under her cake. Jen ate delicately as if she were at a party, she didn't have a spot on her dress from our day's living on the hilltop.

Mother said: I'm going to tell you children a secret; it's something we'll do, just in case . . . she lifted her face to the sky where the arc of red cut across. You mustn't tell a soul, she said, there wouldn't be room, only for us and the Percys. We crossed our hearts and leaned toward her. She paused a moment, looked at the three of us one by one, said: Oh, like a quick embrace, then continued: *If the fire should break over the hill tonight, we're going up the reservoir.* Buzz and I looked guiltily at each other. Mother shooked her finger at him and said: I remember that day you came home rough dried. Well, she went on, we might go up to the reservoir and *fall in again.*

We were too excited to speak. The magnificence of her plan stunned us. We saw ourselves standing chin-deep in water while flames raged overhead. Then Jen spoke: But, mother, you get sick just as soon as water touches your stomach. That was true; we suddenly recalled mother's terror of water, all the vacation-time creeks she had bathed in and how, when we pulled her into waist-deep places, she grew pale with fright and was sick. It was one of our family jokes—You, the daughter of a sea captain, we used to say.

Mother seemed glad that Jen had thought of that; she patted her and said: No, I'd promise not to get sick, I could stand it for a little while, I really wouldn't be a coward, especially if you children were not afraid.

Oh no, we cried. Afraid? How could she ever imagine we would be afraid?

You can't wade in, you know, Buzz said expertly. When you once get in it's all the same, up to here. He touched his throat and made me remember how he looked that day when another six inches would have drowned him. And also, he said you've got the barbed wire to think of.

Barbed wire? Mother looked defeated.

Yes, all around the reservoir, Buzz said. He looked at her, wondering how far he could go, then threw all caution to the winds. But a good thick pad of newspaper will fix that, he said, that's the way we always get over barbed wire.

It was quite wonderful to be able to give away our secrets to mother, to have her so unexpectedly grateful for all the knowledge we had acquired on our trespassing expeditions. We told her everything we knew about the reservoir, the best trails up to it, how rain collected in it, deepening it inch by inch all winter, and spring freshets feeding it from the hills. It was an abandoned reservoir; after it was built it was found to be not high enough to supply the necessary pressure. It has no outlet, Buzz said.

Mother picked a piece of icing off her cake, pretending to examine its consistency. Has it got *things* in it? she asked.

Not a sign of life, we assured her. We could speak with the authority of fishermen. Only lily pads floating around, we said, and mother shivered and looked at the sky.

When Mr. Percy passed on the way back to his house we waved to him and sang out: *Mother, may I go out to swim?* to let him know we knew the secret, and he sang back: *Yes, my darling daughter,* quick and responsive in the way we liked. That'll be our password, Buzz said.

How does it look? mother called down to him.

They're backfiring, maybe it'll hold, Mr. Percy said, but if not . . .

he gave us a significant wave. He would come for us. We had everything ready, four packages of food graded in size, the largest for mother, the next for Jen and smaller ones for my brother and me. I didn't see how we were going to be able to sleep that night. We studied the sky before we went indoors.

It looks a little redder, Buzz said hopefully.

Mother tucked us in bed fully dressed and said she was going out to sit on the porch for a while. Jen and I lay together listening to Buzz's breathing and the murmur of voices from the porch.

Isn't it exciting? I whispered. Will we undress for it, do you suppose? and I floated from her arms into the reservoir and made everybody laugh when I rested my elbows on two lily pads as if they were little green tables.

Laura, are you all right? It was my father's voice on our front, porch, strained and anxious. Then suddenly it grew resonant against the cement walls of the reservoir. And the children safe? he was saying, and saw our heads among the lily pads. No water, they can't fight it, no water, Laura, it's a hell down there. Jen's arm withdrew, a lily stem soft and smooth. Here, father, here, she whispered, and went up toward him against the crimson sky. Come in a moment, do come in, there is cake, mother said. Ah, cake, your cake, Laura— and a round leaf big enough for the five of us came up out of the water, and mother set the table on it, putting a double-sized piece of cake at father's place . . .

Next morning militia men brought the bodies down from the reservoir. We watched them winding a single file down the trail, wondering what they carried wrapped in two khaki army blankets. Everyone guessed aloud until the soldiers were in our street, then we knew, and no one could speak. Two refugee children from the burning Mission, separated from their family in the flight from the flames, had gone up alone to the reservoir the night before. The soldiers spoke tersely as they tramped along. A water main in the hill had burst, filling the reservoir. They had been sent up to investigate. At first they thought the floating faces were water lilies. Mother stood rigid as the damp bundles sent by, then suddenly she crumpled as if every bone in her body had dissolved, falling softly at our feet.

EARTHQUAKE AND FIRE:
THE FIRST NEWS STORY

The Call-Chronicle-Examiner

SAN FRANCISCO, APRIL 19, 1906:—Death and destruction have been the fate of San Francisco.

Shaken by a temblor at 5:13 o'clock yesterday morning, the shock lasting 48 seconds, and scourged by flames that raged diametrically in all directions, the city is a mass of smouldering ruins. At six o'clock last evening the flames seemingly playing with increased vigor, threatened to destroy such sections as their fury had spared during the earlier portion of the day. Building their path in a triangular circuit from the start in the early morning, they jockeyed as the day waned, left the business section, which they had entirely devastated, and skipped in a dozen directions to the residence portions. As night fell they had made their way over into the north beach section and springing anew to the south they reached out along the shipping section down the bay shore, over the hills and across toward Third and Townsend streets. Warehouses, wholesale houses and manufacturing concerns fell in their path. This completed the destruction of the entire district known as the "South of Market Street." How far they are reaching to the south across the channel cannot be told as this part of the City is shut off from San Francisco papers.

After darkness, thousands of the homeless were making their way with their blankets and scant provisions to Golden Gate Park and the beach to find shelter. Those in the homes on the hills just north of the Hayes Valley wrecked section piled their belongings in the streets and express wagons and automobiles were hauling the things away to the sparsely settled regions. Everybody in San Francisco is prepared to leave the city, for the belief is firm that San Francisco will be totally destroyed.

Downtown everything is ruin. Not a business house stands. Theatres are crumbled into heaps. Factories and commission houses lie smouldering on their former sites. All of the newspaper plants have been rendered useless, the "Call" and the "Examiner" buildings, excluding the "Call's" editorial rooms on Stevenson Street being entirely destroyed.

It is estimated that the loss in San Francisco will reach from $150,000,000 to $200,000,000. These figures are in the rough and nothing can be told until partial accounting is taken.

On every side there was death and suffering yesterday. Hundreds were injured, either burned, crushed or struck by falling pieces from the buildings, and one died while on the operating table at Mechanics Pavilion, improvised as a hospital for the comfort and care of 300 of the injured. The number of dead is not known but it is estimated that at least 500 met their death in the horror.

At nine o'clock, under a special message from President Roosevelt, the city was placed under martial law. Hundreds of troops patrolled the streets and drove the crowds back, while hundreds more were set at work assisting the fire and police departments. The strictest orders were issued, and in true military spirit the soldiers obeyed. During the afternoon three thieves met their death by rifle bullets while at work in the ruins. The curious were driven back at the breasts of the horses that the cavalrymen rode and all the crowds were forced from the level district to the hilly section beyond to the north.

The water supply was entirely cut off, and may be it was just as well, for the lines of fire department would have been absolutely useless at any stage. Assistant Chief Dougherty supervised the work of his men and early in the morning it was seen that the only possible chance to save the city lay in effort to check the flames by use of dynamite. During the day a blast could be heard in any section at intervals of only a few minutes, and buildings not destroyed by fire were blown to atoms. But through the gaps made the flames jumped and although the failures of the heroic efforts of the police, firemen and soldiers were at times sickening, the work was continued with a desperation that will live as one of the features of the terrible disaster. Men worked like fiends to combat the laughing, roaring, onrushing fire demon.

"THE DAMNDEST FINEST RUINS"

by

LAWRENCE W. HARRIS

Put me somewhere west of East Street where there's nothin' left
    but dust,
Where the lads are all a'bustlin' and where everything's gone bust,
Where the buildings that are standin' sort of blink and blindly stare
At the damndest finest ruins ever gazed on anywhere.

Bully ruins—bricks and wall—through the night I've heard you call
Sort of sorry for each other 'cause you had to burn and fall,
From the Ferries to Van Ness you're a Godforsaken mess,
But the damndest finest ruins—nothin' more or nothin' less.

The strangers who come rubberin' and a'huntin' souvenirs,
The fools, they try to tell us it will take a million years
Before we can get started, so why don't we come to live
And build our homes and vactories upon land they've got to give.

"Got to give!" Why, on my soul, I would rather bore a hole
And live right in the ashes than even move to Oakland's mole,
If they'd all give me my pick of their buildin's proud and slick
In the damndest finest ruins still I'd rather be a brick!

THE CITY THAT WAS

by

WILL IRWIN

THE old San Francisco is dead. The gayest, lightest hearted, most pleasure loving city of the western continent, and in many ways the most interesting and romantic, is a horde of refugees living among ruins. It may rebuild; it probably will; but those who have known that peculiar city by the Golden Gate, have caught its flavor of the Arabian Nights, feel that it can never be the same. It is as though a pretty, frivolous woman had passed through a great tragedy. She survives, but she is sobered and different. If it rises out of the ashes it must be a modern city, much like other cities and without its old atmosphere.

San Francisco lay on a series of hills and the lowlands between. These hills are really the end of the Coast Range of mountains, which stretch southward between the interior valleys and the Pacific Ocean. Behind it is the ocean; but the greater part of the town fronts on two sides on San Francisco Bay, a body of water always tinged with gold from the great washings of the mountain, usually overhung with a haze, and of magnificent color changes. Across the bay to the north lies Mount Tamalpais, about twenty-five hundred feet high, and so close that ferries from the waterfront take one in less than half an hour to the little towns of Sausalito and Belvedere, at its foot.

Tamalpais is a wooded mountain, with ample slopes, and from it on the north stretch away ridges of forest land, the outposts of the great Northern woods of *Sequoia sempervirens*. This mountain and the mountainous country to the south bring the real forest closer to San Francisco than to any other American city. Within the last few

By permission of The Viking Press

years men have killed deer on the slopes of Tamalpais and looked down to see the cable cars crawling up the hills of San Francisco to the south. In the suburbs coyotes still stole in and robbed hen roosts by night. The people lived much out of doors. There is no time of the year, except a short part of the rainy season, when the weather keeps one from the fields. The slopes of Tamalpais are crowded with little villas dotted through ˌthe woods, and these minor estates run far up into the redwood country. The·deep coves of Belvedere, sheltered by the wind from Tamalpais, held a colony of "arks" or houseboats, where people lived in the rather disagreeable summer months, coming over to business every day by ferry. Everything there invites out of doors.

The climate of California is peculiar; it is hard to give an impression of it. In the region about San Francisco, all the forces of nature work on their own laws. There is no thunder and lightning; there is no snow, except a flurry once in five or six years; there are perhaps half a dozen nights in the winter when the thermometer drops low enough so that in the morning there is a little film of ice on exposed water. Neither is there any hot weather. Yet most Easterners remaining in San Francisco for a few days remember that they were always chilly.

For the Gate is a big funnel, drawing in the winds and the mists which cool off the great, hot interior valleys of the San Joaquin and Sacramento. So the west wind blows steadily ten months of the year; and almost all the mornings are foggy. This keeps the temperature steady at about 55 degrees—a little cool for the comfort of an unacclimated person, especially indoors. Californians, used to it, hardly ever think of making fires in their houses except in a few days of the winter season, and then they rely mainly upon fireplaces. This is like the custom of the Venetians and the Florentines.

Give an Easterner six months of it, however, and he, too, learns to exist without chill in a steady temperature a little lower than that to which he was accustomed at home. After that one goes about with perfect indifference to the temperature. Summer and winter, San Francisco women wear light tailormade clothes, and men wear the same fall-weight suits all the year around. There is no such thing as a change of clothing for the seasons. And after becoming acclimated these people find it hard to bear the changes from hot to cold in the normal regions of the earth. Perhaps once in two or three years there comes a day when there is no fog, no wind, and a high temperature in the coast district. Then follows hot weather, perhaps up in the eighties, and Californians grumble, swelter and rustle for summer clothes. These rare hot days are the only times when one sees women in light dresses on the streets of San Francisco.

Along in early May the rains cease. At that time everything is green and bright, and the great golden poppies, as large as the saucer of an after-dinner coffee cup, are blossoming everywhere. Tamalpais is green to its top; everything is washed and bright. By late May a yellow tinge is creeping over the hills. This is followed by a golden June and a brown July and August. The hills are burned and dry. The fog comes in heavily, too; and normally this is the most disagreeable season of the year. September brings a day or two of gentle rain; and then a change, as sweet and mysterious as the breaking of spring in the East, passes over the hills. The green grows through the brown and the flowers begin to come out.

As a matter of fact, the unpleasantness of summer is modified by the certainty that one can go anywhere without fear of rain. And in all the coast mountains, especially the seaward slopes, the dews and the shelter of the giant underbrush hold the water, so that these areas are green and pleasant all summer.

In a normal year the rains begin to fall heavily in November; there will be three or four days of steady downpour and then a clear and green week. December is also likely to be rainy; and in this month people enjoy the sensation of gathering for Christmas the mistletoe which grows profusely on the live oaks, while the poppies are beginning to blossom at their feet. By the end of January the gentle rains come lighter. In the long spaces between these winter storms, there is a temperature and a feeling in the air much like that of Indian summer in the East. January is the month when the roses are at their brightest.

So much for the strange climate, which invites out of doors and which has played its part in making the character of the people.

The externals of the city are—or were, for they are no more—just as curious. One usually entered San Francisco by way of the Bay. Across its yellow flood, covered with the fleets from the strange seas of the Pacific, San Francisco presented itself in a hill panorama.

Probably no other city of the world, excepting perhaps Naples, could be so viewed at first sight. It rose above the passenger, as he reached dockage, in a succession of hill terraces. At one side was Telegraph Hill, the end of the peninsula, a height so abrupt that it had a one hundred and fifty foot sheer cliff on its seaward frontage. Further along lay Nob Hill, crowned with the Mark Hopkins mansion, which had the effect of a citadel, and in later years by the great, white Fairmont. Further along was Russian Hill, the highest point. Below was the business district, whose low site caused all the trouble.

Except for the modern buildings, the fruit of the last ten years, the town presented at first sight a disreputable appearance. Most of the buildings were low and of wood. In the middle period of the '70's, when a great part of San Francisco was building, the newly-rich perpetrated some atrocious architecture. At that time, too every one put bow windows on his house to catch all of the morning sunlight that was coming through the fog; and those little houses, with bow windows and fancy work all down their fronts, were characteristic of the middle class residence districts.

Then the Italians, who tumbled over Telegraph Hill, had built as they listed and with little regard for streets, and their houses hung crazily on a side hill which was only less than a precipice. The Chinese, although they occupied an abandoned business district, had remade their dwellings Chinese fashion, and the Mexicans and Spaniards had added to their houses those little balconies without which life is not life to a Spaniard.

Yet the most characteristic thing after all was the coloring. The sea fog had a trick of painting every exposed object a sea gray which had a tinge of dull green in it. This, under the leaden sky of a San Francisco morning, had a depressing effect on first sight and afterward became a delight to the eye. For the color was soft, gentle and infinitely attractive in mass.

The hills are steep beyond conception. Where Vallejo street ran up Russian Hill it progressed for four blocks by regular steps like a flight of stairs. It is unnecessary to say that no teams ever came up this street or any other like it, and grass grew long among the paving stones until the Italians who live thereabouts took advantage of this herbage to pasture a cow or two. At the end of four blocks, the pavers had given it up and the last stage to the summit was a winding path. On the very top, a colony of artists lived in little villas of houses whose windows got the whole panorama of the bay. Luckily for these people, a cable car scaled the hill on the other side, so that it was not much of a climb to home.

With these hills, with the strangeness of the architecture and with the green-gray tinge over everything, the city fell always into vistas and pictures, a setting for the romance which hung over everything, which has always hung over life in San Francisco since the padres came and gathered the Indians about Mission Dolores.

And it was a city of romance and a gateway to adventure. It opened out on the mysterious Pacific, the untamed ocean; and through the Golden Gate entered China, Japan, the South Sea Islands, Lower California, the west coast of Central America, Australia. There was a sprinkling, too, of Alaska and Siberia. From his windows on Russian Hill one saw always something strange and suggestive creeping throught the mists of the bay. It would be a South Sea Island brig, bringing in copra, to take out cottons and idols; a Chinese junk after sharks' livers; and old whaler, which seemed to drip oil, home from a year of cruising in the Arctic. Even the tramp windjammers were deep-chested craft, capable of rounding the Horn or of circumnavigating the globe; and they came in streaked and picturesque from their long voyaging.

In the orange colored dawn which always comes through the mists of that bay, the fishing fleet would crawl in under triangular lateen sails; for the fishermen of San Francisco Bay are all Neapolitans who have brought their customs and sail with lateen rigs stained an orange brown and shaped, when the wind fills them, like the ear of a horse.

Along the waterfront the people of these craft met. "The smelting pot of the races," Stevenson called it; and this was always the city of his soul. There were black Gilbert Islanders, almost indistinguishable from negroes; lighter Kanakas from Hawaii or Samoa; Lascars in turbans; thickset Russian sailors, wild Chinese with unbraided hair; Italian fishermen in tam o' shanters, loud shirts and blue sashes; Greeks, Alaska Indians, little bay Spanish-Americans, together with men of all the European races. These came in and out from among the queer craft, to lose themselves in the disreputable, tumbledown, but always mysterious shanties and small saloons. In the back rooms of these saloons South Sea Island traders and captains, fresh from the lands of romance, whaling masters, people who were trying to get up treasure expeditions, filibusters, Alaskan miners, used to meet and trade adventures.

There was another element, less picturesque and equally characteristic, along the waterfront. San Francisco was the back eddy of European civilization—one end of the world. The drifters came there and stopped, lingered a while to live by their wits in a country where living after a fashion has always been marvellously cheap. These people haunted the waterfront and the Barbary Coast by night, and lay by day on the grass in Portsmouth Square.

The square, the old plaza about which the city was built, Spanish fashion, had seen many things. There in the first burst of the early days the vigilance committee used to hold its hangings. There, in the time of the sand lot troubles, Dennis Kearney, who nearly pulled the town down about his ears, used to make his orations which set the unruly to rioting. In later years Chinatown lay on one side of it and the Latin quarter and the "Barbary Coast" on the other.

On this square the drifters lay all day long and told strange yarns. Stevenson lounged there with them in his time and learned the things which he wove into "The Wrecker" and his South Sea stories; and now in the centre of the square there stands the beautiful Stevenson monument. In later years the authorities put up a municipal building on one side of this square and prevented the loungers, for decency's sake, from lying on the grass. Since then some of the peculiar character of the old plaza has gone.

The Barbary Coast was a loud bit of hell. No one knows who coined the name. The place was simply three blocks of solid dance halls, there for the delight of the sailors of the world. On a fine busy night every door blared loud dance music from orchestras, steam pianos and gramophones, and the cumulative effect of the sound which reached the street was chaos and pandemonium. Almost anything might be happening behind the swinging doors. For a fine and picturesque bundle of names characteristic of the place, a police story of three or four years ago is typical. Hell broke out in the Eye Wink Dance Hall. The trouble was started by a sailor known as Kanaka Pete, who lived in the What Cheer House, over a woman known as Iodoform Kate. Kanaka Pete chased the man he had marked to the

Little Silver Dollar, where he halted and punctured him. The by-product of his gun made some holes in the front of the Eye Wink, which were proudly kept as souvenirs, and were probably there until it went out in the fire. This was low life, the lowest of the low.

Until the last decade almost anything except the commonplace and the expected might happen to a man on the waterfront. The cheerful industry of shanghaing was reduced to a science. A citizen taking a drink in one of the saloons which hung out over the water might be dropped through the floor into a boat, or he might drink with a stranger and wake in the forecastle of a whaler bound for the Arctic. Such an incident is the basis of Frank Norris's novel, "Moran of the Lady Letty," and although the novel draws it pretty strong, is not exaggerated. Ten years ago the police, the Sailors' Union, and the foreign consuls, working together, stopped all this.

Kearny street, a wilder and stranger Bowery, was the main thoroughfare of these people. An exiled Californian, mourning over the city of his heart, has said:

"In a half an hour of Kearny street I could raise a dozen men for any wild adventure, from pulling down a statue to searching for the Cocos Island treasure." This is hardly an exaggeration. It was the Rialto of the desperate, a Street of the Adventurers.

These are a few of the elements which made the city strange and gave it the glamour of romance which has so strongly attracted such men as Stevenson, Frank Norris and Kipling. This life of the floating population lay apart from the regular life of the city, which was distinctive in itself.

The greatest beauty-show on the continent was the Saturday afternoon matinee parade in San Francisco. Women in so-called "society" took no part in this function. It belonged to the middle class, but the "upper classes" have no monopoly of beauty anywhere in the world. It had grown to be independent of the matinees. From two o'clock to half-past five, a solid procession of Dianas, Hebes and Junos passed and repassed along the five blocks between Market and Powell and Sutter and Kearny—the "line" of San Francisco slang. Along the open-front cigar stores, characteristic of the town, gilded youth of the cocktail route gathered in knots to watch them. There was something Latin in the spirit of this ceremony—it resembled church parade in Buenos Aires. Latin, too, were the gay costumes of the women, who dressed brightly in accord with the city and the climate. This gaiety of costume was the first thing which the Eastern women noticed —and disapproved. Give her a year, and she, too, would be caught by the infection of daring dress.

In this parade of tall, deep bosomed, gleaming women, one caught the type and longed, sometimes for the sight of a more ethereal beauty —for the suggestion of soul within which belongs to a New England woman on whom a hard soil has bestowed a grudged beauty—for the mobility, the fire, which belongs to the Frenchwoman. The second generation of France was in this crowd, it is true; but climate and exercise had grown above their spiritual charm a cover of brilliant flesh. It was the beauty of Greece.

With such a people, life was always gay. If the fairly Parisian gaiety did not display itself on the streets, except in the matinee parade, it was because the winds made open-air cafes disagreeable at all seasons of the year. The life careless went on indoors or in the hundreds of pretty estates—"ranches" the Californians called them— which fringe the city.

San Francisco was famous for its restaurants and cafes. Probably they were lacking at the top; probably the very best, for people who do not care how they spend their money, was not to be had. But they gave the best fare on earth, for the price at a dollar, seventy-five cents, a half a dollar, or even fifteen cents.

If one should tell exactly what could be had at Coppa's for fifty cents or at the Fashion for, say thirty-five, no New Yorker who has not been there would believe it. The San Francisco French dinner and the San Francisco free lunch were as the Public Library to Boston or the stock yards to Chicago. A number of causes contributed to this. The country all about produced everything that a cook needs and that in abundance—the bay was an almost untapped fishing pound, the fruit farms came up to the very edge of town, and the surrounding country produced in abundance fine meats, game, all cereals and all vegetables.

But the chefs who came from France in the early days and stayed because they liked this land of plenty were the head and front of it. They passed on their art to other Frenchmen or to the clever Chinese. Most of the French chefs at the biggest restaurants were born in Canton, China. Later the Italians, learning of this country where good food is appreciated, came and brought their own style. House-holders always dined out one or two nights of the week, and boarding houses were scarce, for the unattached preferred the restaurants.

The eating was usually better than the surroundings. Meals that were marvels were served in tumbledown little hotels. Most famous of all the restaurants was the Poodle Dog. There have been no less than four establishments of this name, beginning with a frame shanty where, in the early days, a prince of French cooks used to exchange ragouts for gold dust. Each succeeding restaurant of the name has moved further downtown; and the recent Poodle Dog stands—stands or stood; one mixes his tenses queerly in writing of this city which is and yet is no more—on the edge of the Tenderloin in a modern five story building. And it typified a certain spirit that there was in San Francisco.

For on the ground floor was a public restaurant where there was served the best dollar dinner on earth. At least, if not the best it ranked with the best, and the others were in San Francisco. There, especially on Sunday night, almost everyone went to vary the monotony of home cooking. Everyone who was anyone in the town could be seen there off and on. It was perfectly respectable. A man might take his wife and daughter to the Poodle Dog.

On the second floor there were private dining rooms, and to dine there, with one or more of the opposite sex, was risqué but not especially terrible. But the third floor—and the fourth floor—and the fifth! The elevator man of the Poodle Dog, who had held the job for many years and who never spoke unless spoken to, wore diamonds and was a heavy investor in real estate. There were others as famous in their way—the Zinkand, where, at one time, every one went after the theatre, and Tait's, which has lately bitten into that trade; the Palace Grill, much like the grills of Eastern hotels, except for the price; Delmonico's, which ran the Poodle Dog neck and neck to its own line; and many others, humbler but great at the price.

Listen! O ye starved amidst plenty, to the tale of the Hotel de France. This restaurant stood on California street, just east of Old St. Mary's Church. One could throw a biscuit from its back windows into Chinatown. It occupied a big ramshackle house, which had been a mansion of the gold days. Louis, the proprietor, was a Frenchman of the Bas Pyrenees; and his accent was as thick as his peasant soups.

The patrons were Frenchmen of the poorer class, or young and poor clerks and journalists who had discovered the delights of his hostelry. The place exuded a genial gaiety, of which Louis, throwing out familiar jokes to right and left as he mixed salads and carried dishes, was the head and front.

First on the bill of fare was the soup mentioned before—thick and clean and good. Next, one of Louis' three cherubic little sons brought on a course of fish—sole, rock cod, flounders or smelt—with a good French sauce. The third course was meat. This came on en bloc; the waiter dropped in the centre of each table a big roast or boiled joint together with a mustard pot and two big dishes of vegetables. Each guest manned the carving knife in turn and helped himself to his satisfaction. After that, Louis, with an air of ceremony, brought on a big bowl of excellent salad which he had mixed himself. For beverage, there stood by each plate a perfectly cylindrical pint glass filled with new, watered claret. The meal closed with "fruit in season"—all that the guest cared to eat. I have saved a startling fact to close the paragraph—the price was fifteen cents!

If one wanted black coffee he paid five cents extra, and Louis brought on a beer glass full of it. Why he threw in wine and charged extra for after-dinner coffee was one of Louis' professional secrets.

Adulterated food at that price? Not a bit of it! The olive oil in the salad was pure, a California product—why adulterate when he could get it so cheaply? The wine, too, was above reproach, for Louis made it himself. Every autumn, he brought tons and tons of cheap Mission grapes, set up a wine press in his back yard, and had a little, festival vintage of his own. The fruit was small and inferior, but fresh, and Louis, himself, in speaking of his business, said that he wished his guests would eat nothing but fruit, it came so cheap.

The city never went to bed. There was no closing law, so that the saloons kept open nights and Sundays at their own sweet will. Most of the cafes elected to remain open until 2 o'clock in the morning at least.

This restaurant life, however does not express exactly the careless, pleasure-loving character of the people. In great part their pleasures were simple, inexpensive and out of doors. No people were fonder of expeditions into the country, of picnics—which might be brought off at almost any season of the year—and of long tours in the great mountains and forests.

Hospitality was nearly a vice. As in the early mining days, if they liked the stranger the people took him in. At the first meeting the San Francisco man had him put up at the club; at the second, he invited him home to dinner. As long as the stranger stayed he was being invited to week end parties at ranches, to little dinners in this or that restaurant and to the houses of his new acquaintants, until his engagements grew beyond hope of fulfilment. Perhaps there was rather too much of this kind of thing. At the end of a fortnight a visitor with a pleasant smile and a good story left the place a wreck. This tendency ran through all grades of society—except, perhaps, the sporting people who kept the tracks and the fighting game alive. These also met the stranger—and also took him in.

"High society" in San Francisco had settled down from the rather wild spirit of the middle period; it had come to be there a good deal as it is elsewhere. There was much wealth; and the hills of the western addition were growing up with fine mansions. Outside of the city, at Burlingame, there was a fine country club centering a region of country estates which stretched out to Menlo Park. This club had a good polo team, which played every year with teams of Englishmen from southern California and even with teams from Honolulu.

The foreign quarters are worth an article in themselves. Chief of these was, of course, Chinatown, of which everyone has heard who ever heard of San Francisco. A district six blocks long and two blocks wide, housed 30,000 Chinese when the quarter was full. The dwellings were old business blocks of the early days; but the Chinese had added to them, had rebuilt them, had run out their own balconies and entrances, and had given the quarter that feeling of huddled irregularity which makes all Chinese built dwellings fall naturally into pictures. Not only this; they had burrowed to a depth of a story or two under the ground, and through this ran passages in which the Chinese transacted their dark and devious affairs—as the smuggling of opium, the traffic in slave girls and the settlement of their difficulties.

In the last five years there was less of this underground life than formerly, for the Board of Health had a cleanup some time ago;

but it was still possible to go from one end of Chinatown to the other through secret underground passages. The tourist, who always included Chinatown in his itenerary, saw little of the real quarter. The guides gave him a show by actors hired for his benefit. In reality the place amounted to a great deal in a financial way. There were clothing and cigar factories of importance, and much of the Pacific rice, tea and silk importing was in the hands of the merchants, who numbered several millionaires. Mainly, however, it was a Tenderloin for the house servants of the city—for the San Francisco Chinaman was seldom a laundryman; he was too much in demand at fancy prices as a servant.

The Chinese lived their own lives in their own way and settled their own quarrels with the revolvers of their highbinders. There were two theatres in the quarter, a number of rich joss houses, three newspapers and a Chinese telephone exchange. There is a race feeling against the Chinese among the working people of San Francisco, and no white man, except the very lowest outcasts, lived in the quarter.

On the slopes of Telegraph Hill dwelt the Mexicans and Spanish, in low houses, which they had transformed by balconies into a semblance of Spain. Above, and streaming over the hill, were the Italians. The tenement quarter of San Francisco shone by contrast with those of Chicago and New York, for while these people lived in old and humble houses they had room to breathe and an eminence for light and air. Their shanties clung to the side of the hill or hung on the very edge of the precipice overlooking the bay, on the verge of which a wall kept their babies from falling. The effect was picturesque, and this hill was the delight of painters. It was all more like Italy than anything in the Italian quarter of New York and Chicago—the very climate and surroundings, the wine country close at hand, the bay for their lateen boats, helped them.

Over by the ocean and surrounded by cemeteries in which there are no more burials, there is an eminence which is topped by two peaks and which the Spanish of the early days named after the breasts of a woman. The unpoetic Americans had renamed it Twin Peaks. At its foot was Mission Dolores. the last mission planted by the Spanish padres in their march up the coast, and from these hills the Spanish looked for the first time upon the golden bay.

Many years ago some one set up at the summit of this peak a sixty foot cross of timber. Once a high wind blew it down, and the women of the Fair family then had it restored so firmly that it would resist anything. It has risen for fifty years above the gay, careless, luxuriant and lovable city, in full view from every eminence and from every valley. It stands tonight, above the desolation of ruins.

The bonny, merry city—the good, gray city—O that one who has mingled the wine of her bounding life with the wine of his youth should live to write the obituary of Old San Francisco!

BARRIERS BURNED

(A RHYME OF THE SAN FRANCISCO BREADLINE)

by

CHARLES K. FIELD

It ain't such a terrible long time ago
    That Mrs. Van Bergen and me
Though livin' near by to each other, y' know,
    Was strangers, for all ye could see,
For she had a grand house an' horses to drive,
    An' a wee rented cottage was mine,
But now we need rations to keep us alive
    An' we're standin' together in line.

An' Mrs Van Bergen she greets me these days
    With a smile an' a nod of the head;
"Ah, Mrs. McGinnis, how are you?" she says,
    "An' do you like Government bread?"
She fetches a bag made of crockydile skin
    An' I've got a sack when we meet,
But the same kind of coffee an' crackers goes in,
    An' it's all of it cooked in the street.

Sure, Mrs. Van Bergen is takin' it fine,
    Ye'd think she was used to the food;
We're gettin' acquainted, a-standin' in line,
    An' it's doing' the both of us good.
An' Mr. Van Bergen and Michael, my man,
    (They've always been friendly, the men)
They're gettin' together and layin' a plan
    For buildin' the city again!

CITY OF MIRACLES

by

GELETT BURGESS

THERE it lay, a constellation of lights, a golden radiance, dimmed by the distance. San Francisco the Impossible, the City of Miracles! Of it and its people many stories have been told, and many shall be; but a thousand tales shall not exhaust its treasury of Romance. Earthquake and fire shall not change it, terror and suffering shall not break its glad, mad spirit, Time alone can tame the town, rob it of its nameless charm, subdue it to the Commonplace. May Time be merciful—may it delay its fatal duty till we have learned that to love, to forgive, to enjoy, is but to understand!

[1910]

MAMA AND THE BIG CITY

by

KATHRYN FORBES

IN THOSE DAYS, if anyone had asked Mama unexpectedly, "What nationality are you?" I believe she would have answered without hesitation, "I am a San Franciscan."

Then quickly, lest you tease her, she would add, "I mean Norvegian. American citizen."

But her first statement would be the true one.

Because from the moment she was to step off the ferryboat, confused and lonely in a strange land, San Francisco was to become suddenly and uniquely her own.

"Is like Norvay," the Aunts said Mama had declared.

And straightway she'd taken the city to her heart.

Mama learned so many things about San Francisco. She could tell you how to get to Telegraph Hill; what time the boats came in at Fisherman's Wharf; the names of the young boys who tended the steaming crab kettles along Bay Street; and where to find the blue and yellow lupins at Land's End.

The cable cars were an endless delight, and Mama's idea of a perfect Sunday afternoon was for Papa to take us riding on them from one transfer point to another.

Papa would tell of the time Mama took out her citizenship papers and astounded the solemn court by suddenly reciting the names of the streets. "Turk, Eddy, Ellis, O'Farrell," Mama had said proudly, "Geary, Post, Sutter, Bush, and Pine."

Papa said the clerk had quite a time making Mama understand that such knowledge was not necessary for citizenship.

Mama made friends with an Armenian lady who had a store out on Third Street, and gave her her best *lutefisk* recipe. Best of all, though, Mama liked to explore Chinatown. Old Sing Fat and Mama held long conversations over the counters of his Grant Avenue Bazaar. Like as not, she would come home to Castro Street with a tiny bag of lichee nuts or preserved ginger. And if any of us were ill in bed, Mama would go down and get us a small package of those Chinese water flowers that open into amazing beauty when dropped into water.

And if anyone ever asked us where we were born, Mama instructed us, we should say "San Francisco." Didn't copies of our birth certificates, neatly framed and hung on the wall of Papa's and Mama's room, testify to that proud fact?

"After all," Papa used to tease her, "after all, San Francisco isn't the *world*."

But to Mama it was just that. The world.

Papa had been working steadily for a long time now, and for once we had a little money ahead. And Mama had told us that within a few months there would be a new brother or sister.

Then—a Real Estate Salesman got hold of Papa and tried to sell him a chicken ranch across the Bay.

Just a little money down, the salesman said, and Papa could pay off the balance like rent. And just think, he told us, there were also five whole acres of fruit trees.

"Sunshine!" the man said enthusiastically. "No fog."

Mama bridled as if someone had said something against one of her children.

"Fog is good," she declared. "Is healthy."

"But there will be eggs for the little ones," he countered. "And plenty of milk."

"There is a cow?" Papa asked.

Well, no, the salesman admitted, no cow. But there were four fine goats.

I saw Mama wrinkle her nose.

Only after Papa said that it would be nice to be your own boss and have a place of your own, instead of being a carpenter—only after we children and Nels had coaxed and pleaded—did Mama reluctantly agree to the move across the Bay.

It was fun at first, helping Papa to prune the trees and to mend the roof of the sagging little house; fun to carry the water from the well and to chop the wood. I remember what a great time Nels had whitewashing the chicken coop. Dagmar helped Mama to start a little vegetable garden, and Christine and I took turns milking the ever present goats.

But when the cold weather came, our enthusiasm for country life waned rapidly. We children were not used to tumbling sleepily out of bed while it was still dark, eating our breakfast by lamplight, then trudging miles to school.

Nor were we used to a one-room schoolhouse, to playmates who called us "Scandahoovians." Ours had been a more cosmopolitan atmosphere.

"Hicks!" Christine and I retaliated sulkily. "Country hicks!" And knew a deep homesickness.

Dagmar mourned the merry-go-round and the ponies at the park, while Nels spoke often and wistfully of the big city library with its thousands of books.

Christine and I missed the sidewalks. Our beloved roller skates hung idly in the closet, and as we oiled them carefully every Saturday morning, we remembered that once we had been the very best skaters on the block.

Only Mama never complained. But we saw her stand for long moments at the window—looking westward.

Papa worked early and late, but fought a losing battle. We watched the young trees in the orchard, our carefully tended garden, shrivel and blacken with frost. We had not had money enough to provide smudge pots.

The chickens came down with a strange and baffling illness; most of them died and the few surviving hens stopped laying eggs.

Only the goats kept producing. Our pantry shelves were stocked with the brown goat cheese Mama had made.

For the first Christmas in our lives, we children did not get to see the big city stores and the wonderful window displays. And Papa's toolbox was packed away in the closet with our skates.

On New Year's Eve we were allowed to stay up. Mama made "sweet soup" for us, and she and Papa said Skoal! and wished us each a *Godt Nytaar* as they drank their coffee.

At midnight Mama held up her hand. "Listen!" she said.

We couldn't hear anything.

"Bells!" Mama said. "Bells and whistles in San Francisco."

Papa looked worried. "Is too far to hear," he told her gently. "You imagine things."

I thought I saw tears in Mama's eyes, but I must have been mistaken. Mama never cried.

"It is not good," Papa said heavily, "for carpenter to try to be farmer."

"Such talk!" Mama protested. But Papa's shoulders did not straighten. And the next day he went to see the Real Estate Salesman. But the man didn't seem interested in us any more. So then Papa had Nels write out an advertisement for the newspaper. But even that wasn't successful.

We only had one answer, an old couple by the name of Sonderman. They liked the chicken ranch, but as Mr. Sonderman explained, they had their big house on Steiner Street to dispose of first.

"Eleven rooms," Mrs. Sonderman told us, "and since our boys are grown and gone away, Mr. Sonderman and I just rattle around in it."

Of course eleven rooms was too big for us, and never in the world could we get enough money together to put a down payment on it —even counting what Papa had in the chicken ranch.

But Mama never seemed to know when something was hopeless. She made several trips over to the city to see the Steiner Street house and to talk with the Sondermans.

Then Aunt Jenny came over to see us.

"To visit for a while," she said brightly. And we children were much too polite to tell her we knew she'd come to stay with us until after our new baby was born.

Mama made fresh coffee and she and Aunt Jenny and Papa sat down to the kitchen table.

"What is wrong with the children?" Aunt Jenny demanded.

Mama's eyes were worried as she looked at each of us.

"They do not look good?" she asked anxiously.

"Such long faces they have," Aunt Jenny explained.

Mama looked at us again. "I see what you mean," she said slowly. "They have not happiness."

Aunt Jenny told us news of the old neighborhood. We remembered the Andersons? Well, they had moved over to Castro Street.

And Peter Larson, Anna Lundquist's brother, had got the carpenter contract on the new high school, and he had told Aunt Jenny he just wished he had Papa for a carpenter foreman.

Papa held out his earth-stained hands. "Would be good," he sighed, "to hold tools again. To smell the fresh new wood."

Mama stood up suddenly. "I just think," she said. "That Sonderman house—eleven rooms. Jenny, that would make a fine boarding-house."

Aunt Jenny laughed shortly. "Indeed, And where would you find time—*now*—to do the work?"

Mama's face reddened. "But *after*—Papa, the children—all would help. We would work together."

Absolute nonsense, Aunt Jenny declared. Besides, she pointed out, we had only about four rooms of furniture.

"But we could get more, Jenny. With Papa working for Peter Larson."

Aunt Jenny shook her head as if the whole plan was hopeless.

"I think," Mama said stubbornly, "that the Sondermans would be willing to give us three—maybe four—months' rent on the Steiner house for what we have paid on this place. Mrs. Sonderman *likes* chicken farm."

Papa laughed out loud for the first time in months. "And goats," he said. "Old Mr. Sonderman likes goats."

Mama and Papa looked at each other for a long time. Then Papa went down the road to phone. When he came back he nodded his head and said, "Four months' free rent." And he brought his tool chest out of the closet and started sharpening the tools.

"We go," Mama said happily, "we go." And sent Nels for boxes.

"Wait," Aunt Jenny pleaded. "Wait and talk this over. You should think a long time before you make a move like this."

"We go," Mama said again, "we go today." And started taking the dishes off the shelves.

Aunt Jenny choked on her coffee. "Such foolishness! You can't. You must wait until after—"

There was a strange urgency in Mama's voice. "We go *today*. The house is vacant. The Sondermans moved their things over to their married son's last week."

"And what of all your hard work here?" Aunt Jenny demanded. "What have you got out of it?"

"Four months' free rent in a big house in San Francisco," Mama said. "And goat cheese." She pointed to the pantry shelves. *"Lots* of goat cheese." And Mama was smiling.

Late that afternoon, when Papa had brought the last box into what had been the Sonderman's house and was now ours, Mama told Nels he could go to the library, and she sent us children out to play.

Eagerly and joyously we skated up and down the block, exploring the new neighborhood, making plans for the next day.

When it grew dark, we went home for dinner and found that all the Aunts were there. It was Aunt Jenny, however, who told us the news. She looked as if someone had played a trick on her.

"You have a new baby sister," she told us grimly, and took us down the hall to the room that was now Papa's and Mama's.

Mama smiled reassuringly at us as we tiptoed in. She lifted the blanket from the tiny bundle on her arm. "Her name is Kaaren," she said.

Papa turned to beam at us and we saw that he was hanging our framed birth certificates in a neat row against the wall. He took a tack out of his mouth.

Aunt Sigrid came in with soup for Mama. "Say," she said, "isn't it funny how all your children are born in San Francisco?"

"Funny?" Aunt Jenny demanded crossly. *"Funny?"*

"Is good," Mama said happily, "is good."

SAN FRANCISCO

by

WALLACE IRWIN

She laughed upon her hills out there
    Beside her bays of misty blue;
The gayest hearts, the sweetest air
    That any City ever knew.
For I have whistled all the songs
    That thrilled upon her carefree breath,
And I have mingled with her throngs—
    But never in the thought of Death.
Lady of Ventures, Joy of Earth,
    How more the pity for your moans
With all the blossoms of your mirth
    Crushed, like your Youth, beneath the stones!

MY MING COLLECTION

by

STEWART EDWARD WHITE

DIFFERENT people have different things they react to without rhyme or reason. Just touch the button and they do the rest. Why does a miscellaneous movie audience in Minnesota, composed of a mélange of ex-Yankees and squareheads, yell itself red in the face when the band strikes up "Dixie"? Certainly they have no dear old plantation memories. Nor is the phenomenon confined to Minesota. It is a sort of generalized convention which even love of the spirited tune cannot quite explain. There are other, more localized fetishes, that are guaranteed sure-fire in reducing loyal citizens of a particular section or state or city to a mush of sentimentality.

Some of these have a solid foundation. Such as a Californian's love for the old-fashioned Chinaman. By Californian I do not mean your latter-day upstarts who know the Golden State only in the twentieth century. You must go back at least into the Gay Nineties to get the full flavor of the relationship. Not that it has even yet entirely disappeared. Here and there the cockles of your heart may still be warmed by the sight of a survivor of the race, very, very wrinkled, but starched and bland and deliberate and uncompromisingly himself.

For in the Eighties, and for perhaps twenty years thereafter, all Chinamen were like that. You adopted them into your household, or they adopted you—that point has never been cleared—and you were fixed for life. Also that particular department of your life was placidly but firmly removed from your control. Nor, short of abandoning Chinese servants completely, were you ever able to change. If for any reason Gin Gwee had to leave, or desired to leave, he did so without fuss or warning. Nobody even bothered. His "second uncle" slid into his place. And if Gin Gwee, his foreign business terminated, decided to return, there he was! And possibly you never saw the second uncle again. Once completely established in the good graces of one or another of the great families, you need never give the thought of service a moment's worry.

Almost anybody who was started out right, and who was not flagrantly obtuse, or harsh, or unreasonable in other ways, could command this sort of generalized service. If his became known as a good household, he was never unsupplied with a good Chinaman; and that without search or solicitation on his own part. If, on the other hand, he or his womenfolk conducted a bad household, then he was doomed to stupid, slovenly, and incompetent successions, until he gave up Chinese servants in disgust—which settled that situation. This was the plain business aspect, the ordinary run-of-the-mill relationship, easy, efficient, comfortable, pleasant. The element of personal loyalty and affection—on both sides—was its beautiful and by-no-means-uncommon flowering. We shall return to that later.

Many times I have heard one woman say to another that "Chinese servants are the best in the world, if you know how to run them." Know how to run them! Shucks! If you know how to be run by them would be a more accurate statement. They were perfectly willing to do those things you wanted done—even when, evidently, they did not understand why you should desire them—but they did them in their own way. It was just as well for you to make up your mind first as last that that way was your way, for you would most certainly never get anything different. Anyone who had any success at all with Chinese servants understood that. As a consequence, nobody bothered to apologize for the most startling departures from the ordinary conventions of polite society elsewhere. They were small price to pay for the smooth efficiency of comfort. We took them—and it—for granted.

In our early married life we, personally, conducted our whole establishment on a one-Chinaman basis. We had a moderately good-sized house, with two guest rooms that were occupied most of the time by friends who followed the custom of early days by staying with us for months at a time. Toy took care of the whole show. He cooked all meals, served them, and washed the dishes. He cleaned the entire house and made the beds. He could, and did, cook and serve, without a moment's hitch of delay or pause, for dinner parties of ten or twelve. He shopped for our vegetables, and we used to think he counted the green peas, so accurately did he seem able to gauge our exact appetites. Furthermore, by half-past two, or three o'clock at the latest, he was all finished until time to start dinner; the whole place, including his kitchen, spick and span, in apple-pie order. At that hour, dressed in beautiful brocades, snow-white socks, thick-soled Chinese shoes, stiff black skullcap topped with a carved button of coral, his long pigtail down his back, he toddled off down the street to Chinatown on pleasure of his own. He was always calm; he was never hurried. I used to study how he could do it and never did quite make out, except that he never made a false or unnecessary move, and that he was marvelously clever at dovetailing one kind of task with another. We paid him forty dollars a month.

On one occasion we were called upon to entertain at dinner a very important diplomat and his lady. Things went smoothly, as usual. The courses succeeded one another without delay, piping hot. Toy waited faultlessly, slipping in and out so unobtrusively that no one noticed he was ever absent from the room. He paused behind Mrs. White's chair.

"Missy White," he instructed her, "tonight you put on clean nightgown," and proceeded with the business of the dinner.

The Californians present probably did not even notice this astonishing performance, but those diplomats must have been greatly shocked—or amused. Toy had merely, between change of plates, slipped upstairs to turn down the beds. Next day was laundry day. He had laid out a fresh nightdress. He was informing Mrs. White of that fact. He could imagine no reason why he should not do so; nor would he have understood any reproof.

Only once did Mrs. White depart from the entirely commonplace acceptance. She attended a tea of elderly women, all good housekeepers. She listened to a lot of talk. She returned home filled with a new consciousness that she was neglecting her duties by not taking a more personal supervision of how the details of the household were being carried forward. So she summoned Toy and went over the whole place in approved household fashion according to the lights that had been revealed to her at the tea of the elderly ladies. Toy followed, saying nothing. At length he stopped short in his tracks.

"Whassa matter with you, Missy White?" he demanded. "You talk jus' like one old woman!"

She came to. That was exactly what she was doing.

It is natural that, with such picture-puzzle nicety in fitting the day's doings, Toy and his like should develop a keen sense of procedure. They proceed largely by routine; and it is disconcerting when, without warning, that routine is broken. And one who had experienced something like that nightgown episode would be astonished to discover how rigid is their sense of propriety and etiquette.

Two blocks below us, on a corner, stood a bungalow. The kitchen entrance was not in the rear, but in the side of the house on one street; the front door was on the other street.

As the whole place was brightly gardened, a stranger had no evident indication as to which was which. It was opened by Sing.

"Is Mrs. Gilchrist at home?" inquired the visitor.

Sing did not reply. He looked her coldly in the eye.

"You go 'round flont door," he instructed, and closed this one in her face.

Dutifully she plodded around to the other side of the house, rang the bell, repeated to Sing, when he came, the same question.

"No," said Sing blandly; "she gone out."

"Wouldn't you think," lamented the visitor, telling about this, "that he could have told me that in the first place?"

Knowing Chinese servants, we did not.

By the late Nineties, if you could get a good Chinese servant at all, he was trained—at least in his own fashion—and knowledge in our ways. But back in the middle Eighties the case was a little different. Fresh recruits were still coming from China. They were learning our habits and our language. Incidentally, they were learning fast; especially when it is considered how diametrically opposite to ours are so many of their customs. We forget that many of our methods must seem upside down to them. After a time they took it for granted that we did most of our concerns illogically, and ceased to try to reason about them. They just did as they were told, and did not bother to find any logic in it. That is the explanation for most of the "stupid Chinese performances" the newcomer used to talk about.

So well-known was this trait that everybody warned the newcomer of it. Owing to difficulties of language, instruction in duties was always by demonstration.

"They'll do exactly as you show them," was the advice, "but be sure you show them the first time correctly, for you can never change them."

I have seen Gin Gwee placidly watering the lawn from under an umbrella, in a pouring rain. From the practical point of view, it was an imbecile performance, and Gin Gwee knew that just as well as you or I. But in other matters, that seemed to him equally imbecile, he had used his common sense to modify orders—and caught the devil for it! So he had made to himself a resolve that forever after he would follow the letter, for no man can fathom the fantastic ideas of the foreign devil. And when a Chinaman makes a resolve, believe you me it is copper-riveted, and the incident may be considered closed.

My parents rented a small house and acquired Gin Gwee. They showed him his duties in the minutest detail once. That was sufficient. Pending completion of a bin in the corner of the lot, they dumped the wood ashes from the kitchen stove on the ground just outside the kitchen door. The bin was finished of a Friday. Father demonstrated the removal of the ashes from the ground outside the door to the new bin. Thereafter, for as long as we occupied this house, Gin Gwee dumped the ashes beside the door until a Friday, when he transferred them to the bin; nor could he be deflected from that routine. With the first demonstration of duties, whatever the lacks and discrepancies, the incident was finished for all time.

Sometimes mistakes in understanding were amusing. Early in their association Mrs. Gilchrist decided to instruct Sing in the etiquette of formal calls. Therefore, as usual, she demonstrated. She rang her own doorbell, handed Sing her card, showed him what to do with it, and all the rest.

"You *sabe?*" she concluded as usual.

"I *sabe,*" said Sing confidently.

A day or so later Mrs. Gilchrist's next-door neighbor ran across on some errand, after the informal fashion of nextdoor neighbors.

"Good morning, Sing," said she brightly when he opened the door, and made to enter without further inquiry, for she was an intimate of the house. But Sing blocked the doorway.

"You got ticket?" he demanded. "You no got ticket, you no come in."

When one of these old-fashioned Chinamen found a household that suited him, he not only stayed, but he became one of the family. Its interests were his own. He gave its members not only a perfect service, but loyalty that expressed itself in the oddest vigilances and indignations. Nobody put anything over on his people— not so far as he was concerned! He considered it his privilege to examine every purchase that came into the house, of any description, no matter how trivial, or how intimate, or how far remote from his own responsibility.

"How much you pay for dat?" he would demand accusingly, and, on receiving an answer, would shake his head in gloomy disapproval.

"Wong will be the death of my soul!" complained one woman, half laughing. "I'm torn whether to lie to him, or become a niggard in the eyes of my friends, or abandon everything and let him look on me as a hopeless fool! If I give a dinner, I'm in terror always lest there be not enough to go around, but there always is—just," she acknowledged.

Toy never hesitated to advise or correct our guests. Among others, we once entertained a vivacious English-woman of high degree. To her Toy offered a trayful of various hors d'oeuvres. She was telling a story and hovered in hestitation of choice.

"Come on; you hully up," Toy interrupted her finally.

Startled, she stared at him wildly and grabbed in haste the nearest. Toy, undisturbed, went on his rounds.

It was impossible to observe small etiquettes. It must not be thought that Toy ever intruded outside his own sphere of responsibility. Indeed, I doubt if he bothered to listen to what anybody was saying. But within that sphere he considered he had rights.

"You take some," he insisted to one who declined a certain dish. "Him velly good."

Or he would firmly modify one's choice.

"No, you take that one," he ordered, and was meekly obeyed. He moved with a calm dignity that raised anything he said and did miles above gaucherie. In his white starched loose garments and his silent felt-soled shoes, with his carved ivory face and his shaved forehead and his queue down his back, he was a beautiful and soothing presence.

Toy was several steps above the coolie class, probably from the north of China, to judge by his height and the cleancut, aristocratic lines of his face. He was, I think, devoted to us; I know we were devoted to him. When, after many years, there came that mysterious and compelling call that sooner or later takes every Chinaman back to China, we looked after his disappearing back, with the pigtail wiggling, and our eyes were misty. Generally these old Chinamen returned after a time to their families. One of our friends has several of these superannuated ex-servants living in tiny one-room shacks scattered about her extensive place, content to sit in the sun and be near their "missy." If you wish to gauge the sometimes tigerlike loyalty of these people, delve into the true stories of the San Francisco earthquake.

But Toy did not come back; nor did we expect him to do so. Nobody ever gets more than a glimpse of the early lives and circumstances of these men. I do not know whether this is a natural secretiveness, or a taking for granted, or a despair of conveying the picture, but so it is.

However, we did know that Toy had ties in China that must ultimately claim him. It seemed he owned, or had an interest in, a furniture factory that apparently brought him in more money than we were paying him. Also a family. This latter bit of news came to us only toward the last. Toy showed us, proudly, a photograph he had just received—a comely woman with four sons. We gazed on it with slight perplexity, for two of the children were of very tender years.

"These all your family?" I asked.

"My family. All boy," said Toy.

"But, Toy," I expostulated, "how can that be? To my certain knowledge you have not been back to China for ten years."

"Oh, dat all light," said Toy complacently. "I got fliend."

We left it at that.

SAN FRANCISCO

by

PHILIP B. ANSPACHER

How many times have I traversed the bay
  That laps the lovely city of my birth,
  Its waves, its sea-gulls and its rocky girth,
The background of a childhood's holiday.
The winged years have swiftly fled their way,
  And I have traveled over all the earth
  Esteeming each great city at its worth,
The corridors of Venice, the villas of Pompeii;
But thou O goddess, shine the loveliest
  Of all the city-queens beside the sea,
  Thy figure looms aloft in sunlight dressed,
Thy face gleams o'er the waves resplendently;
  Thy prophet lips speak wisdom to the West,
  And sing to Asian shores of Liberty!

[1917]

A LIFE -- A BOWL OF RICE

by

LEMUEL DE BRA

BOW SAM stood in the doorway by his sugar-cane stand and watched with narrowed eyes an old man who shuffled uncertainly down the alley toward him.

"Hoo la ma!" cried Bow Sam, in surprised Cantonese as the old man drew near. "Hello, there! I scarcely knew you, venerable Fa'ng!"

Fa'ng, the hatchetman, straightened his bent shoulders and looked up. There was a gleam in his deep bronze eyes that was hardly in keeping with his withered frame.

"Hoo la ma, Bow Sam," he said, his voice strangely deep and vibrant.

"You have grown very thin," remarked Bow Sam with friendly interest.

"Hi low; that is true. But why carry around flesh that is not food?"

The sugar-cane vendor eyed the other shrewdly. What was the gossip he had heard concerning Fa'ng, the famous old hatchetman? Was it not that the old man was always hungry? Yes, that was it! Fa'ng, whose long knife and swift arm had been the most feared thing in all Chinatown, was starving—too proud to beg, too honest to steal.

"You have eaten well, venerable Fa'ng?" The inquiry was in a casual tone, respectful.

"Aih, I have eaten well," replied the old hatchetman, averting his face.

"How unfortunate for me! I have not yet eaten my rice; for when one must dine alone, one goes slowly to table. Is it not written that a bowl of rice shared is doubly enjoyed? Would you not at least have a cup of tea while I eat my mean fare?"

"I shall be honoured to sip tea with you, estimable Bow Sam," replied the hatchetman with poorly disguised eagerness.

"Then condescend to enter my poor house! Ah, one does not often have the pleasure of your company in these days!"

Bow Sam preceded his guest to the wretched hovel that was the sugar-cane vendor's only home. There he quickly removed all trace of the bowl of rice he had eaten but a moment before.

"Will you take this poor stool, venerable Fa'ng?" said Bow, setting out the only stool he possessed, and placing it so that the hatchetman's back would be to the stove.

Wearily, Fa'ng sat down. Bow put out two small cups, each worn and badly chipped, and filled them with hot tea. Then while the hatchetman sipped his tea, Bow uncovered the rice kettle. There was but one bowl of rice left. Bow Sam had intended to keep it for his evening meal; for until he sold some sugarcane, he had no way of obtaining more food.

Behind Fa'ng's back, Bow took two rice bowls and set them on the stove. One bowl he heaped full for the hatchetman. In the other he put an upturned tea bowl and sprinkled over it his last few grains of rice.

"Let us give thanks to the gods of the kitchen that we have food and teeth and appetite," chuckled Bow Sam, seating himself on a sugar-cane box opposite Fa'ng.

"Well spoken," returned the old hatchetman quickly, filling his mouth with the nourishing rice. "*Aih!* there is much in life to make one content."

With his chop-sticks Bow Sam deftly took up a few grains of rice, taking care lest he uncover the upturned tea bowl.

"I am very grateful," said Bow, "that I have a few teeth left, that I quite often have enough rice, and that I sometimes have meat as often as once a month; but to hear you—a proud old hatchetman—express such sentiments on an empty stomach fills me with admiration."

"It is a virtue to be content with one's lot," remarked Fa'ng quietly.

"*Hi low!* That is true! But the younger generation are always fretting because they think they have not enough; while, as anyone knows, they have much more than we who first came to this land of the white foreign devil."

"They are young," spoke Fa'ng, nodding his head slowly. "For us the days have fled, the years have not tarried. And we have learned that if one has but a bowl of rice for food and a bent arm for pillow, one can be content."

"*Haie!* How can you speak so softly of the younger generation when it is they who have robbed you of your livelihood? I know the gossip. You, the most famous killer in Chinatown, find yourself cast out out like a worn-out broom by these young upstarts who have no respect for their elders. Is it not true?"

With his left hand the old hatchetman made an eloquent gesture, peculiarly Chinese, much as one quickly throws open a fan.

"Of what value are words, my friend? They cannot change that which is changeless. A word cannot temper the wind, nor a phrase procure food for a hungry stomach."

"Nevertheless, I do not like such things," persisted Bow Sam. "I love the old ways. You were an honourable and fearless killer. When you were hired to slay one's enemy you went boldly to your victim and told him your business. Then, swiftly, even before the doomed one could open his lips, you struck—cleaned your blade and walked your way.

"The modern killers!" Bow Sam spewed the words out as one does sour rice. "They are too cowardly to use the knife. They hide on roofs, fire on their victims, then throw away their guns and flee like thieves. *Aih,* what have we come to in these days!

"It was but yesterday after mid-day rice that I had speech with Gar Ling, a gunman of the Sin Wah *tong.* He stopped to buy sugar-cane, and I told him that had I the money I would hire him. There is one of the younger generation, the pockmarked son of Quong, the dealer in jade, who has greatly wronged me and my honourable family name, and my distinguished ancestors. As you very well know, one cannot soil one's own hands with the blood of vengeance. Moreover, I have no weapon, not even a dull cleaver. Neither can I afford to hire a fighting man.

"I was telling all this to Gar Ling," went on Bow, straining the last drop of tea into Fa'ng's bowl, "and he told me he would settle my quarrel, but it would cost one thousand dollars. When I told him I had not even a thousand copper *cash,* he became angry and abusive. As he walked his way, quickly, like a foreign devil, he spat in my direction and called me an unspeakable name."

"*Ts, ts!* You should have wrung his neck. Repeat to me his unspeakable words."

"He said," cried Bow Sam, his face twisted in fury, "that I am *the son of a turtle!*"

"*Aih-yah!* How insulting! As anyone knows, in all our language there is no epithet more vile!"

"That is true. But what is even worse, I did not remember until after he had gone, that he had not paid me for the piece of sugarcane. Such is the way of the younger generation; and we, who have been long in the land can do nothing."

"Yet it is by such things that one learns the lesson of enduring tranquility," remarked Fa'ng, smacking his lips and moving back from the table.

For about the time, then, that it takes one to make nine bows before the household gods, neither man made speech. Then Fa'ng arose.

"An excellent bowl of rice, my good friend."

"*Aih,* it shames me to have to give you such mean fare."

"And the tea was most fragrant."

"*Ts,* it was the only the cheapest *Black Dragon.*"

The two old men went to the door.

"*Ho hang la,*" said the hatchetman.

"*Ho hang la,*" echoed the sugar-cane vendor. "I hope you have a safe walk."

. . . .

Fa'ng, the hatchetman, made his way down the alley to the rear entrance of a pawnshop. There he spoke a few words with the proprietor.

"I know you are honest, old man," said the pawn-broker. "But instead of bringing it back, I hope, for your own sake, you will be able to pay what you owe me."

Then from a safe he took a knife with long, slender blade and a handle of ebony in which had been carved an unbelieveable number of notches. Fa'ng took the knife, handling it as one does an object of precious memories, concealed it beneath his tattered blouse, and went his way.

Near the entrace of a gambling house in Canton Alley the old hatchetman met the pock-marked son of Quong, the dealer in jade.

"For the wrong you have done Bow Sam, his family name, and his distinguished ancestors," said Fa'ng quietly; and before the other could open his lips the long blade was through his heart.

In front of a cigar store in Shanghai Place, Fa'ng found Gar Ling, the gunman. "I have business of moment with you, Gar Ling," said the hatchetman. "Come."

Gar Ling hesitated. He stood in great fear of the old killer, yet he dared not show that fear before his young friends. So with his left hand he gave a peculiar signal. A boy standing near with a basket of *lichee* on his arm turned quickly and followed the two men down the alley. Drawing near his employer, the boy held up the basket as though soliciting the gunman to buy. Gar's hand darted swifty into the basket beneath the *lichee,* and came out with a heavy automatic pistol which he quickly concealed beneath his blouse.

The old hatchetman knew all the tricks of the young gunman, but he pretended he had not seen. As they turned a dark corner, he paused.

"For the insulting words you spoke to Bow Sam," he said calmly, and the long blade glided between the gunman's ribs.

As Fa'ng drew the steel away, Gar Ling staggered, fired once, then collapsed.

.   .   .   .

Bow Sam stood in the doorway by his sugar-cane stand and watched with narrow eyes an old man who shuffled uncertainly down the alley toward him.

"*Hoo la ma!*" he cried, as the old man drew near. "I did not expect to see you again so soon."

The old hatchetman did not raise his head nor reply. Staggering, he crossed the threshold and fell on his face on the littered floor.

With a throaty cry Bow Sam slammed the door shut. He bent over Fa'ng.

"This knife," said the hatchetman; "take it—to Wong the pawn-broker. Tell him—all. Worth—more—than I owe."

"But what's—"

"For the wrong that the pock-marked one did you, for the insult Gar Ling spoke to you, I slew them," said Fa'ng with sudden strength. "My debt is paid. *Tsau kom lok.*"

"*Haie!* You did that! Why did you do that? I could never pay you! And look! *Aih-yah,* oh, how piteous! You are dying!"

With awkward fingers, the vendor of sugar-cane tried to staunch the flow of blood where Gar Ling's bullet had struck with deadly effect.

"Pay me?" breathed Fa'ng the hatchetman. "Did you—not—feed me? Can one—put a value—on food—when the stomach—is empty? *Aih,* what matters it? A life,"—his eyelids fluttered and closed— "a life—a bowl of rice. . . ."

[1920]

THE GIFT

by

CHARLES CALDWELL DOBIE

AT THE bakery where I work there is a Japanese boy named Ito who comes every night at twelve o'clock to clean up the litter we make in our hurry with the baking. The first time I saw him I laughed softly. I had been in San Francisco only two days and I was too busy talking with my friends to go about, so this Japanese boy was the first of his kind I had ever seen. I laughed softly, and I said to myself:

"Josef Vitek, you are a long way from home! Fancy, yesterday you saw for the first time a palm tree, and to-day you look upon a strange human being!"

But to tell the truth, I was disappointed. In the little Bohemian school-house of my native village of Polna we learned many things about distant countries. Every day we studied a large gray book that was filled with maps and wonderful stories and pictures. I have seen pictures of Japanese in this book, but they were gay people dressed in the drollest fashion you can imagine and carrying gaudy umbrellas and fans. Except for the strange shape of his eyes and the bronze color of his cheeks, Ito might have been a countryman of mine, or the sullen Greek who works beside me.

I looked at him many times on that first night in spite of my disappointment, but on the second night he was already an old story. By the end of the week I did not trouble to lift my eyes when he came in.

One hot night when we were very busy with our bread and the big iron kettle had been filled with grease for frying doughnuts, who should trip upon a pan dropped near the ovens but this Japanese boy of whom I speak. He tripped suddenly and gave a cry, and one hand fell in the bubbling grease. I put my fingers before my eyes. When I looked about again the Greek beside me was laughing and all the others had cruel smiles upon their lips. I went forward toward the ovens: Ito was standing up, and his hand hung before him like a dead thing. I opened the cupboard where they keep spice and such flavorings, and in a corner I found a bottle half filled with a sweet oil. Ito was still standing in front of the flaming ovens and the rest of the company smiled over their work. I felt ashamed of my companions.

I called Ito. He came and stood in the shadows beside me, and I poured oil upon his burnt hand and bound it up with an old handkerchief that my landlady had washed only that day for me.

"You should go home," I said to him. "You cannot wash the mixing-bowls with a hand like that."

But he shook his head and answered, "Who will do my work if I go to my home now?"

And I said, "I will."

He put on his hat and left without a word.

Next day as I was leaving my room to go to work I met my landlady in the hall. Every evening at about seven o'clock I leave the house, and every evening at this time I come upon this landlady of mine in the hall, or upon the stairs, or at the front door. She is always bending over some household task, but she is never too busy to stop for a pleasant word with me. This evening I left a few minutes before my accustomed time and my landlady was nowhere to be seen, but as I was closing the front door she came running out. "Josef!" she cried, "Josef, my son, you are leaving early! What is the matter? Are you sick, or in some trouble?"

I stepped back into the hall. "I am never sick," I replied, "and trouble is a matter for those who keep a sharp eye for it."

My landlady shook her finger in the air and her face was sad. "Ah, Josef, my son, you speak as every young person should. If I could say the words as you have said them I should be happy. But remember, the eye of trouble is sharper even than the eyes of those who look for it."

"Well," I said to her, and I laughed as I said it, "perhaps you are right. But my leaving early has to do with none of these things. A man burned his hand at the bakery where I work and I must go earlier for I shall have more than my share to do to-night."

"Wait," my landlady said, "until I go to my room. I have a salve that we use in Alsace and it works wonders. No matter how bad the burn, it will be healed before the week is out."

I waited for her, and she came back and put a small glass jar in my hand. "Before the week is out," she repeated, "the man's hand will be well again, and if he is a good Christian perhaps it will work more quickly."

"A good Christian!" I laughed again. "He is no Christian at all. He is a Japanese who comes to scrub the pots."

She sighed and shook her head. "Well, what is so is so, but I would rather my salve went to one of my own kind. However, God is good, and if He wishes to heal a heathen's hand it is not my affair."

And with that she went to her room.

That night at twelve o'clock Ito came to his work. But, as you have guessed, he could do nothing. I gave him the salve and sent him home again; we had no word of him for three days. I confess that I grew very tired of doing my own work and the work of this Japanese, too.

On this night when I had sent Ito home for the second time I said to myself: "These companions of mine will help me clear away the litter once they are through with their own tasks. Last night it was different—a busy night and every one had his hands full."

But when they had finished with their baking they sat at the long table where we gather after work is done. They sat at this long table, smoking cigarettes, while my Greek friend called me Ito, in a high cracked voice like an old woman's and my companions laughed.

"Ito, Ito—be careful with the mixing-bowls, Ito!" my Greek friend would cry out. "If you should break one of those bowls you would have to live upon rice for a week to pay for it." Or again he would say, mockingly, to the others: "What has become of our Japanese boy, Ito? Is that his brother scrubbing down the kneading-board? Yes, it must be his brother. They look exactly alike. They are like two wrinkled peas in a worm-eaten pod."

While they mocked me my heart grew very bitter, for these men were my comrades. And now, because I did a kindness to one who could not sit with us, they were scornful.

On that second night I had no time to sit in my accustomed place. I worked until daybreak, and one by one my companions rose and left.

I went home at daybreak and a silver mist hung over the city. But here and there the sun shone in little patches of gold, smiling as a woman does through a thin veil. I smiled, too, in spite of what was troubling me, and before I had reached my doorstep the mist was gone.

On the third night a young girl, a friend of Ito's, came to the door of the bakery and asked for me. She tapped upon the side door that leads from the street to the kitchen; my Greek friend heard the noise and went forward and turned the knob. When he saw a Japanese girl standing before him he said at once:

"You do not want *me;* the man you are looking for is Josef Vitek. I am a baker, and a Christian!"

He said this last proudly for all to hear. She did not understand, of course, but I knew his meaning and my heart beat quickly. I did not trouble to wipe the dough from my hands, but I left my task and went out upon the street, closing the door.

"Tell me," I said to this Japanese girl, "how soon will Ito be at work again?"

"Next week," she answered. "His hand is still full of pain. Every morning he rubs it with the salve you gave him. By the end of the week it will be well. You are a kind man. He has sent me to tell you this. But the man who opened the door—I do not like *him!*"

She made a little bow, drawing in her breath as one does when the soup is too hot. I nodded to her and went in the door again, back to my work. My comrades were busy and they were silent for a time, but finally my Greek friend began to speak.

"Is not this Josef Vitek a droll person?" he said to a man standing beside him. "It seems as if he will have none of Christians. Now he is making sheep's eyes at a woman who has skin the color of the citron we put in pound-cakes."

"He says he is a Bohemian," called out another.

"Do you think he has been fooling us? Have you noticed his hair? It is straight and black. Perhaps—"

I looked up from kneading and the anger in my eyes stopped them. But I said nothing and presently they began again.

"Do you not think," said one, "that we should speak to our master about this new Japanese boy? His mind is not on his work. This evening when I broke an egg in one of the bowls it was still filled with crust of yesterday's mixing."

"And the kneading-board," cried my Greek friend, "It is as yellow as the face of his Japanese sweetheart! But what can you expect of a man who can do everything and nothing! He will be mixing his baking and his pot-washing next. We shall find him using soap for greasing the pans and butter for washing them clean again."

I put my lips together tightly; I would not give these comrades of mine the pleasure of seeing how much they hurt. For sometimes comrades are cruel people, and especially my Greek friend who works beside me.

It was Friday night and everyone was busy almost until daybreak. But my thoughts were so pleasant that I worked swiftly; even my pot-washing was finished before the appointed time and the kneading-board scrubbed until it shone like the cheeks of a snow-maiden instead of being yellow like the face of Ito's little friend.

I was glad that I had finished all my tasks so quickly, for now I thought: "I have not had time all week to sit at the table with my comrades. This is Saturday morning and I shall not see them until Sunday evening at seven. Many things may happen in that time and it is well to part friends."

On Saturday mornings we have coffee at this table in the corner, for the Friday's baking is a hard task, and our master rewards us with steaming coffee and bits of hot, buttered pastry. It was Ito's duty to fill the coffee-pot and lay out the table, and pile the buttered pastries in a huge dish where all could reach them. At first I wondered what I should do about this, but at once I said to myself:

"What was Ito's task is now yours." And I began to make everything ready.

I made the coffee and served it to these comrades of mine, and even the pastries were buttered and put in their proper place. They drank quickly and ate the pastries in great haste, and I thought:

"Josef, if you do not hurry they will all be finished, and then it will not be so pleasant for you."

I washed my hands and laid my baker's cap aside. Then I went over to the ovens and lifted up the coffee-pot and poured out a steaming cupful. I walked to the table; my heart beat quickly and my hand shook. My comrades did not notice me and no one moved up to make a place. Finally I laid a hand upon the shoulder of my Greek friend.

"Will you not let me sit beside you?" I asked.

He looked first at my face and then at my feet, and back at my face again; every one at the table followed his example. And at once he rose and left me standing with the coffee-cup trembling in my hand. I bit my lip hard and sat down in his place, and with that every man left his seat and I sat alone.

When I got home to my lodgings who should be at the front door but my landlady. I nodded to her, but not pleasantly, and I began to climb the stairs to my room. But my landlady calls me her son and she does as a mother will, even when I wish it least. So, on that morning, she laid her crooked hands upon mine as she said:

"Josef, my son, I would rather see you in tears than with that look upon your face. How did you come by it?"

"I did a kindness for one who was not a comrade . . . . . You were right—the eye of trouble is sharper than the eyes of those who look for it."

"Josef, Josef," she replied, "you have a good heart, but a good heart has never saved any man from suffering. Why did you not leave this Japanese to his own people? Surely they can help him."

"Who said anything about a Japanese?" I questioned.

"Ah, Josef, my son, do you think that old women are lacking in wit? Have I not watched you going early every evening to your work and coming home long after your time? And have you forgotten my salve? Give any woman two facts and an hour at her knitting and she will do more with it than a judge can with the testimony of a dozen witnesses."

"Well, you are right as usual. I have done a kindness for this man, and my comrades have not ceased making me answer for it.

If I had asked you at the beginning perhaps you would have given me good advice and saved me."

But my landlady shook her head. "It might have happened as you say. But who can tell? I am a woman. Did I not give you my salve knowing it was for one who was not a Christian? I leave some things to God."

"The man's hand is almost healed," I said to her.

Her face was full of smiling. "Ah, Josef, my son, I am glad of that! See, God is with us. It will all come right! After a season everything will be as it once was."

"No," I answered, and my heart was full as I said it, "things are never again as they once were."

My landlady raised one hand to my forehead and she pushed back my hair. "Josef, my son," she said, "when you are as old as I am you will be glad that this is so."

That afternoon I rose early, for I could not sleep, and I went to walk in the Park. I kept to the sidepaths where there were a few people, but in spite of everything whom should I meet but Ito, entering the Park at one of the big gateways.

"How is your hand?" I asked.

He drew in his breath. "I shall come to-morrow to my work," he answered.

I was about to walk on when he bowed again. "Will not Mr. Vitek —who is my friend—drink tea with me? In Japan this is a custom."

I looked about, wondering whether any of my comrades were there to see. "If you wish it," I replied.

We went to the Japanese tea-garden that stands in a sheltered corner of the Park, and I have never seen anything so beautiful. I had looked in at this tea-garden many times, but never when spring was upon it. Along the bamboo trellises purple flowers hung like grapes and filled the air with sweetness; in the pools blue iris made thickets in which the goldfish hid, and at every turn blossomed a cherry tree.

Ito went before me into the little tea-house and drew up a bench so that we could look out over the shaded pool. We sat down. A young woman came with tea and little cakes and tiny bowls, and I almost forgot my troubles, for this young woman was like the pictures of Japanese I had seen in the great gray book at home.

When we had finished our tea we walked among the cherry trees and Ito said to me:

"In Japan the time of blossoms is a gay time. These trees are nothing! You should see them in the gardens of *my* city."

"These are beautiful enough for me," I answered, "and if I might carry a branch home I would be happy."

We went out of the great carved gateway, and Ito bowed, not once but many times, to me at parting, saying as he did so: "You are Mr. Vitek, my friend. Next week, I am told, you have a festival. At that time I shall bring you a gift."

I walked home, and when I arrived I knocked upon my land-lady's door. "I have met the Japanese," I called to her, "and what do you suppose? His hand is well, and he is is to bring me a present at Easter. Can you fancy what it will be?"

"How gay your voice is!" she called back. "It will be something fine I have no doubt. A piece of silk, or yards of fine crêpe, or perhaps a carved box of some sort."

"Those are all women's gifts!" I cried. "No, it will be none of those things, I am sure. But, as you say, it will be something fine."

All that night and all Sunday I thought about Ito's gift, and the more I thought the more puzzled I became. I even walked in the early morning past the windows of a Japanese bazaar, thinking I might see the thing he was to give me. In this window there were all the things my landlady had spoken of—pieces of silk, and yards of fine crêpe, and carved boxes without end. And there were wonderful ivory balls, and carved one within the other; and strange swords in black-and-gold scabbards; and gods with gilt faces sitting on thrones as yellow as their cheeks. But there was not one thing that tempted me, and I thought:

"What is this thing that Ito will bring me? Surely there is nothing made in Japan for a Bohemian like myself. Well, who knows? Perhaps it will not be a Japanese gift, after all." And I went home better pleased.

Now I had been so busy with these thoughts of what Ito was to do for me that I forgot about all my troubles until I came on Sunday evening to the bakery again. I went in through the side door that leads to the kitchen, and I had a pleasant word ready for my comrades. But those who did not frown at me gave me cold greetings, and I remembered what had happened on Saturday morning and my heart was full of bitterness. I knew that they were waiting for me to do the work of two men, and I was glad when, at midnight, Ito came as usual to his tasks.

"Oh," said my Greek friend, scornfully, to me, "so your yellow comrade has come back again! And how is he to reward you? with a week's wages, or a kiss upon either cheek, or will he content himself with saying a good word for you to the family of your Japanese sweetheart?"

"Before the week is out you will know how I am to be rewarded," I replied proudly. "He has promised me a gift, and it will be something fine, I can tell you."

"Listen to him!" my Greek friend cried aloud for all to hear. "This Josef Vitek is expecting a gift from his friend Ito. Can you not fancy what it will be? A cotton wrapper with flapping sleeves, such as these heathens wear. Next week we shall have our friend coming to work in this shroud."

That night I finished my work early, but I did not wait to sit with my comrades. Instead I left before daybreak and Ito followed me out and said:

"I have decided what I am to give to Mr. Vitek, my friend."

"Ah, is that so?" I answered. "Yesterday I looked into a Japanese shop-window, wondering what it would be."

"Mr. Vitek, my friend, will not find what I am to give him in any such place," he replied, smiling. Then he went back to the kitchen again.

When I told my landlady what Ito had said she was as puzzled as I.

"Perhaps he will bring you a necktie with a red rose embroidered upon it," she called after me as I closed the door of my room, "or a frame of sea-shells for your mother's picture—or a leather-covered pillow full of pleasant mottoes. No, I give it up!"

When Friday night came I could hardly keep my thoughts on my baking. At midnight Ito opened the side door and I looked up from my work. He had a big bundle in his hand wrapped in brown paper. The four edges of the paper were pinned together in a point.

"It must be something light," I thought, "and easily crushed, or he would have tied string about it."

But I had not long to guess further. Ito threw aside his hat and made at once for me. I wiped the dough from my hands and stood smiling as he came toward me. All my comrades stopped their work and waited. He stood before me and made a little bow and laid the bundle on the kneading-table.

"Mr. Vitek, my friend," he said, "I have brought you a gift."

I turned toward the table, and my fingers trembled as I took the pin from Ito's bundle. My comrades all leaned forward. The brown paper fell away; I heard my Greek friend laugh. A great branch full of cherry blossoms lay in front of me. I said nothing, but I bowed to Ito, and tears of shame were in my eyes.

"I have had a hard time to get these blossoms for Mr. Vitek," whispered Ito to me. "But I have a friend who knows the daughter of the honorable people who live in the tea-garden. For him they have forgotten their rules."

At this my comrades all turned to their work again; there was no loud laughter, but I could see smiles of scorn upon their lips.

I set the blossoms in a jar of water and left them in a far corner of the kneading-table, but, to tell the truth, I would rather have thrown them in the face of the man who brought them. But I did my best to make a brave show before these men who were no longer my friends. And as I worked I thought to myself:

"Josef Vitek, you must look for another shop in which to earn your bread. These men are silent now because Friday night is a busy night and they have no time for jesting. But when they sit about to drink their Saturday-morning coffee they will hold their sides with laughing at you."

And I remembered all the fine things that my landlady had guessed would be my portion, and I felt my face grow hot with anger.

Toward morning when Ito began to lay the table for the usual feast my heart grew heavy indeed, for was not the next day Easter, and was I not cut off from my companions forever? I set my lips together tightly and washed my hands and got myself ready to leave. I washed my hands and wrapped the blossoms in the brown paper, and put on my hat. But at the door whom should I meet but my German master coming in with a smile on his lips.

"Josef, Josef, where are you going? Surely this will not do! Here I am, ready to eat an Easter breakfast with you, and I find you going home. Come, what have you in the paper?"

I tore the wrapping away. My master took the cherry bough and held it up for all to see.

"Josef," he said, "I have not seen blossoms like these since I left my native village. Surely they have blossoms nowhere in the world such as they have in the country where I came from."

At this my Greek friend spoke up pleasantly. "You have never been in Greece or you would not talk so foolishly. Blossoms in Greece are such as only gods plant."

And another spoke laughingly in praise of *his* country and its blossoms—and another, until the kitchen was merry with their disagreement.

All this time I stood with a heavy heart, wishing that I might be one of them again, and suddenly my master took me by the hand and said in a loud voice:

"Well, my friends, we are *all* right—blossoms in the springtime are blossoms the world over, but there is only one Josef."

With that I burst into tears, and my Greek friend came forward and kissed me upon either cheek. And all the others stood before me while I broke off bits of the blossoms and gave to each of them; and they laughingly pushed me into my accustomed seat.

"Ah, Josef, my son, you are smiling," said my landlady, when she opened the door for me. "Your Japanese friend must have surprised you."

"He has indeed," I answered as I held up the blossoms for her to see.

"My! are they not beautiful? I have not seen such blossoms since I left my native village in Alsace. But, tell me, what did your Japanese friend give you? Was it finer than you imagined?"

"Much finer," I said to her.

And I broke the cherry bough in two and gave my landlady half.

SAN FRANCISCO

by

MARY CAROLYN DAVIES

Sun, and the flash of a seagull's wing
    Aglint with sun.
The throb of the engine's beats that sing,
    The siren's tongue.
A silver flash on the wrinkled blue
    Of the age-old bay;
Then the city's towers spring up to you
    Out of the day.

Night, and the sweep of the seagulls' flights,
    Half-seen, half-guessed:
Night, and the gleam of the restless lights—
    Night, but no rest.
The shy waves whispering to the shores,
    Then a blaze of light—
And the city's face springs up to yours
    Out of the night.

"NO MORE SAD THOUGHTS"

by

GEORGE MARDIKIAN

WHEN I first came to America as a young man of twenty-two, fresh from the horrible wars in the Near East, from murder and torture, I knew what it meant at first hand to be starved and frozen and left for dead in the snows of winter. And when I escaped these tortures and came to America, it was like coming to Heaven. As a child I remember my first glimpse of Mt. Ararat, which is the most majestic sight to every Armenian. Across a hot valley and far up into the sky this snow-covered mountain rises nearly 17,000 feet, with two peaks. This mountain was the legendary resting place for Noah's Ark. I shall never forget it. But there are also bitter memories of Armenia, and I shall never forget the new thrill I had when, as an immigrant boy, I saw the Statue of Liberty as we came into New York Harbor. Here was relief from torture and heartbreak, and I felt it with all my heart. At that moment, I decided to leave all hatred and bitterness behind and begin life anew; like the many wonderful things we had heard about America in Armenia, the Statue of Liberty seemed to symbolize them all that day.

When we arrived at Ellis Island, immigration officers inspected us, gave us a shower and changed our clothes. That shower seemed to wash all the ugliness of the world away forever. My brother Arshag had wired from San Francisco to tell us he had my railroad tickets, and so I set out to cross the United States. Since I could not speak a word of English or understand anything that was said to me, my ticket was pinned to the lapel of my coat; this had my name and destination on it. People were kind and smiled at me; the contrast was so great, it was hard to believe that people could be as happy and cheerful as I saw them that day on the train. Everything I saw inspired me with an ambition to be one of them. I thought of the many things and decided I should go to school immediately, study English and learn how to be a good American.

The cross-country trip was not without momentary excitement and misgivings. Coming into Kansas City, the Traveler's Aid Society took charge of me. During the stopover I looked out into a street and saw thousands of men wearing fezzes marching toward the depot. My God, I thought, are there Turks over here too? And I reached instinctively into my pocket for the rock I invariably carried at home as protection against them. When they came closer, I realized they were not dressed quite right and they seemed too happy to be Turks. I believe the first thing I asked my sister when I reached San Francisco was who these people were. She told me they were Shriners who had been to a convention.

The following day was Sunday. My family took me on a tour of San Francisco, and we went to the beach. It was a bright clear day and it was a marvelous sight to see thousands of people playing in the sand, laughing and having a hilarious time. Women and children were swimming and riding the Chutes, and even old men with whiskers were throwing balls and playing leapfrog. I couldn't understand it.

Are these people crazy? I asked myself. In our country when people grow up they are solemn and have dignity. For years I had not seen them laugh and play. What is the matter with these people? I thought.

This bothered me. That night I couldn't eat or sleep thinking about my first day here. I remember my sister and brother talking about me and wondering what was wrong. The next morning I decided to see the city by myself and walked many blocks until I was exhausted. However, I remained on the same street so I wouldn't get lost. What I saw was amazing. I saw men with pails going to work. They were whistling. Milkmen were humming quietly as they left bottles on the doorsteps. The motorman on the cable car was whistling merrily as he pulled on the brakes. Even the street-sweeper smiled at me as he cheerily called, "Good morning." He didn't even know me. But I smiled back.

Suddenly I had it! I rushed home to my sister, and ran into the kitchen yelling, "These San Francisco people are not crazy. They are right. We are wrong. It is right to be happy. You feel better. You make the other fellow feel better. I am going to be a happy American; no more thinking sad thoughts, making sad music, and dwelling on the woes of our people."

But to get to the subject of food, and one food in particular. I had arrived in New York in the month of July, in 1922, and got on one of those trains that took eight days to get to San Francisco. People could see that I couldn't speak English because I was labeled with a tag showing my name and destination. Fortunately, my brother had sent me money enough so that I could well afford to eat in the dining car, but the trouble was that I couldn't order in English. Being able to read French, I could make out potato salad on the menu. It is practically the same in my language, so I took a chance and ordered it for my first dinner. The next day I was presented with an identical menu. Again I ordered potato salad. This went on for eight days, and it was *bad* potato salad—really terrible potato salad.

Right then and there I resolved that some day when I got the opportunity I was going to serve to Americans the best potato salad in the world. And that is the reason why, in my sandwich shops today, I serve more than a thousand orders of potato salad a day. It is the same potato salad that I serve at outstanding functions. I use it not only as a fine delicacy, but for buffet luncheons I use a large plateful as the table centerpiece, with the message of the day written on it in colored mayonnaise.

. . . .

Potato Salad

    1 pound firm, fresh potatoes
    2 hardboiled eggs
    1 teaspoonful salt
    white pepper to taste
    1/4 cupful vinegar
    1 pimiento (chopped fine)
    2/3 cupful mayonnaise
    1 small onion sliced
    2 tablespoonfuls chopped parsley

Boil potatoes in skins. When cool, peel and cut in quarters. Then slice or dice. Add vinegar, mix well, and let soak. Slice onion, and pour salt over it. Then squeeze out all the juice, and wash salt away with cold water. Mix onion with potatoes; add pimiento, eggs, salt and pepper, parsley and mayonnaise. Mix well and let stand in refrigerator for some time before serving.

"BOSS-MISSY"

THE CASE OF ROSETTA BAKER

by

ALFRED MEYERS

1.

Fantastic is the word to describe the foursome that rallied on Nob Hill on the evening of December 7, 1930.

The hostess was Mrs. Rosetta Baker, one of the canniest business women in the Bay Area. Divorced twenty-eight years before by her husband, she had done well for herself. Long ago she had decided that the safe, sure investment was real estate. Now a string of apartment houses scattered from the east slope of Nob Hill to what is known affectionately as "Polk Gulch" was indicative of her business acumen; a swelling bank account testified to her shrewdness. Assured of a more than ample income, she settled down in one of her apartment houses, on California Street above Old St. Mary's Church, to enjoy life. Well-preserved, dashing in manner and dress, she felt free to indulge herself in two hobbies: amateur theatricals, and the sponsorship of well-set-up, presentable young men. She was sixty-five.

It was her interest in theatricals that had led her to attend a performance at the Green Street Theatre, a somewhat bohemian little playhouse on the far side of Chinatown where the Spanish colony blends into Little Italy. During the performance her fancy had been caught by the leading man, a young actor named Walter Outler, or Middleton, as he was known professionally. She had found the opportunity to make his acquaintance, to introduce him to her

---

From *The San Francisco Murders* by permission of the publishers, Duell, Sloan and Pearce, Inc. Copyright 1947 by Duell, Sloan and Pearce, Inc.

friends. For eight months now he had been her protege. It was he who was her escort the night of December 7th. He was twenty-eight.

The other couple was equally startling. Mrs. Walker Coleman Graves, Mrs. Baker's dearest friend Maud, was a woman well over middle-age and also a divorcee. She had, of course, met Middleton many times at cocktail parties and other gatherings, but she had never seen him in one of his roles at the theatre. The party had been arranged to fill in this gap in Maud's education.

Lest her friend feel neglected, Mrs. Baker had invited Middleton's friend and roommate, Arthur Beale, to make up the fourth. Beale, a young man of twenty-three, was the pianist at the Green Street Theatre.

So it was that the mismatched quartet met at Mrs. Graves' apartment on Nob Hill where they fortified themselves with sherry cocktails. Following the cocktails they drove in Mrs. Baker's car to the Sir Francis Drake Hotel for a hasty dinner and then on through Chinatown to the theatre.

Maud's reaction to Middleton's performance is not a matter of record. It must have been at least satisfactory, though, for at eleven-thirty they were all still together, eating chocolate ice-cream sundaes in a confectionery store on Polk Street. When the ice-cream was consumed, the young men were shepherded into Mrs. Baker's waiting car and whirled away to the Graves apartment for a sherry nightcap.

"The boys left my apartment with Mrs. Baker about twelve-fifteen," Mrs. Graves told the police next day. "About fifteen minutes later Mrs. Baker called me up to say good night. She didn't say anything about the boys being there and I presume they had gone."

And so the two ladies retired to their respective chambers, doubtless reflecting pleasantly on their harmless evening. Mrs. Graves said she went straight off to sleep.

As for Mrs. Baker, it may be that she took up a little volume of poetry to read for a few moments. At least, a volume was found later in her bedroom. One poem in particular had received more than casual attention from her, for the last line had been annotated.

Below that line, which read, "Sex is the curse of life!" she had written in her spidery handwriting: "This is true!"

2.

The following morning a figure was observed in front of the apartment house on California Street. Clad in blue trousers and blouse, a bent old man went methodically about certain routine matters. Slowly, painstakingly, he swept out the vestibule and down the front steps. He connected a hose and flushed off the steps and the sidewalk, carefully watered the two little trees near the curb.

At intervals the rattle and clank of a cable-car bound for Montgomery Street and the brokerage district passed by. Bond clerks and stenographers saw him going about his labors, but he paid them no attention. After all, during the nine years he had been houseboy for Mrs. Baker, Liu Fook, the sixty-two-year-old Chinese, had seen hundreds of the clattering little red cars slide down the hill.

When the outside chores were finished, Liu rolled up the hose, shuffled around the side of the building to Ellick Lane and disappeared into the tradesmen's entrance.

He was next seen in the lobby of the apartment house. Tenants leaving for work observed him straightening chairs and rugs, picking up a few scattered papers. He moved so slowly about his tasks that, as always, a few of the passersby stopped to urge him to take some time off. They all knew he had been ill for some time; it would be wise, they suggested, to relax, to rest and recover his health. Again as always, he shrugged aside these promptings, muttering in his pidgin-English that he had to take care of "boss-missy." And so his well-wishers went their way, smiling fondly at the devotion of the old Chinese.

The next person who saw Liu was a Mrs. Dix, the manager of the apartment house, who occupied the apartment next to Mrs. Baker. It was on her door that Liu pounded frantically, screaming shrilly that she should come at once. Pausing only to put on a wrapper, she hurried after the jabbering Chinese.

The door to Mrs. Baker's apartment was open and Liu pointed in. From the hallway nothing could be seen, however, but an overturned chair and an expanse of bare floor. Urged forward by her excited guide, Mrs. Dix went through the little hallway and on into Mrs. Baker's living room.

There was more than enough to be seen there. The wall-bed was down, occupying one corner of the room. The covers lay on the floor at one side. On the floor at the foot of the bed lay the almost nude body of Mrs. Baker, her nightgown and one of the bed sheets tangled around her neck.

For a moment Mrs. Dix stood stunned by the sight. Then resolutely she stepped around the body of her employer and telephoned the Harbor Emergency Hospital. Fifteen minutes later the police had arrived, and the net had begun to close around Liu Fook.

One glimpse of the death-room was sufficient to indicate that a struggle had taken place, that this was no instance of Desdemona being murdered quietly in her bed. The dead woman had undergone terrific punishment. Her chest was crushed in. Eight ribs had been broken. Her face was smeared with blood, and one finger had been peeled of its flesh. That stripped finger suggested the first motive, which was robbery. Mrs. Baker had worn a large diamond ring which had become so tight that it could not be removed. The murderer, however, had found a way of removing it. He had simply wrenched it off.

The ring was missing. Search of the apartment disclosed that other jewelry had also disappeared: a watch, another and smaller diamond ring, and an amber necklace. Seventy-five dollars in cash, known to have been in the room, was gone also.

While the search for the missing valuables was in progress, other officers were searching every inch of the place for clues. Their first reward was a piece of skin, roughly about an inch square, with a bit of flesh adhering to one corner. It lay on a rumpled rug beside the bed. Near it was a worn thickness of leather from the heel of a shoe. In the center of the room were two shallow scratches in the floor, scratches that appeared to have been made by nails from a shoe. A third find was a button with a bit of shredded blue cloth hanging from it.

Studying the cloth, the officer tried to remember where he had seen a color and material similar to it. His eyes fell upon the figure of Liu Fook huddling against the far wall. The Chinese was wearing a suit of the same blue cloth.

In answer to a brusque summons, the old Chinese limped forward. An examination of his shoes showed that the outer thickness of leather was missing from one of the heels. Two protruding nailheads were spaced the exact width of the marks on the hardwood floor.

When this fact was pointed out to him, the old man flung up his hands in excited protest—and betrayed another fact. On one finger was a wound still oozing serum. The fragment of skin picked up from the floor fitted over it exactly.

Other officers were searching the basement. In the little corridor opening on Ellick Lane they had come across a startling discovery. Just outside the door leading into the little room Liu used during the day was a metal pail full of water. Soaking in the water were a blouse and a pair of trousers, both of blue cloth. When the dripping garments were brought upstairs, the button with the shred of blue cloth was found to have been torn from the right sleeve of the blouse.

Mrs. Dix, meanwhile, had been telling the police a strange story. Three or four times during the preceding two years Mrs. Baker had been forced to discharge Liu Fook for insolent behavior. It seemed that Liu disapproved of his employer's inclination to entertain young men and had told her so in no uncertain terms. The arguments had wound up each time with Liu's being discharged. Each time, however, he had come back, pleading for his job and promising to restrain himself in the future. Each time Mrs. Baker had relented.

Another storm had been brewing, though, for some weeks; in fact ever since Mrs. Baker's friendship with young Middleton had begun. It seemed that so far the old Chinese had succeeded in restraining himself as far as his employer was concerned. But Mrs. Dix told of his coming to her and launching into an almost hysterical diatribe against "boss-missy." Indeed, not two days before, he had gone so far as to predict what would happen if this friendship were not broken off. His hands had closed together as if around a throat; they had shaken, strangling.

That story did it. Protesting his innocence in a screeching blend of Chinese and pidgin-English, Liu was carted off to jail.

The search went on. No trace of money or jewelry could be found, however thoroughly the basement room and corridor were ransacked. After half an hour of upheaval, it was learned that Liu had other quarters. Off went the hunt, through the Stockton tunnel to 841 Stockton Street. There the one shabby room was almost pulled apart. No jewelry was found.

While the Stockton Street search was going on, another figure had entered the case. Lincoln U. Grant, business manager for Mrs. Baker, had arrived at the California Street apartment to take a hand. Upon being informed of the course of the investigation, Grant went down to Liu's basement room to conduct his own search. Sometime later he came back upstairs with the missing two rings, the watch, and the amber necklace.

Grant's story was that he had been prowling about in the rubbish piled along one wall of the Ellick Lane corridor. A heap of discarded telephone directories piled on a rickety chair had attracted his attention. Dust covering the books seemed undisturbed, suggesting that they had been overlooked in the previous search. As a matter of fact, they had. Tucked away between two of the directories down near the bottom of the pile were the missing trinkets.

As Grant handed over the gegaws, it was seen that one of the rings—the large one—was smeared with blood.

The news of the murder and of the subsequent arrest of the Chinese houseboy rocked San Francisco as almost nothing had since the disaster of 1906. The murdered woman had been somewhat of a social figure. Her interest in amateur theatricals had made her many acquaintances. At one time she had even arranged a dancing class as part of the staid Fairmont Hotel's social program. In addition, her wealth gave her a very definite position. She liked people and she mingled with them. People who knew her liked her; in the words of one acqaintance, she was "a sweet old thing with quite a talent for acting—in a small way, of course."

But it was the holding of the Chinese that created the greater sensation. Much was made of an old tradition that never in the history of the Chinese in the United States had one of them killed his employer.

San Francisco was devoted to its Chinese for two reasons. They liked them for themselves. Also they were well aware of the fact that the Chinese are an integral, and probably the most picturesque, part of the city that is renowned for its color. Until that time, too, the Chinese houseboy had been a tradition. Every family of means and position had at least one. They were trusted servants and pampered like lapdogs.

Consequently, at the news that a houseboy had been arrested for

murder, the sensation was terrific. Almost every household felt the
impact in one way or another. Suspicion crept in where, heretofore,
there had been perfect trust. The newspapers whooped it up and
there was chaos, domestically speaking.

Aware of the rising feeling and naturally anxious lest it burst
bounds and engulf the whole Chinese colony, a potent and formidable organization now stepped forward to stand beside Liu Fook.
This was the Six Companies, the group of men supervising all of the
Chinese in the Bay Area.

Their first attempt at stemming the tide, it must be admitted, was
slightly less than successful. It consisted of a melodramatic plea, via
the newspapers, that "their cousin" simply could not be guilty because "it is an old Chinese superstition that a murderer must flee at
once from the scene of his crime and never return. Should he return,
he would be seized by the spirit of his victim in the form of a devil."

The police were not impressed, they insisted doggedly that the
right man had been arrested and went about their business of sewing
up the evidence to prove it. The Six Companies' next step was emi-
nently more practical: they equipped Liu with legal counsel and
provided him with an interpreter. With the arrival of the latter upon
the scene, the old man's chatterings began for the first time to take
on intelligible form.

Heretofore the newspapers had been full of references to Liu's
"boss-missy." Now ten days after the murder, that picturesque and
widely known appellation had fallen by the wayside. Diction and
syntax, in exchange, reared their prosaic heads, and Liu is quoted
as saying:

"Mrs. Baker treated me like a brother. Would I kill a woman who
had been like a sister to me? Always we were good friends through
the nine years and three months I worked for her. Often she laughed
and joked with me, saying, 'Now don't run away with the money,
Liu; I need you too much.'"

During the preceding ten days another change had come about.
The newspapers had veered over to Liu's side. At first they had been
guardedly antagonistic; an objective perusal indicates that all were
convinced of his guilt. Now suddenly the San Francisco public
was bathed in treacle and tears. The first indication of the about-
face was contained in an editorial about whose fairness there can

be no question. "It is," the editor wrote thoughtfully, "too easy to pick upon an Oriental who understands our language none too well and say, 'He did it!' But that will not satisfy the conscience of the citizens of San Francisco. The truth must be known beyond the peradventure of a doubt."

Had all reports of Liu been in the same vein there could have been no criticism. But they were not. The sob-sisters took over and had a holiday. The official reports from police headquarters were dismissed as a necessary evil, to be passed over as quickly as possible. Liu was gradually made to appear a martyred old family retainer, whose sole fault was remaining in the service of a woman ungrateful enough to have allowed herself to be murdered.

The police were still unimpressed. Liu's reference in his interview to Mrs. Baker's money had been meant as a solar-plexus blow to the motive of robbery. It had really been not too much of a shock. Many persons had come forward to testify that the old houseboy had often collected the rents for his employers; had frequently been sent to her bank to cash checks, large and small; had had constant access to the apartment, where her jewelry had always been kept. It was established, too, that the old man had managed to scrape together a bank account in his name totaling over three thousand dollars.

To counterbalance this, though, another bit of evidence had lately been uncovered. The trousers soaking in the pail in the basement corridor had been thoroughly examined. Clinging to the knees were a number of grayish hairs similar in color to the dead woman's. These hairs plus the fragment of skin plus the torn-off button plus the leather heel plus the soaking garments plus the jewelry outside his room plus the threats against Mrs. Baker led the police to feel that now their case was air-tight.

On December 15, 1930, the Grand Jury convened. On the basis of the foregoing evidence it voted to indict Liu Fook for murder.

3.

Each day had brought its sensation. At the funeral of Mrs. Baker the crowds had been so unmanageable that police had been called in. The mourners were almost crowded out of the chapel. The dead woman's family had rallied from Los Angeles and as far east as

St. Louis. Mrs. Dix had had to fight her way through the mob. Lincoln U. Grant, the business manager, was there. Maud Graves attended but was so overcome by grief that she had to battle her way out halfway through the service. Beale and Middleton did not attend.

Beale, the young pianist, was lost sight of in the attendant publicity. That was not the case with Middleton. Shortly after the discovery of Mrs. Baker's body, Maud Graves had informed the press that "the poor boy is heart-broken. He came to my apartment Tuesday night, threw himself on the bed, and cried for hours." She added that he was planning on leaving for Hollywood to have a fling at what she called "the talkies."

Mrs. Dix came forward with a repetition of her story of Liu's disapproval of Mrs. Baker's protege. From his prison cell Liu added his own shrill blast to the publicity whirling around the young actor. He announced to the press that he had frequently seen Middleton kissing Mrs. Baker. Once, he said, they had embraced while he was still in the room. The old man had shown his emphatic disapproval by stamping out, slamming the door after him.

Middleton promptly denied ever having so much as kissed Mrs. Baker's hand. But Liu and his friends were getting under his skin. On December 12th he appeared before the police, complaining that he was being shadowed. Chinese friends of Liu had set up a day-and-night watch over him, two of them always being visible across the street from his front door, keeping alert watch over every person who entered or left his apartment.

One day later Liu uttered from his prison cell a pathetic plea that he be allowed his daily pipe of "yen-shee" or opium. Instantly the cry of "Narcotics!" went ringing through the city. Melodramatic rumblings of dope-rings and opium orgies roared over the hills.

And so it went, up to the day Liu was brought before Judge Lazarus. San Francisco, already confused beyond measure by the red herrings and criss-crossed trails, had still another shock to bear. In an almost unprecedented move, the Grand Jury now announced that, upon further consideration of the evidence, it had reversed itself. The indictment it had already voted was now refused.

Judge Lazarus decided, however, to review the evidence, even though he admitted that he felt the case of the police was weak.

As a result of the review, the judge ruled that the evidence was sufficient and Liu was held for trial in Superior Court. On January 19th he was brought before Superior Judge Harris to be arraigned and instructed for trial. With his interpreter beside him, he took his place in the stand and waited.

Judge Harris turned to the interpreter: "How does the defendant plead, guilty or not guilty?"

Liu was all too familiar with the sound of that last word. Before the interpreter could frame an answer, the old Chinese pounded his trembling fists together.

"I no guilty!" he screamed. " I no kill boss-missy. All time somebody say, 'You guilty?' " The thin voice rose higher. "No! I no kill her."

When the sensation in the courtroom was finally quelled, Judge Harris set the trial for February 24th.

During the interevening three weeks much happened to various persons concerned with the case. And everything that happened was carefully reported to the public. It appeared as if everyone but the police were bound and determined that anyone could be guilty of the murder but Liu.

When Mrs. Baker's will was opened, it was found that the bulk of her estate was bequeathed to a niece living in Los Angeles. "Purposely excluded" were a sister, two nieces and two nephews, all from St. Louis; a niece and a nephew living in San Francisco; and another niece from Oakland, California. A family feud, conscientiously aired in the newspapers, was the cause of this exclusion. A year previous to the murder, Mrs. Baker's brother, a prosperous dentist, had died in Sacramento and left his three-hundred-thousand-dollar estate to his sister. The other members of the family were so little overjoyed at the news that they hinted at the use of undue influence on the part of Mrs. Baker. Her effective retort to the charge had been to cut them off completely in her own will.

The nieces from St. Louis started proceedings to have the will set aside. They suggested that a rapprochement between their aunt and themselves had been reached and that a new will had been in the offing. They implied that the police might well drop the case against Liu Fook and regard with suspicion a certain person who should be nameless but who lived in Los Angeles.

Lincoln U. Grant, too, was having his troubles. His wife announced that she was suing him for divorce. Middleton, the actor, accused him of having marital designs on Mrs. Baker. Grant indignantly denied the whole story, insisting that his relations with the woman had been perfectly platonic and that he had never in the world dreamed of marrying her. He denied that he had ever possessed a key to the Baker apartment. He proclaimed that he had not known of the murder until he had been informed of it late on the morning of the discovery of the body. He insisted that he had spent the night in an apartment he maintained in Oakland.

The police believed him. After a careful investigation they had long ago discarded both him and Middleton as suspects. None of the bickering in the newspapers touched them. They knew they had the right man, the murderer, under lock and key.

On February 24th, Liu appeared in court for his trial. Stolid and indifferent he sat through the tedious process of impaneling the jury. Once he leaned over to whisper to his counsel. A flutter of anticipation went through the room. But the old man was not confessing to the crime; he was only asking for some stamps for a letter he had written to "his wifey-woman," as the newspapers quaintly put it, in Hong Kong. It developed that he had not only a sixty-three-year-old-wife in China, but three sons and two daughters in this country.

By the time the trial began, the city was quivering with anticipation. The courtroom was jammed. The police had, as far as they could see, stopped every gap and loophole in the evidence. The District Attorney was ready with every legal weapon at the command of the law. It remained now only for the jury to listen and decide.

The first evidence concerned the manner in which the murder been committed. Early reports, in fact the coroner's report made immediately after the examination of the body, had it that Mrs. Baker had been strangled with the bed sheet that was tied around her neck. Yet this was demonstrated to be untrue. Photographs of the body show both the nightgown and the sheet to be only loosely wrapped around the throat. Medical authorities testified that the dead woman had been strangled by hand, the larynx squeezed out of shape, the bruises from the hands still remaining in the flesh after death.

Much had been made before the trial of the fact that Liu Fook, a frail man, could not have caved in the woman's chest and broken her ribs. Yet it was pointed out the deceased was far from a young woman; the bones were brittle. If she had been thrown to the floor and knelt upon, it was quite probable that the bony structure should have caved in. Liu could easily have done that.

Defense brought up the matter of the square of skin found on the bedroom floor. Liu insisted that he had sliced the finger while washing windows some days before the murder. The day before the murder he had simply flicked the fragment of dead skin to the floor while he had been talking to Mrs. Baker.

Police produced a photograph of Liu's hand, showing that the wound was not healed but was still an open wound. Witnesses testified that they had gone with Liu to the window upon which he said he had cut his finger. The pane was whole; there was nothing upon which he could have cut it. Spots he pointed to as being blood were demonstrated to be spots of paint.

Liu said he had not gone into Mrs. Baker's room the morning of the murder. With the daily paper in hand, he had unlocked the door, observed the body of his mistress lying on the floor, and flung the paper into the room. He had then run to call Mrs. Dix. Yet Mrs. Dix testified that, standing in the doorway, she had been unable to see anything beyond the hallway. Diagrams of the apartment showed plainly that nothing of the room except a portion of the head of the bed could be seen from that vantage point. Police pointed out that the newspaper Liu said he had thrown into the room was found wedged at the foot of the bed between mattress and bedstead.

The matter of the leather heel has already been mentioned. Liu maintained that it frequently dropped off and that he simply picked it up and pressed it back onto the nails. He maintained that it, like the piece of skin, had been dropped in the apartment the day preceding the murder.

When the button had been torn off the sleeve of the blouse he was unable to say. But this much he did know: he had never put the blue suit to soak in the pail of water; as a matter of fact, he had not even worn it for several days previous. Promptly a chemist was called who testified that he had examined the water from the pail and had found evidences of human blood in it.

Confronted by that testimony, Liu made an adroit turn and blandly denied ownership of the trousers. Two Chinese, friends of Liu's, came to the stand to testify that they themselves had given the trousers to the old man. Mrs. Dix pointed out that she had, only a few days before, mended a rip in the seat of the trousers for Liu and calmly turned them inside out on the stand and pointed to the purple thread with which she had mended them.

The blood on the face of the dead woman was not her own. Prosecution contended that it had been smeared there while Liu was strangling her. It had come from the cut finger, which, the police maintained, had not been cut at all but had been bitten during the struggle. Another smear of blood was seen in a photograph of the Yale lock on the door to the apartment. Prosecution pointed out that the smear could have been made while the old Chinese was opening the door from the inside, holding the injured finger stiffly out to protect it.

A flicker of interest was occasioned by the news that the official record of Liu's fingerprints had disappeared. They had been introduced at the preliminary hearing. Since then no one had seen them. They were never found.

The case wound on. Every new bit of evidence was greeted by a firm denial from Liu. His lawyers hooted at the theory of the police that the murder had been done because the old man was jealous of his mistress's association with young men.

Yet circumstantial as it was, every phase of the evidence pointed to Liu and only to Liu. It seemed there could be no question of his guilt.

But the District Attorney and the police had become increasingly uneasy during the course of the trial. There was nothing they could put their fingers on. Rather it was an intangible antagonism, sensed rather than felt, quivering in the air. Each telling point seemed to fall upon deaf ears. It was almost as if no one were interested in anything but the fact that Liu Fook should be freed.

The trial moved to its close, apathy becoming more and more evident. Despair and desperation tinged the closing remarks of the prosecution.

The jury of ten men and two women filed out. In exactly twenty-one minutes they were back in the jury-box. The verdict was "Not guilty."

On March 22nd, four days after Liu Fook walked out of court, he appeared on the stage of the famed Mandarin Theatre on Grant Avenue in the heart of Chinatown. Two thousand Chinese and many white persons crowded the theatre to the doors. Liu spoke from one side of the stage. It was a short speech. Only a few words. And then he disappeared.

The next day, escorted by his Chinese friends, he journeyed to the Embarcadero. There, in a tumult of goodbyes, he boarded the *President Johnson,* sailing for Hong Kong.

"Well, Liu," asked a reporter, "will you be coming back here some day?"

Liu's eyes turned toward Chinatown, toward California Street hill. "Mebbe I go home China to die. Mebbe I come back again. I dunno."

An hour later, when the *Johnson* sailed, his wizened yellow face could be seen at the railing. He waved his hand slowly, the hand from which a piece of skin had once been missing. He turned away.

And what of Liu's "boss-missy," the woman whose murder had threatened to overturn a tradition? A week or so later one of the papers printed a short paragraph on the case. It wound up: "But who did murder Rosetta Baker?"

Purely a rhetorical question, of course.

[1945]

FROM THE GOLDEN GATE BRIDGE

by

STANTON A. COBLENTZ

This shall remain: the ragged headlands flung
Far out against the sunset-crimsoned sea;
Dim spits and isles; and one star-lantern hung
Over the wrinkled, lone immensity;
These clouds that flare from ruby-red to gray;
Those peaks that stab the violet dusk; and white
Of breakers curving in wide lips of spray
Under the bald and seagull-peopled height.

This shall remain. The phantoms of the dark
Shall whistle in the wind; and fog shall blow
Its shawl round ghostly moons; and day-fire mark
The long east-ranges with a rosebud glow.
But ah that, after all man's strife is through,
More than the terns and hawks may greet this view!

SUN ON FISHERMAN'S WHARF

by

ERNEST K. GANN

THE sun warmed the fog over Fisherman's Wharf and gradually dissolved its heavy content until it became a silver haze. For a time certain units of the fog resisted the attack and hung in tatters from the masts, the tops of the first houses, and the ends of the pier fingers. It was time for basking the body, and so the members of the dock committee came out of the haze one by one and gathered in their accustomed place in the lee of the wall at Standard Fisheries.

A heavy timber stretched almost the length of the wall and the committee sat upon the timber, or put one foot on it, or disregarded its existence, according to precedent and their physical condition. It was understood among them that certain members of the committee had rights, and these were set by seniority, or oratorical ability. It had long been established that Little Bat's place along the timber was at the extreme south end, that is, as far as possible from the north end of the timber, which reached to the very edge of the dock. This precaution minimized the chances of Little Bat falling into the water when he became drunk, which he would certainly manage to arrange by noon. The members of the committee, who had far more important things to think about, were tired of retrieving Little Bat from the bay and going through the dull process of reviving him by artificial respiration.

Spade-face, who had once suffered a brain injury, and so lost his sense of smell, occupied that portion of the timber next to Little Bat. There was never any argument about his right to the position.

His ability to suffer Little Bat at close quarters when he became obstreperous during the afternoon guaranteed his position. For Little Bat persisted in annoying the fish-house workers and his inevitable reward was a bombardment of fish, old eggs, boxes, and smashed crabs. No one contested Spade-face's seat on the timber, though it was recognized that he caught the sun upon his sagging shoulders perhaps five minutes before anyone else did.

Hoolihan normally took his seat on the timber next to Spade-face. It was the best seat on the timber, also held without protest, since Hoolihan was a man of means. It was well known that a sister-in-law sent him money from time to time and this sometimes allowed Hoolihan to sleep in a furnished room at night. The room was on a steep side street behind the chocolate factory and Hoolihan would descend from it each morning promptly at seven-thirty. Hoolihan claimed to have once been a sailor, but everyone knew he had never been any farther to sea than the timber. Nevertheless his opinions on boats, fish, and fishermen were listened to with respect. At some time during the day he might produce a bottle of wine from the folds of his overcoat. It was an important matter. A man who had staggered the streets the long night, a man who finally crept into a packing box, or an empty truck trailer, or a factory doorway—a man who slept outdoors, or worse yet, with the Salvation Army— could develop a powerful thirst by nine o'clock in the morning.

At the far end of the timber, nearest the water, sat Mister Fancy. He was a very small and timid man who wore a tie consistently. The tie was marked "San Francisco World's Fair, 1915." Its faded beauty was responsible for Mister Fancy's title. No one had ever been known to pay the slightest attention to him. He was merely another pair of ears to catch the wisdom of General Ball, and when he disappeared early in the afternoon his absence was seldom noticed. His situation on the timber was exposed to the harbor wind and shaded from the sun except at high noon.

General Ball was the recognized spokesman of the dock committee. He had no specific place on the timber, preferring to sit where he could find an opening for his bulk. Since his duties required him to roam the docks, the boats, and the fish houses throughout the day in search of vital information, he seldom felt it necessary to sit down anyway. He thought and talked with greater emphasis and clarity

standing up. An erect posture allowed him to flay his arms against
the sky as he spoke and so hold the slippery attention of his audience.
General Ball wore the uniform of a regular committee member;
greasy black cap, overcoat hanging almost to his ankles, and shoes
with holes in both bottoms and tops. So clothed, he was immediately
set apart from the irregulars who occasionally found their way to
the special place of the committee—irregulars being, in General
Ball's eyes, any wanderers who had no established retreat in all the
city. The wanderers would come and go, standing for a few hours
with their hands in their pockets, looking at their feet, listening to
General Ball expound the news of the world and the wharf.

"I'll tell you," said Ball on this morning as the sun began to warm
his back. "I'll tell you this, and anybody who don't listen to me is
a ostrich. Now you take a farmer. Go ahead, take him. What does
he dö? He gets up maybe five o'clock in the morning. He goes out
and milks some cows. It ain't a easy life, you understand, and sometimes the cow is sick. But sick or not, the farmer comes back to a
nice hot breakfast. He eats that, then what does he do?" General
Ball examined his audience for a reaction. Receiving none, he cocked
his head to one side and wagged a long grimy finger at the occupants
of the timber. "When a farmer gets through with his breakfast he
monkeys around in the fields—"

"Jush a minute," Little Bat interrupted angrily. "Jush a mo*ment!*
Have you ever *been* on a farm?"

"No . . . no, I never been on no farm, but I say to you, a farmer's
got it easy."

"Yer fruity," mumbled Little Bat. "I ain't gonna listen to you no
more." As if to protect himself from further exposure to General
Ball's views, Little Bat pulled his head down into the collar of his
overcoat and closed his eyes. General Ball ignored him. He addressed
himself to the more dependable ears of Mister Fancy and to three
irregulars who had already gathered to absorb the sun. His voice
assumed a tone that indicated he was prepared to be reasonable.

"A farmer now, he has his problems—sure. But after he eats his
breakfast, what does he do? He goes out and climbs on a nice
comfortable tractor and plows his fields, that's what he does. And
all the time the gov'ment is payin' him to sit on the tractor whether
he raises anything or not. Right?" General Ball did not wait for

any confimation from his audience. It was still too early in his theme to permit interruptions.

"So then this here farmer comes back home and eats a big lunch and takes a snooze afterwards—maybe even has a daytime go at his old lady. He's lyin' there thinkin' what a wonderful gov'ment we got and when he gets tired of thinkin' how swell it is, he goes out in the field and plows some more. Then he comes back home again and has a drink—"

"You gotta clock says it's time for *us* to have a drink?" asked Spade-face.

"No, I ain't got a clock and I never need one because I can always tell exactly what time it is by the sun."

"Yer fruity. Yer jus' fruitier than hell," Little Bat mumbled again. One of the itinerants raised his watery eyes to blink at the sun.

"Then what time is it?" he asked.

"What difference does it make what time it is? You goin' somewhere, mister?"

"No, I ain't goin' nowhere, I just want to know what the hell makes you think you can tell time by the sun."

"I'm talkin' about farmers and if you guys will let me stick to the subject you'll learn a thing or two."

"I still want to know what the hell time you think it is," the itinerant insisted. General Ball scorched him with a look. But he held his hand toward the sun and spread his fingers slowly.

"It's ten minutes past eight," General Ball pronounced.

"That's crap," the itinerant said. General Ball at once took three pugnacious steps in his direction, paused, and then continued his approach until he was in a position to almost touch his own unshaven chin to that of his heckler.

"You callin' me a liar?"

"Yer the biggest liar I ever heerd," said the itinerant, holding his ground. "You want to make somethin' of it?"

General Ball's nose twitched suspiciously. "Where did you get the whiskey?" he asked.

"How you know I got some whiskey?"

"It stinks on yer breath."

"Whiskey don't stink."

General Ball allowed a subtle change to come over his attitude. Then suddenly he placed a friendly hand on the itinerant's arm. He laughed hoarsely.

"Oh, pal! That's a good one, pal! That's the best one I ever heard in a long time. And now just to prove whiskey don't stink, how about divvying with us. We'll conduct sort of a experiment."

"You said it was too early to have a drink."

"I never said that. Little Bat said it."

"I never did!" Little Bat almost raised himself from the timber, so violent was his protest. General Ball increased the pressure of his hand on the itinerant's arm.

"Come on, pal. Bring out the whiskey. Bring it out, pal."

"What'll you pay?"

"Pay?" General Ball was horrified. "Listen, pal. This here is our place, see? We been comin' here every day for years and years. We like to have guests once in a while, see, but usually they got the good sense to divvy."

"This here is the end of a street but it's still a public thoroughfare. Anybody can stand here."

"Maybe so, but we share and share alike. It's a rule."

"You a Communist?"

"What's it to you?"

"I don't like Commies." Now the itinerant pushed his chin toward General Ball's.

"Then I ain't a Commie."

"And *I* ain't got no whiskey left. Frisk me all you want but you won't find none at all."

"Wh' we need is no gov'ment," said Little Bat. "No gov'ment at all."

Breathing deeply to hide his disappointment, General Ball drew away from the itinerant until he again stood in a commanding position before the timber.

"Now we was talkin' about fishermen before this loud-mouth hypocrite interrupted," General Ball began.

"You was talkin' about farmers," Mister Fancy said mildly. General Ball glared at him.

"Shut up, you, and maybe you'll learn something. Now some people say fishermen are just farmers on the ocean. Get the relation?

Well, there ain't no comparison. In the first place the gov'ment don't give the fisherman nothin' but headaches. What they do is help out fishermen of every nation we was fightin' against in the war with money and fine boats. And as if that ain't enough, they allow their fish, these enemy fish mind you, to come into this country and flood the market. Does that make any sense?" No one challenged General Ball and so he was able to continue in a softer tone.

"As if that wasn't enough, the gov'ment throwin' the tax money in the enemies' throats, look at the life they got to lead compared to some farmer. They get up maybe at three o'clock in the mornin', the fishermen that is, and if it ain't too rough maybe they can brew a pot of coffee for breakfast—maybe. Then all day long they got to bounce around in a little boat and they don't dare even take a drink or they fall overboard and drown. So they work all day long until it gets dark, then they got to come in from wherever in the ocean they are. So if they are lucky they get in maybe at ten o'clock, or maybe not even for several days, and then what do they find? I ask you what do they find?"

Hoolihan knew his cue perfectly. "It depends," he said.

General Ball smiled upon him. "You're a hundred per cent correct. It depends on if he's got any fish or not. If he's got any fish he's got to sell 'em before they spoil. He can't be waitin' around for a decent price and the buyers know it. So they give him a first-class screwin'. And what's more, a man that can't steal his weight in fish don't stay weighin' them very long. But now suppose the fisherman don't have no luck? Does he get paid anything for his work all day? Nothin' he gets. Nothin' of course from the dealers and nothin' from the gov'ment. I feel sorry for the fishermen." General Ball reached into the pocket of his ragged overcoat and brought forth the stub of a cigar. He placed it between his yellow teeth and chewed on it reflectively. Then he studied the sun a moment and finally sighed.

"Hoolihan," he said, "have you got any money this mornin'?"

"Of course not."

"Didn't yer sister-in-law send no money at all?"

"No."

"If we could only find some guy who had a job once, we could help him collect his unemployment insurance."

"I had a job once," said the itinerant.

"When was that?" General Ball asked eagerly.

"Nineteen-thirty. I was the bes'—"

"You ain't eligible," snapped General Ball. He at once went back to his examination of the sun. "It looks to me like this is going to have to be a prospectin' day. We got to deploy. And we got to hurry because it's already gettin' late. Spade-face, you work the north side of Jefferson Street, and, Fancy, you take the south goin' the other way. Me and Hoolihan will take Bay Street and—" General Ball paused to frown at Little Bat. "He's too drunk. We may as well leave him lay because he'll never be able to pan a dime." General Ball shivered at the sun. "It looks to me like this is goin' to be a dry day. I just got a awful hunch."

BAGHDAD-BY-THE-BAY

by

HERB CAEN

BY THE dawn's early light Coit Tower standing starkly silhouetted against the first faint flush in the east . . . A sun-and-windswept corner on Montgomery Street, where you can look west and see a wall of thick, dirty fog rising geniilike from the Pacific, while a finger of whiter, puffier stuff feels its way into the Bay, twisting this way and that till it conforms to every contour, snugly and coldly . . . And the poor man's perfume of Skid Road—a melancholy mixture of frying grease, stale beer, and harsh deodorants that clings to your clothes and your thoughts for hours.

The smug majesty of the City Hall's famed dome, higher (and dirtier) than Washington's, and so far above the conniving that goes on beneath it . . . The few surviving little wooden houses of Telegraph Hill, clinging together for mutual protection against concrete newcomers slowly pushing them out on a limbo . . . And Fisherman's Wharf at 7 a.m., with its tiny fleet of tiny ships lined up in neat display, and proud sea gulls strutting past to review them.

The hangers-on outside the Public Library in Civic Center, singing an *a cappella* chorus of futility against the roaring backdrop of a metropolis in motion—Market Street . . . That occasional white ferry-boat drifting over from the Oakland mole and dipping respectfully beneath the aloof bridge that doomed so many of its side-wheeling sisters . . . And block after block of flatiron buildings along Columbia Avenue—sharp edges of a city that grew in too many directions at once.

The incongruity of a lonely foghorn calling somewhere in the

Bay as you stroll hatless down a sun-swept street—and the grotesque sight of this jumbled city from Twin Peaks, a sardonic, hyterical travesty on the dreams of those who stood there after the Great Fire and planned the Perfect City . . . Long-forgotten cable-car slots wandering disconsolately and alone up steep hills that are now flattened, with a contemptuous snort, by high-powered, twin-engined buses . . . And the Saturday-night symphony audiences arriving breathlessly at the Opera House from streetcars, on foot, in shabby automobiles—a far and enjoyable cry from the Friday-afternoon trade slinking slowly up in limousines that actually look bored.

University of California's Medical Center (where they discovered vitamin E) rearing up like a spectacular movie set against the darkness of Mount Sutro and Parnassus Heights, while in the pre-dawn hush of Golden Gate Park, far below, squirrels sit unafraid in the middle of the silent roads, and ducks waddle importantly along the bridle paths . . . The full magnificence of the Pacific bursting into your consciousness as you swing past the Cliff House . . . And the monumental mechanical madness of the Kearny, Geary, Third, and Market interesection, where traffic, honking the horns of its dilemma, squeezes painfully through a bottleneck with a "Stop" sign for a cork.

The too-bright mask of Chinatown's restaurants and bars, sometimes standing half empty, while upstairs, in the tenementlike apartments, live six Chinese in one room . . . The glittering Golden Horseshoe during opera season, a constant reminder that there are Upper Classes even in a public building paid for by the masses . . . And the eye-bulging sight, from atop the Fifteenth Avenue hill, of the little white new houses marching through the Sunset District toward the Pacific like stucco lemmings that decided, just in time, not to hurl themselves into the sea.

St. Francis Wood, Pacific Heights, and Sea Cliff, where the homes have room to puff out their chests in the satisfaction of success; and the ornate frame buildings just west of Van Ness—before 1906 the mansions of the mighty, today living out their long lives as boardinghouses for those who are also merely existing . . . Those two distinguished neighbors, the Mark Hopkins and the Fairmont, staring blankly at each other across California Street in the silence of 5 a.m.

when even the cable slots cease their friendly gibberish . . . And the corner of Jackson and Kearny, a one-worldly blend of China, Italy, and Mexico, where, all within a few steps, you can eat chow mein, top it off with chianti, and then step into a Spanish movie.

The inner excitement of Stockton Tunnel, as the jampacked buses wiggle noisily through, autos somehow squeeze past, and school kids run excitedly along the inside walk; and North Beach, with its 1001 neon-splattered joints alive with the Italian air of garlic and the juke-boxed wail of American folk songs . . . The dismal reaches of lower Market after midnight; the city within a city that is the deep Mission District, and the bittersweet juxtaposition of brusquely modern Aquatic Park against the fortresslike jumble of red brick where Ghirardelli makes his chocolate.

The crowded garages and the empty old buildings above them, the half-filled night clubs and the overfilled apartment houses, the saloons in the skies and the families huddled in basements, the Third Street pandhandlers begging for handouts in front of pawnshops filled with treasured trinkets, the great bridges and the rattletrap streetcars, the traffic that keeps moving although it has no place to go, the thousands of newcomers glorying in the sights and sounds of a city they've suddenly decided to love, instead of leave.

The warm magic of a spring day in "the city that knows no seasons" and all seasons—the children frolicking like sea lions on the Beach, the white-faced office workers turning their eager faces to the sun from the flatness of apartment house roofs, the cops shedding their coats and their dignity at every street corner, the whole city shrinking pleasantly together in the rare wonder of it all . . . The new buses on Market Street, snorting along in the ghostly shadows of streetcars that are no longer there—except in the memories of those who remember the madness of the street with the four-track mind, it's quieter now along the Nightmare Alley that used to frighten timid old ladies—but somehow it's no longer Market Street . . . And the white-stucco false fronts of the Western Addition houses which were mere children in the days of the fire-quake— old relics with their faces lifted, feeling young and popular again in this overcrowded era when there's a sweetheart for every hearth.

The old, bent Italians who have spent the best years of their lives shining shoes at North Beach bootblack stands—still able to smile although the Promised Land has given them not gold in the streets, but boots in their faces . . . The silent sun worshipers who crowd the benches on the tiny plateau of Union Square, comfortably parked for an hour—while in the streets all around them anxious automobiles poke their noses into the garage entrances, then draw back angrily at the implacably pleasant signs: "Sorry—Parking Space Full" . . . And wonderful, parklike Dolores Street, which bobs up and down in its own divided way from Market Street—straight into a past that had time and space for grassy parks in the middle of streets, lawns in front of houses, and sidewalks big enough for games of hopscotch under shade trees.

The picturesque firehouse on California Street, occupied by Engine Fifteen and topped off by the most magnificent weather vane in town —so definitely a part of the past that you expect a horse-drawn engine to come pounding out any moment . . . The oppressive a mosphere of Playland-at-the-Beach on a cold, wet day—the barkers standing still and silent in their overcoats, the Fun House an empty cavern of gloom, the merry-go-round playing a tinny prayer for sunshine . . . The lush green lawns of Julius Kahn Playground in the Pacific Heights sector, where the proletariat may romp in the shadow of mansions which stand coldly with their backs turned . . . And the Russ Building at five o'clock—suddenly becoming a Tower of Babble as the secretaries and stenos, so tired just an hour earlier, clatter out on their high heels like children freed from school.

The mad jumble of architecture that distinguishes Russian Hill— huge apartments and tiny back houses, formal gardens and unkempt patches of lawn, empty lots and mysteriously unfinished apartment houses . . . The garlic-flavored signs on the stores and offices along Columbus Avenue, singing their own Italian Street Song for your eyes and reminding you dreamily of faraway places you've never seen . . . Tenth and Mission, a notable Baghdadian intersection, where there is a service station on each of the four corners—plenty of free air, plenty of free water, plenty of free enterprise . . . And the Nob Hill gentlemen who walk their dogs in Huntington Park on many a midnight—their pajama bottoms peeking out from beneath their overcoats, their manner still as majestic as a floorwalker's.

The "Little Ghetto" of the Fillmore-McAllister area, rubbing narrow shoulders with "Little Osaka" and "Little Harlem"—a few thought-provoking blocks majoring in minorities . . . The massed neon signs along lower O'Farrell Street, their raucous red heightened by the driving rain, their reflections casting a weird upward glow on every strange passing face . . . The little bookshop in Old St. Mary's, always with a half-dozen volumes ranged in its small windows quite conservatively—so that you could never accuse it of advertising . . . And McDonald's fantastic secondhand bookstore on Mission, a cavernous treasure trove for the bargaining literati, stacked from floor to ceiling with everything from *True Detective Tales* to *Das Kapital*—with Mr. McDonald himself, a character straight from Dickens, presiding urbanely over his cut-rate classics.

The lovely homes ranged along the bluffs of Sea Cliff, where the residents may gaze at the Golden Gate Bridge from the ocean side; an exclusive view for the exclusive few . . . The unbathed Skid Rowgues who line up for a sunbath in front of the Salvation Army on Howard Street—men with darkness in their hearts trying to get color in their cheeks . . . The never-changing downstairs lounge at the Mark, where the Same Old Faces sit in the Same Old Places and talk the talk of people with nothing to talk about except each other; the Social Register—ringing up a "No Sale" . . . And the shiny black limousines lined up for rent on Geary Street near Powell—the trappings of millionaires, available for a few dollars to those who need a King-for-a-Day-Dream.

The scores of tiny coffeeshops in the theatrical hotel sector, serving breakfast in the afternoon to pancaked girls who go to work with the sunset and to bed with the sunrise—leading upside-down lives in a world which is hardly right-side up . . . The tiny restaurant that nestles on California Street between the great buildings of the financial district—and is known as "Mom's Home Cooking" . . . That fantastic old theatre 'way out on Mission, which was built solely to put a competitor out of business; when that was accomplished, it closed . . . And the clusters of spotlights which bathe the Shell Building in gold, creating a forever amber landmark on the skyline.

The psychopathic ladies of the night who patrol streets like Larkin and Mission in the endless hours before dawn—speaking to passing men in a dead voice that invites no answer . . . The deadpanned old men sitting silently by the hour in the pool halls of Market Street and North Beach, watching others enjoy themselves from behind Life's eightball . . . The row after row of tiny, all-alike hotels along Turk, Eddy, and Ellis streets—as monotonous, as hard to identify as the men who inhabit them . . . And lower Mason Street at three in the morning—a hurly-burlycue of boisterous soldiers and sailors, double-parked cabs, dames who've had that one too many, all-night drugstores and hamburgers; just about all that's left of the town they called "Frisco!"

Grant Avenue and Post Street, the crossroads of Baghdad-by-the-Bay, where (if you stand there long enough) you can see everybody in San Francisco . . . The always freshly painted buildings of Alcatraz, glowing so brightly in the afternoon sun that for a second you forget it's inhabited by men who are deserted together on an island . . . That institution called the Bay City Grill, where the old-time waiters still follow the ancient habit, at times, of totaling your check for you right on the tablecloth . . . And the shabby gospel singers, shouting out their hearts and the glory of God at Third and Howard—while their audience lounges around on fireplugs and against telephone poles, shutting their ears and listening only with their half-closed eyes.

The frank, open windows of Telegraph Hill's miniature castles, whose occupants gape at the gapers every bit as blandly as the gapers gape at them . . . The "Portals of the Past" service station on the crest of Nob Hill, a stone's throw from the Pacific-Union Club—whose front door is also a portal of the past . . . The death of a dream in cluttered-up-run-down Sutro Heights—once the pride of a millionaire, now a sore sight for eyes that remember its beauties and turn away from its decay of today . . . And the huge neon star that revolves slowly and majestically atop the Sir Francis Drake to advertise a saloon in the sky —easily outshining the small electric cross that marks a church in the dark valley below.

Tourists standing smellbound at Fisherman's Wharf, staring in disbelief at the huge pots of boiling water and asking the question they always ask: "You mean you *actually* throw them in *alive*?"—as the attendant, too bored to answer, nods curtly and reaches for the sacrificial crab . . . The wonderful contrast of that neat little chicken ranch under the massive approach to the Golden Gate Bridge at Fort Point —the chickens cluck-clucking around as though well satisfied that while they might not be able to build such a miracle as the span overhead, neither can a man lay an egg . . . And out-of-townies staring through open mouths at the ring of lobsters on display in the windows of Bernstein's Fish Grotto on Powell Street—tourist-trapped by San Francisco's oldest shell game.

Chinatown's fine ladies and merchants, heading up Grant Avenue around eleven o'clock each morning for the little places that serve a tiffin of tea and steamed buns—an old Spanish custom among the Chinese . . . The shadowy waiting station of the long-dead Powell Street Railroad Company at Fulton Street and Seventh Avenue—a sentimemento of the days when the cable cars ran out to the Park instead of into the red . . . The long-ago-and-faraway atmosphere at Robert's-at-the-Beach on a Sunday night, filled with oldsters who become slightly nostalcoholic and youngsters who aren't yet aware that they're filling up with memories for future use . . . And Kearny Street in the Hall of Justice region, one part of the rundown-downtown sector that preserves some of the rough, tough color of an earlier San Francisco—as unpretty as it's unphony.

The treat of treating your eyes to true magic—at sundown, on the terrace behind the Cliff House, with the endless Beach sprawled out on your left, the Gold Gate yawning with dignity at your right, and Seal Rocks in front of you, thrill-houetted sharply against a sun sinking with amazing swiftness into the great ocean . . . Baghdad-by-the-Bay!

INDEX